Better Teaching, More Learning
Strategies for Success in Postsecondary Settings

James R. Davis

AMERICAN COUNCIL
ON EDUCATION
Series on Higher Education
ORYX PRESS
1993

Copyright © 1993 by American Council on Education and
The Oryx Press

Published by The Oryx Press
4041 North Central at Indian School Road
Phoenix, AZ 85012-3397

Published simultaneously in Canada

Printed and Bound in the United States of America

∞ The paper used in this publication meets the minimum requirements of American National Standard for Information Science—Permanence of Paper for Printed Library Materials, ANSI
Z39.48, 1984.

Library of Congress Cataloging-in-Publication Data

Davis, James R., 1936-
  Better teaching, more learning : strategies for success in
postsecondary settings / James Davis.
    p. cm. — (American Council on Education/Oryx series on
higher education)
  Includes bibliographical references and index.
  ISBN 0-89774-813-1
  1. College teaching—United States. 2. Learning. I. Title.
II. Series.
LB2331.44.D38 1993
378.1′25—dc20   93-9809
                                                                          CIP

In Memory of

Marian Davidson Davis
John Willis Davis

who taught me at an early age to work hard,
to be thorough, to love learning,
and to organize my life and thoughts

Contents

Foreword   *vii*

Preface   *ix*

Clear Thinking about Teaching   1

Part I: The Perspectives   23
The Subject   25
The Setting   46
The Students   60

Part II: The Teaching Strategies   95
Training and Coaching   97
Lecturing and Explaining   133
Inquiry and Discovery   173
Groups and Teams   242
Experience and Reflection   299

Choosing and Using the Teaching Strategies   342

Index   *371*

Foreword

America's 3,000 colleges and universities are remarkably diverse in form and function, yet they all share a common commitment to teaching and learning. Considering the centrality of teaching and learning to higher education's societal mission, it is both puzzling and regrettable that those who bear the primary responsibility for teaching—the college faculty—know so little about it. Indeed, most of the graduate programs that train each new generation of college faculty devote little attention to developing teaching skills, and few graduate departments (outside of the field of psychology) make any effort to teach their students anything about human learning. The unstated assumption seems to be that effective teaching depends only on mastery of the subject matter.

The fact is that a great deal is already known about effective teaching and learning. What James Davis has done in this very readable book is to pull together much of this knowledge and to synthesize and organize it in an original way. Rather than focusing on technique—a favorite approach of many previous treatises on college teaching—Dr. Davis instead puts student *learning* at the center of his discussion. He says plenty about technique, to be sure, but discussions of teaching techniques are typically conducted in the context of how and why the learning process is likely to be affected.

An unique feature of Davis' approach is to acknowledge the central roles of *subject matter, setting,* and *student diversity.* Rather than simply describing "ideal" or "best" techniques and strategies for facilitating student learning, he points out that pedagogy must inevitably vary according to the subject matter, the social and physical setting where learning is supposed to take place, and the individual talents and proclivities of the learner. An especially useful and original feature is his regular use of examples from hypothetical professors in widely varying disciplines to illustrate the importance of subject matter. Because those of us who teach at the collegiate level are strongly identified with our particular subject matter fields and subfields, this feature should make the book especially appealing to college professors.

In the process of highlighting these subject matter differences, Dr. Davis makes a convincing case for the existence of many *principles* that transcend disciplinary differences. Among other things, his discussion of these principles suggests that we should be experimenting much more with *interdisciplinary* courses and programs. Some of my own recent research on undergraduate education indicates that students would benefit substantially from such courses.

Perhaps the most important contribution of the book is that it deals with the practical challenge of developing and implementing effective classroom teaching strategies in the light of what is known from many decades of research on human learning. Davis manages to breathe life into these somewhat abstract theories by showing what they suggest about teaching strategies. For example, in "Lecturing and Explaining" Dr. Davis treats the much-maligned classroom lecture. Rather than joining the chorus of educational critics who have been railing against our heavy reliance on the lecture method, he shows in very practical terms how this time-honored technique can be used to engage students more actively in the learning process. In particular, he shows how the effectiveness of our lectures can be enhanced by a greater understanding of cognitive psychology and the principles of information processing.

This is a book that could only have been written by someone with Jim Davis' unique background. He is not only a scholar and an experienced teacher who loves the craft, but he is also a teacher of teachers who has conducted many workshops for college teachers across a variety of fields and institutional settings. Any college teacher (or secondary teacher, for that matter) will benefit from reading even parts of this book; the prerequisites are simple: an affinity for the art and a desire to make it more enjoyable!

—Alexander Astin
Higher Education Research Institute
University of California, Los Angeles

Preface

This is my only chance to write to you informally about the assumptions I hold about teaching and the decisions I have made about this book. Gaining a better grasp of these assumptions and decisions will help you to read these pages with more understanding.

First, I believe that most teachers who work at the postsecondary level want to be good teachers. Although other interests—scholarly and personal—may drain away energies that could be put into better teaching, most teachers are attracted to postsecondary instruction because of a love for their field of study and their desire to communicate it. Thus, this book is rather upbeat, perhaps even naive in its assumption that most teachers want to improve. Some earlier readers of the manuscript have noted this, pointing out that the tone is overly optimistic. What is the alternative: to write a "gloomy" book about college teaching? That would be out of character for me and probably not very useful for you; so let me acknowledge initially that I seem not to have taken into account the "dark side" of the professorate. I have chosen to write about what *can* be done, not to lament what cannot.

Second, I believe that many teachers are already good at something, but that they tend to do their one good thing over and over again. At the end of one of my workshops on teaching strategies, an economist said to me: "I believe I am very good at the one thing I do. Now I realize that I could do many more things and that I could be very good at them, too." The comment made me happy, because it captured the essence of what I was trying to achieve. The improvement of postsecondary teaching, it seems to me, depends on many teachers using many more options than they currently use.

Third, most postsecondary teachers lack a conceptual framework for thinking about and talking about their teaching. They are deluged with endless exhortation to be better teachers and are given fragments of advice, but no conceptual framework, no consistent instructional model, no system for incorporating the bits and pieces of advice into an overall scheme that makes sense. I have tried to provide that conceptual framework in this book, and I believe that having a framework, with clear reference points, is important for being able to organize and evaluate all the advice we are given about teaching.

Fourth, most efforts to improve teaching focus on teaching, without much discussion of learning. This is a book about how people learn. It is not an educational psychology text, but it is like such texts in emphasizing learning. The goal in writing this book has been to pull together what is known about learning and translate it into a form that is useful for college teachers. Thus, there is a deeper discussion of the relationship of teaching and learning here than is found in most books on college teaching.

Fifth, I included examples in each chapter—examples of teachers and institutions in the "perspective" chapters and examples of actual teaching in the "teaching strategies" chapters. These examples involved some difficult choices. I chose to make the examples fictional, rather than actual, because I wanted to illustrate *ideal* applications of each teaching strategy. I also chose typical subjects, settings, and students, and typical teachers to illustrate the teaching. I wanted typical situations to increase the credibility of the illustration. Unfortunately, "typical" can sometimes be read as "stereotypical," and early readers of the manuscript pointed this out. The last thing I want to do is portray ethnic or gender stereotypes, and I understand clearly that ethnic minorities and women appear in many roles and at all levels of the higher education system today. But for the reasons mentioned above, the illustrations I generated are more typical than atypical. I'm hoping that readers will be able to say, "Yes, that makes sense; I've known someone like that." I also chose to develop in detail three vivid examples for each teaching strategy, rather than to proliferate several examples that are treated only superficially. This choice requires readers to "leap" from the examples provided to their own fields and instructional situations. I believe such a leap is not difficult for most teachers, but it takes some imagination. It is important to read the examples and not skip over them; try to extract from them the principles, techniques, and activities that will work in your own field.

Sixth, I synthesized the work of many scholars in many fields, and quoted, paraphrased, or otherwise "boiled down" in some form original work from many sources. This book is a work of synthesis and translation, and what is "original" in my work is the creation of a conceptual framework, the development of the illustrations, and the clear explication of other people's ideas. For this reason, I am more indebted than most authors to the work of other scholars, the real backbone and substance of this book. I very carefully established exact quotations where they occur, but I also did much summarizing and paraphrasing. Where I did so I tried to indicate clearly in the notes the sources of these ideas. In the cases where extended descriptions and summaries appear, I want to acknowledge, once again, my dependence on the work of these scholars. In my efforts to produce readable and readily understandable summaries, I hope I have not done violence to the authors' original intentions. Where extended summaries are presented, I encourage readers to seek the original text for a deeper and more detailed understanding.

In addition to these many scholars, I wish to thank others who have contributed to the development of this book. In developing the illustrations for each strategy, I sometimes referred to subject matter textbooks, referenced in the footnotes; at other times personal conversations with colleagues augmented my knowledge of a particular subject. I wish to thank these colleagues, particularly LaRue Boyd, of the University of Denver College of Business, for his input on case studies in marketing; Nancy Green, of the Colorado Institute of Art, for her professional knowledge of interior design; and Kathy Scott, of the Community College of Aurora, for her insights on customized training in small business settings.

I also want to thank colleagues who have read selected chapters of the manuscript, particularly Joel Macht for his valuable insights on "Training and Coaching," Al Goldberg for his comments on "Groups and Teams," and Carol Taylor for her guidance on computer-assisted instruction.

I want to acknowledge the resources of the University of Denver in supporting this scholarly activity, particularly the School of Education and the staff and collection of the Penrose Library. I am also deeply indebted to my assistant in the Center for Academic Quality, Marcela Mikkola, for endless hours at the word processor producing an accurate manuscript. I wish to thank the American Council on Education and The Oryx Press for agreeing to publish this book, and in particular I wish to thank John Wagner for editorial assistance.

Most of all, I wish to thank the participants in my workshops, students, and colleagues who have, over the years, allowed me to test these ideas and who through their dialogue have helped me to shape and confirm my views of teaching.

Clear Thinking about Teaching

I went to chemistry class five times a week and didn't miss a single one. Mr. Manzi stood at the bottom of the big rickety old amphitheater, making blue flames and red flares and clouds of yellow stuff by pouring the contents of one test tube into another, and I shut his voice out of my ears by pretending it was only a mosquito in the distance and sat back enjoying the bright lights and colored fires and wrote page after page of villanelles and sonnets.
—Sylvia Plath, *The Bell Jar*

MANY SUBJECTS, DIVERSE SETTINGS

Almost everyone today is teaching someone something somewhere. Teaching has always taken place, of course, in informal as well as formal settings. In traditional societies the wisdom of the elders was passed on informally to the young through various methods of socialization; but today teaching, through institutions explicitly designated "educational," has taken on a startling new importance and undeniable urgency. The widely publicized "crisis in education," so easy to describe, yet so difficult to remedy, has thrown teaching into the glare of a searching spotlight.

Today in postsecondary education, teaching takes place in many unique and diverse institutional settings—in large public universities, in small private liberal arts colleges, in two-year community colleges, in proprietary (trade) schools, and in specialized institutions, such as theological schools or medical centers. The settings vary, and the teachers in these settings teach an array of complex subjects to an increasingly diverse population of students. Who are these teachers, and what is it they hope their students will learn?

To illustrate the teaching strategies set forth in subsequent chapters of this book, fictitious examples of "real" teachers are presented as they teach *their* subjects in *their* settings. Five of these teachers, and the institutions where they teach, are introduced below.

Roscoe Meade teaches sociology at Mid-West University. He does research in population studies and teaches upper-division and graduate level courses in his disciplinary specialty, demographics. Located in a medium-sized city in what is both an industrial and agricultural state, Mid-West is a large, public, land-grant "multiversity," which enjoys a national reputation established equally by a handful of prominent scholars and its athletic teams. The undergraduate students are described by the faculty as "typical college students," full of energy, deeply involved in campus life, and only occasionally (at mid-terms and finals) serious about their studies. The graduate students, of course, are another matter. Attracted from a national and international pool to various disciplinary and professional specializations, they are the inspiration of most of the faculty who are assisted by them in their research and the teaching of undergraduates. Research is, of course, what motivates the faculty, because the reward structure heavily favors scholarly activity in what all agree is a "publish or perish" environment. The campus sprawls across acres of rolling land, dotted with high-rise residence halls, brick classrooms and office buildings, various institutes and research centers, two Olympic swimming pools (indoor and outdoor), an 80,000-seat stadium, and several bookstores, as well as assorted playing fields, lakes, parks, and a golf course. Sometimes, Professor Meade gets caught up in a campus governance issue, but usually he likes to be left alone to pursue his grants and contracts, to conduct his research in Third World countries, and to develop his courses and seminars, which he takes seriously and enjoys.

Edna Wolf teaches classics of literature at Elm Grove College. Like many of the faculty there, she is very broadly educated, having taken her doctorate in comparative literature with a year's post-doctoral work in American poetry. What she enjoys most about her work within the Humanities Division is her role in the team-taught interdisciplinary course in the core curriculum. Located in a small town in rural Iowa, Elm Grove was founded by a Protestant religious denomination before the Civil War. Now independent, private, and governed by a self-perpetuating Board of Trustees, the College is well-endowed and selective in admissions. The students are highly motivated and well-prepared academically, and over 80 percent go on to graduate or professional school within five years of their graduation. Elm Grove has a strong national reputation as a liberal arts college, and is recognized also for its required Work, Education, and Service Off-Campus term (WESOC), through which students are placed in internships, work, or field study experiences all over the country and around the world. The spacious campus contains a tasteful collection of old, stone, ivy-covered administration buildings; modern classroom, laboratory, and studio facilities; and cleverly designed clusters of residence halls gathered around a community center. Students can call up the holdings from the library and a state consortium of libraries from computer terminals in their dorm rooms. The campus is three blocks from the main street of the small town that owes its place on the map to Elm Grove College. For Edna Wolf, it is the perfect place to contemplate what writers of every age and place have to say about life.

Vicki Hastings teaches a course on wellness at Pacific Coast Community College. A former high school physical education teacher, she earned a master's degree in exercise physiology and now enjoys teaching adults of all ages. Her students come in all shapes and sizes and their motivations are all slightly different—lose weight, stay well, reduce cholesterol, stabilize blood pressure. Located in a working class suburb of a major Pacific seaport, PCCC is part of the extensive state-funded community college system designed to provide access to higher education for the general population. The mission of PCCC is four-fold: to provide developmental education to students whose previous learning has not prepared them well for higher education, to provide a college transfer program that is well-articulated with the public four-year institutions, to provide a limited number of occupational programs that offer career-entry skills to business and service providers in the city, and to reach out to the adult community with general courses and programs, such as English language and literacy, health and fitness, child-rearing, public speaking, and oceanography. The students, who come almost exclusively from within the county, range from 18 to 80 in age (with an average of 29), and the student body has a majority of minorities. Many enter as high school dropouts, enroll in developmental English and math, pass the GED, and move into either a college transfer or occupational program. The "campus" consists of four pre-cast concrete buildings and a large parking garage that together consume the equivalent of three city blocks. Vicki Hastings likes the challenge of teaching fitness to so many different kinds of people.

Nancy Green teaches interior design at the Art Institute of the South. She owns a successful interior design business of her own, and it has grown to the point where she has a manager who deals with the day-to-day operation so that she is free to pursue her dream—teaching students what they need to know to enter and be successful in a career in interior design. Located in the heart of a large city in the South, the Art Institute is one of eight campuses in various cities owned by the parent company, Educational Enterprises, Inc. As such, it is a proprietary "trade school," established, like any other business, to earn a profit for its owners. It is heavily regulated by the state and must comply with numerous regulations, including safeguards against fraud, regular reporting of employment prospects for its graduates, and even certain standards established by the state board on "general education" requirements. The students are of all ages and come from all over the state, from adjoining states, and a few foreign countries. They find housing in the community and commute to classes sandwiched between part-time jobs. All of the students have an expressed interest in a career in the applied arts—fashion merchandising, interior design, music video production, visual communication, photography—but they vary widely in artistic aptitude upon entry. The "campus" consists of the first five stories of a downtown high-rise office building. The classroom and studio facilities are excellent, and each year the company pours surplus earnings back into new classroom equipment. For Nancy Green it is a short commute, mentally and actually, from her business to the classroom.

Jonathan Wesley teaches a course entitled "Social and Personal Transformation" at New England Theological Seminary. He earned dual degrees in psychology and divinity and after his graduate studies he worked as a prison chaplain for five years before accepting a post as seminary professor. Located in the comfortable suburb of a now overgrown New England town, the New England Theological Seminary (NETS) is a freestanding professional school, not affiliated with either a university or a single denomination. Drawing support from several denominations, and, over the years, from many wealthy donors, the Seminary has taken on an ecumenical character and has evolved an identifiably liberal, "hands on" approach to the preparation of clergy for a variety of pastoral settings. Although a handful of students come to the Seminary directly from their undergraduate work, most are older career-changers, and now more than half are women. They bring considerable "life experience" to the classroom and, although their basic attitudes and values are well-formed, they are open and searching, willing to consider and reconsider almost everything. The relatively small (350 students) institution prides itself on being both an academic and a spiritual community, although faculty are never able to define community and the students are doubtful whether it is spiritual. Jonathan Wesley hopes that his students will learn to function as change agents in a world badly in need of healing.

What, if anything, do these teachers have in common? They teach different subjects, in radically different types of institutions, to extremely different types of students. If they share anything, it is probably their hope that their students will learn what it is they have to teach. Whatever their subject and wherever the setting, most teachers share at least one common goal: they want their students to learn.

DEFINING TEACHING

What is "teaching?" Is there a definition of teaching so broad as to include all of the types of instruction mentioned above? Are there common elements involved in all teaching?

In 1871 an obscure politician named James A. Garfield remarked at a Williams College alumni banquet that "the ideal college is Mark Hopkins on one end of a log and a student on the other." Mark Hopkins was a former president of Williams College and Garfield's favorite teacher. (In those days, the president of the college was the best teacher.) Garfield, who went on to become the twentieth president of the United States, could think of no better educational situation than to have a student sit on a log and interact with Mark Hopkins.[1]

Actually, the image is a good one for helping to define teaching. It can be converted into a simple model as follows:

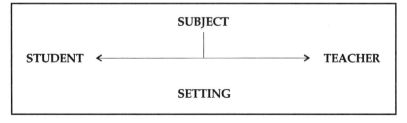

"Teaching", in this model, is defined as the "the interaction of a student and a teacher over a subject."[2] There may be one student or several in a class. The students can be young or old, bright or below average intelligence, "normal" or physically challenged, highly motivated or "turned off," rich or poor, male or female. The subject can be easy and straightforward or difficult and complex. The teacher may not be physically present, as with televised or computer-assisted instruction. But in most situations, the model holds up. A teacher, a student, and a subject. And where is the log? The model is enclosed in a box to represent the setting where teaching takes place. Teaching takes place somewhere, in some specific context. The institution may be highly selective, or "open door" in its admissions policies. The climate for learning may be favorable or destructive, supportive or frustrating. The resources, both physical and human, may be lavish or meager. No teacher teaches in a vacuum. The setting makes a difference. Teaching involves a teacher trying to teach someone something somewhere.

Can there be teaching without students? Probably not. Philosophers may argue about whether a tree falling in the forest makes a sound even if there is no one there to listen; but if there are no students, there is no teaching. Can there be teaching when there are students, but no teacher? There certainly can be learning without a teacher. A great amount of learning goes on without teachers; but the activity is called learning, not teaching. Can there be teaching without a subject? Can a person swim without water? There must be a medium, a subject, about which there can be structured and sustained dialogue. Teaching involves a teacher and a student interacting over a subject in a setting.

But what is this interaction with students that we call teaching? What is the nature of the communication that moves across the log between teachers and students?

AN ART, A SCIENCE, A PROFESSION

Some say that teaching is a science. These people stress the scientific aspects of teaching and focus on ways to systematize the communication between teacher and student. They believe that it is possible, through careful selection and pacing of materials, to regulate interactions among the student, the teacher, and materials to be learned, thus reducing the possibility that learning occurs by chance. They believe that enough is now known about how people learn to develop a technology of teaching. One of the chief advocates of a technology of teaching was B.F. Skinner.[3] He argued that teachers can be trained to employ educational technology or to use "fool-proof" materials that do the teaching.

Others say that teaching is an art. These people believe that "scientific" teaching ends up in formalized, cookbook approaches that force students to perform and bureaucratizes learning. Besides, they argue, actual teaching involves great amounts of intuition, improvisation, and expressiveness, and effective teaching depends on high levels of creativity, sound judgment, and insight. Elliot Eisner, a professor of education at Stanford, has likened the artistic aspects of teaching to the activity of a symphony conductor. The teacher, like the conductor, draws upon a repertoire of skills and orchestrates a highly complex process.[4] Teaching, Eisner argues, is much more like the work of the artist than the scientist. Teaching involves complex judgments that unfold during the course of instruction. Teachers must deal creatively with the unexpected. There are no fail-safe routines and prescriptions. Furthermore, the most important goals of teaching are those events that occur during the process. The outcomes are often embedded in the learning process itself.[5]

Perhaps the controversy about teaching should not be cast as an either-or debate. Is it not possible that teaching may be some art and some science? If so, what is the relationship of the art and the science? When is the art employed? When is the science employed?

Perhaps it would be more accurate to say that teaching involves artistic judgments that depend on science. As N.L. Gage notes, there is a "scientific basis for the art of teaching."[6] For teachers, this scientific base is found chiefly in the social sciences, in the research on learning generated by the disciplines of psychology, sociology, and speech communication. Naturally, the "knowledge" produced by the social sciences, like that of the physical sciences, is growing and ever-changing, subject to correction and open to new findings. But a knowledge base exists and is there to be known and understood by teachers. One of the major purposes of this book is to make that knowledge base available to those who teach at the college level. To be effective, we need to know what is known about how people learn.

Perhaps the best way to think about teaching is to call it what it should be called, not an art, not a science, but a profession. Teaching involves professional judgment. Teaching calls for the trained eye to see what is actually happening, and the trained mind to decide what to do next. In fact, the mark of a profession is that its knowledge can not be reduced to fail-safe rules and universal prescriptions. Most of us think of ourselves as professionals "in our field," that is, as chemists, sociologists, accountants, or nurses, but do we think of our *teaching* as professional activity? Do we believe that teaching requires the same sophisticated levels of knowledge and the same complex choices made by other important professionals: attorneys, physicians, clergy, psychologists, engineers, architects?[7] Professionals cannot rely on guesswork; as teachers, there are things we need to know. Scientific knowledge and a keen sense of how to apply it are both required for making well-informed professional decisions about teaching.

TOUGH DECISIONS, LITTLE FEEDBACK

What are these professional decisions, and how do teachers make them? Most teachers in colleges and universities play out complex roles where teaching is only one of the many things they do, along with research, advising, professional service, consulting, and involvement in the governance process of their institution. In most proprietary institutions and in some community colleges, many teachers also manage a business, practice a trade, or carry on a professional practice "on the side." As teachers, we are busy with many things besides teaching. Because of this, there is a great temptation for us to "wing it," to go into the classroom and improvise.

Life in the classroom can be hectic.[8] Before class students have questions about assignments and grades, they ask for handouts from the previous class (which they missed), or they want to know if the tests were handed back and what's going to be on the next one. During class teachers dispense information, ask questions, give answers, respond to comments, guide discussions, and referee arguments. We try to get the silent students to talk and the loud-mouths to pipe down. We set up, use, and take down various kinds of media. We look for barometers of the classroom climate—signs that the work is too easy, too hard, or just boring. We give encouragement and feedback. We give and hand back tests, make assignments, mark our recordbooks, and otherwise monitor student progress. After class there are more questions. Classrooms are busy places!

In class, teachers do a lot of "thinking on their feet" in the midst of the act of teaching.[9] We are constantly considering one or more alternatives, choosing between continuing on one path or selecting another. Important decisions are being made every few seconds. We are busy gathering information, seeking cues, and monitoring what is happening to individuals or within groups. We look for discrepancies between what should be happening and what is happening so that we can intervene. We are making distinctions, translating observations into useful concepts, and making rapid-fire choices. Unfortunately, the choices are often between two "goods." We have to choose between encouraging the rough-shod flamboyant initiative of a young man of limited ability versus the shy genius of a retiring older woman. We have to choose between spending the rest of the hour nailing down statistical formulas for students having trouble with them or moving on to the more challenging process of application. Is it best to keep discussion on track or follow an interesting diversion? It is hard to choose the "right" alternative when both alternatives are "right." Teachers are busy decision makers.

Because classrooms are busy places and teachers are preoccupied with the decisions they are making, teachers are not always aware of what is actually happening. Most of us consistently underestimate the amount of time we talk; we are seldom aware, even in "discussion classes," of how we monopolize the conversation. We are blind to the fact that we interact with some students much more frequently than others—more with men than women, more with bright students than poor students, more with those seated front and center than in the back row or on the periphery. Some teachers experience shock when they are told these things. When we see a videotape of our teaching we are often horrified to discover halting speech, out-of-control gestures, constant pacing, poor eye contact, or other disturbing mannerisms.

Unfortunately, teachers don't get much feedback on their classroom behavior because their teaching is done in relative isolation. In most colleges and universities, the old adage still applies: "My classroom is my castle." We may talk with other teachers about our subject, but we seldom talk about how we teach our subject. When we receive feedback from students through end-of-the-term course evaluations, it is usually in the form of Likert-scale responses to items about "preparedness," "knowledge of the subject," and "respect for student opinions." Although this information from course evaluations can be very valuable, faculty often find reasons to discount (or repress) this feedback. It is a rare professor who asks students, "What do you really think about my teaching?" Even when students are given an opportunity for candid constructive criticism, it is usually not early enough in the term for the teacher to do anything about it. For the most part, the academic world of higher education is simply not structured to give teachers regular, meaningful, sophisticated feedback about their teaching. Therefore, most of us struggle along in splendid isolation, working as independent practicing professionals, without supervision (even as a novice) and without built-in mechanisms for generating new ideas and techniques.

GAINING PERSPECTIVE, USING STRATEGIES

An apparent contradiction emerges from these observations about the life of teachers in college classrooms. On the one hand, teachers are too busy to think, they are driven by day-to-day tasks, and they are sometimes dreadfully out of touch with reality.

On the other hand, teachers are thinking all the time, making quick and frequent *ad hoc* decisions, trying to resolve dilemmas and explain to themselves what's happening. If this is what teaching is, being partially blinded by the dazzling glare of the classroom, but struggling to use what vision we have to see, what can be done to help us restore our sight? How can we learn to see more clearly what is happening in our classrooms and regain more control over our teaching?

Thomas Good and Jere Brophy put the matter succinctly: "If you don't know how to look, you don't see very much."[10] If you don't know what a play action pass is, you won't see it on the football field. If you don't know what a checkmate is, you won't see it on the chessboard. Similarly, there are certain things that we need to be able to see in our classrooms; and to see them, we need to know what to look for. Teachers need perspective.

In the research on the differences between beginning and experienced teachers in school settings, one of the clear and conclusive findings is that inexperienced teachers lack the conceptual structures to make sense of classrooms events. Beginning teachers simply do not extract the same levels of meaning from what they see. Experienced teachers see better what is happening.[11] True, they have more knowledge about the subject, but experienced teachers also have more perspective on the instructional process. They know how to "read" the classroom like a football quarterback reads the defense. One might expect a similar difference between novice and experienced college teachers; and in fact the gap may be more pronounced, because most college teachers have had no formal training whatsoever in what to "see." Effective teachers of whatever level, like connoisseurs of fine wine, need to know how to spot the little differences that are, in fact, the big differences.

The primary purpose of Part I of this book is to help those who teach in higher education settings to gain perspective, so that they can see better what's happening in their classrooms. To see more clearly, there are certain things teachers need to know about the subject, the setting, and the students. In the next three chapters the focus is on seeing—understanding what to look for. Among others, the following questions are addressed:

- **Perspective 1: The Subject:** What is the subject? What is the curriculum? How are the objectives of instruction established? How does the teacher make decisions about the scope and sequencing of material and the appropriate amount of breadth and depth? What is the overall organizing principle of the curriculum and how can it be discovered? What are the deeper values underlying instruction and how does the teacher recognize them?
- **Perspective 2: The Setting:** How is teaching affected by the setting in which it takes place? How do arrangements of physical space and social structure affect classroom communication? How do patterns of organizational mission, culture, and climate shape the setting? How does the setting provide limits for what will be attempted in the classroom? Why is it important for there to be a good fit between the teacher and the setting?
- **Perspective 3: The Students:** How does developmental life stage affect learning? What are the social and emotional developmental tasks that adults face as they move through the life cycle? Are there stages of cognitive development and differences in the way students engage in thinking? What is intelligence and how do students differ in the types and amount of intelligence, aptitude, and motivation they possess? How do physical differences in sensory capacity affect learning? Do students have different learning styles? How do differences in ethnic background, social class, and gender affect learning?

The primary purpose of Part II of this book is to help those who teach in higher education settings to develop teaching strategies, so that they can control, focus, and organize their communication with students. As teachers, we not only need to be able to see what is happening in our classrooms, we need to know what to do about what we see. We need to be able to think more clearly about the *activity* of teaching itself. Teachers need some means of organizing their efforts, some ways of conceptualizing the activity *they* initiate in the classroom. Therefore, effective teachers use teaching strategies. They don't walk into the classroom with some fuzzy idea like . . . maybe we'll have a discussion today. They don't ask, midway through a lesson: What was it we were supposed to be doing? They know, because they are working within the framework of a consciously selected teaching strategy. Effective teachers have a game plan for success, a method for organizing the choices they make. Their teaching is under control.

Most of what teachers do can be conceptualized under five strategies. The dictionary definition of strategy is "a plan, a method or series of maneuvers or stratagems for obtaining a specific goal or result." Applied to college teaching, the term "strategy" refers to a plan and a series of activities used to facilitate a particular kind of *learning*. The choice of the term "strategy" is intentional. The more commonly used term "method" usually refers to approaches to teaching such as "lecture," "discussion," or "laboratory" methods.[12] Although this is a common way of thinking about postsecondary teaching, "methods" usually are not based on a paradigm of how people learn. For example, a "discussion" could involve either an inquiry or group strategy. The term "discussion method," therefore, is not very useful for thinking about how to organize teaching. A more valuable approach—with more intellectual substance to it—is to base teaching on conceptions of how people learn. Oddly enough, a great amount of "teaching" takes place without much thought about how students learn. In this book, each of the five strategies is related to a learning paradigm, a base of knowledge in the social sciences about how learning takes place.

The term "paradigm" has been used in a technical way by Thomas Kuhn in his book *The Structure of Scientific Revolutions*.[13] Kuhn uses the term "paradigm" to describe the acknowledged bodies of belief and theory that undergird the activities of "normal science." Thus a paradigm is an accepted way of looking at the world out of which grow the questions, observations, and analyses of various forms of scientific endeavor. Newton and Einstein used different paradigms for "doing" physics. Paradigms shift, and eventually new paradigms replace the old, hence the occurrence of "scientific revolutions." In this book the term "paradigm" is used for the accepted models or patterns that describe the way people learn. In one sense, these are more than just "theories of learning." They involve, as Kuhn suggests, ways of looking at the world that determine what questions get asked and what research gets done. The behaviorist, for example, thinks of learning in a very different way from the way the communications expert looks at the learning that occurs in groups. The kind of learning that occurs is different, the way it takes place is different, the uses to which it is put are different, and the kind of research that has been done to elaborate "how it works" is different. Learning paradigms are based on different assumptions about what learning is and how it takes place. On the other hand, "paradigm" is used in a much less technical and more modest way in this book than in Kuhn's treatise on the philosophy of science. A "learning paradigm" is not in the same league intellectually with Einstein's reordering of the way we look at the universe. Learning paradigms are "lower case p" paradigms.

As will become evident in the five chapters on teaching strategies in Part II, each of the strategies is based on a different paradigm of the way people learn. The important thing to understand at this point is that the strategies grow out of these paradigms, and the paradigms are different. The underlying assumption for this book is that better teaching will result when postsecondary teachers begin to get a better grasp of how *learning* occurs. We will become more effective when we consciously choose to employ teaching strategies, when we broaden our repertory of strategies, and when we become more skilled in using these strategies. The five strategies are identified as follows:

- **Strategy 1: Training and Coaching:** Developing basic and advanced skills by using clear objectives, breaking instruction into steps, and reinforcing progress. Based on the findings of behavioral psychology.
- **Strategy 2: Lecturing and Explaining:** Presenting information in ways that it can be attended to, easily processed, and remembered. Based on research in cognitive psychology.
- **Strategy 3: Inquiry and Discovery:** Teaching thinking skills, problem-solving, and creativity through inquiry and discovery. Based on studies of thinking processes and the psychological research on reasoning and creativity.
- **Strategy 4: Groups and Teams:** Sharing information, working cooperatively on projects, and exploring attitudes, opinions, and

beliefs through group processes. Based on research on group communication and teams.

- **Strategy 5: Experience and Reflection:** Enabling students to reflect on learning that takes place in work settings, internships, travel, or outdoor activities. Based on holistic learning theory and theories of counseling that facilitate insight and self-understanding.

These five strategies provide useful conceptual frameworks for organizing instruction. They can be employed with any subject in any setting and across any age group of students, from college freshmen through senior citizens. The five strategies, together with the three perspectives (on the subject, the setting, and the students) provide the basic professional information that any postsecondary teacher needs to become more effective as a teacher. The rest comes through practice, patience, and perspiration.

THE CASE FOR BETTER TEACHING

Is there a renewed interest in college teaching today? Is the professor's task in the classroom being taken more seriously? Although there is sharp disagreement about whether there is a renaissance of interest in better teaching—depending on which professors one talks to in which types of institutions—there seems to be a growing case, put more persuasively, that there *should* be more interest in better teaching.[14]

The case is made in various ways. First, there is the "new-learners-in-the-classroom" argument, the idea that professors today are increasingly perplexed by the students they are expected to teach. College teachers are encountering increasing numbers of students they don't understand very well—minority groups, disabled students, older students, and women. Furthermore, they are encountering across the board, with representation in all groups and ages, students who are simply not well-prepared for academic study at collegiate institutions. Acknowledging this new student generation, more diverse and perhaps more difficult to teach, some professors are beginning to call for help.

Second, there is the "student-as-consumer" argument. Currently, fewer students are in the traditional college-going age group. The enrollment of students in the 18-24 group peaked in 1980, has declined by 10 percent since then, and is projected to decline by another 15 percent until the mid 1990s when enrollments will increase again.[15] Although more students within the age group attend some form of "college" today (especially women), the absolute number of students is not sufficient, relative to the available capacity of the system to deliver higher education. This means that all institutions (public, private, and proprietary) are scrambling for students. One way or another, students drive the system, as FTEs, payers of tuition, or "satisfied customers." Institutions are concerned, more than ever before, about enrollments—attracting and retaining as many qualified students as possible. One key to attractiveness is a reputation for good teaching. At least some institutions are sending the message through appointment, promotion and tenure procedures, and through the annual salary review process: Good teaching is important!

There is also the "accountability" argument. The higher education enterprise has become incredibly expensive. Tuition skyrockets at double the rate of the cost of living.[16] Personnel costs consume the largest share of institutional budgets. What does the money buy? One thing it *should* buy is good teaching. Most institutions are trying to hold faculty accountable for their teaching, and many are engaged in new efforts to measure student learning. Accreditation agencies are examining what institutions are doing to assess student outcomes and are seeking new ways to hold institutions accountable for having in place mechanisms to measure the impact of instruction.

There is also the "quest for quality argument." In an age of no growth, characterized by such phrases as "steady state" or "managed decline," it becomes clear that the rewards in most sectors of higher education are not going to come from program expansion or new program development. There is a growing awareness that institutions *are* now about what they are going to be in the immediate future, and that real growth will come not in numbers, but in quality. Although there are interesting exceptions to the "no growth" trend, many institutions are focusing inward with renewed interest on the curriculum and the way it is delivered through teaching. The important satisfactions will come from the increase in quality arising from improvement in teaching.

Although these arguments may add up to a "good case" for focusing on the improvement of teaching, and may, in fact, be the practical concerns that will fuel renewed interest in teaching, they fall short of the best case. A far more persuasive and intellectually substantial case can be made for the improvement of teaching in collegiate institutions. That case rests on the acknowledgement that sweeping changes have occurred within society and have drastically altered the context within which professors teach. The transformation of society is surely one of the root causes of the general concern that "something is wrong" with the educational system today. It is not so much that the system has decayed, but that a once vigorous and adequate system has been outrun by phenomenal changes in society that place new demands on education in general and on teaching in particular.

What are these changes in society and how does an awareness of them lead to a sense of urgency about the importance of improving teaching?

First, the role of knowledge in society today is vastly more important than ever before, and knowledge is conveyed, analyzed, criticized, and re-examined through effective teaching. Knowledge is what professors presumably have, and knowledge is now extremely important in society. Knowledge today is what copper, bauxite, coal, and iron ore were during the industrial era. Knowledge is the new precious metal, more valuable than gold or silver; and teaching is the way knowledge is mined and refined. The agricultural era has given way to the industrial revolution, which, in turn, has been superseded by the "information society."[17] This last transformation, a "system break" like the human milestone that occurred when nomadic hunters became farmers, has produced profound changes in the way most of us work and live.[18] What were once science fiction fantasies are now commonplace occurrences. Today, 50 percent of the people who work in offices use computers, satellite receivers dot the landscape, robots produce manufactured goods, instant photocopies are "faxed" anywhere in the world, and phone calls are made from cars and airplanes. The heavy reliance on knowledge in this new age has created a veritable explosion in teaching and learning. For teaching, this means not only helping students learn new skills in identifying, accessing, and retrieving information, but also enabling students to criticize and utilize that information so that it becomes valuable knowledge. The professor's role, as the purveyor of knowledge, is being altered at the same time it is being given new importance.

A second societal change makes the improvement of teaching urgent today: The shrinking world, sometimes referred to as the "global village," and the need for human understanding.[19] People from all over the world are encountering each other with greater frequency and in new ways. Sometimes referred to as "global confluence," this encounter is driven primarily by the internationalization of the business environment and the opening up of a world market, but also by such other activities as inter-governmental relations, cultural exchanges, the work of various service organizations, and even athletic competition.[20] Hardly any human activity today is left untouched by "globalization." Many of today's environmental problems have a global dimension—the destruction of the ozone layer, the management of the oceans, the human uses of outer space. Since the early 1970s "world conferences" have been held on issues that cut across national boundaries—population, hunger, water, the status of women, health care, human rights, and children.[21] On the one hand, there is an emerging core of human values, such as political self-determination, maximizing economic productivity, and basic standards of literacy, health, and well-being; at the same time, people continue to live in ethnocentric "envelopes" of culture, characterized by language, race, religion, customs, and a shared past. People need to learn, as never before, how to deal with each other as human beings, across, within, and in spite of their differences. For students, this is a different kind of learning, one that involves the heart as well as the head. For professors, this calls for new ways of teaching. Students sense that they need a global perspective and that it can be learned. Teaching is the key, therefore, not only to conveying new knowledge, but to bringing about an urgently needed better understanding of the "new people" one encounters in a globalized environment.

A third societal change provides still another reason for improving teaching. Along with the new importance of knowledge and the impact of cultural diversity has come a collapse of traditional norms and values, the sources of meaning for the individual. At the turn of the century, the famous sociologist Emile Durkheim prophetically described the condition of modern man as "anomie," a situation marked by the breakdown of the traditional norms governing behavior.[22] Sometimes labeled "modernist," sometimes "post-modernist," this outlook on the human predicament might simply be described: Nobody knows what to think! The intellectual activity of the contemporary university, with its fragmented and specialized approaches to the generation of knowledge, contributes to this confusion. For every theory or interpretation that scholars construct, another scholar is waiting to "de-construct" it. It is a confusing intellectual landscape, surely for professors, but especially for students. In an age where not much makes sense, how are students to find the concepts, values, and activities that become the sources of genuine meaning in their lives? Although education has always involved the pursuit of wisdom as well as knowledge and understanding, this function of education is being stressed with new urgency today. The old questions—Who am I? Where am I? How did I come to be here? How shall I live my life?—demand fresh answers. Is it so odd that students would turn to their professors for guidance as they seek to examine the meaning of life? Although it is not necessarily our job to provide the answers, it is surely within our role to help students find *their* answers. This role will surely require better teaching.

As society changes, becoming more dependent on knowledge, more globalized, more permeated with a sense of anomie, institutions of higher education, and the professors who teach in them, are called upon to produce students who can cope more successfully in this new age. Ultimately, the strongest argument for the improvement of teaching is embedded in the broader case for educational reform: To create a better fit between what it takes to live in today's society and what educational institutions provide.[23] The improvement of teaching is just one aspect of this larger task.

NOTES

1. The anecdote about James Garfield is reported in Frederick Rudolph, *The American College and University: A History* (New York: Alfred Knopf, 1965). I am indebted to my colleague, Linc. Fisch, who has identified a source that suggests that what was actually said was more likely to be "A log cabin (in the woods), with a pine bench in it with Mark Hopkins at one end and me at the other, is a good enough college for me." For a full discussion of the apparent misquotation see Carroll A. Wilson, "Familiar Small College Quotations II: Mark Hopkins and the Log." *The Colophon* (New Series), Spring 1938, 3:2. Whether a bench or a log, the image is one of close face-to-face communication with a teacher about the subject in a setting.

2. I am indebted to my close colleague, Dr. Allan Pfnister, for drawing my attention to this basic model of teaching. Professor Pfnister originally developed an idea similar to this in an article entitled "Toward a Theory of Teaching," which appeared in *Improving College Teaching*, Winter 1963, pp. 31-35. In the article Pfnister sets forth a model of teaching that stresses communication between teacher and student about a subject.

3. B.F. Skinner has been the chief advocate of a technology of teaching. A collection of his writings appeared in *The Technology of Teaching* (New York: Appleton-Century-Crofts, 1968). The work of Skinner is dealt with in

great detail in the first teaching strategy chapter of this book, "Training and Coaching."

4. Elliot W. Eisner, "The Art and Craft of Teaching," *Educational Leadership*, January 1983, p. 10. For a recent discussion of the teacher as an artist, particularly as dramatist, see Louis J. Rubin, *Artistry in Teaching* (New York: Random House, 1984). See also Joseph Axelrod, *The University Teacher as Artist* (San Francisco: Jossey-Bass, 1973).

5. Elliot W. Eisner, *The Educational Imagination*, 2nd ed., (New York: Macmillan Publishing Company, 1985), pp. 175-77. Some of the more interesting theorizing about the nature of teaching comes from the literature on elementary and secondary teaching, rather than from the higher education literature.

6. N.L. Gage, *The Scientific Basis of the Art of Teaching* (New York: Teachers College Press, 1978), p. 20. For Gage's more recent plea for the "artistic application of scientific knowledge" to teaching, see N.L. Gage, *Hard Gains in the Soft Sciences: The Case of Pedagogy* (Bloomington, IN: Phi Delta Kappa, 1985).

7. The comparison with physicians is not accidental. See Lee Shulman, "It's Harder to Teach in Class Than to Be a Physician," *Stanford School of Education News* (Stanford, CA: Stanford University, Autumn 1984).

8. The ideas for this section come from two studies of elementary and secondary school classrooms: Philip Jackson, *Life in Classrooms* (New York: Holt, Rinehart and Winston, 1986) and Thomas L. Good and Jere E. Brophy, *Looking in Classrooms* (New York: Harper and Row, 1973). Although postsecondary classrooms are somewhat different from the classrooms of public schools, they are only slightly less hectic. The main point of both books is that classrooms are very busy places and teachers don't have either the time or the mechanisms for feedback. These ideas "fit" postsecondary classrooms as well, and, in fact, the isolation of college teachers may be even greater than that of school teachers.

9. The ideas for this section are based on an important article by Christopher M. Clark and Penelope L. Peterson, "Teachers' Thought Processes" in Merlin C. Wittrock, *Handbook of Research on Teaching*, 3rd ed., (New York: Macmillan Publishing Company, 1986). The research on teachers' thought processes summarized there is based on studies of elementary and secondary classroom teachers. The general idea is that teachers engage in interactive thinking (on their feet) to explain what is happening in their classrooms, and that these processes can be documented. Postsecondary teachers engage in similar, though perhaps somewhat different, thinking processes.

10. Thomas L. Good and Jere E. Brophy, *Looking in Classrooms*, p. 36.

11. See Christopher M. Clark and Penelope Peterson, "Teachers' Thought Processes," p. 279. The reference is to studies of school teachers. Because most postsecondary teachers have no training in teaching at all, the gap

between novices and those with experience may be even greater. Postsecondary teachers are largely self-taught through on-the-job training; their development of sophisticated observation skills is an individual and largely chance matter.

12. There are some valuable books in which "teaching methods" are discussed. See especially Wilbert J. McKeachie, *Teaching Tips* (Lexington, MA: D.C. Heath and Company, 1978); Kenneth E. Eble, *The Craft of Teaching* (San Francisco: Jossey-Bass, 1977); and Joseph Axelrod, *The University Teacher as Artist* (San Francisco: Jossey-Bass, 1973). These books contain some excellent practical suggestions, and are good as far as they go, but no attempt is made to relate what the teacher does to fundamental theories about how people learn.

13. Thomas Kuhn, *The Structure of Scientific Revolutions*, 2nd ed., (Chicago: University of Chicago Press, 1970), Chapter 3, "The Nature of Normal Science."

14. See Ernest Boyer, *College: The Undergraduate Experience in America*, The Carnegie Foundation for the Advancement of Teaching, (New York: Harper & Row, 1987), p. 141. This is clearly the best, most recent, comprehensive book on the undergraduate experience in higher education with excellent chapters on the status of teaching. See especially Chapter 8, "Faculty: Mentors and Scholars," and Chapter 9, "Creativity in the Classroom."

15. The figures on enrollment of the traditional college-age cohort are drawn from the report from the Commission on National Challenges in Higher Education, "Memorandum to the 41st President of the United States," American Council on Education, 1988.

16. Arthur M. Hauptman, "Why Are College Costs Rising?" *Higher Education and National Affairs*, August 14, 1989.

17. The original description of a rapidly changing, future-oriented society uniquely dependent on knowledge was presented by Alvin Toffler in *Future Shock* (New York: Random House, 1970) and *The Third Wave* (New York: William Morrow, 1980). The idea was further elaborated as the "information society" by John Naisbitt in *Megatrends* (New York: Warner Books, 1982). For a further elaboration of the implications of the "information society," see John Naisbitt and Patricia Aburdene, *Megatrends 2000* (New York: William Morrow, 1990).

18. The description of the information age as a "system break" comes from Harold G. Shane, *Teaching and Learning in a Microelectronic Age* (Bloomington, IN: Phi Delta Kappa Educational Foundation, 1987).

19. It is difficult to trace the origin of the term, but in 1964 Marshall McLuhan wrote, "Our special and fragmented civilization of center-margin structure is suddenly experiencing an instantaneous reassembling of all its mechanized bits into an organic whole. This is the new world of the global village." See Marshall McLuhan, *Understanding Media: The Extension of Man* (New York: McGraw-Hill, 1964), p. 93. He also wrote in the preface (p. 20)

to that book, "As electronically contracted, the globe is no more than a village."

20. The concept of global confluence comes from Theodore Von Laue, *The Global City* (New York: Lippincott, 1969).

21. Harlan Cleveland, *Humangrowth: An Essay on Growth, Value and Quality of Life* (Palo Alto, CA: Aspen Institute Publication, 1978), pp. 34-38.

22. Emile Durkheim, *The Division of Labor in Society* (Glencoe, IL: Free Press, 1983 and 1933).

23. Some of the recent reports in higher education which call for reform are "Involvement in Learning: Realizing the Potential of American Higher Education," National Institute of Education, October 1984; "Integrity in the College Classroom," Association of American Colleges, February 1985; and "To Reclaim a Legacy," National Endowment for the Humanities, November 1984; "The Challenge of Connecting Learning," Association of American Colleges, 1991.

Part I
The Perspectives

The Subject

Now what I want is Facts. Teach these boys and girls nothing but Facts. Facts alone are wanted in life. —Charles Dickens, *Hard Times*

BROAD AND NARROW DEFINITIONS

In common usage the term "subject" refers to the content of an academic discipline, such as chemistry, history, or mathematics. This emphasis on content is the narrower definition of subject. A good teacher needs to know the subject. As one teacher put it: "You can't teach without some stuff." Effective teachers know the intellectual turf, and they know it well enough to make complex explanations and take on challenging questions. It is assumed, *a priori*, that before teachers begin to think about selecting teaching strategies, they must know their subject in some depth.

Most of us have spent years learning a specialization in a "subject" major and in academic programs leading to advanced degrees. Sometimes we have also accumulated significant levels of experience with the subject in professional or commercial employment settings. Most of us know how to continue to increase our knowledge of the subject as content. What we often lack, however, is a way of thinking more systematically about the purpose of our subject, that is, what we hope students will learn *through* the subject.

A broad definition of "the subject" may include not only content (information), but also such things as skills and abilities, thinking processes, and values and attitudes related to the content. Although students today expect and need information, they will need more than that. One might say, the subject is whatever the teacher hopes will be learned and whatever the students are willing to learn. This broader way of looking at the subject is more useful, but it opens a floodgate to a deluge of possibilities. We are then confronted with the question: What should be included?

ESTABLISHING GOALS

Because no teacher can teach everything, the key question, framed aptly by the nineteenth-century philosopher Herbert Spencer, becomes the following: What knowledge is of most worth?[1] In the information age, when new knowledge is generated at an ever-accelerating rate, Spencer's question takes on new urgency. Conscientious teachers struggle with this question to delineate the subject more precisely for the purposes of instruction. This deliniation involves setting goals. Consider how each of the following teachers addresses Spencer's question.

At Mid-West University, Roscoe Meade is one of 16 professors in a department that has a very carefully sequenced curriculum designed to serve undergraduate majors, master's degree students, and doctoral candidates. The goal, throughout the curriculum, is to help students "think like a sociologist thinks"; that is, to expose students to the topics that sociologists study and the ways they go about conducting research. For Professor Meade, the discipline of sociology is extremely useful for "packaging" the knowledge he most wants his students to have.

At Elm Grove College, Edna Wolf wants to expose students to the very best classic works of literature with the hope that her students will not only appreciate the technical craft and aesthetic grace of the writing, but will also gain some deeper vision of the meaning of human existence. She knows that her colleagues in the Humanities Division at Elm Grove share this goal, because together they have carefully selected the "great works of art" most worthy of study in the coordinated series of courses that make up the "core curriculum" in the humanities. For Edna Wolf, the knowledge most worth having is the classical wisdom that addresses ultimate concerns.

When people ask Vicki Hastings what she teaches at Pacific Coast Community College, she replies, "students." Her goal is to get to know each one personally in her wellness classes and to select the kinds of activities and topics that will best meet their individual needs for personal and physical development. For Vicki, the needs of her students play an important role in determining what knowledge is of most worth.

When Nancy Green teaches interior design at the Art Institute of the South, she sometimes feels inexperienced as a teacher, but she knows that she is an expert in her field, because she has lived it for 15 years. Her goal is to teach the skills that she knows will be needed on the job. She hates the thought of sending her students into the field poorly prepared. For Nancy, the knowledge of most worth is the information and skills that will make her students competent designers.

At New England Theological Seminary, Jonathan Wesley wants to help students understand themselves as agents of social transformation by experiencing what it means to change—beginning with their own attitudes, opinions, and beliefs. To help others change, one must first experience the process of transformation within one's own self. For Jonathan Wesley, the knowledge of most worth is that which will enable his students to become effective advocates of social change.

All these teachers answer the question, "What knowledge is of most worth?" in very different ways. They all arrive at different conclusions about goals; and their goals, naturally, determine what will be included in their courses. It is often a painful process, this business of articulating goals, but this is the place to begin, because it is the foundation of all instructional activity. Curriculum specialists—people who do research and write in a sub-field of education known as "curriculum theory"—have provided a number of useful concepts for helping teachers select the "knowledge of most worth" and organize it for instruction.

CLARIFYING OBJECTIVES

The process of clarifying objectives is simply a matter of making goals more specific. A teacher without objectives—some basic plan for what is to be accomplished—is like a traveler without a destination; not only is it hard to get there, it is also difficult to know when you have arrived. Sometimes objectives will be very concrete delineations of what the students will be able to do as a result of learning; at other times objectives may be more open-ended, flexible descriptions of a situation or problem, out of which various kinds of learning might arise. Either way, a teacher needs some clarity about desired learning outcomes—what the student will learn from instruction.

Teachers are often tempted to teach more than can be learned because there is so much "out there" that could be learned. An effective teacher learns to narrow learning outcomes to a manageable list. Usually we are forced into choosing among desirable outcomes of various kinds. *Cognitive outcomes* have to do with thinking and conceptual abilities; *affective outcomes* have to do with attitudes, values, and feelings; and *psychomotor outcomes* have to do with movement or activity, such as the ability to perform a skill.[2] Although all of these outcomes are desirable, forced choices often have to be made in prioritizing the most desirable outcomes.

When effective teachers seek to define objectives, they ask a series of probing questions about the subject.[3] Where does the subject begin and end? This is usually referred to as *scope* in curriculum planning. How much of the delineated subject should be included in instruction? This is usually called *breadth* in curriculum planning. How deeply should the teacher go into a particular aspect of the subject? This is usually called *depth*. Of the many things to be covered, how much time should be devoted to some things as opposed to others? This is usually called *centrality and balance* in the curriculum. To what extent should students be required to study certain things as opposed to being allowed to pursue their own interests? This is usually called *flexibility* in the curriculum. Which things should be taught first and which second, that is, are there certain topics or skills that are prerequisite to other topics and skills? This is usually referred to as *sequence* in curriculum planning. What is the teacher intentionally leaving out? This is the matter of identifying *gaps* in the curriculum. What is the teacher forgetting to include? This is called the *null* curriculum. What is the teacher unwittingly and unintentionally teaching? This is called the *hidden* curriculum.

As teachers make plans for a class or a course, they must make decisions about all of these matters. These are all difficult questions to answer, and may never be answered fully or finally, but they are useful guides for selecting and organizing the subject for instruction. The answers to these questions help teachers in framing their objectives. Consider the examples presented earlier.

Professor Meade focuses primarily on cognitive outcomes in his upper division course in demographics. He uses a standard textbook and takes up the topics in the order in which they are presented in the book. This is not a "survey" course, so his object is depth and his central focus is on methods of acquiring and interpreting demographic data. Students are permitted some flexibility in selecting a term project topic, but there is also a final exam, along with several quizzes, to ensure that students have a grasp of all the essential information. There is general agreement in the discipline of sociology about what a course in demographics should contain, and it is a fairly self-contained field, so Professor Meade doesn't need to worry much about duplication of material presented in other courses. His colleagues can count on him to cover the essential content and not leave any gaps.

Edna Wolf focuses on affective as well as cognitive outcomes in her literature course, that is, she hopes that students will have opinions and feelings about the classic works of literature she presents. The order of the material is not important; she gave up historical chronology years ago in favor of in-depth study of a few key selected works. Students have no choice of what to study; after all, she and her colleagues have spent considerable time in selecting the most appropriate classics. There is no chance of duplication from course to course this way, and there is little concern about gaps, since chronological survey is not the goal. The central focus is on using great works of literature to help students "examine their unexamined lives." The most important objective is to enable students to gain a deeper vision of the meaning of life in a rapidly changing post-modern society characterized by normlessness.

Vicki Hastings focuses on affective and psychomotor outcomes in her course on wellness. She hopes to help students forge new commitments about eating, mental attitudes, and exercise habits. Because she focuses on the students and their needs, she "covers" various topics when students express interest, not going into much depth on any one subject with the whole group, but conferring after class with students who want to learn more. She knows that she can't teach everything in one course and encourages students to register for the advanced course in the following term. Because her course is not a "talk course," the central focus is on getting people moving, enabling them to experience the new-found sense of well-being that comes with becoming more physically fit by practicing fitness. And above all, Vicki knows that she can't come to class 50 pounds overweight and smoking like a chimney; because if she does, the "hidden curriculum" will override everything else she tries to do or say about fitness.

Nancy Green is interested primarily in cognitive outcomes, but she also wants her students to develop the interpersonal skills needed for working as members of a team and for working with clients. She knows that her students must be able to solve "real world" design problems, and that to do so, they must become experts in dealing simultaneously with the functional use of space, with aesthetic concerns, and with financial considerations. This becomes her central focus and these are the topics she wants to include, but she knows that flexibility can be introduced into the course as students work together on a final team project that addresses these topics.

Jonathan Wesley knows that the commitment to social justice is already implanted in his divinity students; his concern is in helping them to understand how people come to change their attitudes, opinions, and values as they make personal and social transformations. To gain this understanding, his students are given the opportunity to experience what it is like to reexamine their own position on various social questions. The focus of the course, therefore, is on affective outcomes, what Wesley calls "the transformation of the heart." He selects a few social issues to study in depth—capital punishment vs. rehabilitation of offenders, "pro-choice" vs. "right-to-life," public vs. private approaches to social welfare—and uses these as the vehicle for exploring where attitudes about public policy come from and how they can be changed. The sequence of the study of these issues is immaterial, and the coverage of all the important current issues is not the goal, because the central focus is on learning first-hand how personal transformation takes place.

Every teacher needs to be able to identify immediate and long-range objectives—for each class and for the course as a whole—as the first step toward carrying out instruction. Teaching often breaks down right at the beginning when we have not clarified our primary goals and expressed them as objectives. When we lack a clear sense of the desired outcomes of instruction, we often try to do too much and our teaching gives way to random (often frantic) activity. Effective teachers know what they are trying to achieve, and they consciously select and continually refine their objectives.

IDENTIFYING THE ORGANIZING PRINCIPLE

Course objectives are important, but they exist in a broader context. Most courses have their niche within a broader set of organizing principles and educational philosophies. The organizing principle of a course, or set of courses, may or may not be well-articulated; but it is usually there, determining, often in subtle ways, what happens day after day in the classroom.

One place to look for the organizing principle is in the core of required courses that students must take, sometimes referred to as the general education requirements.[4] What is it, if anything, that the institution identifies as essential for all students? In a large, public university this may take the form of a distribution requirement, such as 12 credit hours in each of the areas of the sciences, social sciences, and humanities. Such a requirement sends the message that the academic disciplines are important and that students should be exposed, usually through introductory courses, to several of these disciplines. On the other hand, a small liberal arts college may require that all students take a series of interdisciplinary, often team-taught, courses, especially designed as a core curriculum. Through such courses, the faculty sends the message that a liberal education has at its core certain essential knowledge found through acquaintance with the great books or seminal thinkers of an intellectual tradition. Students are expected to obtain a "general education" or a "common learning" as well as the specialized knowledge that comes through a disciplinary major or professional training. The transfer program of a community college, likewise, may have certain required courses, which are part of an articulated transfer agreement with the public, four-year institutions in the same state. For the occupational programs of a community college or a proprietary school, the core requirements may be in certain basic skills, such as reading, writing, and speaking or in mathematical computation. A theological seminary will usually identify certain courses in the Bible, theology, and church history as "foundational" to all further study. The way an institution identifies its "required core" of studies will often provide some insight into the educational philosophy or key organizing principle of the curriculum in that institution.

It is important, however, to look beyond the core, beyond the general requirements, to identify a more comprehensive principle used to organize subjects for instruction. Five organizing principles may commonly be found in the curricula of postsecondary institutions, and one or more of these principles will surface in most institutions as the key organizing principle or as the "philosophy" of the curriculum.[5]

The most frequently observed principle is the organizational system of the academic disciplines. Most colleges of arts and sciences are organized according to a disciplinary system, and the disciplines usually correspond to departments, such as chemistry, sociology, history, or biology. But what is a discipline? One comprehensive description suggests that a discipline is a community of persons; an expression of human imagination; a domain; a tradition; a syntactical structure and mode of inquiry; a conceptual structure; a specialized language or other system of symbols; a heritage of literature and artifacts and a network of communication; a valuative and affective stance; and an instructive community.[6] A discipline is all of these things, but a simpler definition might be this: A discipline is a specified academic domain with agreed-upon rules for discovering and transmitting knowledge.

Neither the number of disciplines nor their boundaries has ever remained static over time. Old disciplines die out as new disciplines emerge, providing the basis for new methods of inquiry and new knowledge. But at any given point in time, there is general (if not absolute) agreement within a discipline about what is to be studied and how it is to be studied. The professional associations of the major disciplines play a key role in this process of definition.

There are, of course, great advantages to the organizational system of the academic disciplines. As Philip Phenix notes:

> The most impressive claim the disciplines have upon education is that they are the outcome of learning that has actually been successful. A discipline is a field of inquiry in which learning has been achieved in an unusually productive way. Most human efforts at understanding fail. A very few succeed, and these fruitful ways of thought are conserved and developed in the disciplines. Every discipline is simply a pattern of investigation that has proved to be a fertile field for the growth of understanding.[7]

Furthermore, the disciplines provide a common understanding (a lingua franca) for stable interchange among institutions and teachers. A course in introductory sociology is likely to be relatively the same from institution to institution. Most chemists will have at least general agreement about what is taught in organic chemistry.

Although most postsecondary teachers have had a significant exposure to the academic disciplines in their own education—

enough to appreciate the value of the disciplinary system—many teachers today raise questions about the predominance of the disciplines as the exclusive organizing principle for the curriculum. While the disciplines may serve well the "academic priesthood," most of life's problems in the information age, both in the world of work and in the society at large, do not come in the tidy packages suggested by the academic disciplines. Students trained exclusively in a system of academic disciplines may be ill-equipped to deal with the problems of the real world. Students often have trouble seeing the relationships among disciplines, and the rigid boundaries and specialized language of the disciplines often hinder communication. Although the academic disciplines provide an excellent framework for the discovery of knowledge, they do not necessarily provide the best (and certainly not the only) means for the transmission and application of knowledge.

Some colleges organize the curriculum around a different principle, using a list of selected "great books."[8] In the earliest colonial colleges of America, students studied (usually in Greek or Latin) the "classics," a series of great works that embodied the roots of Western thought. Proponents of this view today argue that the wisdom of the past is distilled in selected great books that have become classics. Although the knowledge of the world is always expanding, they argue that the important problems confronting human beings have already been dealt with by the great minds through the ages. While the form of the problems may change, the substance will not. Thus, the foundation of learning should be found in the great books—or other works of art and music—that represent the best of a long tradition. The great books curriculum helps students to distinguish between genuine knowledge and the superficial accumulation of information. It also addresses directly the problem of normlessness by introducing students to the cultural norms and values that have come to be considered timeless.

The most ardent defenders of the great books organize the entire curriculum around a list of classics. Most often, only a course, or a series of courses (often within the general education curriculum) are organized around the great books theme. In either case, it is in the discussion of these works, usually in small seminars, where the essence of the educational experience lies. The strength of this approach is in the development of critical thinking, speaking, and writing skills—the traditional foundations of liberal learning—and in the humanizing effect of such learning.

It can be argued, however, that a curriculum with such a strong historical orientation shortchanges the study of the present and the future and does little to prepare students to enter the highly specialized and increasingly technical job market of the information age. If there has been a true "system break" with the past, perhaps the extraordinary emphasis on "classics" in the great books approach is dysfunctional for students in the information age. Today, there is also much controversy about the works that truly belong on the list, with some critics of the great books curriculum suggesting that more works from non-Western cultures and more works by women and members of minority groups should be included for study.[9] The widespread and frequent encounter today of diverse groups of people suggests that knowledge of Western culture alone is insufficient.

Another way of organizing the curriculum is to focus on the personal development of students. Here the organizing principle is shifted from the content of the subject to the growth of the individual student. The subject becomes the medium for personal development. Through recent research on human development, particularly (post-adolescent) adult development, key developmental tasks of college-age students (establishing identity, becoming autonomous, etc.) have been identified. Theories of social-emotional, ethical, and cognitive development provide insights into the stages of normal development through which most college students are passing.[10] Advocates of what is often called a "student-centered curriculum" argue that the primary purpose of education is to facilitate human development, and that nothing is truly learned unless it involves the maintenance or enhancement of the self in some way.[11] Courses should include subjects that address students' personal concerns, and the curriculum should not be a series of requirements but a list of opportunities from which students choose those studies that best meet their needs. Through extensive consultation with faculty mentors, students and faculty together design a program of studies— courses, independent study projects, work experience, internships, travel—that facilitates the development of students here and now rather than preparing them for some remote indescribable future.

Although student development as an organizing principle for the curriculum maximizes opportunities for personalizing education, critics argue that the substance of education, particularly the development of academic skills in some depth in a selected field, is often neglected. Students may too easily avoid what is new, difficult, or of future (rather than present) interest or value. They may complete their program of studies lacking the technical knowledge (gleaned through sometimes distasteful discipline) so essential for the information age.

Still another organizing principle for the college curriculum is the development of selected competencies. Proponents of what is often called a "competency-based curriculum" contend that education should be functional and students should be prepared for specific roles, particularly occupational roles, which they will begin to fill upon completion of their studies. Competency-based curricula are most often found in professional schools and in majors designed to prepare students for a specific occupation, but some efforts have also been made to establish competency-based curricula in liberal arts colleges.[12] The most important questions in a competency-based curriculum are the following: What should graduates be able to do? What competencies should they have? What educational experiences will assure specified outcomes? In a competency-based curriculum the starting point is usually some occupational or "real-life" activity or skill. If it is possible to specify what a teacher, nurse, accountant, or parent or citizen, actually does when he or she is doing it well, then it is possible to work backward from those activities to the educational experiences that will produce those competencies. Students work through a series of course and other educational activities that have been carefully designed to develop (and test) selected competencies.

The great strength of a competency-based curriculum is its emphasis on results—specific, testable, clearly defined educational outcomes. Students often are allowed to work at their own pace, focusing on what they really need to learn to become competent. Teachers and students both know the goal and when they reach it. Critics of this approach, on the other hand, argue that the focus is too narrow and too future-oriented. Students fail to gain a sufficient appreciation of their cultural heritage and the ways knowledge comes into being. When the focus is exclusively on pre-selected competencies, the educational experience becomes routine and unimaginative. Students will settle for learning only what they need to know rather than developing a love of learning for its own sake. It is sometimes argued that students in such programs trade away an education for the accumulation of a handful of currently marketable but soon-to-be-outdated skills. As for exploring the deeper meaning of life, the important questions may not even be raised.

A final theme sometimes used as an organizing principle for the curriculum is social change. Here the emphasis is on developing individuals who are able to help build a better society. The assumption, of course, is that the present society is far from perfect, producing too many unresolved social, economic, political, and environmental problems. Some argue that because education is increasingly funded by society, a collegiate education ought to result collectively in the betterment of society. For this to occur, it is necessary to use an interdisciplinary approach and to attack the problems of society by studying those problems directly. In what is sometimes called a "social problems curriculum," courses are organized around problem themes, such as urban problems, environmental issues, criminal justice, or Third World problems. Some institutions even organize into "cluster colleges" or "colleges within a college" where students of similar interests can live and study together.[13] Usually, a challenging out-of-the-classroom internship or service experience is also associated with these programs.

The great advantage to this approach is that by emphasizing the present and the future, a social problems curriculum prepares students to take active roles as citizens in the community and gives them the knowledge and skills they need to become leaders and change-agents in the information age. To the extent that this curriculum also addresses problems from a global perspective, students are also better prepared to grapple with life in the global village. Those who criticize this approach, however, point out that an *a priori* commitment to change seriously threatens education as a "value-free" process. The highly desirable academic value known as "objectivity" is often replaced with a conscious nurture of commitment. Furthermore, the study of the historical heritage and great works of the past is often shortchanged in the rush to cast everything as a contemporary problem. By overemphasizing "problem solving," other academic skills are neglected. A preoccupation with social problems, it is argued, leads to an overemphasis on the utilitarian function of education, while neglecting deeper academic values, such as the development of a philosophy of life or the cultivation of the "life of the mind" for its own sake. Consider once again the examples provided earlier.

Professor Meade's sociology courses are part of a curriculum that uses the academic disciplines as the chief organizing principle. He wants to introduce students to sociology as a discipline and to "socialize" them into the modes of academic inquiry that sociologists use to go about their studies. Edna Wolf's courses in the Humanities Division at Elm Grove College have been organized around the great books theme. She believes that most of the important human concerns have been expressed already in the classics; and she wants her students to share with her and with each other their personal responses to these works. To the extent that Vicki Hastings' courses at Pacific Coast Community College are part of any organized set of offerings, they reside within a student-centered curriculum. Her courses are there for students to choose when they feel a personal need to live happier, healthier lives. Nancy Green's courses at the Art Institute of the South are part of a competency-based program in interior design. As an experienced designer herself, she has a clear concept of what jobs in this field are and what skills are needed to perform these jobs well. She knows that functional, aesthetic, and financial considerations come into all design decisions, and she wants her students to have the competencies to deal effectively with these problems. Jonathan Wesley organizes his teaching around the theme of social change. His course in personal and social transformation at the New England Theological Seminary is designed to provide students with first-hand knowledge of how people come to hold social attitudes and what mechanism can be used effectively to help people reexamine their attitudes.

Most teaching is brought into focus by an organizing principle that governs the "how and why" for the way things are done. The organizing principle does not always appear in its pure form, and in some cases two or more principles are combined in creative ways. Nevertheless, teachers need to become aware of and be able to articulate clearly the dominant organizing principles governing their teaching.

AGREEING TO DISAGREE

Where do these organizing principles come from? Surely they do not appear one day out of thin air! Curriculum themes have their origins, of course, in many places. John Dewey once identified the sources of curricular goals as "the students, the society and organized subject matter."[14] In higher education, these origins take on their own peculiar form, but in general, Dewey's assertion holds.

Students exert their influence directly, as the "peaceful protestors" did in the 1960s, or indirectly, as the "calculating consumers" did in the 1980s. The most important, but perhaps most subtle, influence of students is through the *a priori* decision that the institution has made about what students to serve and how to serve them. By agreeing to serve a particular kind of student, the institution has opened the door to a big influence on the curriculum. The underlying themes and organizing principles usually arise at least in part from the way the institution defines what students to serve and how to serve them.

Societal influences are also important, because the dominant values of society are quickly turned into expectations for education. In the late 1950s, the launching of Sputnik by the Soviet Union produced a wave of anxiety in the United States about training more and better scientists and technicians. In the 1960s, the civil rights and women's movements generated a high level of concern about equal educational opportunity. In the 1970s and 1980s, as the employment market underwent important structural changes, a new emphasis was placed on career education and job preparation.[15] In the years ahead, the emphasis will be on new knowledge, new abilities to derive and manage technical information, and new interpersonal skills necessary for working in a globalized environment. In the United States today, where change is very rapid and there is a frequent turnover in ideas, values, and technology, the curriculum is often strongly impacted by the shifting expectations of a rapidly changing society.

The curriculum is also influenced by the ways in which "subject matter" is conceptualized, formalized, and emphasized. In higher education this takes place chiefly through a host of academic professional associations and accrediting bodies. These are essentially voluntary associations of scholars with similar interests, but they now have a profound influence upon the curriculum through their reports, recommendations, and annual meetings. What would the language curriculum be without the Modern Language Association? How would the business curriculum be different without the American Assembly of Collegiate Schools of Business? What influence takes place through the accrediting processes of the American Psychological Association or the American Chemical Society?

Teachers in postsecondary institutions today must take into account a broad array of outside factors that influence the curriculum. The subject, in the broader sense, involves a balance between what the teacher wants to teach, what someone else wants taught, and what students want to learn. Even in the most prestigious colleges and universities, where the curriculum has long been the sacred prerogative of the faculty, student needs, societal pressures, and changing conceptions of the subject increasingly determine what is taught. The curriculum exists in a social context.

Ultimately, however, the organizing principles of the curriculum have their origins in a "philosophy of education." Whenever choices are made about what to include in instruction or how to go about instruction, values are at stake; and values—what is real, true, good, and beautiful—rest ultimately on one's personal philosophy. Many decisions about what should be included in instruction are governed by philosophical considerations. Differences in curriculum orientation, therefore, ultimately involve disagreements about the underlying purposes of education.[16] Disagreements about educational purposes, in turn, involve fundamental philosophical controversies about the nature of reality, what constitutes knowledge, and how to define human nature. Is knowledge gained primarily from sense experience? Is the world we see the real world, or is there more to the world than meets the eye? Are human beings more emotional than rational? Is the individual more important than society, or society more important than the individual? Are students naturally good and internally motivated, or are they essentially lazy and perverse? Is there such a thing as progress? These are the great, unanswerable human questions—issues that philosophers have struggled to clarify through the ages—but the tentative answers we provide to these questions determine in large measure how we will organize our subject for instruction.

Sometimes our colleagues will ask, "What evidence is there that the curriculum should include one thing as opposed to another?" Usually this is the wrong question, because "evidence" of the kind that will settle the argument is not forthcoming. Most curricular decisions are based on a commitment to particular values that become the criteria for "what's important." If Roscoe Meade, Edna Wolf, Vicki Hastings, Nancy Green, and Jonathan Wesley were all brought together in the same room, it would not be long before they would be at each other's throats, because they all have different ideas about what is important in their teaching. It is not difficult to predict what would happen if they were all asked to serve on the same curriculum committee. There would be, no doubt, heated arguments about vocational vs. liberal education (the "cash vs. culture" debate), egalitarian vs. elitist education (the "all vs. best" debate), and applied vs. basic education (the "useful vs. theoretical" debate). Hopefully, these teachers would grow to appreciate the strengths and weaknesses of their varying and sometimes opposing viewpoints. Maybe they would be able to generate some creative synthesis of their differences. But more likely they would simply have to agree to disagree. Perhaps it is best that they all teach at different institutions. Agreeing to disagree is what Americans have chosen to do about higher education. That is why there is no national system of higher education, no national examination for entrance, no national university, and so many different kinds of institutions. The great achievement of American higher education is its diversity; it's great challenge will be in generating diverse responses to the demands of a new era.

Will a new curriculum theory emerge for the information age? Will the older organizing principles—the disciplines, the great books, the student-centered approach, the competency-based system, the social problems curriculum—give way to some new organizing principle, based on a yet to be articulated futuristic philosophy of education? In an age of such rapid change, filled with so many surprises, it is imprudent to answer with an unequivocal "no"; but the organizing principles have deep roots, and because education has been a conservative and conserving enterprise, it is unlikely that these principles will suddenly drop out of sight. What is more likely, instead, is that they will take on new forms, become more highly elaborated, differentiated, and synthesized. The disciplines will not go away; to the contrary, there will probably be more of them, but more interdisciplinary studies surely will be elaborated. The list of "great books" will become longer and longer (because truly new knowledge has been generated in the twentieth century), and the list will surely be broadened and integrated to include the great works of other cultures and sub-cultures. There will be many student-centered curricula, based not only on the developmental needs of traditional-age college students, but also on the needs of mid-career adults and senior citizens, and members of different ethnic groups and genders. And so on. Some of the best aspects of the various organizing principles may be connected in creative new ways to overcome the shortcomings of each alone. It may be possible within a disciplinary framework to introduce students to the "great books" of that discipline, or to strike a balance somehow between what a student needs to know (competency-based curriculum) and wants to know (student-centered curriculum).

A new curriculum, better suited to the present and the future, will be a protean curriculum that changes shape to fit the needs of many different subjects being taught to many different kinds of students in a variety of institutional settings. It will be "pluralistic," achieving many goals and connecting in creative and enriching ways the singular strands of earlier organizing principles. The new curriculum will respect (and teach respect for) cultural pluralism within a nation and cultural diversity among many nations. Through the pluralistic curriculum, students will develop an awareness that many kinds of knowledge are of great worth. Greater efforts will be made to connect the learning that occurs in general education with the major and across majors, and more attention will be paid to assessing learning outcomes at all levels.[17] Above all, the curriculum of the new era will reflect diversity—the diversity of the peoples of the world, and the diversity of ways of learning in a world governed less by tradition and more by existential choices growing out of well-articulated needs.

As teachers we need to know what our role is and where we fit in all of this diversity. We are likely to be most effective in a setting where our goals and abilities are relatively compatible with the curriculum we are trying to implement, where there is a high level of correspondence between our philosophy of education and what we can reasonably expect to achieve with the students we teach. Because the philosophical questions are for the most part unresolvable, they keep coming around again and again, like the decorated horses on a merry-go-round. It is important to realize that the significant philosophical issues in education have their historical antecedents.[18] What most people argue about today in education has been argued about many times before. Effective teachers know how and when to take a stand, and they know what their institution stands for; but they also know that reasonable people will disagree about what is most valuable in education, and that certain arguments won't be settled. They know how to get off the issue merry-go-round and get on with their teaching; they know how to keep from going in circles and how to make commitments to what is important in their classroom, at their institution, and for their students. Effective teachers are able to see the subject in perspective.

CONCLUSIONS

Before selecting a teaching strategy, we must surely know the subject, not only in the narrow sense of content, but also in the broader and deeper sense of a medium for what is to be learned. In addition, we must be able to think systematically about organizing the subject for instruction. What are the goals? What are the long-range and immediate objectives of instruction? What are the organizing principles upon which goals and objectives are based? What, also, are the deeper, underlying purposes of education? What are the origins of these purposes? What is the educational philosophy undergirding the curriculum? And, above all, we need to ask ourselves these questions regularly and systematically: When I teach, what am I really trying to do? What is my subject and what am I trying to teach *through* my subject?

All serious thinking about teaching appropriately begins with the subject.

NOTES

1. Herbert Spencer, *Education: Intellectual, Moral and Physical* (New York: Appleton, 1860); quoted in Daniel Tanner and Laurel Tanner, *Curriculum Development: Theory into Practice*, 2nd ed., (New York: Macmillan, 1980), p. 143. The work by Tanner and Tanner is perhaps the most useful single volume on general curriculum theory and is recommended for those who wish to pursue the subject further.

2. The designation of outcomes into "cognitive," "affective," and "psychomotor" domains is commonly found in curriculum textbooks. Efforts to establish a series of taxonomies of outcomes appear in Benjamin Bloom, *Taxonomy of Educational Objectives: Cognitive Domain* (New York: David McKay, 1956); David Kathwohl, *Taxonomy of Education Objectives: Affective Domain* (New York: David McKay, 1964); and Nita Harrow, *Taxonomy of Educational Objectives: Psychomotor Domain* (New York: Longman, 1972).

3. The concepts for analyzing the curriculum (scope, sequence, breadth, depth, etc.) are found scattered about in the basic standard curriculum texts. This list is a composite developed by the author from William H. Schubert, *Curriculum: Perspective, Paradigm and Possibility* (New York: Macmillan, 1986); Daniel Tanner and Laurel Tanner, *Curriculum Development*, and Paul Dressel, *College and University Curriculum* (Berkeley, CA: McCutchan, 1968). The concept of the hidden curriculum comes from Benson Snyder, *The Hidden Curriculum* (New York: Alfred Knopf, 1971), and the idea of the "null curriculum" is derived from Elliot Eisner, *The Educational Imagination*, 2nd ed., (New York: Macmillan, 1985). For a guidebook on planning courses and

curricula in higher education, see Robert Diamond, *Designing and Improving Courses and Curricula in Higher Education* (San Francisco: Jossey-Bass, 1989) and William Berquist, Ronald Gould, and Elinor Greenberg, *Designing Undergraduate Education* (San Francisco: Jossey-Bass, 1981).

4. The concept of "general education" has been elaborated in many sources and over a long period of time. The idea has its roots in the early twentieth century and was a response in part to the elective system established under Charles Eliot at Harvard and also a reaction to the apparent "normlessness" of the World War I period. A brief conceptual treatment can be found in a report of the Carnegie Foundation for the Advancement of Teaching, *Missions of the College Curriculum* (San Francisco: Jossey-Bass, 1977), Chapter 8, "General Education: An Idea in Distress," and in Ernest Boyer, *College: The Undergraduate Experience* (New York: Harper & Row, 1987), Chapter 6, "General Education: The Integrated Core." For historical treatments, see especially Daniel Bell, *The Reforming of General Education* (Garden City, NY: Anchor, 1966) and Ernest Boyer and Martin Kaplan, *Educating for Survival* (New Rochelle, NY: Change Magazine Press, 1977). For examples of current programs, see Zelda Gamson and Associates, *Liberating Education* (San Francisco: Jossey-Bass, 1984). For guidelines on curricular change in general education, see Jerry Gaff, *General Education Today* (San Francisco: Jossey-Bass, 1983).

5. The organizing principles developed in this section were originally developed by the author for a course and shared with a colleague. The same structure was used by that colleague, Clifton Conrad, in *The Undergraduate Curriculum: A Guide to Innovation and Reform* (Boulder, CO: Westview Press, 1978). For a fuller treatment of curricular issues in higher education and an interesting collection of source materials, see Arthur Levine, *Handbook on Undergraduate Curriculum* (San Francisco: Jossey-Bass, 1978), the best single-volume work on higher education curriculum.

6. Arthur King and John Brownell, *The Curriculum and the Disciplines of Knowledge* (New York: John Wiley, 1966), p. 95.

7. Phillip Phenix, *Realms of Meaning* (New York: McGraw-Hill, 1964), p. 36.

8. The college that uses the great books curriculum in its purest form is St. John's College with campuses in Annapolis, Maryland, and Santa Fe, New Mexico. For a historical treatment of the origin of the great books curriculum and a listing of the classics used for study, see Arthur Levine, *Handbook on Undergraduate Curriculum* (San Francisco: Jossey-Bass, 1978), pp. 356-58 and 592-96.

9. "The Canons Under Fire," *Time*, April 11, 1988, p.66. The article contains a summary of the struggles at Stanford University to revise the list of books used for its Western culture courses.

10. The classic formulation of student development needs appears in Arthur Chickering, *Education and Identity* (San Francisco: Jossey-Bass, 1969).

A presentation of the case for a student-centered curriculum is found in Arthur Chickering and David Halliburton, et al., *Developing the College Curriculum: A Handbook for Faculty and Administrators* (Washington, DC: Council for the Advancement of Small Colleges, 1977). A more recent summary of developmental needs of nontraditional as well as traditional age students can be found in Arthur Chickering, *The Modern American College* (San Francisco: Jossey-Bass, 1981), Chapter 1, "The Life Cycle," by Arthur Chickering and Robert Havinghurst. The volume also contains excellent chapters on emerging theories of ego development, cognitive development, and moral development.

11. Carl Rogers, *Client-Centered Therapy* (Boston: Houghton-Mifflin, 1951), Chapter 9, "Student-Centered Teaching." As Rogers puts it: "A person learns only those things which he perceives as being involved in the maintenance of, or enhancement of, the structure of self."

12. Competency-based curricula in teacher education date back to the work of W.W. Travers in the 1920s. The best-known recent effort to establish a competency-based curriculum in a liberal arts college is at Alverno College, Milwaukee, Wisconsin. See Bob Knott, "What is a Competency-Based Curriculum in the Liberal Arts?" *Journal of Higher Education*, 1975, 64, pp. 25-39.

13. The University of Wisconsin, Green Bay, was originally organized around the theme of "environmental problems" and some of the "cluster colleges" at the University of California, Santa Cruz, have social problems themes as their organizing focus. John Dewey is the key resource on education as "social reconstruction." See John Dewey, *Democracy and Education* (New York: Macmillan, 1961).

14. An application of Dewey's model of the forces that shape the curriculum can be found in Denis Lawton, *Social Change, Educational Theory and Curriculum Planning* (London: University of London Press, Ltd., 1973). See also Carnegie Foundation, *Missions of the College Curriculum*, Chapter 3, "External Forces that Shape Curriculum," and Tanner and Tanner, *Curriculum Development*, Chapter 5, "Curriculum Sources and Influences—Society, Knowledge and Learner."

15. For a discussion of the passage of student generations from one era to another see Arthur Levine, *When Dreams and Heroes Died* (San Francisco: Jossey-Bass, 1980).

16. The best single volume for introducing the classical "philosophers of education" is Robert Ulich, *Three Thousand Years of Educational Wisdom* (Cambridge, MA: Harvard University Press, 1954). An excellent exposition of the relationships of philosophical issues and curriculum theory is found in Robert Zais, *Curriculum: Principles and Foundations* (New York: Harper & Row, 1976).

17. Association of American Colleges, *The Challenge of Connecting Learning*, Vol. I, *Liberal Learning and the Arts and Sciences Major* (Washington, DC: Association of American Colleges, 1991).

18. For those seeking an understanding of the historical roots of contemporary issues in higher education, the following sources are recommended: Frederick Rudolph, *The American College and University: A History* (New York: Knopf, 1965); Frederick Rudolph, *Curriculum: A History of the American Undergraduate Course of Study Since 1636* (San Francisco: Jossey-Bass, 1977); and John Brubacher and Willis Rudy, *Higher Education in Transition* (New York: Harper & Row, 1958). A useful historical chronology and a brief description of 12 important events in the development of the undergraduate curriculum in the United States can be found in Levine, *The Undergraduate Curriculum*, p.484 ff. and p. 538 ff.

The Setting

It seemed impossible that modern thought could house itself in such decrepit and superseded chambers. —Thomas Hardy, *Jude the Obscure*

THE IMPORTANCE OF SETTINGS

Teaching takes place in some specific setting. As teachers we communicate with our students about our subject within some institutional context. What influence does the setting have on how we teach? The setting may be conducive to learning or not; it may support instruction or interfere with it. In many ways the setting determines what can and can not be done. It sets the boundaries, physical and psychological, for what will be attempted. The physical space affects arrangements for communication, opportunities for various activities, and general morale. The class, however it may be composed, takes on a social structure. Norms are set for acceptable and unacceptable behavior, for "what's in" and "what's out." Teachers and students take on and play out various roles. Classrooms and entire institutions have a "culture" and a "climate." Social interactions may foster or inhibit communication, growth, and change. We all teach in some setting: new or old, traditional or innovative, large or small, affluent or impoverished. What we may expect to achieve as teachers depends at least in part on the setting within which our instruction takes place.

Seymour Sarason describes a setting as "any instance in which two or more people come together in . . . relationship over a sustained period of time in order to achieve certain goals."[1] The smallest setting is a marriage, the largest, a society. In between, are the settings of schools, universities, hospitals, clinics, companies, factories, government agencies, towns, and cities. A setting includes social as well as physical characteristics. Rudolph Moos, a Stanford psychiatrist who has examined many educational, correctional, and treatment environments, suggests that in assessing settings we should look not only at architectural and physical surroundings, but also at organizational factors, social climate, and the human aggregate that occupies the setting.[2] Effective teachers become sensitized to the physical and human aspects of the classroom as well as to the organizational and social climates of the institutions within which their classrooms reside.

CLASSROOM SETTINGS

Consider the classroom setting. Ideally, as we learned from the great American architect, Frank Lloyd Wright, form and function ought to be united in the design of physical space for human environments.[3] Unfortunately, the physical space in which most teaching takes place has been designed with a rather limited idea of what teaching is and with little imagination about what might take place there. The form of the classroom seldom follows the function of teaching; to the contrary, the form of the space often inhibits the function of teaching. Even good space—a well-designed lecture hall—limits the range of teaching strategies that can be employed comfortably there. Many teachers simply accept the conditions of classroom space as a given, drifting unconsciously into patterns that soon become identified as established custom. As Mark Knapp notes, ". . . some people will accommodate themselves to anything, no matter how uncomfortable or dysfunctional, either because they do not know how to improve the situation or believe that rules forbid them to alter the arrangement."[4] Effective teachers, however, don't accept the given physical environment; they establish the setting they need. They learn to own their rented space, to take charge, to make their own rules. Nothing is sacred—not the arrangements of chairs and tables, not the location of equipment, not the lighting, not the ventilation. Effective teachers aren't afraid to come into a room and totally rearrange it. And if the alterations still leave the room unsuitable for instruction, a new setting is found. Sometimes we need to become very aggressive about creating suitable settings for the teaching strategies we wish to employ.

The setting, however, includes not only the physical space itself, but the way people are arranged within the physical space. This is very important because the arrangement of people in classroom space affects the nature of the communication that will take place.

The teacher sits behind a big desk at the front of the class, a space that may take up as much as one-third of the classroom. Why? Students desks and chairs are arranged in horizontal and vertical rows. Why? The teacher chats informally with students in the front rows. Less interested students arrange themselves around the edges and may even fall asleep at the back. Teachers occasionally sit on their desks, but no students dare to sit on the teacher's desk, or their own desks, for that matter.

Arrangements of space affect people's behavior, and people's behavior affects how space gets arranged. The science of proxemics (the study of human uses of social and personal space) provides three concepts teachers can employ as they think about human behavior in classroom settings: territoriality, dominance, and distance.[5] Human beings, like other animals, stake out a territory that they "own." They develop social arrangements involving dominance and submission—a pecking order. And they employ rules about personal space and distance, which vary from culture to culture. Classroom spaces become the stages where the little dramas of territoriality, dominance, and distance are acted out. Students quickly decide where "their seat" is in the classroom and will stay there for the whole term unless someone moves them. Students know where the professor's space is and will often apologize or say "excuse me" if they feel they are intruding. Students who sit in more prominent spaces may participate more actively and in subtle ways discourage the participation of others. Sometimes students need to be asked to make room for a late-arrival at the seminar table, especially if it's crowded. These natural human behaviors are there to see for the teacher who knows how to look. Becoming aware of these behaviors is a prerequisite to influencing them.

The arrangements of people in space are important because they affect communication. The relationship of space and communication has been studied in educational settings, and some of the important results have been summarized by Mark Knapp:

> In classrooms, there is a center of activity with more student participation from people seated front and center; participation decreases towards the back. In seminar settings, most of the participation comes from students directly opposite the leader. Students tend not to sit in the seats on either side of the leader. In organizational settings, superiors will sit at the head, or front, of a rectangular table and subordinates will sit at the sides. People seated at the head, foot and middle of the sides do more talking. Participation decreases as group

size increases, being greater in seminars than in large classrooms. Communication when people are sitting around a table is more focused and sustained than in a "cocktail party" situation. When the topic is difficult and causes stress, or when people are viewed as unfriendly, participants choose to sit farther apart. Communication with handicapped or otherwise "stigmatized" persons is carried on at a greater distance.[6]

Spatial arrangements and communication patterns are closely linked.

The classroom setting is also shaped by the roles that people are assigned or voluntarily accept. Obviously, teachers and students play their respective roles, but it is useful to think more deeply about *how* teachers play their role. For a study of college classrooms Richard Mann created a classification system of the following six "teacher-as" typologies:[7]

- **The Teacher as Expert.** The teacher is an expert within certain defined areas of knowledge. This presumed subject matter expertise creates a "right to be there" and an expectation from students that they will learn something about that subject. Within this role the disparity between teacher and student is heightened with regard to the differing amounts of knowledge, experience, and wisdom they have.
- **The Teacher as Formal Authority.** The teacher is also "in charge" of the classroom, which means that the teacher has control over content of presentations, readings, grading, standard of excellence, deadlines for assignments, who will and won't speak, and, ultimately, who is permitted to be there. Within this role there are certain assumed hierarchical relations among students and teachers.
- **The Teacher as Socializing Agent.** The teacher is a gatekeeper to the academic and professional world, and a representative of a field. Teachers introduce students to the language, values, and behaviors appropriate to an imagined professional life, occupational goal, or discipline, and to the intellectual community generally. In this role, hierarchy is less pronounced, but students still look up to and often mimic the vocabulary, intellectual pose, and (sometimes) the personal demeanor of the teacher.
- **The Teacher as Facilitator.** The teacher attempts to determine what students have come to learn, what they can do already, and what they need help in doing. As facilitator the teacher helps to open opportunities and help students define their own roles and

needs as learners. In this role the teacher becomes more closely identified with students and their potentialities and aspirations.

- **The Teacher as Ego Ideal.** The teacher often provides a model of the good biologist, well-educated scholar, or "nice person" that the student might like to be. Although this idealization may be limited to only certain aspects of the teacher's performance, and may occur only in certain students at certain times, students tend to find things in their teachers (intellectual passion, drive, self-discipline, encyclopedic knowledge, memory, patience) that are impressive, desirable, and worthy of emulation. The teacher, whether unintentionally or by choice, becomes an ego ideal for students to imitate, envy, or reject. In this role, the identification between student and teacher can become very close.

- **The Teacher as Person.** The teacher also functions out of role, simply as a person, often expressing personal values, opinions, and feelings and validating students also simply as persons. The desire for trust, respect, and affection are human needs of all students and teachers and are also a part of the teaching-learning process. In being simply a person, the teacher may bring some welcome relief from the hierarchy of defined roles and may puncture some myths about being a teacher.

In the way that teachers choose to play each of these roles, and to the extent that certain roles are emphasized more than others, the classroom environment is further defined. If a teacher chooses to emphasize the role of expert and authority, for example, and to down-play the role of facilitator, that influences the social structure of that classroom. In short, teachers not only adapt to settings; they also help to create them, including the social structure of those settings.

The physical space, the arrangements of people within that space, and the various roles that people play within the micro-social structure of the classroom all combine to produce a "climate." Although it is not easy to define precisely what is meant by climate, most people who visit classrooms know that each has its own climate—a particular mood, atmosphere, or emotional tone. Ask any student; they can tell you about the climate in each of their classes. The goal, it would seem, in creating a classroom climate favorable to learning is to avoid extremes: classrooms that are too filled with threat or devoid of challenge, overly serious or frivolously social, unproductively chaotic or rigidly formal.

As teachers, we need to learn to read the classroom environment and become alert to our own behavior in responding to and creating the settings where teaching takes place. But this is only one part of the setting. Classrooms are embedded in institutions, and the institutional context also helps set the stage for, and partially determines, what happens in classrooms.

INSTITUTIONAL SETTINGS

Are institutions of higher education distinctly different from one another? If so, in what ways? Do differences in institutional settings make any difference in the way teaching is approached and carried out? Burton Clark, who has written extensively on the nature of the American system of higher education and has compared it with other national systems, suggests that they do.[8]

> The academic profession is shaped by many social settings. Prominent among them is national context: the profession takes a different shape, even radically so, in France than in the United States, in Mexico or Brazil than in the United Kingdom or Somalia. . . . Discipline or field of study, is a second primary setting: the profession takes a different shape in physics than in political science, in biology than in classics, in engineering than in education. . . . Increasingly, institutions are a third structuring context: in France the academic occupation is different in the grand ècoles than in the universities; in the United States it is radically different in community colleges than in research-based universities.

The American higher education system, by far the largest in the world, and also the most decentralized and diverse, is made up of many different kinds of institutions. Consider again the five different examples of institutions presented initially in the first chapter of this book: Mid-West University is a large, public land-grant university; Elm Grove College is a small, private liberal arts college; Pacific Coast Community College is a large, public two-year college; the Art Institute of the South is a proprietary trade school; and New England Theological Seminary is a private, free-standing specialized professional school. Obviously, these institutions appear to be quite different from one another. But *how* are they different, and how might this difference affect teaching? Is there a way to examine institutions more closely and more systematically to understand the nature and extent of their diversity?

In an enlightening chapter entitled "What Makes Institutions Different?," Robert Birnbaum develops and spells out a set of categories for examining institutional differences.[9] To begin with, there are differences in programs. Institutions vary in the types and levels of degrees they offer (associate, bachelor's, master's, professional, or doctoral). Institutions also differ in the areas in which degrees are offered (occupational, liberal arts, professional) and in the types of majors and concentrations available (history, chemistry, women's studies). They differ in their comprehensiveness (how many different types of degrees and programs are offered—few or many) and in their basic purpose or institutional mission. In addition to these programmatic differences, institutions also vary on their instructional delivery systems (types of classes, uses of technology, off-campus programs), in their policies with regard to students (admissions, grading, initiatives permitted), and in their administrative processes (calendars, general requirements). Institutions also vary in their systemic characteristics. Although several different systematic classifications have been proposed, the most widely known and used is the one developed originally by the Carnegie Council in 1976; it divides institutions into six major categories: 1) doctoral-granting, 2) comprehensive, 3) liberal arts, 4) two-year, 5) professional and specialized, and 6) nontraditional. In addition to type, institutions can be distinguished by size (large or small) and control (public, private, proprietary, religious). Institutions can also be compared on the basis of constituents served, with some institutions varying by sex (male, female, coed), ethnic background, socioeconomic status, religious affiliation, and selectivity. Most institutions also vary in their culture or climate and their set of distinctive values and attitudes. These seemingly ephemeral differences have been subjected to empirical study, and convincing documentation has been provided to support the idea that different institutions have a distinctive environmental press, student orientation, or campus culture. Institutions also exhibit structural diversity depending on whether they stand alone or belong to some larger system of institutions.

Colleges and universities also vary in their prestige and selectivity. In a classic essay entitled "The Academic Procession," sociologist David Riesman described the status system of American postsecondary institutions as a snake-like procession, with a small number of prestigious institutions at the head, a larger group in the middle trying to emulate the leaders, and a few in the tail struggling along behind.[10] Colleges and universities can also vary in their visibility, that is, in how well they are known, which, of course, also is related to their prestige. A classic study by Alexander Astin and Calvin Lee discovered that institutional size and selectivity based on student entrance scores served as the defining variables for how well an institution was known.[11]

Four aspects of institutional setting deserve further elaboration: mission, culture, climate, and academic discipline. Most institutions, wherever they fit in the classification system, have some distinctive mission or purpose that is peculiar to them as an institution. For most institutions this mission is the "glue" that holds everything together. Some institutions are tight and cohesive, others are more loosely coupled. Expressed simply, the institutional mission consists of stated purposes and intended outcomes of activity, the consequences of educational efforts.[12] Sometimes the institutional mission is referred to as the "academic strategy"—the institution's answer to the question: What business are we in?[13] Most institutions try to capture their distinctiveness in a formal mission statement. Written or unwritten, every institution *has* a mission, and what that mission is has a great influence on the scope of the curriculum and the delivery of instruction.

When the institution's mission has been successful over an extended period of time, people speak of the mission as the "organizational saga."[14] This somewhat embellished institutional history becomes a legend, retold with a high degree of loyalty and romance. Teachers who are sensitive to the setting in which they teach try to learn about the institutional mission and organizational saga.

"Organizational culture" is a much broader concept than mission and saga. The idea of culture has been around for many years, of course, coming originally from anthropology as a concept used to describe the norms, beliefs, values, customs, and artifacts of a society. In recent years the concept of culture has been applied to organizations. Terrence Deal and Allen Kennedy studied successful businesses and concluded that a major key to success was having a "strong culture," that is, a well-articulated paramount belief, a superordinate goal and widely shared philosophy that guides the activities of employees.[15] As Ellen Chaffee and William Tierney note in their study of collegiate culture and leadership, a quick way to focus on the culture of a college or university is to ask, "what gets done, how does it get done, and who does it?"[16] Chaffee and Tierney suggest where one should look for the answers to these questions.

The culture of an organization is grounded in the shared assumptions of individuals participating in the organization. Often taken for granted by the actors themselves, these assumptions can be identified through stories, special language, norms, institutional ideology, and artifacts that emerge from individual and organizational behavior. The socialization process used to introduce new members to the culture and maintain continued loyalty and morale are also significant cultural mechanisms in organizational life. That is, the way faculty and administrators become and remain socialized to an institution is a critical element of culture.

In addition, organizations, like classrooms, also have a "climate." Climate refers to the way the people in the institution feel about the organization. The climate induces those who work and study in the institution to feel "satisfaction, dissatisfaction, high morale, low morale, anxiety, stress or motivation."[17] Whereas culture, as a construct, stresses deeply embedded patterns of shared values, assumptions, and beliefs; climate refers to current perceptions and attitudes and what it is like to be at the institution at this point in time. Climate has a more psychological base, is more easily changed, and will fluctuate over time. Teachers must be able to read the institutional cultures and assess the climates of the settings where they teach.

Within a specific institutional setting every teacher is also a member of an academic field. This may be one of the formal academic disciplines (chemistry, psychology, history), a professional field of study (business, nursing, education), or an occupational area (interior design, law enforcement, drafting). The disciplines and professions are so much a part of academic life today that it is hard to imagine a time when they did not exist, but there was such a time. In a fascinating history of the disciplines and professions, Burton Clark points out that they are a relatively recent development.[18] Although the "classical" professions of law, medicine, and theology have roots that go back eight centuries, the disciplines and "modern day" professions as we know them emerged in the mid-nineteenth century. As they developed, each of these fields came to provide a home for its adherents, and these fields developed into markedly different worlds. As Clark notes:

> The daily rounds of the professor of classics do not lead to the corridors of the management school, where the strange ways of this neighboring tribe could be observed. The medical school anesthesiologist has no reason, in the normal course of affairs, to become acquainted with the working life of a political scientist expert in voting behavior, let alone that of a scholar immersed for all time in Dante.

Teachers think differently about their teaching—content, thinking skills, habits of mind, attitudes toward the subject—depending on their discipline or professional field. There is a kind of epistemology of the workplace that makes life for some academics quite different from others. How we approach our teaching depends to some extent on our membership in an academic field and the way that field takes its place among the others in a particular institutional setting.

It is clear, then, that institutions vary by degree level, by program, by comprehensiveness, by selectivity, and by size. They can be classified by type. They can be categorized by constituents served, campus environment, type of support, and system membership. They vary in status and visibility, in mission, and in culture and climate. Within these institutions, academics find their peculiar home in a discipline, profession, or occupational area. Of what importance are these differences in institutional setting to the teacher? How might these institutional differences impact the setting in which teaching occurs?

The level of degree offered will determine whether one is teaching graduate students, majors, or lower division students; and as most experienced teachers know, there can be an enormous difference. The kinds of programs offered and the comprehensiveness of the institution can create a campus environment that tends toward the aesthetic, the technical and scientific, or the professional, which in turn creates certain expectations about the emphasis of classroom instruction. Similar expectations will develop around the importance attached to the theoretical and applied, the long-range or immediate usefulness of knowledge. Institutional size can impact class size, the number and quality of human interactions, the superficiality or depth of acquaintance with students. Size can also affect the type of interactions among faculty, the degree of cooperation in planning the curriculum, and the opportunities for team teaching and cross-disciplinary instruction. Size, control, and prestige can work together to affect the availability of resources—classroom, laboratory, and studio facilities; the availability of media; and other resources (human and technological) to support teaching. Prestige and resources affect the overall morale of the faculty. Selectivity and prestige will affect the kinds of students attracted to the institution, their general and specific aptitudes for learning, the strength of their motivations, and the degree of rigor and challenge that may or may not be reasonably expected in the presentation of material or the evaluation of student learning. The mission and saga of the institution shape the nature of the campus community, the values that are cherished, the learning outcomes to be most valued, and the student accomplishments most rewarded. Institutional mission will also affect the emphasis and support given to teaching—whether teaching is to be rewarded or endured, whether students are to be nurtured or tolerated. The organizational culture determines which classroom roles the teacher may most comfortably play and what norms will govern classroom behavior, right down to dress, acceptable language, appropriate use of illustrations, and the intensity of classroom discussion. All of these variables will function in their unique way in different disciplines, professions, and occupational areas.

A GOODNESS OF FIT

Teaching takes place in a setting and the kind of setting makes a big difference. The setting produces expectations, and expectations set the boundaries for what *must* be done and *can't* be done. The key issue, once again, is fit. How do one's hopes, dreams, and aspirations as a teacher fit with the realities of the institutional context? If there is a goodness of fit with regard to goals and the means for reaching those goals, then teaching can proceed smoothly; the task is to move on, to refine and elaborate the use of various teaching strategies, to become proficient. If the fit is not good, if there is an incongruity between what the teacher is trying to do and what the setting calls for, there will be problems—sometimes serious, paralyzing problems that overwhelm other efforts to improve.

"Badness of fit" or dissonance between teacher and institution can occur in three ways. The first of these concerns teachers who are new to the institution; they may lack the time or the skill to assess the institutional setting. New teachers coming to an institution directly from their graduate studies may still be psychological captives of the institution where they have been studying. ("At ____ we did it this way.") A dissonance may develop that can be remedied by better acquaintance with the new setting through effective orientation, a skillful mentor, or the mere passage of time. A second, more enduring dissonance may occur when teachers are operating in the present setting as if they were in the setting where *they* went to college. ("When I went to college we ____.") Most teachers, especially beginning teachers, teach the way they were taught. Until teachers have had some opportunity to reflect on the nature of teaching, they will tend to draw on the familiar—the teaching they watched—which may or may not be appropriate in their current setting. The last, and often most difficult dissonance, occurs when the teacher wishes that he or she were in some ideal (often idealized) environment and is unable to accept the realities of the present setting. In this situation, the teacher is often capable of reading the present setting, but is emotionally unwilling or unable to accept the givens of that setting. ("This place is impossible, these students don't even ____.") In this case the dissonance will eventually prove to be frustrating to the students and the teacher, and may eventually produce a problem for the administration.

This is not to suggest, of course, that teachers ought not to try to change the settings where they teach. All settings are dynamic, subject to modification, and evolving. Some settings are more open to change than others; some settings need to be changed more than others. But most settings where teaching takes place are fairly stable, if not downright unmovable; and because they are social structures, with all of the meaning that implies, they are not easily changed. Moreover, those who would change the settings where they teach might be more effective if they are first able to show that they truly understand these settings.

CONCLUSIONS

As we aspire to better teaching, it is useful to cultivate a sense of the importance of the setting where instruction takes place. Classrooms consist of physical space, more or less adequate to teaching, which is probably more amenable to rearrangement than we realize, if we are willing to overcome the inertia to change it. Classrooms also include arrangements of space for communication; they are microsocial settings where teachers and students take on and play out various roles. Classrooms exist in some larger institutional context, and the nature of the institution—its degrees, programs, size, control, mission, culture, and climate—can have an important effect on what can and can not be done in that setting. What one does as a teacher also varies by academic field. Settings help to set the parameters for teaching: the kind of learning that is most desirable, the upward and downward limits to rigor, the most effective techniques to be used, and the most desirable relationship between teacher and student. A certain amount of goodness of fit, between the teacher and the setting, is necessary if teachers are to be effective. On the other hand, teachers also create the setting, collectively, as a faculty, and individually, within their own classrooms, and are at least partially responsible for the settings where they teach.

Effective teachers know where they are and why they are there.

NOTES

1. Seymour B. Sarason, *The Creation of Settings and the Future of Societies* (San Francisco: Jossey-Bass, 1972), p. 1.

2. Rudolf H. Moos, *Evaluating Educational Environments* (San Francisco: Jossey-Bass, 1979). See especially pp. 6-10.

3. Frank Lloyd Wright, *Frank Lloyd Wright on Architecture* (New York: Duell, Sloan, and Pierce, 1941), p. 189.

4. Mark L. Knapp, *Non Verbal Communication in Human Interaction* (New York: Holt, Rinehart and Winston, 1972), pp. 37-38.

5. Robert Sommer, *Personal Space: The Behavioral Basis of Design* (Englewood Cliffs, NJ: Prentice-Hall, 1969), pp. 12-38. For a classic discussion of the key concepts of proxemics, see Edward T. Hall, *The Hidden Dimension* (Garden City, NY: Doubleday and Company, 1969).

6. Mark L. Knapp, *Non Verbal Communication*, p. 55. See also Chapter 6, "Environment," in Loretta A. Malandro and Larry Baker, *Non Verbal Communication* (Reading, MA: Addison-Wesley, 1983).

7. Richard Mann, *The College Classroom: Conflict, Change and Learning* (New York: John Wiley & Sons, 1970), p. 212 ff.

8. Burton Clark, *The Academic Profession: National, Disciplinary and Institutional Settings* (Berkeley: University of California, 1987), p. 2.

9. Robert Birnbaum, *Maintaining Diversity in Higher Education* (San Francisco: Jossey-Bass, 1983), Chapter 2, pp. 37-56. Birnbaum also explores other interesting issues not as relevant to this chapter, such as whether and to what extent diversity is desirable, and whether colleges are becoming more alike.

10. David Riesman, *Constraint and Variety in American Education* (Lincoln: University of Nebraska Press, 1956).

11. Alexander Astin and Calvin Lee, *The Invisible Colleges: A Profile of Small Private Colleges with Limited Resources* (New York: McGraw-Hill, 1972), pp. 1-23.

12. Carnegie Commission for the Advancement of Teaching, *Missions of the College Curriculum* (San Francisco: Jossey-Bass, 1977), Chapter 7, "The Mission of Undergraduate Education."

13. George Keller, *Academic Strategy: The Management Revolution in American Higher Education* (Baltimore: The Johns Hopkins University Press, 1983), Chapter 4, "Slouching Toward Strategy."

14. Burton Clark. *The Distinctive College: Antioch, Reed and Swathmore* (Chicago: Aldine Publishing Company, 1970), p. 235.

15. Terrence Deal and Allen Kennedy, *The Corporate Cultures: The Rites and Rituals of Corporate Life* (Reading, MA: Addison-Wesley Publishing Company, Inc., 1982). George Kuh and Elizabeth Whitt, *The Invisible Tapestry: Culture in American Colleges and Universities* (Washington, DC: Association for the Study of Higher Education, ASHE-ERIC Higher Education Report No. 1., 1988), p. 12.

16. Ellen Chaffee and William Tierney, *Collegiate Culture and Leadership Strategies* (New York: American Council on Education/ Macmillan, 1988), p. 7.

17. Marvin Peterson, et al., *The Organizational Context for Teaching and Learning: A Review of the Literature* (Ann Arbor: Regents of the University of Michigan and NCRIPTAL, 1986), p. 32. See also Marvin Peterson and Melinda Spencer, "Understanding Academic Culture and Climate" in William G. Tierney, ed., *Assessing Academic Climates and Cultures* (San Francisco: Jossey-Bass, 1990), New Directions for Institutional Research, No. 68, pp. 6-8.

18. Burton Clark, *The Academic Life: Small Worlds, Different Worlds* (Princeton, NJ: The Carnegie Foundation for *The Advancement of Teaching*, 1987), Chapters 2-4. The quotation is from pp. 69-70.

The Students

Mother is putting my new secondhand clothes in order. She prays now, she says, that I may learn in my own life and away from home and friends what the heart is and what it feels.
　　　　　　　　—James Joyce, *Portrait of the Artist as a Young Man*

DIVERSITY IN THE STUDENT BODY

A student is anyone the teacher is trying to influence through teaching. In certain colleges, usually the more selective ones, faculty play some role in setting and carrying out policies for choosing the students who will be taught. In many settings, however, teachers have no choice at all in choosing the students they will teach. As one teacher put it, "You get what you get. On the first day you go into the class and there they are; it's up to you to teach them." Who are these students we get in our classes, and how can we understand them better?

One thing we know is that the American higher education system serves a wide variety of students in many settings. The catch word today is "diversity." Students vary considerably by age, gender, ethnic background, home country, or region of the country. They are a diverse population, becoming more diverse. Those who were once called the "new students" are today familiar faces on most campuses.[1] "Traditional" students are becoming hard to find. "In 1989, only about one-sixth of the 12.7 million college and university students were between eighteen and twenty-three years of age, enrolled full-time, and lived in campus housing."[2] Diversity in the student body gets expressed in different ways, of course, in different institutional settings. As noted earlier, the kinds of students to be found at a particular college or university will vary with the location, environment, culture, and mission of that institution.

STUDENT CULTURES

Students, like institutions, are described as having "cultures." Student cultures exist at the national level, at the institutional level, and within institutions as subcultures. At the national level, student cultures shift from year to year or over a period of years.[3] Sometimes it is possible to describe the end of one student generation and the beginning of another, and it is common to speak of student generations by decades—the 60s, the 70s, etc.[4] By examining yearly data gathered by the Cooperative Institutional Research Program (CIRP), it is possible to "take the national pulse" of the changing values and attitudes of entering freshmen.[5]

The student culture at a particular institution may be quite different from that at a neighboring institution and both may be different from the "national trends." Various instruments have been developed to assess student cultures at the institutional level.[6] Although each measure differs in important respects, in general each measures the institution's perceived environmental press, that is, whether the students on a particular campus tend to emphasize such things as academic, scholarly, social, or career interests. Qualitative research methods have also been employed to understand student cultures at particular institutions.[7]

The research at postsecondary institutions has revealed that student cultures are not monolithic and that more often than not, various subgroups, or subcultures, exist side by side on the same campus. One interesting study of Stanford undergraduates during the 1980s found five distinct types of students: careerist, intellectual, striver, unconnected, and other (students not fitting the other four types). These students all attend the same institution but have very different goals and use the institution in different ways.[8] Sometimes student subcultures are consonant with and enhance the main thrust of the institutional culture; sometimes they go off in another direction.[9] Effective teachers try to stay informed about student cultures, not only at the national level, but at the institution where they teach.

STUDENTS AS INDIVIDUALS

Ultimately, however, students show up as *individuals* in classrooms. The generalities represented through demographic surveys and the descriptions of student cultures and subcultures, however insightful, take teachers only so far in understanding students. Most teachers want to understand the individuals they teach—*their* students. Although several students in any given class may share certain common characteristics, such as age, gender, or ethnic background, students are also different from each other, right down to their fingerprints. What is it that we want and need to know about our students if we are going to be more effective in teaching them? How can we gain perspective on the students in our classroom?

When college teachers are asked what they would like to know about their students, they usually can generate a long list of questions. Usually these questions can be reduced to several categories for more systematic investigation. Questions about "age" usually lead to some discussion of social and emotional development. Questions about "how students think" lead to discussions of cognitive development. Questions about "how slowly or rapidly students learn" lead to discussions—often quite heated—about intelligence, aptitude, and motivation. Questions about differences in "visual/auditory, concrete/abstract" approaches to learning lead to discussions of sensory modalities and learning styles. Questions about "background" lead to discussions of ethnicity, social class, and gender. All of these questions are important. Although immediate and specific answers will not always be found—some students forever remain a puzzle—these are, nonetheless, the right questions to ask. Most of us want to gain a clearer perspective on our students.

UNDERSTANDING SOCIAL AND EMOTIONAL DEVELOPMENT

Although some institutions still enroll a majority of students aged 18-24, most colleges and universities today are serving large numbers of older students. What difference does it make how old a student is? How can age affect the learning process?

Developmental psychologists have demonstrated how people of different ages tend to have different preoccupations. What interests a student at 21 may not interest a student at 43. Thanks to the pioneering work of Darwin, Freud, Piaget, and Erikson, and those who followed their lead, the idea of separate stages of development from birth to death—now known as life cycle development—has been quite well established. The stages of human development have been charted and described in great detail by observing, systematically, what people focus on at different times throughout their lives.[10] Psychologists are able to build up theories of development empirically by observing what people of a particular age group—adults as well as children—are working on and struggling with, and those preoccupations are generally referred to as "developmental tasks."[11]

Developmental psychologists once thought that individuals moved systematically, task by task, through each stage, and that a person could not progress to the work of the next stage until the work of the previous stage was complete. The tendency today is to view stages less rigidly, noting that there is some truth to the idea of progression, but recognizing that there is also great unevenness in growth. People move forward, then backward, then forward again, sometimes getting stuck, sometimes skipping ahead. Individuals can also be at various stages of different kinds of development simultaneously.[12]

It is also recognized today that some kinds of development, particularly physical development, are maturational, proceeding at a natural pace from within the individual, and not subject to much environmental influence. Other forms of development, however, are highly susceptible to education and experience, and, in fact, depend on them. Teaching, when it is appropriately timed with developmental capability and motivation, is very important in facilitating learning, but when inappropriately timed can lead to great frustration both for the learner and the teacher. Effective teachers learn to tell the difference between what growth they can facilitate and what maturation they must wait for patiently.

Although a great amount is known and has been written about the social and emotional development of children, most college teachers are interested in adult development. Erik Erikson was among the first to write extensively of adult development, and he adds to the early childhood stages additional categories to describe the development of adults.[13] It is useful to begin with a brief review of adolescence, because the youngest of college students may still be dealing to some extent with unresolved issues of adolescence. The adolescent (roughly 12-17 years old) is struggling with identity formation. Here the primary task is to forge a consistent and continuous view of the self that also survives the close scrutiny of others. Adolescents, in their own words, are "trying to find themselves" and "get it together." They are self-absorbed and believe (mistakenly) that other people are as preoccupied with their behavior and appearance as they are, thus creating an "imaginary audience" before whom they act out their fishbowl lives. Hence, the persistent testing out of new images of self with clothing, hairstyles, fads, and slang.

The adolescent is "on stage" enacting a "personal fable" with a leading role full of exaggerations and fantasies. Not fully accepted yet in adult society, adolescents create "subculture" groups that set them apart from their parents. When a consistent personal self comes together, the adolescent achieves a sense of identity; the failure to achieve a sense of identity leads to inner turmoil, a sense of being lost or "out of it," and possibly to more serious consequences. Most students, by the time they come to college, have made at least some basic resolution of the "identity crisis" of adolescence, though they may also be carrying into college some unfinished business.

The task of the post-adolescent young adult shifts from identity formation to finding one's niche with others and within the society as a whole. The young adult (hopefully by now) has a self able to relate to another self, and the primary task becomes the development of successful intimate relations with others. If the adolescent asks "Who am I?" the young adult asks "Where am I going and with whom?" The opposite of intimacy is isolation, and some young adults feel they are "out of phase" if they don't resolve these issues as quickly as they would like.

In *Education and Identity*,[14] his classic, but still valuable, formulation of developmental tasks for traditional-age college students, Arthur Chickering describes seven "vectors" of development as follows:

- **Achieving Competence.** Developing basic abilities—intellectual, physical and manual, social, and interpersonal—and the confidence to achieve what one sets out to do.

- **Managing Emotions.** Learning how to become more aware of feelings, to trust them more, and to manage them more effectively—particularly feelings associated with sex and aggression—and to learn, eventually, what can be done with whom, when, and under what circumstances.

- **Becoming Autonomous.** Learning not only how to live away from parents, but becoming emotionally independent, freed of continual and pressing needs for reassurance, affection, and approval.

- **Establishing Identity.** Building on the work of adolescence to further clarify a sense of one's own characteristics, physical needs, personal appearance and sexual identification.

- **Freeing Interpersonal Relations.** Learning to become less anxious, less defensive, less burdened by inappropriate past reactions, and more spontaneous, friendly, warm, and trusting.

- **Clarifying Purposes.** Developing a clearer sense of vocational plans and aspirations, avocational and recreational interests, and lifestyle goals.
- **Developing Integrity.** Elaborating a personally valid set of beliefs and values that have some internal consistency and serve as a tentative guide for behavior.

Although not all students are working on all seven of these tasks at the same time, and although each student addresses these tasks in different ways, Chickering's framework provides a useful description that has a positive resonance for those who work with traditional-age students.

Chickering's framework of developmental tasks may be thought of as an "age theory," as opposed to a "stage theory," which focuses on a sequence of steps through which people may pass more independent of their age. One such theory is Jane Loevinger's stage theory of ego development.[15] She describes stages through which people pass on the road to developing a strong (healthy) ego, generally recognized as the ability to mediate between conflicting aspects of the self and the self and the external environment. Loevinger suggests six stages as follows:

- **Self-Protection Stage.** Concerned with control and advantage in relationships, opportunistic in following rules, thinks in stereotypes, sees life as a zero-sum game and blames others and external circumstances.
- **Conformist Stage.** Concerned with appearances and social acceptance, lacking in introspection, still thinking in cliches, conforming to external values, perceiving group differences in stereotypes with little appreciation of individual differences.
- **Self-Aware Stage.** (Conscientious-Conformist) Increasing self-awareness and ability to see alternatives and exceptions, concerned with solving problems, finding reasons for the way life works, and adjusting to new situations.
- **Conscientious Stage.** Concerned about mutuality and responsibility in relationships, seeing that there are exceptions to rules, that life involves choices, that self-respect and long-term goals are important, and that events are part of a larger, social context.
- **Autonomous Stage.** Making choices within a framework of recognized complexity, acknowledging inner conflict and respecting the autonomy of others.

- **Integrated Stage.** Concerned with the reconciliation of inner conflicts and cherishing individuality within a broad social context.

Loevinger's empirical research on adults has established that most traditional-age college students are either at the "Conformist" or "Conscientious" stage or are squarely between them in the "Self-Aware" stage. Interestingly, Loevinger estimates that the Self-Aware stage is the most frequent "stopping place" for ego development in most adults in our society. For teachers it is important to note that, depending on where students are in terms of ego development, they are likely to have different attitudes about education. People at the lower stages tend to view education as external to the self, as something to get or to have. At the middle stages education is seen as a goal or asset, an investment in one's future, something to make one's life more enjoyable and worthwhile; whereas at more advanced stages education is seen as having intrinsic value apart from goals, as leading to creativity and deeper values.

Other stage theorists have developed different concepts (and use different words) to describe social and emotional development. Whatever the particularities of the descriptions, college students, as they move out of adolescence and into young adulthood, appear to be struggling with various aspects of the transition that have to do with relating to self, to others, and to society, and there appears to be a strong emphasis on becoming more autonomous in the sense of being controlled from within.

Not all students today, however, are of the traditional age group. Many are older and find themselves in later developmental stages working on other developmental tasks. What are the stages of adulthood that follow those described above? Three key studies by Gould, Levinson, and Sheehy appeared in the 1970s, elaborating in detail for the first time the developmental tasks of adulthood.[16] The findings of this research, based on interview studies of men and women in various occupations and of different social backgrounds, are pulled together and summarized succinctly by Arthur Chickering and Robert Havinghurst:[17]

> During the mid twenties—a period of *provisional adulthood*—first commitments to work, marriage and family, and to other responsibilities are explored. Then another transitional period occurs during the late twenties and early thirties, when these initial commitments are reexamined and their meaning questioned. The long-range implications of continuing with the current work, spouse, community or life style have become apparent; one or more of these may look less

challenging or satisfying than at 22. In some cases changes must be made. In others, reaffirmation and renewed commitment occur, sometimes after flirtations with one or more alternatives.

The thirties are a time for *settling down*, for achievement, for becoming one's own person. But as the forties approach, time becomes more finite. Responsibility for parents begins to be assumed, while responsibilities of adolescent or college-age children continue. The likely limits of success and achievement become apparent, and the *mid-life transition* is at hand. Major questions concerning priorities and values are examined. Unless a change in work is made now, the die is cast. Affirmation of the earlier career most frequently occurs, but with moderated expectations and drive. A long-standing marriage may be temporarily or permanently upset. Friends, relatives, and spouse become increasingly important as *restabilization* occurs during the late forties and fifties. Interests forgone in the service of work receive more attention. Mellowing and increasing investment in personal relationships characterize the fifties.

Studies of older (post-60) adults indicate that developmental tasks are focused on planning for and adjusting to retirement, coping with declining health and strength, making new friends and becoming affiliated with late-adult age groups, establishing satisfactory (sometimes new and less spacious) living arrangements, coping with the death of a spouse, and developing a broader religious or philosophical perspective. The task for older adults has been summarized as "do less and be more."[18]

The question arises whether developmental tasks are "different" for women and men. Although there is no agreement on this sticky issue, it seems that men and women may respond to the same tasks in different ways and with different timing. Some studies indicate that women face the same tasks, but may work them through, particularly if they have spent time in child-rearing, as much as a decade later. Of special interest is the "match" between when a woman may be working on certain developmental tasks and when her spouse is working on the same tasks; the degree of match sometimes produces conflict and sometimes greater facilitation.[19] More significant, perhaps, than gender differences is what happens when a life event occurs that seriously disrupts the developmental process. Bernice Neugarten stresses the importance of having functional events in adulthood "happen on time."[20] When life events—the death of a spouse, the loss of a child, a promotion or being fired, a divorce, moving to a new city, not being able to retire—upset normal development, a crisis can occur. Interestingly, the research on adult continuing education indicates that many adult learners seek out education when a major life event has produced a crisis in their lives.[21]

As teachers, most of us recognize the descriptions of these stages of social and emotional development in ourselves as well as our students, and many of the tasks have a "common-sense" ring to them. What we are usually not as good at is understanding how to tie our instructional efforts into these developmental needs. Once having identified the stage at which a student seems to be, the next step is to think about what might nudge (or jar) the student into the next stage of development. If a traditional-age student is working on "managing emotions" and "freeing interpersonal relations," what can the teacher do to provide experiences that will challenge the old patterns of behavior and stimulate the formation of new ones? If a traditional-age student appears to be in the "conformist stage," would it not be appropriate to challenge the student's stereotyped thinking about groups and rules and to draw the student's attention to individuals and exceptions? Most of the social and emotional developmental tasks cry out for human interaction, for testing out ideas, values, and modes of behavior within a safe environment. This hunger for interaction extends well beyond the desire for interaction with the teacher. Most students are seeking more frequent and far deeper opportunities for relationships with other students than most classroom environments permit.

Another important lesson to be drawn from the literature on student development is that developmental level affects, to a large extent, how students perceive the education in which they are engaged and what they expect from it. As teachers, we may have goals for our students that they simply don't share, and they may have goals for their education that we don't comprehend or value. As teachers coping with our own developmental tasks, it is easy to forget, or simply ignore, the developmental niche of the students we teach. Having, or regaining, this perspective is important, if teachers and students are to connect in an effective way on teaching and learning.

UNDERSTANDING COGNITIVE DEVELOPMENT

Thus far the discussion of adult development has focused primarily on the tasks related to social and emotional development. College teachers also want and need to know something about the way students think. Are college students capable of abstract reasoning, and if so, to what extent? What level of complexity can be expected in the thinking of college students? Do students pass through certain stages in the way they think, just as they do in their social and emotional development?

A fruitful line of inquiry on this problem was begun by William Perry at Harvard with the publication of *Forms of Intellectual and Ethical Development in the College Years: A Scheme*.[22] Based on some loosely structured interviews, Perry elaborated an outline for a series of categories to describe the way students think. Some students, he noticed, seem to be what he called "dualistic" in their thinking, tending to see things as black or white, right or wrong. Others are more relativistic, uncertain about whether anything could be "true" or "right" apart from its context, while still others—the more mature thinkers at the upper end of the continuum—are more capable of making sustained arguments and ethical commitments. Perry's scheme was elaborated, researched, and revised by a network of scholars who developed and employed a set of interview techniques and a carefully crafted rating scale known as the "Reflective Judgment Model."[23] Karen Kitchener and Patricia King, the leading researchers in this area, have established and spelled out the stages of reflective judgement by tracking their occurrence in adults of various ages and educational levels and have begun to explore the implications of their work for teaching and learning.

Kitchener and King view the reflective thinker as "someone who is aware that a problematic situation exists and is able to bring critical judgement to bear on the problem." In making critical judgements, similar to what Dewey called the "grounded" or "warranted" assertion, thinkers are called upon to engage in such operations as "evaluation of evidence and consideration of expert opinion," and they must evaluate the "adequacy of argument" and "implications of the proposed solution." To conduct their research, Kitchener and King gave their subjects ill-structured problems (issues about which there can be honest disagreement); they listened carefully to their subjects' answers, which revealed their subjects' assumptions about "the sources and certainty of knowledge" and "about the role of evidence, authority and interpretation in the formation of solutions to problems." What Kitchener and King found was that people vary significantly in the way they think about thinking, and there is a clear pattern of progression—a set of stages—that people go through as they become more complex thinkers. The stages are summarized as follows:

- **Stage One.** The single-category belief system: what is true is true. Beliefs need not be justified. No acknowledgement of problems for which there are no absolute answers.
- **Stage Two.** Truth is ultimately accessible but not available to everyone. Some people are "right"; some are "wrong" (what Perry called dualism). All problems are solvable; the task is to find the right answer, and the source for the answer will be an authority.
- **Stage Three.** Some truth is temporarily inaccessible, even for authorities, but the truth can be found in the future. In areas of uncertainty, because evidence is incomplete, no one can claim authority beyond one's personal impressions and feelings. What is right is what feels right at the moment.
- **Stage Four.** The uncertainty associated with knowing is acknowledged, but is attributed to the limitations of the knower. Knowledge can not be validated externally and is, therefore, idiosyncratic. Authorities are to be questioned.
- **Stage Five.** Knowledge is relative to context. Knowledge depends on interpretation and interpretation grows out of a perspective. But it is difficult to weigh and evaluate two alternative interpretations of the same problem.
- **Stage Six.** Knowing is interpretive and contextual, but some perspectives, arguments, and points of view are "better" than others. Evidence can be compared across contexts.
- **Stage Seven.** Knowing is interpretive, but justifiable claims can be made about the better or best solution to the problem. Through critical inquiry and synthesis of evidence, certain claims have a greater "truth value" and are "more warranted" than others.

Most of us, as college teachers, know that not all of our students are at Stage Seven. What we may be surprised to find out, is how *low* most college students test out on this Model of Reflective Judgement. Consider the descriptions of the stages again as they are given below.

- **Stage One.** In its purest form, probably found only in children.
- **Stage Two.** Most typical of young adolescents, though some college students hold these assumptions.
- **Stage Three.** Most characteristic of students in the last two years of high school and first year of college.
- **Stage Four.** Most typical of college seniors.

- **Stage Five.** Most typical of graduate students.
- **Stage Six.** Typical of advanced graduate students.
- **Stage Seven.** A rarity even in advanced graduate students, but found in some educated adults as they mature into their thirties and beyond.

Kitchener and King have discovered (through their research and that of their students and colleagues in 16 studies on over 1,000 subjects) that subjects will test three out of four times at the same level; that when they test out of a level, it is usually only one stage above or below; and that subjects will test at the same stage even when given problems from disciplines as diverse as history and science. Furthermore, the stages appear to have their "age limits" with very few 13- to 20-year-olds being capable of Stage Six or Seven reflection and the majority of subjects not reasoning higher than Stage Four prior to age 24. Furthermore, changes in reflective judgement patterns involve a sequential movement from stage to stage, rather than brilliant leaps.

The educational implications of the work on Reflective Judgement are just beginning to be understood. What Kitchener and King advocate is "transformative learning," where teaching is targeted to helping students move toward the next stage of cognitive development. This can be done by challenging students at a particular stage with the kinds of activities that are likely to stimulate them to evaluate "where they are" and consider the next alternative. For example, students who are typically at Stage Three (first-year college students) have trouble distinguishing fact from opinion, differentiating the use of an authority and the evidence the authority uses, and using evidence to evaluate their own intuitive beliefs. Appropriate assignments would involve evaluating arguments in terms of their use of evidence and authority, identifying what makes the evidence strong or weak, and trying to identify two or more points of view on an issue. Students at Stage Five, on the other hand, understand that arguments are based on interpretation, but they have trouble evaluating competing evidence-based interpretations, and endorsing one view as better than another. They can be asked to compare and contrast competing points of view and to determine which author makes a better interpretation of the evidence and draws the best conclusion. What Kitchener and King suggest is that teachers need to provide experiences that not only challenge the student but support the student in exploring the next stage. Because challenge often creates a frightening disequilibrium, it needs to be accompanied by support. Transformative learning, they suggest, involves creating "an educational milieu that is developmentally appropriate."

If postsecondary students continue to develop cognitively as well as emotionally, what can teachers do to be "developmentally appropriate"? It is probably safe to say that most college teachers target their instruction at developmental levels that their students have not achieved or are generally unable to achieve, that is to say, too high. This often leads to frustration, both for the teacher and the student; but even more important, given the findings just reported, it leads to ineffectiveness in bringing about *any* movement in the direction of more complex thinking. To begin with, then, we can do a better job of getting "rough estimates" of the cognitive level of our individual students, by looking for clues in the answers they provide to questions in class and to their work on written assignments. Furthermore, we can make better efforts to avoid becoming captives ourselves of the lower stages of development, by being more careful about the textbooks we select and the way we regard them, by presenting multiple points of view in class activities and lectures, and by developing examination questions and assignments that require more than "multiple guess" recall. Although we need not forsake our chance to produce an Einstein, collectively, the postsecondary enterprise might be far better off if we could all be more effective in nudging our students ahead by one or two developmental stages, so that they become at least somewhat more complex thinkers.

UNDERSTANDING INTELLIGENCE, APTITUDE, AND MOTIVATION

As teachers, we know that students vary greatly in intelligence, aptitude, and motivation. In general, the three words are used to describe discrete categories that actually overlap and interact in various ways in the classroom. "Intelligence" usually refers to the raw material of thinking power brought to bear on intellectual operations; "aptitude" refers to the specific skills, abilities, and level of background brought to intellectual tasks; and "motivation" has to do with the will or desire to put forth effort to learn.

Many teachers will admit in private that "intelligence" is important to think about and that it varies widely in their students, but it is not something they are eager to talk about in public. Why?

Intelligence, and its measurement, is a sensitive issue in a pluralistic society. Intelligence testing is less than an exact science and culture-fair tests are hard to produce. Furthermore, intelligence testing has been used thoughtlessly (and sometimes viciously) to attempt to substantiate claims about differences between ethnic groups and to "track" individual students on the basis of supposed "ability." Most college teachers are sophisticated enough to know that they can get "burned" in discussions of intelligence, so they keep quiet. But the *fact* of differences in intelligence won't go away, and the importance of intelligence as *one* of the variables that enters into the learning equation cannot be denied. As college teachers, we need to have some perspective on intelligence.

Unfortunately, even very intelligent people have trouble defining intelligence. Much of the recent discussion of intelligence centers on one issue: Is intelligence one thing or is it several things? If it is one thing, what are its sub-parts? If it is more than one thing, how many things is it, and how different are they from one another? The classic theories of intelligence run the full gamut of possibilities from 1 factor to 120. In a recent work on intelligence, Yale scholar, Robert Sternberg, sets forth a three-part (triarchic) theory of intelligence, the idea of a general intelligence made up of three different components.[24]

First, intelligence involves purposive adapting to, selection of, and shaping of real-world environments relevant to one's life. This "everyday" intelligence involves seeking a good fit between one's self and the environment, either through adapting (adjusting), selecting (choosing or learning), or shaping (changing) one's environment. The requirements for this kind of intelligence change across cultures, time, and age levels. Thus, this kind of intelligence is relative to context (culture or class background) and is difficult to measure. It is the kind of intelligence, however, that everyone knows exists. Second, intelligence is the ability to deal with novel situations and unfamiliar tasks, to cut through to the best solutions using automatic systems for processing information. This kind of intelligence shines in out-of-the-ordinary complex tasks, where the process for dealing with the problem is fast, automatic, and seemingly effortless. Third, intelligence also involves a set of governance and coordination mechanisms through which intelligent behavior is accomplished. Sternberg here refers to aspects of mental activity such as planning, monitoring, and evaluating one's performance, and the speed of acquiring knowledge and performing intelligent acts. The three components, while working together, can also be measured separately. Sternberg's theory takes into account the recent work of cognitive psychologists on information processing and gives greater weight than in the past to "practical" intelligence.

Another, much broader view, a theory of multiple intelligences, has been set forward by Harvard scholar Howard Gardner.[25] According to Gardner's theory, intelligence involves the ability to manipulate symbol systems (linguistic, musical, mathematical, etc.), some of which differ widely enough to be regarded as unique domains of intelligence. Support for the theory of multiple intelligence comes from the study of child prodigies, who can be very bright and precocious in one area, but rather average in another; and from recent efforts to map the brain, which have shown that the abilities to use different symbol systems reside in specific, localized areas of the brain. Gardner goes on to describe six different types of intelligence as follows:

- **Linguistic.** Special ability to deal with the semantic (meaning), phonetic (sound), syntactic (ordering), and pragmatic (useful) properties of words. This intelligence is highly developed in poets and novelists.
- **Musical.** Special ability to hear and generate pitch, melody, tone quality, rhythm, and harmony. This intelligence is highly developed in musicians, performers, conductors, and composers.
- **Logical-Mathematical.** Special ability to manipulate numbers and other abstract symbols in long and complex chains of logical reasoning involving deduction and proof. This intelligence is highly developed in mathematicians.
- **Spatial.** Special ability to perceive the world visually, to produce visual images and geometric forms, to "mentally rotate" or otherwise manipulate those forms in space, to perceive them from other angles or in different contexts. This form of intelligence in highly developed in scientists, inventors, engineers, architects, and artists.
- **Bodily-Kinesthetic.** Special ability to project, carry out, and receive feedback on gross and fine movement. This intelligence is highly developed in actors, athletes, dentists, surgeons, and other people who use tools.
- **Personal.** Special abilities to have access to and act on one's own feelings (intrapersonal skills) and to notice and make distinctions among the feelings and behaviors of others (interpersonal skills).

This intelligence is highly developed in political and religious leaders, teachers, therapists, and others in "helping professions."

Although some would say that the theory does not address "intelligence," but rather classifies different kinds of human intellectual competencies—a phrase Gardner uses occasionally—the trend in thinking about various mental abilities, classically known as intelligence, is toward a greater, rather than lesser, inclusion of abilities.

In either case, whether intelligence is broadly or narrowly conceived, the distribution of various mental powers is spread out somewhat unequally throughout the population. Although we need to be careful in defining intelligence and jumping to conclusions about where it resides, we also need to be sensitive to certain variations in the amounts and types of intelligence found in our students.

"Aptitude" is a somewhat related, but perhaps even more slippery, concept than intelligence. Aptitude is one of two ability measures; the other is achievement. Because they are closely related concepts, they are not easily separated.[26] In general, aptitude refers to the capacity of an individual for learning at some time in the future, while achievement refers to learning previously accomplished. Aptitude is often further divided, conceptually, into general and specific aptitude. General aptitude, as it relates to postsecondary students, involves the ability to succeed in college. Specific aptitude involves the projected ability to learn in a specific field of study or to be successful in a particular professional field, such as art, music, medicine, or law. The two most widely used measures of general aptitude for college are the Scholastic Aptitude Test and the American College Test.[27] As teachers in postsecondary institutions, we are not likely to have much access to formal information about the specific aptitudes of our students. It is useful, nonetheless, to keep a watchful eye out for clues about specific aptitude. We have all known students who seem to be bright, well-motivated, and generally successful in college, but without much aptitude for mechanical engineering, figure drawing, or the flute. On the other hand, we want to be alert to our misuse of "low aptitude" as an excuse for ineffective teaching.

"Motivation" is another concept that appears simple on the surface but becomes more complex as we think about it. Everyone wants highly motivated students, and most of us have succumbed at one time or another to fruitless discussions of our "poorly motivated students." What is meant by motivation? Raymond

Wlodkowski suggests that motivation refers to "those processes that can (a) arouse and instigate behavior, (b) give direction and purpose to behavior, (c) continue to allow behavior to persist, and (d) lead to choosing or professing a particular behavior."[28] Wlodkowski has developed useful categories and a stimulating set of questions for elaborating the concept of motivation and describing its component parts:

- **Attitudes.** Motivation is affected by the attitudes the student brings to the learning situation. What are the student's attitudes about the teacher, the subject, and the setting? What does the student expect to do in this situation?
- **Needs.** Motivation is influenced by the nature and strength of the student's physical and psychological needs. How is the learning situation structured to bring about a sense of belonging, self-respect, and growth of the student's full potential?
- **Stimulation.** Motivation is influenced by the type of and degree of stimulation provided. How are classes organized to provide variety, interest, involvement, provocation, and novelty?
- **Affect.** Motivation is influenced by the feelings the student is having about the situation. How does the student feel about what is being learned, the climate for learning, and the relevance of the experience to daily life?
- **Competence.** Motivation is influenced by the type and degree of competence the student perceives to be gained from the learning experience. How does the student gain feedback about what is being learned and foresee opportunities for applying it in new environments?
- **Reinforcement.** Motivation is influenced by the concrete rewards that follow learning. How do grading procedures and the system of natural consequences provide concrete rewards for learning?

Seen in this way, motivation is not something that students simply have or lack; it is a complex interaction of what the student brings to the situation and what the situation brings out of the student. Some of the elements of the situation can be altered, and may in fact alter the motivation; some may not. Ultimately, teachers can't "motivate" students, they can only influence the variables that may stimulate motivation.

The problem of motivation is frustrating to teachers because certain aspects of it appear to be beyond their control. The frustration is particularly intense with students who appear to be extremely unmotivated and are difficult to reach. Two concepts from the psychological literature may be useful.[29] One is "locus of control," a concept used to describe the degree to which people believe that they have control over their environment. When students come to believe that the locus of control resides primarily in the environment, rather than within themselves, they become less and less motivated to action. If they perceive the world to be governed primarily by fate or chance connections, rather than by outcomes contingent upon effort, they are likely to have a fairly deep-seated, difficult-to-change problem of motivation. A related concept is "learned helplessness," the idea that people have gone through certain extreme "no-win" situations where they have actually learned to be helpless. Students who have an external locus of control or who manifest learned helplessness present an unusual challenge. Sometimes they must be taught, very slowly and patiently, how to alter their fundamental perceptions of the world, including the contingency of effort and outcome.

Consider how the three variables—intelligence, aptitude, and motivation—may interact by examining the extremes of performance. Sometimes students of lower intelligence and aptitude display that "something extra" in motivation that enables them to succeed. But more often than not, when low intelligence and low aptitude are brought to the academic tasks of postsecondary education, there is marginal achievement, failure, and subsequent discouragement, which in turn lead to lower motivation. To reverse this cycle it is often necessary to provide more structure, more time, and a variety of teaching strategies, sometimes addressing the same content in different ways, and perhaps restructuring basic attitudes that affect motivation. At the other extreme are students of high intelligence, aptitude, and motivation, sometimes known as the intellectually gifted, often showing up in college as "honor students."[30] These students are usually successful in their intellectual undertakings and their motivation is fed by success. Although they may have encountered problems in school, depending on the match of challenge and talent, many gifted children grow up to be gifted adults. For them, the instructional problem is different and may call for "acceleration," letting them move rapidly through the subject to advance more quickly to higher levels, or "enrichment," to undertake additional, more challenging work that supplements the usual study of the subject.

Teachers who make special efforts to find out about the intelligence, aptitude, and motivation of their students (and the way these variables interact) may be able to make better decisions about how to select and apply appropriate teaching strategies.

UNDERSTANDING LEARNING STYLES AND SENSORY MODALITIES

In recent years the concept of "learning styles" has captured the attention of many educators. Teachers have been urged to take an interest in students as individuals and to discover their students' individual learning styles. The basic idea is that certain students prefer certain styles of learning just as they might prefer a certain style of dress or model of car. Learning style theories can be grouped into three basic categories: those that deal with brain functions, those based on personality differences, and those addressing differences in sensory modalities.[31]

One group of learning style theorists has stressed the importance of differences in left-brain and right-brain functions.[32] It has been argued that the left hemisphere of the brain is predominantly involved with analytical, logical thinking, especially in verbal and mathematical functions, while the right hemisphere is specialized for orientation in space, artistic endeavor, body image, recognition of faces, and holistic and rational thinking. When students appear to exhibit pronounced individual differences in their preferences for linear (analytic) thinking as opposed to holistic (artistic) thinking, these differences are often referred to as a learning style preference. The preferences may, indeed, be there, but whether they are related to the way the brain hemispheres function is open to question. As Carl Sagan has noted in the conclusion of his study of the evolution of the human brain, "the coordinated functioning of both cerebral hemispheres is the tool Nature has provided for our survival."[33] Perhaps the best way to think of left-brain/right-brain learning style theory is as a metaphor for preferences.

In postsecondary settings, the two most prominent learning style theories based on personality types are David Kolb's "Learning Style Inventory" and the learning style theory growing out of the Myers-Briggs Type Indicator. Kolb notes that most people differ along two dimensions in their learning preferences, from Abstract to Concrete and from Reflective Observation to Active Experimentation.[34] Kolb has used these two sets of polarities to develop the

Learning Style Inventory, a nine-item self-description questionnaire that asks the respondent to rank in order four words (in each item) that describe his or her learning style. Because all people fall somewhere on *both* dimensions, scores will cluster in one of four quadrants as follows:

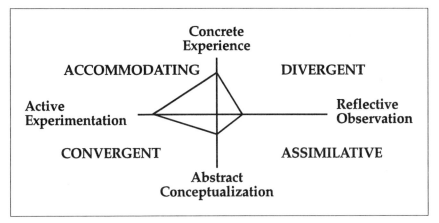

In the example above the respondent has scored high on Concrete Experience and Active Experimentation and will have what Kolb has designated as an Accommodating Learning Style. The four learning styles, made up of the combined emphases of the two dimensions, are summarized briefly as:

- **Convergent.** Prefer problem-solving, decision making, practical application of ideas, finding a single correct answer or solution, working on technical tasks.
- **Divergent.** Prefer organizing many specific relationships into a meaningful gestalt, generating alternative ideas and implications, brainstorming, imagination.
- **Assimilative.** Prefer reasoning, creating theoretical models, integrated explanations, working with ideas, concepts, sound and precise theories.
- **Accommodating.** Prefer doing things, carrying out plans, seeking opportunity and risk, taking action, fitting the theory to the facts, relying on other people for information.

The four learning styles grow out of preferences that in turn grow out of personality characteristics. The implication is that certain people will prefer to approach learning either as convergents, divergents, assimilators, or accommodators.

A second prominent learning style theory is based on the My-ers-Briggs Type Indicator. The dedicated work of a mother-daughter team, Kathleen Briggs and Isabel Briggs-Myers, the personality inventory is based on categories developed by the famous psychoanalyst, Carl Jung.[35] The personality theory includes Jung's familiar categories of "Introvert" and "Extrovert," as well as polarities relating to sensing, intuition, thinking, feeling, judging, and perceiving. The learning style theory is extrapolated from the personality theory, the idea being that people with certain personality characteristics will have related orientations to learning as follows:[36]

- **Extrovert.** Learns best in situations filled with movement, action, talk. Enjoys discussion groups, cooperative projects. May have trouble sitting still, reading books, writing.
- **Introvert.** Learns best alone in periods of concentrated study. Teacher-centered, enjoys lectures, may not like discussion. May not share what is known. Thinks before speaking.
- **Sensing.** Likes to focus on concrete here-and-now, facts and details, putting knowledge to use, learning skills and procedures, being precise and accurate.
- **Intuition.** Likes to gain general impressions, the entire gestalt, concepts, theories. Dislikes structured and mechanical approaches to learning, prefers open-ended assignments, opportunities for imagination. May be careless about details.
- **Thinking.** Prefers performance criteria, wants to know how learning will lead to a deeper understanding of how things work. Likes rule-based reasoning.
- **Feeling.** Wants to know how learning will affect people, interested in process of learning, motivated by learning that touches convictions and values.
- **Judgement.** Prefers structured learning environments, goals, deadlines. Enjoys accomplishment, getting assignments done, achievement.
- **Perception.** Prefers more free-wheeling learning environment, working on several things at once, delaying closure until the deadline. May feel imprisoned in highly structured classrooms.

Although these personality types appear to be measurable by the Myers-Briggs Type Indicator, and although there appears to be a logical connection between personality type and learning style preference, it is not always clear what the teacher is to do with this information.[37] Unfortunately, most of the constructs used in such theories are very broad and unspecified. What does it mean, really, to be more of a "thinking" person than a "feeling" person, when most people do both frequently and usually simultaneously. Moreover, because personality is such a complex thing, teachers need to be careful about typing and labeling students, and treating them as if they were forever a certain way. ("Here comes my intuitive learner.") On the other hand, different people do have different personalities, and personality is one of the variables to consider in thinking about students as learners.

A third category of learning styles involves sensory modalities, the preferred senses for learning. Of the five senses—taste, smell, touch, sight, and sound—the last two, sight and sound, are very important in most postsecondary settings. There are, of course, various forms of musical, dramatic, athletic, and artistic expression that draw on other senses, but in the vast majority of the learning tasks, students take it in through their eyes and ears and put it out through writing and speaking. Students vary significantly, however, in their sensory capacity for input and output, in what educators call their "sensory modalities."

Building on the earlier work of the famous preschool educator, Maria Montessori, Walter Barbe and Raymond Swassing, researchers at Ohio State University, have used the idea of sensory modalities as the basis of a learning style theory.[38] All learners, they point out, have differences in ability in using sensory modalities. These differences can be expressed as preferred styles of learning. The styles are categorized as auditory, visual, and tactile-kinesthetic. Auditory learners (more precisely, those who prefer using auditory channels) like to use their voices and ears and they learn best by talking and listening. They like to "talk it through" and enjoy lectures and class discussion. Silence can be disturbing for them. Visual learners like to see the words written down. They like pictures, charts, diagrams, graphs, time lines. They like the assignment written out and they enjoy written assignments. Tactile-kinesthetic learners like to be "up and doing." They like projects—to build, to handle materials, to act out. They don't want to be told about the computer; they want to try it. When they *do* it, they learn it and remember it. They hate sitting still.

There is a common-sense validation for the idea of learning styles based on differences in sensory modalities. Consider the situation of students with serious physical disabilities. Some students have speech and language disorders, some are deaf, some are blind, others have learning disabilities. Increasingly, these students have been identified and served through special education arrangements in elementary and secondary schools, and are finding their way into postsecondary settings. In recent years, the emphasis has been on the "normalization" of the lives of students with disabilities, encouraging them to lead as normal a life as possible, outside of special instructional settings, within the "least restrictive environment" for learning, if possible within the "mainstream" of the school or college environment.[39] In fact, "mainstreaming" is national policy in the United States, supported by federal and state legislation and a growing body of case law. Increasingly, teachers in postsecondary settings will encounter students with deficits in sensory modalities (and preferences for compensating modalities), and in most cases there are things teachers can do—often little things—that make a big difference for such students.

The teacher's attitude, of course, is important—not labeling, stereotyping, and stigmatizing; not conveying a low estimate of the student; not expecting less (and therefore getting less); not letting the student "play the role" of being disabled.[40] Whether a student's disability becomes a problem depends on the teacher's ability to adapt instruction appropriately (both inputs and outputs) to the student's needs. For example, for students with speech disorders, it is important to provide a risk-free environment where the teacher (and the students) are willing to go slower, take time for repeating, and are willing to find in "imperfect expression" the student's intended meaning. Written outputs will be an important alternative to "class participation." For the deaf and hearing impaired, it is important to assign front row seating, perhaps use an individualized electronic "broadcaster" or an assistant to provide "signing," add supplemental visual materials, employ written testing, and give clear written instructions. On a more practical level, it is important not to stand in front of a window with glaring light or to talk while facing the chalkboard. For the blind and visually impaired, it is important to provide extended verbal explanations, advanced notice (1-3 months) on reading assignments to allow for procurement in Braille or for taping, provision for audio taping of classes, and special arrangement for testing and generation of papers and assignments. For students with learning disabilities, a highly structured, distraction-free work environment may be necessary along with special tutoring in areas of difficulty as well as special arrangements for testing. As federal and state laws provide increasing protection for the disabled, adaptation and "special provisions" to assist these students will no longer be a matter of choice, but a necessity and obligation.

Consider once again the idea of learning styles based on differences in sensory modalities. Whether the differences lead to what may be called "learning styles" is open to debate. What should be clear, however, is that all people, the "normal" as well as the "disabled," vary on a continuum of ability with regard to the use of their sensory modalities. Effective teachers are sensitive to the strengths and weaknesses in the use of sensory modalities that students bring to the learning situation. All students are in this sense special learners.

RESPONDING TO ETHNICITY, SOCIAL CLASS, AND GENDER

There are, of course, other individual characteristics a teacher needs to take into consideration, such as ethnic background, social class, and gender. Students can vary on all of these dimensions.

The United States has often been described as "the great melting pot," but most sociologists agree that the melting never occurred. Although there is a national American culture and identity shared by most citizens, many Americans function also, in varying degrees, within ethnic sub-societies that determine, to a large extent, their values and behavior. Most nations today, however dominant in their long cultural traditions, contain ethnic groups. China, the oldest continuous civilization in the world, is today a nation of over 50 ethnic groups. Membership in an ethnic group is influenced both by how individuals see themselves and how they are seen by others.[41] An individual may have low or high affiliation with an ethnic group, that is, ethnicity can be unimportant or very important. Many Americans do not identify with an ethnic group; they see themselves as "mainstream Americans." Others identify strongly and regard themselves as Italian-Americans, Japanese-Americans, Chicano, Polish, Jewish, etc. The behavior of individual students is often determined by the degree to which they identify with and are influenced by a particular ethnic group.

Effective teachers are aware of ethnic differences; they avoid racial and ethnic stereotyping, and they won't permit it by students in their classrooms, even if this produces some "tense moments." They do, however, encourage the legitimate expression of ethnic differences, and draw upon these differences in creative ways to enrich the cultural awareness of all students. Sometimes teachers will effectively draw out of students some particular aspect of their ethnic experience that will enrich the discussion or enlarge the perspective on the issue at hand. This can be done by simply asking how the issue (the norms, customs, attitudes, or actions) might be viewed differently by members of another ethnic group. Sometimes that question is a general question to the class or (given an established comfort level) a specific question to an individual of an ethnic minority background. Sometimes teachers also acknowledge language differences (particularly with foreign students) and make special efforts to ensure that technical language or culture-laden concepts are being understood. Knowing how to respond to each individual "without regard to race, color, or creed," while at the same time being sensitive to important ethnic differences, is a tightrope walk. Effective teachers learn to tell when ethnic differences should be recognized and responded to and when they should be ignored. The key to success is in reading the degree of identification. People want to be able to define their own ethnicity, not have it thrust upon them. They should be called what *they* want to be called, and students will usually provide some guidelines about this when asked.

Individuals also vary according to social class, sometimes referred to as socioeconomic status (SES). The chief determinants of class are occupation, educational attainment, and income. These factors, in turn, tend to determine where one lives, the cost of housing and cars, other patterns of consumption, memberships, and where one goes to school or college. There are social classes, of course, in all societies, and these are more pronounced where there are great variations in income and wealth.

Side by side in the same classroom may be one student who drives a Porsche and spends spring break in Bermuda, and another who works full-time to put bread on the table and pay the tuition bills. Does it make a difference? Differences in income and wealth have important impacts on what resources are available to an individual, not only for the basics such as food and shelter, but for those things that enrich life: travel, cultural experiences, books, magazines, music lessons, summer camp, etc. Some students have very limited resources and have had little opportunity in their lives for certain kinds of enriching experiences that have a high educational impact. Social class can also affect language usage, behavioral norms, lifestyle, attitudes, and values. In many research studies, sócial class and educational attainment are highly correlated. For those families who are continually in the bottom one-fifth of income and wealth, the effects of cultural deprivation tend to accumulate across the generations. Effective teachers are aware of the relative wealth and impoverishment of their students, how this determines their life experience, and how this enriched or limited exposure influences learning.

Individuals also vary by gender. Does being a female or male make a difference in the way a student learns? Should female students be treated any differently than male students in the classroom? Although the intuitive response to such questions may be "no," there is at least some evidence that female students are already being treated differently in classrooms, and have been so treated through much of their educational experience in elementary and secondary schools. Research suggests that elementary school teachers tend to[42]

- talk more to boys.
- ask boys more "higher order" questions.
- give boys more instructions, while *showing* girls how to complete the task, or *doing it* for them.
- praise boys for the content of their work and criticize them for form and neatness, while doing the opposite for girls.

One comprehensive study of teachers in fourth, sixth, and eight grade classrooms in four states plus the District of Columbia concludes that "male students received significantly more remediation, criticism and praise than female students."[43] An extension of this study at a major American university found that the patterns established in elementary and secondary school persist—male students receive significantly more attention.[44]

Effective teachers are aware of this "different experience" that women have had and make special efforts to free themselves of the "everyday inequities" that may creep into the classroom unnoticed. The project on the Status and Education of Women, sponsored by the Association of American Colleges, lists, among others, some behaviors to be *avoided*.[45] Although these are behaviors male faculty are most likely to exhibit, female faculty may also at times unconsciously

- make disparaging remarks about women in general.
- make disparaging comments about intellectual ability, seriousness, or commitment.
- make comments that divert discussion of a female student's work to her physical attributes.

- use sexist language (girls, gals, or generic "he").
- use sexist humor.
- make more frequent eye contact with and responsiveness to men.
- use modulating tones for women (patronizing, impatient).
- respond more frequently to men's questions and comments.
- ignore women students, even when they volunteer.
- call directly on men, but not women.
- call men students by name more often.
- wait longer for men to respond.
- interrupt women students more frequently.
- ask women lower order questions, while asking men higher order questions.
- respond more extensively to men's comments.
- use classroom examples that reinforce stereotypes about gender.

In the current discussion of gender the focus has been on understanding women, as if men were somehow a given, a stable anchor point that everyone understands. This is, of course, a dangerous assumption. Issues about gender *identity* are now also debated on most college campuses. What we do know is that women have not always been treated fairly by the society and its educational system, and a disproportionate amount of power in the hands of males has shaped an educational context to which women are now calling attention with deep concern. The important point for teachers to remember is that gender socialization is quite different for males and females, and the gender socialization experiences of *individual* students, both males and females, often will be quite different. Effective teachers continue to ask: How has gender socialization influenced important attitudes about the self in this student as learner? This is, of course, an important question to ask about both men and women students.

It is important to note that ethnicity, social class, and gender are also variables that often interact. One must ask not only what it means that the student is male or female, but what it means that the student is a black male or Hispanic female—and beyond that, a lower class black female or upper class white male. (Or to break the stereotype—an upper class black man, the son of a wealthy Atlanta professional family, or a middle class Hispanic woman with ancestral roots in the Southwest that antedate the American Revolution.) The background characteristics of individual students are rooted in social phenomena. The groups—ethnic, social, gender—to which students belong and have belonged during their childhood, can greatly influence the characteristics they bring to the classroom as learners as well as their overall attitudes toward "knowing" and the process of learning.

PEDAGOGIES AND TEACHING STRATEGIES

Some very valuable concepts and theories are available for deepening our understanding of students as learners. It is tempting to fasten upon one or more of these concepts or theories and to build upon it a pedagogy—a theory of teaching. One may, for example, entertain the possibility of developing an entire pedagogy around the "left-brain, right-brain" theory of brain dominance, or a learning style theory based on sensory modalities. An example of one such effort has been the attempt to build a pedagogy around age differences—the so-called adult learning theory of "androgogy."

Malcolm Knowles, in his very stimulating writing about adult education, has catalogued what he and many of his colleagues have identified as the characteristics of adult learners.[46] Over the years, people who had been working with adults noticed that adults seem to bring to the learning situation attitudes and characteristics that are different from children and adolescents. Knowles believed that it was possible to pull these characteristics together into a comprehensive theory of adult education. He borrowed a term just emerging in Europe—"androgogy"—and used it to describe a theory of teaching adults that differed from the traditional theory of teaching children, known as pedagogy. (The Greek roots are *paid* for "child" and *andr* for "man, not boy," and *agogus* for "leading.") Knowles then drew some comparisons between pedagogy and androgogy.

In pedagogy, the learner is dependent and the teacher is responsible for seeing that learning occurs. In androgogy, the learner is self-directed and the teacher facilitates. In pedagogy, the student has little experience to bring to the learning situation and stands to profit most from the teacher's experience and the materials the teacher provides. In androgogy, people bring more experience to the situation and value experience more, accordingly expecting more "hands on" learning through discussion, laboratories, cases, simulation, and field experience. In pedagogy, students must learn what society expects them to learn, and students of the same age are exposed to a fairly standard, step-by-step curriculum. In androgogy, real-life situations and problems create a readiness to learn, and learning is arranged by categories and in a sequence determined by this desire to learn. In pedagogy, students acquire an ordered subject content that they understand will be useful later in life. In androgogy, students want to be able to apply immediately what they are learning and are performance-centered in their orientation to learning. And so on. This polarization of differences between child learners and adult learners, however, has some problems and Knowles himself was clever enough to see them. He notes:

> Then an increasing number of teachers in elementary and secondary schools (and a few in colleges) began reporting to me that they were experimenting with applying the concepts of androgogy to the education of youth and finding that in certain situations they were producing superior learning. So I am at the point now of seeing androgogy as simply another model of assumptions about learners. . . . For example, taking the assumption regarding dependency versus self-directedness, a six-year-old may be highly self-directing in learning the rules of a game but quite dependent in learning to use a calculator; on the other hand, a forty-year-old may be very dependent in learning to program a computer, but completely self-directing in learning to repair a piece of furniture.

Although it may be useful to think carefully about the characteristics of older students—particularly their developmental needs—it is unlikely that one can build a "pedagogy" on these characteristics.

In this book the term "teaching strategy" is used in preference to any kind of "gogy." As described earlier, a teaching strategy is based on and grows out of a paradigm of how people learn. These are broad paradigms that describe how learning takes place with people in general. These paradigms of how people learn have grown out of different assumptions about what kind of learning is taking place (acquiring skills, processing information, thinking, examining attitudes, reflecting on experience) and the contexts in which the learning is occurring. The paradigms encompass what may be thought of as the "primary variables" that determine how learning is taking place. It is obvious, however, that there is no such thing as a "human being in general." This is why it is important to begin by asking about the characteristics of the students to be taught. Student characteristics, however, are the "secondary variables"—sometimes referred to by researchers as the "intervening" or "carrier" variables—that mediate the primary variables of any learning situation. Student characteristics are important, therefore, but they should not be elevated to greater importance than they deserve. Student characteristics will influence, sometimes greatly, how a particular teaching strategy is employed and how successful it will be. Student characteristics will also enter into the selection of a teaching strategy. (For a more complete discussion of the relationships among the strategies, and the relationship of the strategies to the subject, the setting, and the students, see the concluding chapter, "Choosing and Using the Teaching Strategies.") The important thing to note here is that teaching strategies derive from broad paradigms of how people learn; student characteristics, while important, are an insufficient base for pedagogies.

CONCLUSIONS

Before teaching proceeds, while it is being anticipated and planned for, we need to think carefully about the individual characteristics of the students to be taught. It is important to ask the right questions, and formulate tentative answers, about student cultures and subcultures; about the social and emotional development of students; about their level of cognitive development; about their intelligence, aptitude, and motivation; about their learning styles and sensory modalities; and about their ethnic background, social class, and gender.

Effective teachers know whom they are trying to teach.

NOTES

1. K. Patricia Cross, *New Students and New Needs in Higher Education* (Berkeley, CA: Center for Research and Development in Higher Education, 1972).

2. George D. Kuh, "Assessing Student Cultures" in William G. Tierney, ed., *Assessing Academic Climates and Cultures* (San Francisco: Jossey-Bass, 1990), New Directions for Institutional Research, No. 68, p. 52.

3. Ibid. pp. 48-50.

4. Arthur Levine, *When Dreams and Heroes Die: A Portrait of Today's College Student* (San Francisco: Jossey-Bass, 1980).

5. Alexander Astin, William Korn, and Ellyne Berz, *The American Freshman: National Norms for Fall, 1990* (Washington, DC: American Council on Education and Westwood, CA: University of California, Los Angeles, 1990).

6. This research is summarized well in George Kuh, "Assessing Student Cultures," p. 52 ff. The references for the instruments are R.E. Peterson, *College Student Questionnaire: Technical Manual* (Princeton, NJ: Educational Testing Service, 1968); C.R. Pace and G.G. Stern, *College Characteristics Index* (Syracuse, NY: Psychological Research Center, Syracuse University, 1958);

C.R. Pace, *College and University Environmental Scales: Technical Manual*, 2nd ed., (Princeton, NJ: Educational Testing Service, 1969); and C.R. Pace, *CSEQ: Test Manual and Norms: College Student Experiences Questionnaire* (Los Angeles: Center for the Study of Evaluation, Graduate School of Education, UCLA, 1987).

7. Michael Moffatt, *Coming of Age in New Jersey: College and American Culture* (New Brunswick, NJ: Rutgers University Press, 1989). In addition to Moffatt's work, my own earlier effort to study the college experience would today be categorized as a qualitative study: James Davis, *Going to College: The Study of Students and the Student Experience* (Boulder, CO: Westview Press, 1977).

8. Herant Katchadourian and John Boli, *Careerism and Intellectualism Among College Students: Patterns of Academic and Career Choice in the Undergraduate Years* (San Francisco: Jossey-Bass, 1985).

9. George Kuh, "Assessing Student Cultures," p. 56.

10. The discussion of development is based on David Brodzinsky, Anne Gormly, and Sueann Ambron, *Lifespan Human Development* (New York: Holt Rinehart, Winston, 1986). I have also employed two other widely used texts on human development for general background: Paul Mussen, John Conger, and Jerome Kagan, *Child Development and Personality*, 4th ed., (New York: Harper & Row, 1974) and Kurt Fisher and Arlyne Lazerson, *Human Development from Conception to Adolescence* (New York: W.H. Freeman, 1984).

11. The concept of "development task" is elaborated in Robert Havinghurst, *Development Tasks and Education* (New York: Longman's, 1972).

12. For a discussion of stage theory, see "Neo-Piagetian Theory" in Fischer and Lazerson, *Human Development*, pp. 223-24.

13. Erik Erikson's chief writings are *Identity and the Life of Cycle: Selected Papers by Erik Erikson* (New York: International Universities Press, 1959); *Childhood and Society*, 2nd ed., (New York: Norton, 1963); and *Identity, Youth and Crisis* (New York: Norton, 1968). The general framework for adult development and the description of adolescence are drawn from David Brodzinsky *et al.*, *Lifespan Human Development*. See especially pp. 309-23.

14. The vectors of development are drawn from Arthur Chickering, *Education and Identity* (San Francisco: Jossey-Bass, 1969). Chickering appears to have revised and modified the list somewhat in a later work. See "Developmental Change as a Major Outcome" in Morris Keeton and Associates, *Experiential Learning* (San Francisco: Jossey-Bass, 1976). The more recent list is not elaborated fully and has not had the visibility of the earlier formulation, which has been widely referred to in the literature on student development.

15. I have drawn heavily on Rita Weathersby's valuable elucidation of Loevinger's theory by paraphrasing the descriptions set forth in Weathersby's Chapter 2, "Ego Development," in Arthur W. Chickering and Associates, *The Modern American College* (San Francisco: Jossey-Bass, 1981).

The original work is found in Jane Loevinger, *Ego Development: Conceptions and Theories* (San Francisco: Jossey-Bass, 1976).

16. The works referred to are R. Gould, "The Phases of Adult Life: A Study in Developmental Psychology," *American Journal of Psychiatry*, 1972, 129, pp. 521-31; Daniel Levinson, *The Seasons of a Man's Life* (New York: Knopf, 1978); and Gail Sheehy, *Passages: Predictable Crises in Adult Life* (New York: Dalton, 1976).

17. Arthur Chickering and Robert Havinghurst, "The Life Cycle," Chapter 1 in Chickering and Associates, *Modern American College*, pp. 21-22.

18. Ibid., pp. 46-47. The quotation is from p. 46.

19. Ibid., pp. 22-23.

20. Bernice Neugarten, "Personality and Aging" in J.E. Birren and K.W. Schaie, eds., *Handbook of the Psychology of Aging* (New York: Von Nostrand, 1977).

21. Ron Zemke and Susan Zemke, "30 Things We Know for Sure about Adult Learning," *Training*, July 1988, pp. 57-60.

22. William Perry, *Forms of Intellectual and Ethical Development in the College Years: A Scheme* (New York: Holt, Rinehart and Winston, 1970). For a concise introduction to Perry's work, see William Perry, "Cognitive Ethical Growth: The Making of Meaning," Chapter 3 in Chickering and Associates, *Modern American College*, pp. 76-116.

23. The main categories of the Reflective Judgement model are spelled out by its developers in Karen Kitchener and Patricia King, "The Reflective Judgement Model: Transforming Assumptions about Knowing" in Jack Mezirow, ed., *Fostering Critical Reflection in Adulthood* (San Francisco: Jossey-Bass, 1990), pp. 159-76. I have drawn heavily on and have paraphrased sections of that chapter in presenting the Reflective Judgement Model. Readers interested in a fuller elaboration of the Reflective Judgement Model should refer to this chapter for the authors' own words.

24. The classic theories of intelligence are described in Part I, Chapter 1, of Robert Sternberg, *Beyond IQ: A Triarchic Theory of Intelligence* (New York: Cambridge University Press, 1985). Sternberg's own "theory of intelligence" is elaborated in the remaining parts of that same work.

25. Howard Gardner, *Frames of Mind: The Theory of Multiple Intelligences* (New York: Basic Books, 1983).

26. The distinctions between aptitude and achievement are drawn from the American College Testing Program, *Assessing Students on the Way to College*, Technical Report for the ACT Assessment Program (Iowa City, IA: ACT Publications, 1973). See Chapter 2, "Rational for the Content of the ACT Assessment Program," pp. 13-28.

27. Brief descriptions of the SAT and ACT can be found in Ernest Boyer, *College: The Undergraduate Experience in America* (New York: Harper and Row, 1987), p. 33 ff.

28. Raymond Wlodkowski, *Motivation and Teaching: A Practical Guide* (Washington, DC: National Education Association, 1978.) The definition is found on p. 12. The questions below are drawn from an extended chart on pp. 24-32, but have been condensed greatly through paraphrasing and combining. Although the book is intended for teachers in schools, the categories and questions appear to be equally applicable to postsecondary settings and provide a useful elaboration of the concept of motivation.

29. John P. Dworetzky, *Psychology*, 2nd ed., (New York: West Publishing, 1985). See Chapter 9, "Motivation," especially pp. 287-88.

30. For further information on definitions of "giftedness" and the nature of education for gifted children in school settings, see James Gallagher, *Teaching the Gifted*, 3rd ed., (Boston: Allyn and Bacon, 1985); Barbara Clark, *Growing Up Gifted*, 2nd ed., (Columbus, OH: Charles E. Merrill, 1983); and Abraham Tannenbaum, *Gifted Children* (New York: Macmillan, 1983). For an interesting debate on the merits and shortcomings of acceleration and enrichment, see Section III of June Maker, *Critical Issues in Gifted Education* (Rockville, MD: Aspen Publishers, 1986).

31. For an interesting review of several learning style theories, see Pat Burke Guild and Stephen Garger, *Marching to Different Drummers* (Washington, DC: Association for Supervision and Curriculum Development, 1985.)

32. Robert E. Ornstein, *The Psychology of Consciousness* (New York: Viking Press, 1972). Ornstein is representative of left-brain/right-brain learning style theorists.

33. Carl Sagan, *The Dragons of Eden* (New York: Ballantine Books, 1977), p. 248.

34. David Kolb, *Experiential Learning* (Englewood Cliffs, NJ: Prentice-Hall, 1984), p. 67 ff. The category descriptions have been paraphrased and condensed. For a fuller description, see pp. 68-69. The chart is modeled after one that appears on p. 70, but the learning style categories (pp. 77-78, 81) have been added to present all of the essential information in one place.

35. John B. Murray, "Review of Research on the Myers-Briggs Type Indicator," *Perceptual and Motor Skills*, 1990, 70, pp. 1187-1202. The conclusion of the study is that the Myers-Briggs Indicator does measure important dimensions of personality that approximate Jung's typology.

36. George Jensen, "Learning Styles," Chapter 9 in Judith Provost and Scott Anchors, eds., *Applications of the Myers-Briggs Type Indicator in Higher Education* (Palo Alto, CA: Consulting Psychologist Press, 1987). The descriptions are paraphrased and condensed from Jensen's presentation of the categories, p. 183 ff., and from Figure 1, p. 186.

37. Ibid. Jensen raises some important questions about responding to identified learning styles on pp. 188-89.

38. Walter Barbe and Raymond Swassing, *Teaching through Modality Strengths: Concepts and Practices* (Columbus, OH: Zaner-Bloser, 1979). The Swassing-Barbe Modality Index can be used to test modality strength.

39. Nettie Bartel and Samuel Guskin, "A Handicap Is a Special Phenomenon" in William Cruikshank, *Psychology of Exceptional Children and Youth*, 4th ed., (Englewood Cliffs, NJ: Prentice-Hall, 1980).

40. Ibid., p. 80.

41. For the discussion of ethnicity and social class, I have drawn on Donna Gollnick and Phillip China, *Multicultural Education in a Pluralistic Society*, 3rd ed., (New York: Macmillan, 1990). See Chapter 2, "Class," and Chapter 3, "Ethnicity and Race."

42. Roberta Hall (with assistance of Bernice Sandler), *The Classroom Climate: A Chilly One for Women* (Washington, DC: Association of American Colleges, 1982), p. 5. The research on elementary teachers is cited as Myra Sadker and David Sadker, *Sex Equity Handbook for Schools*, pp. 107-09.

43. Myra Sadker and David Sadker, "Sexism in the Classroom: From Grade School to Graduate School," *Phi Delta Kappa*, March 1986, 67.7, p. 32.

44. Isaiah Smithson, "Introduction: Investigating Gender, Power and Pedagogy" in Susan Gabriel and Isaiah Smithson, eds., *Gender in the Classroom: Power and Pedagogy* (Urbana: University of Illinois Press, 1990).

45. Hall, "Classroom Climate," pp. 6-9.

46. Malcolm Knowles, *The Modern Practice of Adult Education* (Chicago: Follett Publishing, 1980). See especially Chapter 4, "What is Androgogy?" The characteristics of androgogy and pedagogy are paraphrased from Exhibit 4; the quote is from p. 43.

Part II
The Teaching
Strategies

Training and Coaching

"Fetch that stool," said Mr. Brocklehurst, pointing to a very high one from which a monitor had just risen: it was brought.
"Place the child upon it."
And I was placed there, by whom I don't know. I was in no condition to note particulars...
Mr. Brocklehurst hemmed.
"Ladies," he said, turning to his family; "Miss Temple, teachers, and children, you all see this girl?
Of course they did; for I felt their eyes directed like burning-glasses against my scorched skin." —Charlotte Bronte, *Jane Eyre*

SKILL DEVELOPMENT

As postsecondary teachers we are often called upon to teach our students specific skills. Sometimes these are what educators call "motor skills," activities that involve particular movements of the body, such as swimming, hitting a tennis ball, playing a musical instrument, using an air brush, or giving an injection. At other times these are what educators call "cognitive skills," such as verbal or quantitative academic skills. These skills include such things as mathematical operations used in arithmetic or algebra, learning to read music, recognizing and using basic grammar and punctuation rules, and being able to use a program on a computer. Many of these are "basic skills" and are taught in the elementary or secondary school, sometimes over and over again; but often they are not "caught" and need to be "re-taught" at the postsecondary level. There are, of course, heated arguments about who should be teaching (and learning) what at the various levels of the educational system; nonetheless, most of us find ourselves, like it or not, teaching basic skills.

The teaching of skills, however, is not limited to basic skills; many advanced skills are also taught in higher education. These skills include both advanced psychomotor and cognitive skills, such as learning to operate an electron microscope, calculating analysis of variance in statistics, using four-color lithography, operating ultrasound equipment, or executing a triple-axel on ice skates. Unfortunately, the teaching of skills is often looked down on as an inferior activity, and the word "training" is sometimes used to designate a kind of teaching that occupies a rung on the status ladder somewhat below its more lofty cousin "educating." The folly of the distinction is obvious: certain skills, like performing brain surgery or flying an airplane, are life-and-death matters! It is important to have a brain surgeon or a pilot who is not only well-educated but also "well-trained" in the particular skills performed. In the teaching of skills, we are often concerned about results and efficiency—seeing that the skill can be performed with a high level of accuracy, and getting the skill taught in the most efficient manner possible. Consider the following examples.

Beth Anderson is a swimming instructor at Mid-West University. Students at Mid-West are required to take two units of physical education activity as part of their general education (graduation) requirements, and often they elect swimming. After an initial placement test to see if they can swim, and if so, how well, students are assigned to beginning, intermediate, or advanced classes. Beth teaches all levels, but the students she enjoys most are the beginners. "It's hard to believe that students get to this point in their lives without knowing how to swim, but I have to admire them for wanting to try. I tell them that we aren't looking for Olympic form; the goal is to swim the length of the pool and back with safety and confidence, so they can enjoy it." Beth is interested in the progress of each student and prides herself on their success. One day a few years back, she told the students she had a treat for them. "It was dumb—just an apple for them to swim to, placed in the water at the right distance for their ability. It seemed to have an amazing impact on their motivation," she observed. "That's what got me started on this reinforcement stuff."

Tony Clementi teaches "Music Appreciation" at Elm Grove College. He lives to share the wonder of music with his students, to help them understand how music works, and to enable them to discover its power to reach the emotions. In addition to introducing students to various stylistic periods and to the major works of the great composers, Professor Clementi likes to analyze the scores of selected works to help students see the ways in which various compositional forms and musical elements appear on the page and sound in performance. For students to do this, they must have at least a basic grasp of the system of musical notation and the way the elements of music are expressed on the printed score. When Professor Clementi began teaching at Elm Grove, he discovered, quite to his surprise, half way through the course, that approximately 15 students out of his class of 50 could not read music. As he tracked the progress of these students, he discovered that they all did poorly on his tests, and worse yet, that they ended up disliking, rather than "appreciating" music. Professor Clementi realized that "reading music" was a prerequisite skill for doing well in his course.

Jolene Jefferson teaches "Developmental Mathematics" at Pacific Coast Community College. How many times have her students "been exposed" previously (like a disease) to the basic math skills she teaches? "Don't even ask," she says, "because that's an irrelevant and irreverent question. Obviously all the previous teaching didn't result in learning. Never mind laying the blame. The way I look at it, here's one more chance—my chance, maybe the last chance—to help them learn it. That's my challenge!"

Jolene covers the basics, weaving her way slowly and skillfully through place value, whole number operations, exponents, factors and multiples, and fractions and decimals. One of the places where students seem to get stuck is in the practical uses of percent. Jolene likes to use very concrete story problems to teach percent examples that her students might encounter in their occupational programs. She knows that students tend to get confused. In the first problem she asks:

> You are a drafter. The architect tells you that 15% of a building totalling 30,000 square feet must be set aside for hallways, restrooms and utilities. The architect asks you to check the preliminary drawings to see if the required space is being reserved.

In the second problem, the situation is similar but the mathematics is slightly different:

> You are a drafter. The architect wants you to check a floor plan to see if the correct percentage of space has been set aside for hallways, restrooms, and utilities. You find that 4,500 square feet

have been reserved. What percent is that of the total 30,000 square feet?

These problems are fairly easy, and Jolene uses them to develop skill in using percent. But she has other problems, where the situation gets more complicated and the numbers don't come out even.

B.F. SKINNER AND BEHAVIORISM

Next to Sigmund Freud, Burrhus Frederic Skinner is perhaps the world's most famous psychologist. It is not completely clear how behaviorism became so thoroughly identified with B.F. Skinner, but he became, before his recent death, its foremost spokesperson.[1] Skinner did not, of course, invent behaviorism, nor did he discover it; it is simply a paradigm of one of the ways that people learn. The principles of operant conditioning have been around for a long time; B.F. Skinner was their most effective and articulate advocate.

Skinner's work is an elaboration of ideas found in the research of John B. Watson and E. L. Thorndike. Watson hoped to establish a science of behavior and believed that psychology would be better if it were "never to use the terms consciousness, mental states, mind, content, will, imagery and the like." His books contain wonderful illustrations of ingenious types of apparatus to measure sight, smell, and sound, including mazes and a "control box" for experimental research on animals, known today as the "Skinner box," but which might more accurately be named the "Watson box."[2] Skinner is indebted to Watson for establishing psychology as a science of human behavior, hence, the term "behaviorist" applied to B.F. Skinner and his colleagues. Skinner is perhaps even more indebted to E. L. Thorndike, who had already outlined, at the beginning of the twentieth century, the basic relationship (connection) between response and consequence that is the foundation of operant conditioning. In Thorndike's day, the leading educational theorists still thought of the mind as a muscle that profited from general exercise. It was commonly believed that each bit of training improves general ability, so that if a student studied enough Latin grammar (and it was hard enough) the faculties of the mind would be appropriately exercised and thus be fit for any intellectual task. Thorndike was able to see the fallacy in this traditional view and established the idea that mental capacities are highly specialized. By examining behavior, Thorndike was able to identify the relationships between rewards and specific learning. Thorndike is remembered for his "Law of Effect." If the consequence that follows a response is satisfying, he notes, the behavior is likely to be repeated. If the "after-effect," as he called it, is annoying, the behavior is not likely to be repeated.[3]

Skinner followed through on the work of Watson and Thorndike by conducting extensive research on animals to establish the principles of operant conditioning experimentally.[4] He investigated the relative effects of punishments and rewards and described the ways in which the rate and persistence of learning are affected by different schedules for delivering reinforcement. He wrote extensively about the implication of his ideas for education, developed simple teaching machines, initiated "write and see" materials for teaching handwriting, authored a text on operant conditioning, coauthored a programmed text on conditioning techniques, and, in his later years, began to speculate on how to apply behavioral principles in forming a more just and humane society.

SHAPING COMPLEX BEHAVIOR

Teaching a rat to press a bar or a pigeon to peck a disc is fairly simple in an automated "Skinner box." The animals more or less stumble onto what produces reinforcement and a food pellet pops out at the right time. What is involved in teaching more complex tasks? Many teachers are hoping to have their students learn fairly complicated things, such as how to swim 100 meters, how to read music, or how to perform basic skills in mathematics. A teacher could spend a good part of the day waiting for a student to "catch on" accidentally to what is expected.

In the laboratory, psychologists have learned an effective way to teach an animal a complex task through a process known as shaping.[5] Suppose that the task is to train a pigeon to turn a complete circle in a clockwise direction. How might a psychologist train a pigeon to turn circles? The first thing the trainer must do is to describe (or operationalize) the goal clearly in "behavioral terms," so that observers can agree upon whether the pigeon is performing the desired behavior. The trainer needs to spell out in some detail what that final behavior is—in this case a clockwise full circle, executed rapidly enough and with appropriate precision so the movement can be recognized as a circle. Next, the pigeon is put in the Skinner box to see if it is already able to turn clockwise circles. Psychologists call this "operant level" or "taking the pigeon's base rate." Teachers would call it "establishing present performance level" or "seeing what the student already knows." Assume that the pigeon does not turn circles and that it just walks around poking its beak into every nook and cranny of the box. How will the trainer get it to turn clockwise circles? The answer is to break the task into a series of steps—successive approximations of the goal. Thus, when the pigeon makes its first move—it may simply shift its weight to the right foot—it is reinforced with food. Next the pigeon steps to the right and leans to the right. More food appears. Then the pigeon takes two steps to the right and twists its neck back and to the right. Food drops into the tray and is eaten. The process continues for a few minutes through a series of successive approximations until the goal (a clockwise circle) is attained.

A similar shaping process is adapted for various forms of instruction involving people. The procedures are relatively simple:

1. A clear agreed-upon observable goal is identified.
2. A base rate measure of existing skill or present performance level is taken.
3. The task is broken into subtasks of appropriate size and difficulty so that the shaping can take place in steps.
4. Successive approximations of the goal are reinforced in some way, providing incentive and feedback until the goal has been reached.

A simple model of the shaping procedure appears below:[6]

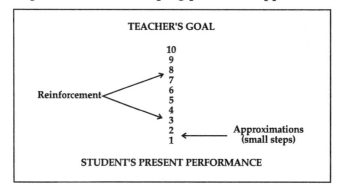

The training and coaching strategy has as its foundation this simple model drawn from behavioral learning theory. The theory "works" and the strategy can be used for very simple or highly complex tasks. Pigeons, for example, have been taught to distinguish circles, squares, and triangles and to peck a triangle to get food.

Perhaps there is hope for students who need to learn how to swim 100 meters, read music, or work math problems. Consider the three examples presented earlier.

Beth Anderson sets a modest goal for her beginning swimmers: to swim 100 meters, the length of the pool, down and back once. There are several ways to achieve the goal, each involving different strokes; and she selects the elementary backstroke as the option she will teach. No student—especially not these students—will just jump in the pool and start doing the elementary backstroke correctly. The stroke has to be "shaped" by breaking it into steps. A student must be able to float, learn to do specific movements correctly with the legs and arms, and breathe correctly. Beth "thinks out" these steps, and she jots down some detailed notes about each of these parts of the task and how she might teach these "sub-tasks" in a step-wise manner.

Beth knows that the students can't perform the task, but that doesn't tell her much about a student's present performance level (PPL); she needs to check out each student individually. As she does this she discovers that some students know how to float, others don't. Some students can float on their stomach, but not on their back. Some have a good frog kick, but they have no confidence when combining the kick with the arm movements. Other students only get in the water and stand near the edge, a few are reluctant even to get into the water! Keeping the goal in mind—getting down and back—and noting the present performance level of each student, Beth thinks about the gap. What are the steps she will need to use to help each student close the gap between PPL and the goal?

For some students, the very first step may simply be to lean over the edge of the pool and put their hands in the water, then their feet, then gradually the rest of their body. When the students get more comfortable in the water, she explains to them about buoyancy and shows them how to take a big breath and use their own lungs for a flotation device. They gradually learn to float on their back, helping to provide physical support for each other until they are comfortable enough to have it taken away. Beth also takes them step by step through the leg and arm strokes. She teaches them outside the pool and gradually transfers them from dry land to the water. In this way she "shapes" swimming behavior, leading students from their present performance level through a series of successive approximations to the goal.

Professor Clementi wants his students to understand the basic elements of music and to be able to recognize how these elements are presented on a score of sheet music. But what, exactly, does he mean by the elements of music? First, there is pitch. He will need to help students learn what pitch is and introduce them to the notation system of lines and spaces that is used to show how one note is higher (or lower) than another. Then there is rhythm. The notes can be "sounded" for different lengths of time and combined in such a way as to make rhythmic patterns. He will need to show the students how time is divided up on a page of music by bars and how each note has a shape that indicates how long it is to be held within the framework of bars. What's left? Loudness and softness, what musicians call "dynamics." How does the composer tell the player how loud or soft to play the notes? This part is easier; there are some recognizable signals on the score.

Professor Clementi gives a simple paper and pencil test on "reading music" during the first class session. Usually, the students who can read music do very well on this test, and those who can't, score very low, getting only a few items correct. Professor Clementi uses the test results to select what turns out to be the 15 students who need special instruction. He announces the formation of a tutoring group—probably no more than four, one-hour sessions.

When he meets the group for the first time, Professor Clementi has already analyzed each student's test paper, but he checks present performance level again by asking each student certain questions about a musical score. Some students know that the lines and spaces help tell what note to play, but they confess that they don't really know about pitch. Others know that the vertical lines make bars, but they don't know what a quarter note or half note looks like. Now Professor Clementi is ready to begin. He knows what the gap is between PPL and the goal. He breaks the task into three parts—pitch, rhythm, and dynamics. One session on each, with one final session to put it all together.

Professor Clementi knows that some students don't want to sing, and he doesn't want to bother with musical instruments, like recorders. Besides, it's the *concept* of pitch he wants to teach, not how to play an instrument. So instead of a pitch, he assigns each student a body movement to represent a pitch, like slapping their knee for "A," patting their head for "C," rubbing their stomach for "E," and so on. Then he shows the students how these letters are represented on the system of lines known as the treble clef. When he points to the notes located on the various lines and spaces, the students assigned to those letters (A, C, E, etc.) are expected to respond with their movement. The students think this is quite hilarious, and they have a good time with it. One student dubs the class "Music for the Deaf." In a short time, Professor Clementi is playing a simple tune with them, by pointing to the notes on the staff as they respond with their movement. In the next session, Professor Clementi tells the students that they must learn how to "perform" their movements within a prescribed length of time, and he warns them that they may be called on for one long "rub" or four short "rubs." He shows them about bar lines and the time signature that indicates how many "beats" within a bar. After he establishes how to make movements according to a regular pattern of 2, 3, or 4 "beats to a bar," he shows the students the notation system for making whole notes, half notes, quarter notes, etc. Then they are ready to practice making their movement, when called upon, the right number of times and for the right length of time.

During the third session of "Music for the Deaf," students learn to make their movement in very small contained strokes, or in big sweeping strokes to represent "soft" and "loud." Professor Clementi introduces the symbols "*p*" and "*f*" and the markings < > and shows the students what a conductor does to get an orchestra to make the music (gradually or suddenly) louder or softer. By this time the students have become quite proficient at playing their "note" in the proper rhythm at the proper dynamic, and the final class session turns into a dress rehearsal for a "concert." Professor Clementi knows that the graduates of the tutoring session will now have the prerequisite skill (reading musical notation) and a fair opportunity for getting a good grade in his course.

Jolene Jefferson wants to teach her students in developmental math the functional uses of percents. She realizes that she has to think carefully about what students are actually doing when they are using percents correctly. First, she notices that she is teaching two related but separate operations. The first task, the simpler of the two, involves identifying a larger number and taking a percent of it. What the student does is to identify the larger number (30,000 square feet) and take the percent by multiplying by the decimal that represents the percent. To do this, a student must first be able to find the percent (15%) and convert it into a decimal (.15) by moving the decimal point two places to the left. From there, the multiplication of 30,000 x .15 is quite easy, resulting in 4,500.

The second part of the task is a little trickier. There are two numbers in these problems, a big number and a little number, in this case the 30,000 square feet and the 4,500 square feet. There is no % number because finding that number is the goal. To perform the task students need to be able to divide the smaller number by the larger number. This will seem odd, but this is how a decimal (and then a percent) is derived. When the big number (30,000) is divided into the little number (4,500), a decimal is produced (.15). This decimal is then converted to a percent by moving the decimal two places to the right.

Once Jolene has the actual behavior of the two tasks clear in her own mind, she gives the students sample problems that will require them to perform the tasks. She checks their present performance level (PPL). A few students get all the problems right. They must already know how to do them and aren't going to require much, if any, teaching, maybe just some clarification. She watches the other students as they work and examines their calculations carefully. By watching for "what goes wrong" (formally called "error analysis") she can determine where students get stuck and why. For each student she analyzes the present performance level and compares it with the goal to determine the size of the gap between where the student is and where the student needs to be.

Then Jolene tries to think about the steps that students need to go through to get to the goal. She realizes that some students get stuck on identifying from the problem the right numbers—the big number and percent or the big number and the small number. Then some students don't seem to know whether to multiply or divide. Others have problems converting the percent to a decimal or the decimal to a percent. These are the problems that Jolene finds in the gap between PPL and the goal, and this area is where she focuses her teaching, on these steps. She takes them up one at a time. She shows the students how to "read" the problem by looking for what information is there. If there is a big number and a percent, then it will be necessary to multiply. If there are two numbers, but no percent, then it will be necessary to divide the little number by the big number to get the decimal. When the task is broken into small steps like this, Jolene discovers that the students aren't so anxious. Now all they need is practice!

USING REWARDS AND PUNISHMENTS

The process of operant conditioning itself has several important steps: setting measurable goals, testing for present performance level, breaking the task into steps, and managing consequences. What are consequences? How do they work? Do they work on everyone the same way?

Consequences can be divided into two basic classes: rewards and punishments. Behavior that precedes a reward is likely to be repeated, hence a reward is often referred to as a "positive reinforcer." Positive reinforcers are anything that an individual is willing to put forth effort to obtain. Punishments, on the other hand, are those things that an individual is willing to work hard to avoid. Behavior that proceeds these consequences is not likely to be repeated.

Does this sound like a circular definition? Behavior will be repeated when followed by a reward; a reward is anything that increases the likelihood that behavior will be repeated? What sort of definition is that? Actually, the definition is framed this way intentionally. The process of reinforcement does not depend on the intrinsic properties of the reward or punishment itself. In fact, a reinforcer probably has no "intrinsic properties." Consider why. When people have just pushed back from the Thanksgiving Day dinner table, they probably will not find food to be rewarding. Remember, Skinner deprived his pigeons of food before they could serve as subjects in his experiments. The degree to which something is reinforcing depends on the internal state of the organism, its relative hunger and satisfaction. Furthermore, there will be considerable variation in tastes. Some people like giblets in their gravy and some do not. For a consequence to work as a positive reinforcer, it must be satisfying to that particular individual. Some students will find it satisfying to be praised for their good work in front of the class, while others will perceive it to be quite embarrassing. Some students will work hard for grades; others find them of little value. It is not accidental, therefore, that behaviorists define consequences in terms of the behavior they produce. If the behavior is repeated, the consequence that brought about the repetition of the behavior can be regarded as reinforcing. If the behavior is not repeated, the consequence—to that individual under those conditions—is not reinforcing, or at least not reinforcing enough to bring about that behavior again.

There are two simple methods for initiating, speeding up, and maintaining desirable behavior and two simple methods for slowing down or stopping undesirable behavior. To initiate, speed up, or maintain desired behavior, a teacher uses "positive reinforcement" or "negative reinforcement." To slow down or stop undesirable behavior, a teacher either uses either "extinction" or "punishment." (Negative reinforcement is often confused with punishment, but the differences between the two will become clear as they are further defined.)

To keep these simple methods in mind, refer to the chart below:

Methods for Initiating Speeding Up Maintaining DESIRABLE BEHAVIOR	
Positive Reinforcement Giving a Reward	*Negative Reinforcement* Threatening Something Unpleasant

Methods for Slowing Down Stopping UNDESIRABLE BEHAVIOR	
Extinction Withholding All Reinforcements	*Punishment* Doing Something Unpleasant

The four types of reinforcement are used in the following ways:

- *Positive reinforcement* is used as a reward for behavior that a teacher wants repeated. Depending on the age or developmental stage of the student, positive reinforcers are likely to be such things as praise, attention, recognition, a warm touch or pat on the back, confirmation of right answers, positive comments on a paper, successful performance of a task, solving a problem, free time or a day off, time for social interaction with peers, points, trophies, various types of food, grades, honor roles, deans' lists, certificates, awards, promotions, pay increases, and anything else that might convey approval or generate satisfaction. Although positive reinforcement often comes from the teacher, some of the best reinforcement comes naturally from the task itself, when the student gets things right, finds out how something works, or successfully performs a skill. In this case, reinforcement is usually referred to as "intrinsic," a natural consequence of the activity. Sometimes the teacher simply tells the student, "You are getting it right," and sometimes the student simply knows. Positive reinforcement may take the form of an incentive ("If you do this, then..."), operating according to what is known as Premack's Principle, or, more affectionately, Grandma's Rule.[7] The teacher's role in using positive reinforcement is to provide incentive to do the task and to reward correctly performed approximations of the task.

- *Negative reinforcement* involves setting aversive conditions that an individual will work hard to avoid. It is like punishment, in that the prospect is unpleasant, but it is unlike punishment because it is never applied. It is best thought of as the threat of punishment, because the emphasis is on avoidance. Like positive reinforcement, it can be "used," or it can occur naturally. Typical types of aversive conditions are those things students will work hard to avoid, such as low grades, suspension, critical remarks, check marks or negative comments on papers, not getting the task done right, having to repeat the task, the loss of self-esteem that accompanies poor performance, staying after class, visiting the dean, a reprimand, embarrassment before one's peers or superiors, and demotion or losing one's job. Although negative reinforcement is unpleasant, it is the possibility of avoiding it that controls the behavior. Studying for a test is often motivated by the threat of negative consequences. The problem with threats, of course, is that sometimes they must be carried out, at which point they turn into punishment.

- *Extinction* is the process of withholding reinforcement selectively. "Extinction" is a somewhat outdated term originally used in laboratory experiments, and teachers today are more likely to say that the behavior is simply being ignored. Behavior is neither punished nor rewarded, but is passed over with the hope that it will slow down or go away. An athletic coach will ignore certain mannerisms associated with a particular skill, knowing that certain "wasted motions" will cease when the trainee discovers they are nonfunctional. Not all behaviors need to be provided with consequences. Any of the things normally used as rewards or punishments can be withheld. Extinction works, however, only when all sources of consequences are withheld. If a teacher withholds consequences from a student who consistently disrupts the class, the process is effective only if the other students are also withholding these rewards, sometimes referred to as "social reinforcement." A student who receives positive reinforcement from his peers for disruptive behavior is not an extinction.

- *Punishment* is the direct application of an unpleasant stimulus. Most people need no further definition of punishment.[8] Although it is strictly forbidden in its physical forms in schools in most states, some students may have a "previous history" that has involved psychological punishment, such as sarcasm, ridicule, or unwarranted criticism. Such students are often anxious about learning new things and tend to be unwilling to risk a mistake. Unfortunately, in some postsecondary institutions punishment in its various psychological forms may still be found, and certain professors become well-known for their acts of public humiliation and classroom terror.

The use of punishment, as one type of consequence, warrants further discussion. Does it work? If so, should it be used? The basic research on punishment shows that it "works," if by "work" one means that it will stop the behaviors with which it is associated. A behavior that is punished is not likely to be repeated. So in certain desperate situations, where something must be stopped, punishment may be a last resort. But in most postsecondary teaching, the goal is not "stopping" behavior, but getting it started in the right direction and continuing it. Here again the research is clear, punishment is good for stopping behavior, but not for establishing it. Positive reinforcement, in generous quantities, is needed to establish new patterns of behavior, i.e., for learning new things.[9] Punishment also poses another problem. The effects of punishment are not easily contained. Punishment has a way of generalizing and escalating, and it produces an emotional response in the learner. Although the teacher may have meant to provide a carefully targeted punishment to stop a specific behavior, the student will often associate other things with that punishment. A student who is punished can learn quickly to hate the teacher, the classroom, the subject, and the entire setting, because each has become associated with the punishment. Effective college teachers use punishment sparingly, if at all, and focus their energies instead on imaginative ways of using positive reinforcement.

Will the conscious employment of consequences, such as praise, grades, time off, honors, and certificates, etc., erode a student's so-called natural incentive or intrinsic motivation for the subject? This is a highly controversial issue. Some teachers are troubled by the use of external rewards. They view them as bribes, and they fear that students will become dependent on them and lose their internal motivation. Many teachers want students to engage in "learning for learning's sake," because students find the activity novel, interesting, exciting, pleasurable, or fulfilling. The last thing they want is to diminish students' natural incentive for learning. Unfortunately, the natural incentive of many students often gets crushed early by the educational system. Furthermore, not all instructional tasks are exciting and pleasurable; some are hard and boring. If students are permitted to learn only what they wish, extrinsic rewards might never be necessary. But in the real world of most postsecondary classrooms certain kinds of learning seem to require external rewards. The question is, "will their use stifle the natural love of learning, if and when it is there?" A quantitative review of 10 studies drawn from journal articles concludes that combinations of praise and other external rewards not only do not reduce natural motivation, they produce and maintain intrinsic interest in the behaviors for which the rewards are given. Tangible reinforcement combined with praise does not appear to undermine intrinsic interest.[10] Effective teachers are sensitive to this issue, however, and they know when the system of reinforcement has become the preoccupation of the students. Reinforcement is used to help students focus on learning; it is a means, not the end. Consider again the three examples presented earlier.

Beth Anderson knows that most of her students are internally motivated and really want to learn to swim; for them feedback on "getting better at swimming" will carry them along. Others in the class are fighting their fears or their awkwardness; for them various forms of external reinforcement are going to be very important. The ultimate reinforcement, of course, is achieving the goal—getting down the pool and back. But some students perceive this goal as very remote, perhaps even beyond their reach. They need extensive reinforcement at each step. Beth has learned that generous amounts of precisely directed praise work well; she tells the students they are "doing well," that they are "getting it," that they are "brave" when they float unassisted, and that they should be "proud" for overcoming their fears of the deep end. Beth also uses "time off" effectively as a reinforcer, by letting students out early (for hard work) or giving them a day off (for achieving one of the steps). Sometimes Beth turns certain subskills into a game, providing a buoy with a flag on it as a "goal" to kick to or float toward. She also sets up small contests (mini-meets) where students judge each other for the best kick or the best stroke. The students who achieve the overall goal quickly and find that they are now enjoying swimming are used as peer tutors to provide individualized reinforcement for others who are slower at developing their skills. Beth has learned not to be a perfectionist about form, so she lets certain awkward and inefficient movements (a kick where the knees come up out of the water) extinguish. Occasionally, when students "test" her to see if they can disrupt her class (wrestling, splashing, horsing around) she will identify that behavior as inappropriate and ask firmly that it be stopped. If it occurs again, she requires "extra time" after class for the students who are wasting class time, but she watches carefully to praise them for appropriate class behavior as well.

Tony Clementi has set up his music appreciation class so that the crazy, improvised body movements themselves become a reinforcement system. The whole idea creates a classroom atmosphere that is positive and rewarding. When students slap their knee or pound their chest, at the right time and with the right intensity, they know they are "getting it"; when they miss, the awesome gap in the "music" becomes a humorous punishment, a mildly embarrassing silence that lets them know that they have missed something. Tony also dispenses well-timed praise for catching on to the more subtle aspects of musical notation. If a student is having trouble at a certain point, Tony gives specialized personal attention; when the group does well as whole, he applauds and shouts "Bravo!" Tony seldom has the need for anything resembling punishment, but he will occasionally address a persistent mistake with "no, you are confusing quarter notes and eighth notes." Tony finds that the avoidance of a low grade in the rest of the course serves as a strong motivator for most of the students to learn to read music. In other words, Tony arranges the class itself to make clever use of reinforcement principles.

Jolene Jefferson knows that her students need huge amounts of praise and support, because they come to her having "failed" before, perhaps many times, and their failure has all the emotional overtones that punishment carries with it. They have learned, through their failures, not to like the subject or the teacher, and their previous experience with embarrassment and humiliation may be sufficient to make them very anxious about what is going to happen in math this time. Jolene knows that she can't rely on unpleasant consequences, and she also knows that for many of her students the usual reinforcers are not rewarding. Praise may seem phony or childish, the number correct on a test may not have much affect, and grades—are you kidding? So Jolene listens hard to discover what might be reinforcing for each of her students. She learns their names, and before class, after class, and as she roams around the room, she tries to find out what they like—posters of sports cars, old Batman comics, Twinkies, dangling earrings, pictures of rock groups. She has set aside a small fund of her own money for buying "reinforcers." Then she listens and watches . . . for success, for something done right, for a whole set of problems done right. Then . . . out comes a prize: a poster, picture, or set of earrings! The students love it. Here is a teacher who cares about them enough to remember their peculiar likes and dislikes. They can't believe that she really goes and picks out that stuff! They call her the "little lady with the big surprises," and soon they are working for one of her prizes. They love her, and, in spite of themselves, they start to learn math. They understand it for the first time ever. What could be more rewarding!

Teachers who use training and coaching strategies learn to use reinforcement effectively. They think up creative possibilities for reinforcement and test them out to see if they are, in fact, truly reinforcing. They know how to time reinforcement with the behavior to be established. They know how much reinforcement to use and how strong to make it. They know how to set up classrooms so that the arrangements themselves will be reinforcing.

SPECIFYING BEHAVIORAL OBJECTIVES

Behavioral learning theory has a number of widely used instructional applications that work like or are indirectly related to operant conditioning. Some of the applications involve one or more aspects of the shaping process—the setting of objectives, the management of reinforcement, the analysis of the task to be learned. Other applications involve technological extensions of behavioral learning theory, such as computer-assisted instruction.

One of these applications is the use of a planning device known as a "behavioral objective." Teachers who use training and coaching strategies often develop and use carefully stated behavioral objectives to guide their teaching.

Educators usually make a distinction between instructional goals and behavioral objectives.[11] Curricular goals, as mentioned earlier, are often expressed in broad, abstract terms. Teachers may say they want their students to "swim confidently" or "appreciate music" or "be able to use percents." Broad goals may be useful in planning a curriculum, but when teachers get down to instruction, they usually need something more specific. The idea of behavioral objectives is closely related to an old concept in the sciences known as "operational definition," and sometimes behavioral objectives are referred to as "operationally-stated instructional objectives."[12]

Behavioral objectives have been formally defined as "relatively specific statements of learning outcomes expressed from the learner's point-of-view and telling what the learner is to do at the end of instruction."[13] Note that the emphasis in the definition is not on what the teacher does and not on what the student does to get to the objective, but on the objective itself—what the student is able to do when the learning has been completed. The classic specifications for formulating behavioral objectives were developed by Robert F. Mager in 1962.[14] To help teachers write objectives that are precise and specific, Mager developed two lists of verbs, vague infinities in one list, specifics in another:

Words Open to Many Interpretations	*Words Open to Fewer Interpretations*
to know	to write
to understand	to recite
to really understand	to identify
to appreciate	to differentiate
to fully appreciate	to solve
to grasp the significance of	to construct
to enjoy	to list
to believe	to compare
to have faith in	to contrast

Mager urges teachers to develop behavioral objectives expressed in very specific language. Mager also suggests that a well-written behavioral objective should contain a statement of terminal behavior, what the learner will be doing when the objective has been achieved; a statement of conditions under which the behavior will be expected to occur; and a statement of criteria, the standards of acceptable performance. Consider the following example:

> Given a 50-meter swimming pool and appropriate training and practice sessions, students will swim down and back (100 meters) uninterrupted using the elementary backstroke.

The terminal behavior is "swim down and back . . . using the elementary backstroke." The conditions are "a 50-meter pool and appropriate training and practice." The criteria are "100 meters" and "uninterrupted." Well-stated objectives contain all three parts: terminal behavior, conditions, and criteria.

Consider another example:

Students will be able to really appreciate music.

The objective sounds good (except for the split infinitive), but there are several things wrong with it. The terminal behavior is "to appreciate music," but that is a very broad activity which may include understanding musical notation, stylistic periods, and composers, and may even mean developing certain attitudes about music. The objective needs to be narrowed, and the construct "appreciate" needs to be elaborated as a set of behaviors. Furthermore, the conditions are omitted. Is this a classroom activity, something that happens at concerts, or a daily ritual in the shower? Also, the criterion "really" is not useful. How might a teacher know when a student is "really" appreciating music? A more clearly stated behavioral objective narrowed to one aspect of learning to appreciate music would be:

Given a sheet of music for a classical composition for the piano, the student will be able to identify by circling on the sheet of music with 90 percent accuracy examples of the following elements of musical notation: sharps, naturals and flats; key signature; indication of meter; bar line; lines and spaces of the treble and bass clefs; whole, half, quarter, and eighth notes; whole, half, quarter, and eighth rests; tempo markings and dynamic markings.

This narrowly defined, measurable objective states what the student will be doing, the conditions under which the task will be performed, and the criteria used in evaluating acceptable performance.

Consider a third example:

Given a paper and pencil test with 10 appropriate items, 30 minutes for completion, and a hand-held calculator, the student will accurately distinguish between two types of problems involving percentage and will be able to complete with 80 percent accuracy the computations needed to arrive at correct solutions for the percent of a number and what percent one number is of another.

This objective is longer and somewhat more complicated because the task is complex. It takes more words (and a great deal of thought) to cover all the bases—the terminal behavior, the conditions, and the criteria.

For teachers who use training and coaching strategies, behavioral objectives are beneficial in planning instruction, essential in designing and evaluating instruction, and useful for students as guides in study. When used effectively, behavioral objectives link together the goals of instruction and the means of evaluation, which, when shared with students, give them insights about how to study. The case for behavioral objectives is hard to refute. An effective behavioral psychologist would never think of asking a pigeon to "really appreciate circles" or to "develop a love for the subject of circle-turning," yet that is what we often do with our students. Although stating objectives in behavioral terms is only the first step in using training and coaching strategies, it is, nevertheless, an important step. The most effective reinforcement ever devised will not be of much use unless we first clarify and understand the objectives of instruction.

DOING TASK ANALYSIS

Setting behavioral objectives is an important first step in the effective use of training and coaching strategies. It is important to specify the objective of instruction, but the objective is seldom achieved in one leap. One-leap learning is reserved for crossing narrow canyons and carries high risks. An objective, as a destination or end, is also logically distinct from the means of getting there. The objective may be "to swim 100 meters," but the steps involved in learning the skill (the stroke) that takes the swimmer down and back are something different. Similarly, the objective, "being able to iden- tify the elements of musical notation," is different from the proce- dure that leads to actually being able to do so; one is the end, the other is the means. Certain kinds of learning, therefore, must ad- vance in small steps toward the objective.

The shaping process, as noted earlier, involves steps—succes- sive approximations that lead to the objective. Once an objective has been stated clearly, it is often useful to break the learning task itself into its component parts. The process for breaking a task into its parts is called "task analysis" or "behavioral analysis."[15]

In some tasks there are several ways to reach the objective. The learner takes the lead, and the approximations that the learner presents are reinforced. In teaching a new student to go to the bookstore several blocks away, it doesn't matter whether the route the student takes is west three blocks, then north two, or north two blocks, then west three; either route will get to the destination. When the goal is the key, the route for getting there is often unimportant. But sometimes the route *is* important, and sometimes the goal can't be reached unless the steps are followed in the exact order. In cooking, for example, the recipe often must be followed step by step—sift the dry ingredients together *before* adding the liquid. Some tasks, therefore, are designated "variable sequence tasks" and others are called "fixed sequence tasks." Also, in some kinds of fixed sequence tasks, the student must learn the last step of the sequence first, even though it comes last temporally in performing the task. For example, with parachute jumping, it would be a mistake to teach "jumping" without first having taught "landing." Task analysis is employed to break learning into its component parts so that steps can be identified and, where necessary, learned in sequence.

Task analysis itself has certain steps:

1. Set the behavioral objective.
2. List all component parts (sub-tasks) of the learning task.
3. Arrange the sub-tasks in sequential order and identify prerequisites.
4. Test the routine for correct order and omissions.

The key to task analysis is in gathering up all of the sub-tasks and getting them in the right order. The sub-tasks can be collected in several ways: by talking with people who know how to perform the objective, by watching people who are proficient at performing the objective, by consulting manuals and books that describe the objective, and by logically analyzing the steps needed to perform the tasks leading to the objective. The teacher may or may not be an expert in performing the task. An expert may perform the task automatically and may not be able to describe what goes into the performance. Most Olympic coaches are not themselves good performers of the event. The successful coach or trainer develops a perspective on the task and is able to analyze it.

Once the components of the task are defined and listed in order, they must be tested against an actual performance. A task analysis is seldom done in the abstract, and when it is done that way, steps are usually omitted. A complete task analysis usually takes several trys.

A typical task analysis for the elementary backstroke is presented below:[16]

Elementary Backstroke—Task Analysis

1. Inhale and float comfortably on back with arms at side, feet together and pointed.

2. Slowly extend arms straight overhead, while
3. Spreading legs, bending knees lightly upward and outward to prepare for
4. Frog kick, pulling legs back together with sharp, whipping action of the feet, while simultaneously
5. Pushing arms (hands cupped) in a broad sweeping motion from overhead to side, while
6. Exhaling.
7. Glide and repeat.

In doing a task analysis, decisions need to be made, of course, about the level of detail to be used in breaking the task into steps. It would be possible, in the task analysis presented above, to take some of the steps (such as the kick) and break them down into much greater detail. Some tasks may have more than one level of activity taking place at once, for example, leg and arm movements.

When the task analysis has been completed, decisions still need to be made about which parts of the task to teach first and how to coordinate the various parts of the task into one smooth functioning whole. The order for teaching the task may not be the same as the order for performing the task. The order for teaching is sometimes referred to as a "learning hierarchy."[17] The development of a learning hierarchy involves asking: What would the students have to know first in order to perform "x," then what would they need to know next to perform "y"? One skill may be subordinate (or prerequisite) to another skill. The focus is on the behavior the individual has to be able to perform at one level in order to be able to advance to the next level. A logical learning hierarchy for the elementary backstroke would be:

Elementary Backstroke—Learning Hierarchy

1. At shallow end teach floating on back, arms extended overhead, using a kick board for support, gradually removing it as swimmer becomes secure.
2. At shallow end teach arm movements.
3. On deck teach leg movements, spreading legs into frog position and whipping together in kick.
4. Transfer kick to water and practice, with swimmer holding on to edge of pool, arms extended overhead.
5. In shallow end, put all parts of movement together and practice.
6. When swimmer is confident, practice in deep water.

Doing a task analysis and developing a learning hierarchy may be especially useful for gaining a better understanding of how to teach a complex skill.

Sometimes it is also useful, once a task analysis and learning hierarchy have been developed, to demonstrate or model the task to be performed and to talk about it. The common sense inclination to demonstrate and describe the activity is supported by research on modeling.[18] The classic studies, reported by Albert Bandura, suggest that subjects who watch a task being performed actually benefit from watching and are likely to do better with the task than those not having been able to watch. This does not mean, of course, that a novice, watching an Olympic swimmer, will suddenly be able to perform the breaststroke. It does mean that some gains in learning may occur that might not otherwise occur without the modeling. Variously known as "imitation," "observational learning," or "vicarious learning," modeling tends to augment the shaping process through visual and verbal mediation that take place within the learner. Furthermore, it has been found that the learner is not only more likely to do better with the skill, but also learns about the contingency of the task and the reinforcement. Thus swimmers, who may be fearful of swimming, may also begin to learn to overcome their fearfulness of swimming by watching others learning to swim who are being reinforced for it. In addition, certain behaviors, already learned, will be manifest more frequently when others are doing it and being reinforced for it.

Teachers who employ training and coaching strategies become proficient in breaking complex instruction into its component parts through task analysis and the development of a learning hierarchy to be used as a basis for the shaping process. They also find appropriate ways to model and describe the task.

USING COMPUTER-ASSISTED INSTRUCTION

Behavioral learning theory has also served as a foundation for the development of computer-assisted instruction (CAI). The next logical step, after specifying objectives and breaking the learning task into its component parts, is to develop and present lesson materials that actually take the learner step by step to the goal. Today, this is done with great sophistication on the computer, but it took several years for the hardware, software, and learning technology to come together.

In 1961, B. F. Skinner published an article in the *Harvard Educational Review* entitled "Why We Need Teaching Machines."[19] This article marked the beginning of efforts to use various forms of technology to extend the principles of behavioral learning theory. Skinner's teaching machines were based on earlier versions by Sidney L. Pressey in the 1920s, which required students to push buttons corresponding to items of a multiple-choice test and would advance the student to the next item only when the correct button was pressed.[20] Skinner's teaching machines were more sophisticated, drawing upon a format for carefully developed textbooks called "programmed instruction." Programmed instruction is a system for presenting lesson materials through small steps called "frames." In each frame some information is presented, and the student is called upon either to select from provided answers or fill in a blank. The student is referred either to the bottom of the page or the back of the book for the right answer. Thus, students are able to get immediate confirmation of right and wrong answers and are able to move through the material at their own pace.[21] The statements in the frames contain clues, technically known as "thematic prompts," which are like the hints a theater prompter gives to aid the actors in remembering their lines.[22] A good program utilizes these techniques to ensure that the proper information is systematically embedded within the frames.[23] Skinner and his colleagues developed the "frames" of programmed instruction into sequences of visual materials stored on disks, cards, and tapes (mechanical as yet, not electronic) and fed them into teaching machines that presented the material one frame at a time. The student made a trial "guess" about how to fill in the blank, then turned the material in the machine upward for comparison with the correct answer. Of course, neither mechanical teaching machines nor programmed instruction are used today because they have been replaced by a far more powerful tool—the electronic computer.

There are many ways to use computers in classrooms, including techniques for supporting lectures and conducting case studies (to be discussed with other teaching strategies), but one common use is still CAI, the drill-and-practice and tutorial applications growing out of behavioral learning theory. Anything a teaching machine could do, a computer can do better.[24] As with Skinner's crude teaching machines, students are presented with frames that display information on a screen and ask questions that call for a response. When the student responds, the computer replies either with a confirmation of the right answer, accompanied by appropriate praise, or with some suggestions about how to get the right answer. Because the computer can be programmed, it can be ready for a range of typical student responses and "make decisions" about replying with appropriate responses. For example, a student might make any of five answers to a single question; the computer can be programmed with five different responses, including where to look for help, how to try again, or brief instructions on how to correct what went wrong. Some CAI incorporates an "expert system" that catalogs and analyzes student responses and offers appropriate help based on the analysis.[25] It can branch the student back for review or forward for more challenging material.

Tremendous advances in computer technology and programming are made each year. It is now possible to move beyond the frame-oriented CAI described above with techniques known as generative CAI. The computer constructs questions as it goes, based on what it "knows" about the subject matter through sophisticated algorithmic descriptions of classes of problems. It is called "generative" because the program can operate on the lesson content in such a way as to generate forms of output that are structurally similar but functionally unique, thus producing the "right stuff" for lesson material.[26] Generative CAI has the obvious advantages of using more varied and interesting material, and increasing the opportunity for individualization of learning.

Another recent application of computers is in the linking of visual materials to CAI. A videodisc or CD-ROM disc can store thousands of frames of visual information, including slides, films, videotapes, and graphics, as well as large libraries of text. Real images, not just computer graphics, appear on the screen. It is possible to jump forward and back through this information very rapidly and with precise control. The implications for branching CAI are tremendous. It is possible to present information, for example, in a film; to ask questions about the information; and depending on the responses to the questions, to move in and out of the text or graphics to seek definitions, to review information previously presented, or to seek new visual material on a related topic or subtopic. Software is now available (such as hypermedia and authoring programs) to link visual materials with computers. These types of software provide authoring tools so that teachers can learn to create their own lesson materials without extensive technical background. The most powerful teaching technology ever created is now available to teachers and it is usually received enthusiastically especially by younger students in the "video generation."

Consider how Jolene Jefferson uses computer-assisted instruction in teaching developmental mathematics. First, she explores whether appropriate software on the topics she teaches already exists. She consults a comprehensive index of software such as *ICP Software Directory* or *Datapro Directory of Microcomputer Software*.[27] Next she looks for reviews of software and examines the *Digest of Software Reviews: Education* or seeks out reviews in selected journals that review software, such as *The Computing Teacher, The Journal of Educational Multimedia and Hypermedia*, and *T-H-E Journal*.[28] She also writes for catalogs of major software producers such as Lotus, Sunburst, Apple, or IBM by consulting the Courseware Directory of the *T-H-E Journal Annual Source Guide of High Technology Products for Education*. For videodisc or CD-ROM materials she consults *Videodisc Compendium* or a multimedia magazine such as *New Media*. Jolene also uses the computer services of her college to gain access to Internet, an international computing network where she can read bulletin boards, such as ISAAC; contact newsgroups and view discussion lists on academic software; and stay in touch with colleagues at other institutions through electronic mail.[29] If a systematic search for existing software results in identifying some promising products, Jolene then reviews the software to see if it is compatible with the available equipment and to see (more importantly) if it addresses her original objectives. She finds that in mathematics there is an outpouring of software options, but she has to look carefully for materials that are suitable for adults.

In areas where no appropriate software is available, Jolene creates her own. This involves developing a "learning program" and then a "computer program."[30] Because she doesn't know a computer language, such as BASIC, she searches for one of the many available authoring tools, which allow her to create lessons with a minimum of technical knowledge.[31] She seeks out colleagues at her institution— experts on computers, graphics, and learning—to work with her as a team. With their advice, Jolene first creates a "learning program" which is in many ways like the frames used in programmed instruction, but more sophisticated. As she develops the learning program, she decides whether the main focus of the materials will be on drill and practice, which simply goes over material that has already been learned, or on tutorial materials, which actually teach the concepts involved in learning different functional uses of percent. Jolene has to decide whether she wants a linear program, where students are drilled in sequence on a fixed series of problems, or a branching program, which allows students to identify and work on their problem areas independently.

It may take Jolene a long time and a great amount of effort to create a CAI program, but the long-term savings of time and effort and the gains in learning are well worth the investment if the program is well-designed. Now she can spend more time in diagnosing the specific problems that students are having so that she can prescribe just the right practice materials for their needs.

USING CRITERION-REFERENCED EVALUATION AND MASTERY LEARNING

Another application of behavioral learning theory is found in an approach to evaluation of student achievement known as "criterion-referenced evaluation." In training and coaching, evaluation becomes a matter of measuring proficiency or competency, that is, evaluating learning by referring to stated criteria. Although this idea seems obvious enough, it has been a long time in coming and its arrival at the college level was met with a storm of controversy.

Over the years, teachers, in a variety of settings from elementary school through college, have used another form of grading called "norm-referenced" evaluation.[32] The central question has been how well the student is doing compared to another student, or to most of the students. What most students do on a test becomes the "norm" or standard. The norms are based on data about performance of a number of individuals. If most students get 60 percent of the problems correct, then those become the "C's" and the few students who do somewhat better get the "A's" and "B's" while those doing somewhat worse get "D's" and "F's." The reference is always the standard (norm) set by other students, hence the term "norm-referenced" grading. Most teachers recognize this practice as "grading on the curve." There is one serious fallacy to this method, however. With regard to the stated criteria for performance, all of the students could be missing the criteria, and missing by a lot! Criterion-referenced evaluation places the focus on the stated criteria—the original behavioral objective—and asks: How many students can actually perform what is called for in the objective?

The use of criterion-referenced evaluation has led logically to the idea of mastery learning.[33] The concept of mastery learning was elaborated convincingly by Benjamin Bloom and his colleagues at the University of Chicago in the 1960s.[34] All levels of schooling, including most forms of postsecondary education, are under pressure today to demonstrate that students are actually learning—not just some of the students, but most of them, and if possible, all of them. Mastery learning is an effort to deal with the practical problem of getting most of the students to master most of the material most of the time. In recent years this has been labeled the problem of "accountability," and in many postsecondary, competency-based training programs some form of mastery learning has been adopted to demonstrate accountability.

Bloom argues that students vary widely according to aptitude, ability and motivation when they enter the classroom. The mistake teachers make is in treating all students the same, in effect, giving them all the same instruction, when, in fact, what is needed is differential (differing amounts and types of) instruction. Students with less aptitude need more instruction. Students who are slower need more time. With the right instruction, Bloom argues, a very high percentage of students—as high as 80 percent to 90 percent—can master the material. The most important ingredient in mastery learning (after setting clear objectives and determining acceptable levels of mastery) is the quality of instruction.

Bloom's ideas have been controversial, and although mastery learning has been widely implemented in elementary and secondary schools, many postsecondary teachers back away from the full implications of it. The reason? Mastery learning requires a redefinition of "equal opportunity." Throughout the history of American education, "equal opportunity" has generally meant giving all students the same chance, which usually means, the same instruction. Bloom's suggestion is that equality of learning should become the goal, not just equality of opportunity for learning. This means that teachers must find ways of giving each student not (just) equal treatment, but what each student *actually needs* to be successful. Thus, *inequality* of treatment may be necessary—in materials, time, instruction, reinforcement—if *equality* in learning is to result. This is a new concept of fair treatment: those who need the most must get the most.

These ideas are no doubt unsettling to many postsecondary teachers. For many years higher education relied on lower levels of the educational system to "sort out" the college bound. There was a time when postsecondary teachers assumed that those who entered their classrooms were "college material" and had relatively the same aptitudes and abilities. It was the teacher's role to give them all "the same fair shot at it." Today, the postsecondary population more nearly reflects the secondary population, and with the addition of many older adult learners, the "college population" has become extremely heterogeneous. It is because of these new students that many postsecondary teachers are struggling to reorient their thinking about the meaning of equal opportunity in the classroom. Increasingly, postsecondary teachers are being called upon to provide inequality of treatment to ensure equality of educational outcome. "Not I," one might protest in indignation, but one must keep in mind that in the "information society" the graduates of postsecondary programs will design the robots, monitor the life-support systems, process the financial information, and read the radar scopes that hold an advanced technological society together. Perhaps some inequality of treatment will be necessary if students are going to be able meet the educational criteria that will enable them to perform these highly skilled tasks in today's society. Or to put the question differently: What level of incompetence can a high-tech society tolerate? Consider once again the examples.

Beth Anderson knows that "grading on a curve" won't work in swimming. The average performance could be 25 meters, which is unacceptable. Beth also knows that she can't work only with the high aptitude swimmers, while letting the rest (excuse the pun) sink or swim. She can identify rather quickly the students who are going to catch on rapidly and those who are going to need a great amount of help. She will have to give much greater amounts of time and effort (unequal treatment) to the poor swimmers, if there is to be equality of outcome.

Although Elm Grove College is highly selective in its admission policies, Tony Clementi knows that the students in his Music Appreciation course, however capable in verbal intelligence, vary widely in their aptitude for and background in music. He realizes that he is going to have to give some extra instruction to those who need it. Now he is generally more sensitive to variations in aptitude and notices much more closely the individual responses that students make to different parts of the course. As he grades quizzes, papers, and exams, he ponders the ways that he can provide additional help for students who need it. Do more students earn A's now? Yes, and that's something he has been meaning to talk over with the dean.

Jolene Jefferson has been using mastery learning with her students for years, although it was only recently that she heard the term and associated it with what she was doing. She knows that her students will not perform perfectly all the time, so she sets different mastery levels for different types of mathematical operations—95 percent for place value, 75 percent for exponents, 85 percent for factors and multiples, etc. Then she sets another goal for herself: she wants 100 percent of her students to reach the designated mastery levels. She knows this will be tough. The key to success, as she sees it, is in finding the areas where students are getting stuck and diagnosing their problems through error analysis. For students that get stuck—this usually shows up on one of their quizzes—she offers extra tutorial time. Do 100 percent of her students reach mastery level? Yes, if not in one term, then in two. Why? She frets about them!

EMPLOYING INSTRUCTIONAL DESIGN

The ultimate application of behavioral learning theory is in large-scale instructional systems in which an attempt is made to control as many of the variables in the learning process as possible: objectives, tasks and sub-tasks, materials, reinforcement, and evaluation. The goal is to guide the learning process completely from beginning (objectives) to end (evaluation). Such efforts are sometimes referred to as a "systems approach" to learning.

A "systems approach" usually involves an organized attempt to account for the whole instructional process by keeping in mind the dynamic interactions among its different parts. A cybernetic system is one that employs feedback and is self-correcting.[35] A systems approach to learning simply means making sure that the process of instruction is carried out according to a detailed plan that follows a series of steps and provides adequate feedback about the learner's progress. Ultimately, knowledge about how the learner is doing becomes the feedback loop that lets the teacher know how the teacher is doing; this, in turn, becomes the basis for correcting the system.[36]

At the college level there has emerged a specific form of instructional design known as Personalized System of Instruction (PSI). PSI originated in a psychology course at Arizona State University developed by Fred Keller, one of B. F. Skinner's graduate students.[37] PSI was first used primarily in psychology courses, but it is adaptable to any discipline or professional field. A PSI course can have many variations, but most involve a precise set of objectives and a series of self-paced learning modules designed to help students reach the objectives. Students are expected to work through the course one unit at a time, progressing at their own pace. Before moving on to the next unit, students must pass a readiness test to demonstrate that they can perform the objectives of the past unit, which is the prerequisite to the next unit. Instruction is provided in many forms—reading, laboratory work, lectures, demonstrations, discussions, films, videotapes, audiotapes—and is made available as a majority of the class is ready for it. PSI is designed to maximize success and reduce failure and allows some students to finish before the end of the term of instruction or to extend the time needed. Variations of the PSI approach are used on many college campuses today. Consider how instructional design can be used by the three teachers in the examples.

Beth Anderson's classes in beginning swimming are only part of her teaching assignment. She also teaches one section of intermediate and one section of advanced swimming. She has done a task analysis on all of the basic swimming strokes and keeps laminated (waterproof) summary sheets of these analyses in a notebook. She can take any swimmer at any level, run them through a quick set of tests to measure their present performance level and plug them into an appropriate set of training routines for the strokes they wish to learn or improve. What was once a hit-and-miss, trial-and-error approach for Beth has become a full-scale systems approach to teaching swimming.

Tony Clementi is now using a Personalized System of Instruction (PSI) format for the Music Appreciation course. He still holds the "music for the deaf" tutoring sessions, but he has also analyzed other parts of the course more carefully and has created a series of auto-tutorial lessons and self-administered quizzes to supplement what he does in class. Students go to the music department listening laboratory and check out supplemental lesson materials on "counterpoint," "sonata form," and "12-tone serialization." Each lesson consists of some additional written materials (including sections of musical scores) and questions to help guide listening activities. Some of the audiotapes include voice-over instructions from Tony that point out where certain things on the score are happening in the performance. He gets feedback on his quizzes that tell him where students are having problems. Now he has a system for keying errors on quizzes to the PSI tutorial materials, and refers students to specific sections of the PSI lessons to correct their errors.

Jolene Jefferson has developed a mathematics practice laboratory where students come to study and check out supplementary materials as needed. The lab is filled with shelves and cabinets marked by topic—place value, whole number operations, fractions and decimals. As students walk around the room, they literally walk through the units of the course. On the shelves and in the cabinets are the special materials related to the concepts in the course—special manipulatives (geoboards, attribute blocks, fractional models) for concrete, hands-on illustrations; computer software for drill and practice; and games that make the learning fun and social. It took a long time for Jolene to build up her collection and organize it systematically into a lab, but now teachers come from the other community colleges to visit and find out what she's doing.

CONCLUSIONS

Teachers who employ training and coaching strategies can become more effective by understanding behavioral learning theory. Operant conditioning is an observable, measurable phenomenon, a true "scientist's science." The theory has been thoroughly described and well-documented in the laboratory, and its practical applications are extensive and very useful. Objectives can be operationalized and clearly stated, and complex activities can be broken into their component parts through task analysis and taught through a shaping procedure. The powerful technology of the computer can be employed to manage the learning process and a mastery learning approach can be developed to ensure that most of the students learn most of what is being taught. In some cases, entire courses can be developed more thoroughly by using a systems approach. Teachers who value a rational, data-based approach to teaching that provides a framework for measured progress and ultimate accountability usually like the training and coaching strategy.

NOTES

1. The discussion of behaviorism is based on the actual writings of B. F. Skinner. His work is summarized in most textbooks on educational psychology, but the clearest introductory explanation of behavioral learning

theory is found in the work of one of his students: Fred S. Keller, *Learning: Reinforcement Theory*, 2nd ed., (New York: Random House, 1969). The most accessible work by Skinner is *About Behaviorism* (New York: Knopf, 1974).

2. John B. Watson, *Behaviorism* (New York: The People's Publishing Institute, 1934) reprinted in New York by W. W. Norton, 1970, p.2. Watson's desire to establish psychology as a science is also expressed in *Psychology from the Standpoint of a Behaviorist* (Philadelphia: J.B. Lippincott, 1919) and *Behavior: An Introduction to Comparative Psychology* (New York: Henry Holt & Co., 1914).

3. E.L. Thorndike, *The Psychology of Learning* (New York: Teachers College, 1921), p. 237. Thorndike understood the relationship of consequences and learning and referred to "associative learning," "connection forming," and "laws of habit," p.17. The "Law of Effect" is explained in *Human Learning* (New York: The Century Co., 1931), pp. 58-61. See also Thorndike's *The Fundamentals of Learning* (New York: Teachers College, 1932).

4. B. F. Skinner was an enormously productive scholar. The basic principles of behaviorism are outlined in *The Behavior of Organisms* (New York: Appleton-Century-Crofts, 1938). The relationship of behavior and reinforcement is described in *The Contingencies of Reinforcement* (New York: Appleton-Century-Crofts, 1969). The effects of different systems of rewards and punishments are spelled out in *Science and Human Behavior* (New York: The Free Press, 1953) and in *Schedules of Reinforcement*, coauthored with C. Ferster, (New York: Appleton-Century-Crofts, 1957). Skinner's essays on education are collected in *The Technology of Teaching* (New York: Appleton-Century-Crofts, 1968). His article, "Why We Need Teaching Machines," appeared in the *Harvard Educational Review*, 1961, 31, pp. 377-98. His texts on operant conditioning are *About Behaviorism* (New York: Knopf, 1974) and *The Analysis of Behavior*, coauthored with J. Holland, (New York: McGraw-Hill, 1961). His work on language is found in *Verbal Behavior* (New York: Appleton-Century-Crofts, 1957), and his utopian ideas are explored in *Walden II* (New York: Macmillan, 1948) and *Beyond Freedom and Dignity* (New York: Knopf, 1971). The "outside interests" appear in *Cumulative Record* (New York: Appleton-Century-Crofts, 1959). A collection of Skinner's essays may be found in *Upon Further Reflection* (Englewood Cliffs, NJ: Prentice-Hall, 1987), and his work on old age, coauthored with M.E. Vaughan, is *Enjoy Old Age: A Program of Self-Management* (New York: Norton, 1983).

5. The shaping process is described by B. F. Skinner in *Science and Human Behavior*.

6. The model for shaping is borrowed from Joel Macht, *Teacher, Teachim* (New York: John Wiley & Sons, 1975), p.177.

7. David Premack, "Toward Empirical Behavior Laws: 1. Positive Reinforcement," *Psychological Review*, 1959, 66, p. 219.

8. Skinner discusses punishment in *The Technology of Teaching*, p.96. For a review of forms of corporal punishment, see A. Maurer, "Corporal Punishment," *American Psychologist*, August 1974, pp. 614-26.

9. G. Walters and J. Grusec, *Punishment* (San Francisco: W.H. Freeman, 1977).

10. E. A. Workman and R. Williams, "Effects of Extrinsic Rewards and Intrinsic Motivation in the Classroom," *Journal of School Psychology*, 18(2), pp. 141-47.

11. R. Davis, L. Alexander, and S. Yelon, *Learning System Design* (New York: McGraw-Hill, 1974).

12. Paul Dressel, "The Nature and Role of Objectives in Instruction," *Educational Technology*, May 1977, 17(5) pp. 7-15. See also W. James Popham and Eva L. Baker, *Systematic Instruction* (Englewood Cliffs, NJ: Prentice-Hall, 1970), pp. 20-24, for a discussion of operationally stated instructional objectives.

13. R. Burns, *New Approaches to Behavioral Objectives* (Dubuque, IA: William C. Brown, 1972), p.5.

14. Robert F. Mager, *Preparing Instructional Objectives* (Palo Alto, CA: Fearon, 1962), p. 11.

15. The discussion of task analysis is based on Robert H. Davis, et al., *Learning System Design*, Chapter 5 "Task Descriptions."

16. The task analysis for swimming is based on similar task analyses for swimming, standing long jump, 50-yard dash, and golf presented in Beth Sulzer-Azaroff and G. Roy Mayer, *Achieving Educational Excellence: Using Behavior Strategies* (New York: Holt, Rinehart & Winston, 1986), see Chapter 17 for task analyses based on unpublished papers by A.J. Cuvo, et al.; T.L. McKenzie, et al.; and R. M. O'Brien, et al.

17. See R. M. Gagne, "Learning Hierarchies," *Educational Psychologist* 1968, 6(1), pp. 1-6.

18. The classic research on modeling and modeling effects is presented in Albert Bandura, *Principles of Behavior Modification* (New York: Holt, Rinehart and Winston, 1969).

19. B. F. Skinner, "Why We Need Teaching Machines."

20. B. F. Skinner, *The Technology of Teaching*.

21. L. Stolurow, "Programmed Instruction" in R. Ebel, ed., *The Encyclopedia of Educational Research* (London: Macmillan, 1969), pp. 1017-1021.

22. J. Taber, R. Glasser, and H. Schafer, *Learning and Programmed Instruction* (Reading, MA: Addison-Wesley, 1965).

23. C. Thomas, I. Davies, D. Openshaw, and J. Bird, *Programmed Learning in Perspective* (Chicago: Educational Methods,1964).

24. For an interesting history of the conceptual roots of the computer, see Christopher Evans, *The Micro Millennium* (New York: Washington Square Press, 1979). The idea for the computer dates back (at least) to the hand-

powered "Difference Machine" of Englishman Charles Babbage (b.1791), who created a mechanical monster designed to do complex calculations.

25. Neill Graham, *The Mind Tool: Computers and Their Impact on Society* (St. Paul, MN: West Publishing, 1986).

26. P. McCann, "Learning Strategies and Computer-Based Instruction," *Computers and Education*, 5, pp.133-140.

27. *ICP Software Directory, Microcomputer Systems*, published semiannually by International Computer Programs, Inc., 9000 Keystone Crossing, P.O. Box 40946, Indianapolis, IN 46240. Software Hotline: 1-800-428-6179. See also *Datapro Directory of Microcomputer Software*, Delran, NJ 08075, 1-800-328-2776.

28. A digest that contains abstracts of software reviews that have appeared in various computer magazines is *Digest of Software Reviews: Education*, published by School & Home Courseware, Inc., 301 W. Mesa, Fresno, CA 93704. Expecially useful are *The Journal of Multimedia and Hypermedia* (JEMH) P.O. Box 2966, Charlottesville, VA 22902; *T-H-E Journal*, 150 El Camino Real, Suite 112, Tustin, CA 92680-3670; and *Computing Teacher*; International Council for Computers in Education; 1787 Agate; University of Oregon; Eugene, Oregon 97403. Other examples of computer magazines that typically review software are *BYTE*, McGraw-Hill, Inc., One Phoenix Mill Lane, Peterborough, NH 03458; *Software News*, Sentry Publishing Co. Inc., 1900 West Park Drive, Westborough Office Park, Westborough, MA 01581; *Personal Computing*, Hayden Publications, Inc., 10 Mulholland Drive, Hasbrouk Heights, NJ 07604; *Compute*, Compute Publications, Inc., 825 7th Avenue, New York, NY 10019; *Classroom Computer Learning*, 2451 East River Road, Dayton, OH 45439; and *Computers in Education*, Moorhead Publications, Ltd., 1300 Don Mills Road, Toronto, Ontario M3B 3M8, Canada.

29. *T-H-E Journal, Source Guide of High Technology Products for Education, Videodisc Compendium*, Emerging Technology Consultants, Inc., P.O. Box 12044, St. Paul, MN 55112. *New Media*, Hypermedia Communications, Inc., 901 Mariner's Island Blvd., Suite 365, San Mateo, CA 94404. ISAAC is a communications service funded by IBM and operated at the University of Washington, Seattle, WA.

30. Neill Graham, *The Mind Tool*, p.322.

31. A wide selection of authoring systems is now available, some for foreign languages as well as English. *T-H-E Journal, The 1986-87 Source Guide*, lists 19 sources of authoring systems appropriate for teachers.

32. The discussion of norm-referenced and criterion referenced evaluation is based on Robert Glaser and David Klaus, "Proficiency Measurement: Assessing Human Performance" in Robert M. Gagne, ed., *Psychological Principles in Systems Development* (New York: Holt, Rinehart and Winston, 1962), pp. 419-74. The selection is also found in M. David Merrill, *Instructional Design: Readings* (Englewood Cliffs, NJ: Prentice-Hall, 1971), pp. 331-56.

33. James Block, *Mastery Learning* (New York: Holt, Rinehart and Winston, 1971).

34. Benjamin Bloom, *Human Characteristics and School Learning* (New York: McGraw-Hill, 1982). See also Benjamin Bloom, *All Our Children Learning* (New York: McGraw-Hill, 1981).

35. M. David Merrill, "Components of a Cybernetic Instructional System" in M. David Merrill, ed., *Instructional Design: Readings.* This is an excellent sourcebook of readings for those who may wish to study further the techniques and processes of instructional design.

36. For models of a systems approach to instructional design, see R. Davis, L. Alexander, and S. Yelon, *Learning System Design*, and W. Dick and L. Carey, *The Systematic Design of Instruction* (New York: Scott Foresman, 1978).

37. K. Johnson and R. Ruskin, *Behavioral Instruction: An Evaluative Review* (Washington, DC: American Psychological Association, 1977). See also Ohmer Milton, *Alternatives to the Traditional* (San Francisco: Jossey-Bass, 1972). Keller's own description of PSI can be found in "Good-Bye Teacher . . . ," *Journal of Applied Behavioral Analysis*, 1968, 1, pp. 79-88.

Lecturing and Explaining

"What's a lecture like?"
Nacib twisted his mustache . . .
"I'll explain it to you. Pay attention. There's a man, a poet, who talks about something."
"Talks about what?"
"About anything. This one is going to talk about tears and longing. He talks and you listen . . . "
"Is that all? Nothin' else?"
"That's all. But the thing is, what he says."
"And what does he say?"
"Beautiful things. Sometimes the way they talk, it's hard to understand what they mean. That's when it's best."
　　　　　　　　　　—Jorge Amado, *Gabriela, Clove and Cinnamon*

PRESENTING INFORMATION

As postsecondary teachers we spend a significant amount of classroom time presenting information through lectures. In the "information age" having the right information, understanding it, and being able to remember it is increasingly important. Sometimes the information we present is basic and uncomplicated, but more often than not, the information that is the "subject" of instruction in postsecondary settings today is quite complex, involving technical language, difficult concepts, and complex relationships among ideas.

In college and university settings, extended and formal explanations are known as "lectures," but explanations are also given in less formal settings, in a laboratory, on a practice field, or even in the professor's office. In postsecondary education, lecturing is still the most widely used "classroom teaching method," and for some teachers it is their only strategy.[1] One of the oldest methods of instruction, lecturing entered American higher education in the mid-nineteenth century as a "German import," gradually replacing the recitation method handed down from the colonial colleges.[2] The great scholars of the German universities delivered lectures on their own research, but today the lecture is used to summarize the work of a great many scholars in a particular field.

Because of its widespread use and deep historical roots, lecturing is often viewed as the most "traditional" teaching method and has fallen out of favor among those teachers who consider themselves to be "creative" or "innovative." If anyone needs information, they say, let them look it up in a library or call up a database on a computer. But an effective lecture, to the contrary, while it may involve information, goes well beyond providing "facts" that might better be gleaned from a textbook or library assignment. An effective lecture can have many purposes, such as stimulating interest; focusing attention on what is important; introducing new terminology; presenting, analyzing, and criticizing ideas; offering a new perspective; demonstrating how something works; or tracing the steps of a discovery or creation. Viewed in this way, lecturing can be the means to many ends, and the role that information plays in the lecture can be quite varied. Lecturing, therefore, is neither intrinsically "good" nor "bad"; its success depends on how it is done. It is one among other strategies available to us. Consider the following teachers who employ the lecturing and explaining strategy.

Pierre de Chardin teaches Visual Communication at the Art Institute of the South. Most of his students have an identifiable talent in at least one medium—painting, drawing, photography, design—but sometimes their ideas about talent get in the way of their learning. Pierre lets his students know on the very first day what he thinks about talent: that success in art is 98 percent perspiration and 2 percent inspiration, that talent can be taught, and that the craft of the artist—the toolbox of techniques—can be learned. "In school," he tells his students, "teachers spent years teaching you the alphabet, how letters make words, and how words can be made into sentences. Why is it that you spent all of this time studying the craft of verbal communication, but no one ever taught you the basic tools of visual communication?" Pierre de Chardin's challenge is to develop a series of effective lectures on the elements of visual communication.[3]

At Mid-West University Roscoe Meade teaches an advanced course in the sociology department on demographics. The course is required for upper division majors and master's degree candidates; and because it deals with quantitative analyses of populations, it has the potential, at least as it is initially perceived by students, for being dry. Professor Meade knows that he has his work cut out for him, but he also believes that the study of demographics, to which he has now devoted 15 years of scholarship, is anything but boring. His challenge is twofold, to model for students how sociologists generate and analyze demographic data, and to show that both the subject and the methodology are interesting and useful. He has introduced the students to basic demographic concepts, leading them carefully through the characteristics of populations (absolute size, density, distribution, composition) and has introduced simple formulas for analyzing population growth in terms of natural increase, fertility, mortality, and migration.[4] The evidence from the first quiz suggests that students understand how these variables interact and how demographic and nondemographic factors are related. Now Professor Meade is ready to plunge into one of the big issues—trends in world population growth, what has come to be known as the "population bomb."

John Newton teaches physical science in the core curriculum at Elm Grove College. In the astronomy portion of the course, he has gradually worked his way "outward" from the earth and the moon, to the solar system and its movements, to the location of the solar system on the edge of the earth's spiral galaxy, to the super cluster of galaxies "nearby" that harbor another 40,000 galaxies, and on out to the estimated 100 billion more galaxies.[5] As he moves though this material, Professor Newton reviews the scientific evidence and the people and experiments that helped to generate it. Along the way, in almost every class, students raise questions about the beginnings of the universe. And so the time has now come to deal with that topic. He knows that the students are generally interested, but he asks himself what it is he most wants to communicate to them and what he hopes they will understand and remember. It will take some boiling down of the highly technical material on the "big bang" to make it comprehensible to freshmen.

COGNITIVE PSYCHOLOGY

As any student knows, a lecture can be brilliant or dull, entertaining or boring, enlightening or deadly. What makes it so? Lecturing is a particular form of communication, primarily auditory, but also visual, and to learn how to lecture well we need to know what transpires when people are communicating. How is it that people come to "learn" when they are listening to and watching a lecture? What takes place when students attempt to pay attention to, process, and remember information?

These are areas that have been investigated extensively by cognitive psychologists, scholars who study mental processes. Effective lecturers know something about the processes going on in their students' heads and will organize and deliver their lectures in such a way as to maximize the probability that the information will be attended to, processed, and remembered, or, in other words, learned! The ultimate goal is that the lecture will impact students in such a way that at some future point in time they will be able to use the information they have encountered, that is, to act upon what they have heard and respond to what they have seen. The basic paradigm of learning for the lecturing and explaining strategy is the information processing model drawn from cognitive psychology.

Cognitive psychology has no B. F. Skinner, no single figure who can be said to be its foremost spokesperson. The study of mental processes has its roots in the work of Wilhelm Wundt, William James, F.L. Bartlett, and the European movement known as Gestalt Psychology, but from the turn of the century until the end of World War II the behaviorists dominated psychology, insisting that human consciousness was a "black box" and that behavior—both animal and human—was the only appropriate subject of scientific psychology.[6] What occurred in the period from 1950 to 1980 in the area of cognitive psychology was nothing short of an intellectual revolution.[7] An area that had been beyond the proper domain of study for psychologists—human consciousness—now became the focal point for an outpouring of scientific investigation and theory-building. The field attracted some of the best scholars and became an area of intense and exciting activity.

Behaviorism had reached its zenith. But more important, an increasing number of psychologists found the operant model inadequate for fully describing human learning. Although learning is certainly influenced to some extent by "connections" and "consequences," human beings, they argued, tend to act upon and reorder the stimuli that constitute the environment, largely through the uniquely human instrument of language. Through language and other symbolization processes, humans engage in complex, covert mental activity called "mediation." A new breed of psychologists became convinced that the behaviorists were wrong about the "black box" of the human mind. They came to believe that covert mental processes—the things that go on in the head—were the key to understanding human behavior. It was as if the behaviorists were leaving out the most important thing just because it was hard to study.

Other forces combined to stimulate new interest in cognitive psychology. A science of human engineering was emerging from military applications of psychology. Verbal learning theorists and linguists were developing new models to explain language behavior.[8] Communications engineering developed as a new science, spawning jargon that psychologists were eager to appropriate: "signal," "noise," "coding," "channel capacity," "serial and parallel processing," "information bits," and others. Computer science added its own terminology: "algorithms," "flow charts," "subroutines," "programs," "inputs," and "outputs." As systems analysts began to describe what took place between "input" and "output" in a computer, cognitive psychologists began to speculate about the processes that occur between human "input" and "output." It was only a short leap from thinking of the computer as a "complex information-processing system" to conceptualizing the human mind as a "complex symbol manipulation system."[9] If one were to attempt to assign a date for the emergence of cognitive psychology as a recognized field, it would probably be 1958, the date of the now-famous conference sponsored by the Rand Corporation, a meeting of the leading psychologists of the day, from which emerged the influential "metatheory" of Newell, Shaw, and Simon.[10] Their work stimulated a flurry of research.

THE INFORMATION PROCESSING MODEL

One of the things that differentiates human beings from most "lower" animals is the ability to mediate, that is, to use cognitive processes to enter between stimulus and response. Because these processes are covert, they are difficult (behaviorists say impossible) to study. What methods did cognitive psychologists develop to study mediation? Assume for a moment that a spy is assigned to a hillside to observe an industrial factory through a pair of binoculars.[11] He sees railroad cars arriving all day long with raw materials at one end of the factory. Trucks pick up the completed products at the other end. He can make whatever observations he wishes from the hillside, but can't go inside the factory. He must send off regular reports on what takes place inside. How will he go about it? He would begin to make and record observations. He would find out what raw materials are processed. He would note the number of workers and would observe their comings and goings. He would observe the glow of light from the windows and listen to the noises from inside. He would examine the products closely. And so on. Eventually he would begin to make some inferences—speculations, intelligent guesses, and conclusions based on what evidence was available. When enough speculations from different viewpoints begin to add up, he can write the first draft of his report. As his observations continue, he may even be able to include a model or diagram of what he thinks is going on in the factory. Scientists call this process, when evidence comes together to support a conclusion, "convergent validation."

The technique of convergent validation and the problem of the "black box" are widespread in the physical and social sciences, and are by no means limited to cognitive psychology. Scientists have determined that the interior temperature of the sun is 25,000,000 degrees, but no one has set foot on the sun with a sun thermometer. Physicists develop models of the atom that include subatomic particles, such as the quark and neutrino, without actually being able to measure and observe these particles directly. Astronomers compute the magnitude of stars without visiting them and postulate "black holes" without getting sucked into them. Anthropologists reconstruct life in primitive cultures by inference from the secondary evidence of artifacts. So what is so difficult about the problem of illuminating the "black box" of human consciousness?

In the 1960s cognitive psychologists began to produce the first basic models of human information processing. Those models have been revised and elaborated, and today some of them are so sophisticated and mathematically complex that even other cognitive psychologists have trouble understanding them. After 25 years of research there is still disagreement about the details, but there is also fairly consistent agreement about the main elements of these models. The diagram shown below is a composite and simplified version of human information processing models that appear regularly in textbooks and journal articles on cognitive psychology.[12]

Information Processing Model

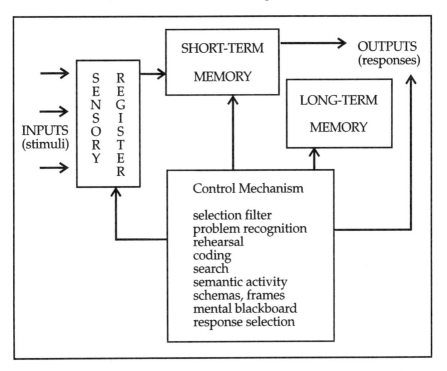

According to these models, information comes in through any of the five senses and impinges on a sensory register. Filters are activated and let pass or screen out what a person will pay attention to based on interest. The main features of the information are extracted, abstracted, and encoded. They are held in short-term memory for a few seconds while a "decision" is made about what to do—respond directly, think about them, integrate them with new information, or store them in long-term memory. Perhaps the new information requires a search for old information held in long-term memory. Although the process is enormously complex, there appears to be general agreement about functions called "sensory register," "short-term memory," "long-term memory," and various "filters" and "control mechanisms." These are not places in the brain, of course, but rather sets of interrelated processes that go on in the head to facilitate the symbolic manipulation of information.

ATTENTION MECHANISMS

How do the component parts function in this fantastic symbol-manipulation system that human beings carry around on their shoulders? Consider the mechanisms that govern attention. People are bombarded by a huge variety of sensory inputs (especially visual and verbal) each day. Why do people pay attention to certain things and not others? How many things can a person pay attention to at once? Will students pay attention if they are told to pay attention? What must we do to get students' attention and hold it? How can we help students focus on the important parts of a lecture or explanation?

Some of the earliest experiments on attention were designed to examine what happens when people try to listen to more than one thing at a time. Cherry called this the "cocktail party phenomenon."[13] Most people have had the experience of standing around at a party listening in on one conversation, but then being drawn off to another. What does a person hear in one conversation that tends to make them lose what they hear in another? Cherry and others simulated the party situation by having subjects listen to two separate but comparable messages through earphones, one message in one ear, another message in the other ear. In these "dichotic presentations" the subjects were directed to shadow (repeat aloud) the message they were hearing in the designated ear. It is not surprising that subjects usually could report in great detail afterward what they heard in the designated ear; but when asked what they heard in the unattended ear, they floundered. Sometimes they couldn't even tell if the message had been switched to another language or played backwards. In other words, their attention was relatively undivided.

Experiments like these became the basis of "switch" theories and "filter" theories of attention. If two messages (stimuli) arrive at the same time, one will get through and the other won't, as if there were a switch to turn one channel on and another off.[14] Apparently when attention is focused on something (the selected stimulus), it is focused there almost exclusively. Notice the word "almost." More recent studies suggest that attention is not so much like a switch that is on or off, but like a filter that selectively lets through the important information while screening out most (but not all) of the rest.[15] Additional dichotic listening experiments confirmed this view—subjects heard at least some things (like their own name) in the unattended ear or would cross channels to follow an interesting story.[16] But in general, attention tends to be highly focused.

Other experiments on attention have dealt with the amount of attention required (and available) for different kinds of tasks. Some tasks, simply require less attention than others, and when that is the case, attention can be divided up somewhat among tasks. Capacity for attention, though limited, is not a fixed entity; it varies with the difficulty of and familiarity with the task. Some tasks, when sufficiently practiced, are almost automatic; others are deliberate.[17] It may be possible to carry on a heated debate while driving on the open thruway automatically, but nearly impossible to speak at all while negotiating a crowded intersection.

It seems reasonable to conclude that the human capacity for attention is a limited resource, perhaps far more limited than intuition would suggest or multimedia adolescents would admit. On the other hand, when it is necessary to attend closely to something, human beings have a rather remarkable capacity for attending to what they want and need to see or hear.

The lessons in this for teachers are quite clear. We can't teach students anything unless we first get and hold their attention. When we are competing with strong distractions, we are probably going to lose out. (The student who comes late, interrupting the lecture, will probably attract more attention than the lecturer.) The first rule, therefore, is "Get the students attention!" It is encouraging, however, to note that once students have directed their attention to the desirable point, they can become well-focused and single-minded. The second rule is "Tell students what to pay attention to!" They probably will do it. An effective teacher helps students distinguish the trivial from the important. To do this, teachers need to be careful not to supply too much information, that is, not to deluge students with too many sources of information at once. This is especially true if the subject is new or difficult. The third rule, then, is "Don't overload the system!" Attention is a limited resource. In other words, the content of a lecture should be as uncomplicated as possible, precisely focused, and carefully organized. Consider once again the three examples.

When the students amble into Pierre de Chardin's Visual Communication class, they hear soft music playing, Debussy's "Afternoon of a Faun." They pick up a "handout" at the front desk and make their way to their seats. They look up and notice slides being projected automatically, one after the other, on the screen at the front of the room. The music creates a mood and the slides capture their attention. The slides, it turns out, are the visual illustrations that will be used during the lecture. They are presented in the same order and under the same topic headings as they will be shown in the lecture. The students begin to "try to make sense" of what they are seeing and notice that the slides and topic headings correspond to the headings provided on the "handout"—dot, line, shape, tone, and color. They are getting a preview (sometimes called an advance organizer) of the lecture. When the last slide is projected, Pierre turns the music and the projector off, so as not to divide their attention, and begins drawing with magic markers on a big newsprint pad held by an easel. His "drawing" consists entirely of dots, and the room grows silent as the students watch his composition take shape. He does not need to tell them that the class is beginning; it has begun.

Professor Meade alternates (one at a time) between an overhead projector and slides to present demographic information through various charts, graphs, figures, and tables. He knows that the displays are not always easy to read, so he tries to point out what is important with a beam of light pointer. To open the lecture, he selects a line graph that he knows will capture the students' attention, flips a switch on the projector, and dims the lights slightly. He moves directly into a discussion of the data. "On the left," he points out as he faces the graph, "from pre-history going back as far as you wish, up to around 1650, the world's population (those alive at anyone time) grew from about 300 million to 500 million people. That is why you see this thin black line rising only slightly across all those years. In the years after that time, since 1650, more than four billion people have been added; so that, as you can see on the right, the thin black line shoots almost straight up, reaching almost 5 billion people. You will note that this is a point more than nine times as high as the thin line that demarcates the population of most of history prior to the modern era. The figures for the earlier years are, of course, estimates, based on inferences from existing data, such as cultivated land areas, military records, and human remains. So I ask you, as you gaze at this nearly vertical line, which stands for nearly 5 billion people, how is a demographer to think about this data? What has caused this tremendous growth? Will it continue? Can we predict future population growth? If so, what variables will be involved in the prediction? Will the world become overpopulated? And what does 'overpopulated' mean?" Professor Meade looks out over the class in what might seem to be an embarrassingly long pause, but he knows what he's doing; he is giving the students time to think about the questions, time to focus on the topic.

Some of the students, brows furrowed, eyebrows knit, look genuinely worried as they stare at the graph.

Professor Newton knows that his students are fascinated with the general problem of cosmology and the specific topic of the origin of the universe, but he wants to begin with an illustration that rivets their attention. He asks each student to take the hand they are not writing with and to hold it up in front of them, as if to examine it closely, and to keep one eye on the projection screen at the front of the classroom. Then he tells them to imagine that he has provided them with a super magnifying device that allows them to increase the power of magnification upon demand.[18] He establishes the general principle that the more closely they examine their hand, the further back they will peer into time. At a relatively low level of magnification, he tells the students, they will see the individual cells of the skin. A still shot of skin cells appears on the screen. "If we increase the magnification greatly," he continues, "each cell will appear as complex as a city, with specialized neighborhoods full of complex apparatus to deal with the respiratory, sanitary, and energy-producing functions of the cell." Another image appears on the screen, a slide of a poster-size model of a cell provided by a textbook publisher. He notes that even though this cell is only a few years old, its architecture goes back a billion years to the time that simple cells evolved on earth. Within the nucleus of the cell, in the contours of the DNA, is an even more complex chemical inheritance that spells out how to make a cell, indeed, how to make a human being from skin and bones to brain cells. The DNA model appears on the screen. Now he invites the students to turn up the magnification some more, so that they can see the atoms and their whirling electrons. He points out that some of the electrons joined up with their atomic nuclei more than 5 billion years ago, in the nebula from which the earth was formed. "By increasing the magnification by a hundred thousand times, the nucleus of a single carbon atom comes into view, the product of a star that exploded before the sun was born, perhaps as much as 15 billion years ago." A model of the carbon atom appears. Finally, urging the students to increase the magnification and take a closer look still, he reminds them about quarks, the subatomic particles that make up each proton and neutron in the nucleus. A model of a configuration of quarks appears. "The quarks have been bound together since the universe was a few seconds old. With these quarks we have reached the origin of the universe. And those quarks that you are staring at in your own hand are, by the way, the same quarks that were there at the beginning of the universe." Professor Newton pauses, rubs his bald head, removes his glasses, and looks out over the class. He sees students still staring, wide-eyed at their hand, as if like an infant they had discovered it for the first time and realized what it was. After a brief pause he continues, and in that silence, Professor Newton knows that he has his students' attention.

INFORMATION PROCESSING

What happens once a person "decides" to pay attention to something? How does perception actually take place? Once a stimulus enters some part of the sensory register and is selected for attention, how is it acted upon? For the teacher, this becomes the more practical question: How do students comprehend what they see and hear?

A traditional, common-sense view of perception is that a person simply sees what is out there. Philosophers have struggled for centuries with this problem—the subject-object relationship of the mind to the "real world." Today, cognitive psychologists join those in this debate who emphasize subjectivity, the importance of what the "mind" does in information processing. In fact, cognitive psychologists today would say that there is no one-to-one (isomorphic) correspondence between what is "out there" and one's perception of it. Rather, perceptions involve a highly complex mental interpretation of sensory stimuli.

What is involved in this process of interpretation? How does a person come to recognize and make meaning of the sounds, words, sentences, and images that are the building blocks of communication? As with many other breakthroughs in cognitive psychology, the story begins with the computer.[19] In developing the technology for scanning, now widely used to read zip codes, grade sheets, and the numbers and names on bank checks, it became necessary to learn how to develop programs that would "read" letters and numbers. A process known as template matching was developed to search for and match a pre-determined shape. Thus, an electronic template for the number 3 was created to correspond to the shape of the number 3 used in the account number on the check. It is not surprising that this crude model of template matching was proposed as a way of thinking about how people process information; and there is, indeed, some support for it in lower animals.

The template matching process works well for what are called invariable sets, that is, when the pattern to be registered is always the same. But the problem becomes more complex when the scanner must read a variety of stimuli (variable sets) and make correct discriminations of letters and numbers. Such a scanner could read the type from many different printing styles, and even handwriting. For example, what does a scanner have to do when it is asked which of the following figures are A's:

$$A \triangle V A_a F_a$$

In this situation the electronic device does not have a template but a bank of features that has the characteristics of A's. For example, A's have some of these characteristic features:

$$/ \; , \; \wedge \; _\sigma \; \gamma\Gamma$$

This more complex scanner looks for features, not an exact template; it looks for the abstract characteristics of "A" not just a specific "A."

Selfridge and his colleagues developed for hand-printed characters an electronic scanner that employed what came to be known as the Pandemonium system. In this system, certain "feature demons" are created to look for the features of A's. A program is created to test for the features located by the feature demons, such as long diagonal lines and short horizontal lines. As the feature demons locate the features appropriate to the letter A, they are checked off by a computational demon. At the top of the system is the "decision demon" that determines whether the feature demons have accumulated enough evidence to "read" the stimulus as "A." Using a "best-bet" probability principle, the decision demon bases its decision on the statistical evidence gathered by the feature demons.

Not surprisingly, the Pandemonium system became a useful model for describing human information processing as well. If this was what was necessary for "electronic intelligence" to read the features of a stimulus, surely something very similar must go on in the heads of human beings. Humans apparently have a highly complex feature-based pattern recognition system for information processing, too. Cognitive psychologists have done research on various aspects of this system and the findings tend to support the model. For example, people make more errors and are slower at making fine discriminations, such as those between C, Q, and G than they are at simple discriminations between A, C, and N. In general, the Pandemonium theory holds up as far as it goes; the problem is that it does not go far enough to account for even more complex phenomena.

Up to this point, this description of information-processing has centered on what cognitive psychologists call "bottom-up" processing, those aspects of the system that are "data driven" and guided by the features of the stimulus coming into the system. Operating simultaneously with this bottom-up system is a "top-down" system, which is more concept driven or hypothesis driven, and seems to come more from within the individual than from outside stimuli.[20] While processing outside stimuli, the individual simultaneously marshals ideas, thoughts, and meanings from prior knowledge and tests the new inputs against experience. "Top-down" theorists emphasize what the individual brings to the information during processing. These researchers have found that context, meaning, and prior knowledge affect information processing directly and deeply.

Drawing on the work of Gestalt psychologists who preceded them, cognitive psychologists have been able to establish that perception is greatly influenced by context. For example, the length of a line will appear to vary (though it actually does not) according to what lines appear adjacent to it, as part of the overall context:

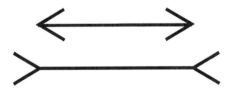

Likewise, small circles of equal size will appear to vary depending on the size of the circles around them:

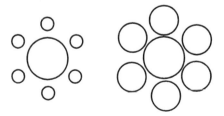

Similarly, groups of dots, five rows of four, will tend to be perceived as rows or columns depending on the way they are arranged:

Such phenomena are said to obey the law of proximity. In a similar way elements of a like kind tend to be grouped together, even if their proximity is held constant:

X X X X
O O O O
X X X X
O O O O

The rows predominate over the columns in what is known as the law of similarity. The legacy from Gestalt psychology is that individuals organize their perceptions according to the whole configuration (gestalt), and context is, therefore, very important. The perceiver puts individual perceptions into the "big picture" and sees things as part of a larger whole.

Top-down processing theory also emphasizes the importance of "meaning-making" in the processing of information. Individuals work hard to discover the meaning of what they are seeing and hearing, especially semantic meaning, and then process that information as part of an overall pattern of meaning. For example, for processing the word "ice," in the sentence, "The car slid on the ice," a great deal of help is provided by the earlier part of the sentence, "The car slid on the . . . . " That part of the sentence almost cries out for the word "ice." Not so much help is provided if the sentence ends in the word "banana." Even though a person might slide on a banana, a car usually would not, and the statement begins to border on nonsense, causing the reader to slow down and take a second look. Research bears out the importance of semantic meaning in information processing. Word pairs that are meaningful, such as "Nurse-Doctor," are processed and pronounced more rapidly than nonmeaningful pairs such as "Nurse-Tree." Similarly, lists of words presented in a meaningful order, such as "dog, chased, cat, tree," are more rapidly processed than unrelated words presented in random order, such as "tree, boat, pickles, sheep."

The place of semantic meaning-making has been widely examined by cognitive psychologists interested in the study of reading. Although reading surely involves to some degree the bottom-up functions of learning the alphabet and certain phonic rules, there is growing evidence that readers also depend to a large extent on context for establishing meaning. For one thing, it is not necessary to have every letter of every word to read a sentence:

Thix examplx xhould proxe xhe poixt.

Sometimes the reader makes the same symbol into different letters as needed, according to the context:

T/\E C/\T

Clearly, when people read, they process words, groups of words, and phrases—chunks of information, not individual letters. In fact, once one has learned to read and practiced it considerably, it is very difficult to process individual letters accurately. Consider the point by counting the number of "f's" in the following passage:

> Finished files are the result of years of scientific study combined with the experience of many years.

A count of less than six requires some careful rereading. As most writers know, proofreading goes much slower than reading for meaning, and most cognitive psychologists would agree that different processing activities are involved. In most processing of information, an attempt is made by the individual to "make sense" of what is being processed.

Of course, not all individuals will arrive at the same meaning at the same time. In auditory experiments, subjects were asked to listen to a speech synthesizer that was gradually being speeded up, so that the sounds gradually changed from a low unintelligible rumble to the meaningful sentence, "I am a computer." As one might suspect, individuals perceived the sounds first as language and then as a meaningful message at quite different points in the "speeding-up" process. People make meaning in their own way at their own pace.

Where does the meaning that is imposed on the stimulus come from? It does not come from thin air, but from somewhere within the individual. Top-down theorists have also stressed the importance of prior knowledge (experience) in information processing. What a person "knows" about the stimulus and is able to bring to it will greatly influence the speed and ease of processing. For example, when subjects are given a very brief glimpse of a flash card containing three rows of nonsense letters, such as:

G J Y
Q D P
L Z V

they have a great deal of difficulty in processing the information quickly and accurately. They may get one row or a few letters in a couple of rows. But when exposed for the same length of time to another set of letters:

I B M
S O S
I O U

the processing is rapid, easy, and accurate. In the last set of letters, of course, most subjects would have a high degree of familiarity—previous learning and experience—with the letter sets. Cognitive psychologists have tried to describe how previous knowledge is stored and called forth to assist in information processing. What previous knowledge does it take, for example, to understand a simple passage like the following:[21]

> Jack was invited to Jill's birthday party. He wondered if she would like a new pail. He went to his room and shook his piggy bank. It made no sound.

The reader (processor) of this passage must understand what a birthday party is and what the expectations are about presents. In addition, the reader must know something about "real" pails and "play" pails, not to mention piggy banks, coins, the sounds of coins, and so on. Obviously, if none of this information is in place, it will be difficult to understand the passage. If it is in place, what place is it in, and how does it come into play in processing?

Cognitive psychologists (with some help from linguists) suggest that individuals organize their prior knowledge into "scripts," "frames," and "schemas" and that they call up this knowledge in pre-organized "knowledge packets" when they encounter new information.[22] Although the distinctions among scripts, frames, and schemas are not always precise (different terms are used by different theorists in their own ways), in general, these are simply different packaging devices for prior knowledge. In layperson's language, these are categories of ideas used for clustering information.

A script, for example, is used to organize information about a familiar series of events. When a person is learning about going to a Chinese restaurant, the "restaurant script" is called into play. It already contains information about general restaurant experience such as getting seated, reading a menu, ordering, being served, paying the bill, etc., as well as the proper sequence for doing these things. When one learns something new about how this is done in a Chinese restaurant, the basic restaurant script is used and serves quite well for making sense of the new learning that takes place. If there is no restaurant script to begin with, then there will surely be problems in learning about a Chinese restaurant.

Scripts provide not only information (facts) but also knowledge of processes and expectations. There are various types of scripts, such as situational scripts (for such situations as restaurants, movies, dances, etc.), personal scripts (for roles such as teacher, bank robber, lover), and instrumental scripts (for actions and processes, such as boiling an egg or kicking a football). Scripts are a short-hand way of packaging knowledge. As new information comes in, the processor has to search for scripts that are already in place to make meaning of it.

Sometimes a schema or frame provides the overall context within which an entire passage (written or spoken) can be understood. Consider, for example, the following:

> The procedure is actually quite simple. First, you arrange things into different groups. Of course, one pile may be sufficient depending on how much there is to do. If you have to go somewhere else due to lack of facilities, that is the next step; otherwise, you are pretty well set. It is important not to overdo things. That is, it is better to do too few things at once than too many. In the short run this may not seem important, but complications can easily arise. A mistake can be expensive as well. At first the whole procedure will seem complicated. Soon, however, it will become just another facet of life. It is difficult to foresee any end of necessity for this task in the immediate future, but then one never can tell. After the procedure is completed one arranges the materials into different groups again. Then they can be put in their appropriate places. Eventually they will be used once more, and the whole cycle will then have to be repeated.[23]

The passage cries out for a schema, perhaps expressed as a title, such as "Doing the Laundry." Although more than one schema might be provided for this passage, without some schema, the reader flounders and seeks to impose one. When a schema is provided, the information is processed more rapidly and remembered more accurately and in greater detail. (Read the passage again using the "laundry schema.") The important contribution of schema theory is that it reemphasizes the fact that prior knowledge is important to new understanding. If there is no existing knowledge base to which the new knowledge can be related, there is probably no understanding![24]

More recently, cognitive psychologists have begun to acknowledge the importance of both bottom-up and top-down aspects of information processing. Although the exact relationship of the two aspects is poorly understood, it appears that both are important. Drawing on the earlier Pandemonium theory, some information processing theorists are suggesting a "blackboard model" wherein there are a large number of demons at work, some assigned to gathering "evidence" about the features of in-coming sensory stimuli,while others are busy calling up old information to aid in generating hypotheses about the new.[25] Both old and new information is put up on a mental "blackboard" to allow examination of hypotheses in light of the evidence. A "specialist demon" known as a "supervisor" manages all the other demons, makes sure that nothing is being overlooked, weighs the evidence, judges its sufficiency, and makes decisions—a flurry of simultaneous activity.

Needless to say, this is an imperfect system. The previous "knowledge" may be grossly inaccurate, perceptual sets may interfere with making distinctions, perceptual defenses may interfere for emotional reasons (so that the individual refuses to"see"), and the "evidence" may be improperly weighed and the wrong conclusions drawn. Nonetheless, with all of its imperfections, the human information processing system, as described by cognitive psychologists today, is remarkable for its potential to handle extremely complex inputs. In short, it is designed for learning! In drawing conclusions from information processing theories, one must be careful about unwarranted leaps in application and overgeneralizations, but the main outlines of the theories surely have some important implications for teaching. It is important, first, to recognize that there is no one-to-one correspondence between what a teacher provides (in words and visual illustrations) and what a student sees, hears, and, more importantly, understands. The student is an active interpreter of the information being provided, seeking out the main features of the information, boiling it down into a more manageable form, while trying to make judgements about the sense of what is actually being perceived. While acting on in-coming sensory stimuli (both visual and auditory), the student is also trying to put it in context, see the big picture, make semantic meaning of it, and relate it to previous knowledge. This is done by bringing into play various frameworks and packages of previously acquired knowledge to help make sense of what is new and often strange. If there is one conclusion that a teacher can surely draw from these theories, it is this: Students are by necessity (and usually desire) active processors of the information presented to them.

How can teachers facilitate that activity? First, by being aware of how information processing works, but also by engaging in a form of communication in lectures that presupposes mental interaction on the part of the student with the information being presented. The structure of a lecture must correspond to the apparatus that a student has for receiving it. The lecture should be given in a way that it can be received. Giving a lecture, therefore, should be more like throwing a frisbee than a shotput. A shotputter spends a considerable amount of time in getting set to fling a very heavy object. The purpose is simply to fling it—as hard and as far as possible. Everyone stands back and watches to see how far the shot has been put. There is no intention that it be caught; no one in their right mind would try to catch a shot. With a frisbee, on the other hand, the purpose is to throw it in such a way that it can be caught and even thrown back. In general, the message of a lecture needs to be light enough to be caught and organized in such a way that it can be easily grasped. Consider how the professors in the previously stated examples give their lectures.

Pierre de Chardin knows that his students are more likely to excel in visual processing of information (as opposed to verbal processing) so he uses a number of carefully selected slides and some drawings that he creates on his newsprint pad as the primary focus of his lecture. To help students process what he has to say, he provides them with a "handout" that contains a detailed outline of the lecture (six main headings—one for each point) with certain technical words, key concepts, and important names already written in. He encourages students to write down, as they go along, their own "short-hand" version of what he is saying. He urges them to note key words and phrases (not full sentences) and to make an occasional sketch if it helps.

Pierre finishes his composition of dots and turns the page on the easel to a blank sheet. "The dot," he points out, "is the simplest, minimum form of visual communication."[26] He shows how the placement of a single dot on the page can make a difference, and that when two dots appear, the eye wants to connect them. When three or four dots appear, they form a relationship and there is the beginning of a picture. He turns on the slide projector and shows some slides that illustrate how the arrangement of dots, close together or far apart, can give the appearance of light or shade, and he reminds the students that they have all seen the black-and-white pictures in newspapers that are essentially arrangements of dots. Then he projects a slide of Seurat's famous painting, "Sunday Afternoon on the Island of La Grande Jatte," and explains how Seurat painted almost entirely with dots. Another slide, showing an enlargement of a section of that painting, illustrates how the dots work as a part of the whole. Then for comparison, Pierre projects some slides of familiar fashion advertisements that have "borrowed" Seurat's Pointillist technique of using dots. Pierre points out that Seurat was really the forerunner of the idea of the four-color half-tone printing process used for color brochures in design work today. He holds up some examples of large colored posters that he has gathered from museums in his travels around the world. "And its all done with dots!" he exclaims.

Pierre moves over to the easel again, pauses to give students a chance to get their notes down, and begins dabbing a series of dots along one horizontal axis. He adds more and more dots, making them closer and closer until, finally, he announces, "A line is just a series of dots." He reminds the students that the next topic on their outline is "line." He knows they have a schema for "line," but he hopes they will start to think of line in a new way. Then he takes the marker, puts it down to make a dot and starts drawing it along the surface of the paper to make a line. He tells the students that another way to look at a line is as a dot in motion over time. He shows, through a series of slides of works by Durrer and Rembrandt, how lines are used to convey a simple but complete and often dramatic effect in drawings, woodcuts, and etchings. He urges the students to let their eyes linger on the details to see how the lines work as a part of the whole. He reminds the students that they have seen many different types of line drawings before, and shows them new examples of fashion ads, perspective renderings, floor plans, and designs for cars, where the dominant visual element is line.

In a similar way, Pierre moves on through the other elements of design, being careful to orient students each time he makes a transition to a new topic. He introduces "shape" with slides of the basic shapes—circle, square, triangle—and illustrates how shape is used as a pictorial element. Then he moves on to "movement"—vertical, horizontal, diagonal, and circular—across the surface of the picture. Slowly and carefully he explains "tone" as variations in light and dark, and shows slides that illustrate the variations. Pierre ends the six-point lecture with an explanation of "color," introducing the differences between hue, saturation, and brightness, topics he will discuss in more detail in a future lecture.

Throughout the lecture Pierre has been very careful in introducing new terminology, trying always to relate a new idea to an existing base of knowledge. He has provided names and labels for new concepts on the written outline. He has provided definitions where necessary and vivid illustrations. He knows that the words he speaks and the slides he shows on the screen are also being projected on the individual "mental blackboards" of each student, and that their "supervisor demon" is working hard to sort out all of the verbal and visual images to make sense of them. His students have begun to learn some new ways of seeing.

Professor Meade knows that the students in his lectures on demographics are busy "talking in their heads," so he designs his lecture to stimulate that "talk." He does this by posing questions. He doesn't answer most of these questions, nor does he expect the students to do so; that is not his purpose. What he wants to do is to actively engage his students in processing the information he presents. His questions provide a framework for organizing the subject and serve to activate a mental response. Professor Meade knows how to get the "supervisor demons" in his students heads to ask: What am I seeing? What does this information mean? Where have I seen this before? This is new, what shall I do with it?

Beside the lecturn, Professor Meade has a personal computer, which is attached to a simple pad that slips onto an ordinary overhead projector. Whatever appears on his monitor is projected on a large screen at the front of the classroom for all the students to see. He turns off the slide with the line graph of world population growth throughout history and switches on the computer. He asks the students if they think that the world population will continue to grow as it has in the last century, and as they think about that, he enters some figures into the computer.[27] Using a simple computational program, he fills in a formula that includes the present growth rate, the present population, and (as an unknown) the years it takes to double the population. He presses RETURN and the results flash on the screen: "At the present rate of growth, the population will double by 2024, reaching 9.4 billion." Realizing that some students are catching on faster than others, he asks them if they understood what he did with the formula and explains it once again for those who missed it. Then he asks the students if they think the population will double like that again. Some nod yes, some no. As they are reflecting on this he enters a command to double again and a new set of data flashes on the screen. He pauses to give the students time to process it. "According to present growth rates, the population will redouble to 18.8 billion by 2065. What do you think about that?" He pauses to let them formulate their mental reactions. He repeats the operation. "It will be 37.6 billion by 2106. Do you want me to go on or shall I stop?" A student quips: "Stop, we'll all be dead by then anyway." Professor Meade replies, "maybe sooner," and cracks one of his rare half-smiles.

He looks around the room for a while, then asks, "Well,what's wrong with this?" He pauses to let the students reflect; then, without looking up, proceeds to answer his own question. He asks the students if they remember what the textbook says about how fertility and mortality work together to produce natural increase. He turns off the computer and flips on a colored slide for which he has already provided the context. He sets forth the main features of the line graph. "The red line of the deathrate," he points out, "drops off dramatically then evens out—people can only live so long even with modern medicine. The blue line, which indicates the birthrate, continues upward; but then it gradually drops, too. The big increases occur in the transition phase, when the deathrate drops and the birthrate rises. As a result of this natural increase there are a lot more people to have babies, and they do!" He senses that he needs a concrete illustration. "For that period it's like compound interest at the bank. That's why the birthrate soars. But eventually it stops and stabilizes, or at least that's what it has done in the more developed countries." He has given them a script for the process of increase and stabilization. He ties it down with another illustration. "It's like an adolescent growth spurt—several inches all at once, and then a leveling off." Then he asks, "Do you think that is what will happen in the less developed countries as they get more developed?" Some heads shake yes, some no. By now, all of the feature demons and supervisor demons are making pandemonium in his students' heads.

Professor Meade moves on to another chart of population growth by country that appears on the screen. He explains that the main idea of the chart is that population growth today is very uneven from country to country and region to region. Then he points out the details. "The growth rates for countries, such as the U.S.A. and what was formerly the U.S.S.R. are less than 1, but in regions such as East Africa and Middle America, growth rates are as high as 3." The table is replaced with two pie diagrams that show that by the year 2025 certain regions of the world will have a much larger slice of the world population pie than they do at present, particularly South Asia and Africa. Then Professor Meade asks the students if they think those trends will continue. "Will the growth rates in those regions eventually stabilize?" Some nod yes, some no.

The rest of the lecture proceeds in a similar manner. The question of overpopulation is raised and addressed. Professor Meade knows that the students already have a schema for "overpopulation," but it may be inadequate and he wants them to examine it carefully. The concept of "population density" is brought into the discussion and a bar graph showing population density per square kilometer is projected. Huge differences in the length of the bars appear between Bangladesh, Japan, and the Netherlands, on the one hand, and Australia, Canada, and the U.S.A, on the other. "Population density is one way of thinking about overpopulation," Professor Meade points out, "but would the Japanese say that they are overpopulated? Probably not." He points out that "overpopulation" may not be related as much to land mass as to economic conditions, to such things as the ratio of work force to available capital or the ratio of population to means of subsistence.

Professor Meade ends the lecture with a flurry of questions. "So what do you make of all this? Will the population of the world continue to double? When will the world be 'overpopulated,' or is it already? And who is to say that the world is overpopulated? Is it only the more developed countries that view these trends with alarm! Do shifts in the balance of population necessarily produce shifts in the balance of political power?"

What students "learn" from Professor Meade's lecture is how to process the information, how to grasp its inner meaning, and how to use it. What Professor Meade hopes his students will learn, day by day, is a method for looking at population information, the demographer's method, the sociologist's method—skeptical, rational, objective, disciplined.

Professor Newton knows that today there is something lurking in his students' heads, perhaps something troublesome to them, that could disrupt the processing of all of the remaining portion of the lecture unless he deals with it—their previous learning about "creation." He knows that the word "creation" will call up a different schema for each student. He decides to deal with the potential problem directly, pointing out that many pre-scientific cultures developed "creation myths." He knows that "myth" will call up still another schema, so he pauses to point out that myths are literary, as opposed to scientific, attempts at cosmology, which summarize what matters most to the societies that have preserved them. "For the Hebrews, Adam was made of dust; for a Tahitian fisherman, an angler god tugged the islands up from the ocean floor; for the African Bushman, the Milky Way came from the sparks flying upward from the fire." Without devaluing these myths, Professor Newton urges the students to set them aside for a moment, including those of their own religious traditions, and suggests that comparing pre-scientific literary myths to scientific, empirically derived theories of cosmology is like comparing apples and oranges. He urges the students, "Hang up your hang-ups, at least temporarily, so that you can hear and examine what the scientific method is able to tell us about this."

Having set aside, if not resolved, this initial source of distraction, Professor Newton plunges into the big-bang theory.[28] He realizes that the concept is new and somewhat abstract, so he searches for a concrete illustration, a new schema the students can use to understand a difficult concept. "It is as if," he explains, "the Milky Way galaxy were to be enclosed in a gigantic hydraulic press, like those used for crushing old cars into scrap metal, as it were, a huge trash compactor. Picture, then, the Milky Way being squeezed down to about one cubic foot." He pauses, realizing that this is a new idea put into a bold image. "With this compression taking place, the stars and planets would be pressed together, the molecules and atoms would break down and the nuclear structure of subatomic particles would decompose into a hot, dense gas of subatomic particles called 'plasma.' Now reverse the process and let this highly compressed cubic foot of hot plasma explode. Everything starts moving out from the center of the blast until eventually it arrives at the the Milky Way again. If you can picture that for the Milky Way, then try to picture it for the whole universe."

Professor Newton then asks, "What is the scientific evidence for this and how could such evidence be gathered? Think of it this way. If you examined the results of an atomic explosion, you would look at the devastation and then work backwards to describe the source by inference." Professor Newton has video projection capability in his lecture hall, and he pauses to run a brief videotape of an atomic explosion, playing it first forward and then backward. "The universe we have today is what came after the explosion, and the scientific problem is to use the existing evidence to reconstruct the explosion."

Professor Newton notes that there are many sources of evidence to support the theory, but he lets the students know that there are only two that he wants them to understand today. The central portion of his lecture is used to elaborate these two points. He gives the students these two main headings: the idea of the "Expanding Universe," and the concept of the "Evolution of the Elements."

He introduces the work of George Lemaitre, a Belgian priest and mathematician, who first elaborated the idea of an expanding universe. "You will remember that we learned earlier in this course that everything in the universe is moving away from every thing else. Well, if it is," Professor Newton explains, "Lemaitre reasoned that there must have been a time when everything was much closer together. In fact, so close together as to occupy a single pinpoint in space called a singularity." He puts a dot on the chalkboard and writes "singularity" beside it. "And when was this?" he asks. "At a point in time with no yesterday. That's all! Lemaitre reasoned that there was some kind of a primordial atom and that a big initial event, later dubbed the 'big bang' by Fred Hoyle, set it off." Professor Newton then reviews how later scientists accumulated the physical evidence to support Lemaitre's mathematical theory, mostly from observations of stars in the expanding universe.

Then he lets the students know that he is moving to the second point, the "Evolution of the Elements." He begins to explain how the elements that are known today have emerged at different points in time, relative to the big bang at the beginning. He knows that the students already have a framework for understanding the elements and the structure of atoms from their previous study of chemistry in this course. "To unravel the mystery of the big bang," he continues, "the astronomers had to call in the physicists who had studied sub-atomic particles. The physicists knew what conditions were necessary for various elements to form and the relative abundance of the various elements in the universe today. The more abundant elements, hydrogen and helium, which make up 96 percent of the matter of the universe, were formed in the big bang, but other, less abundant elements were created later by the burning of stars. The mix of elements found in the universe today is the result of how they were created, with different elements emerging at different points in time over billions of years. That's why we began the lecture today by taking a trip backwards in time while looking at your hand. The nature and progression of the development of the elements, along with atomic and sub-atomic particles, is like a 'second proof' for the idea of an expanding universe set off by a big bang."

Professor Newton pauses, removes his glasses, and comes out in front of the lectern to field questions. He knows that not all students have heard and processed what he has said in the same way, so he is interested in their questions. Now the hands are shooting in the air and the questions are popping:

Will the universe just keep expanding?
Will the universe collapse in on itself again someday?
Has it expanded at exactly the same rate since the beginning?

Did the elements in our hand really come from the stars?

What was there before the big bang?

Professor Newton likes the students' questions. They are not questions growing out of confusion; they aren't resulting from inadequacies in his explanation or their processing of it. These are the questions born out of understanding. Yes, most of the students have caught the main features of the idea and now, in their own way, are trying to throw the idea back to him. Ah, yes, even a "heavy subject" can be made into a frisbee toss.

MEMORY

Cognitive psychologists have been able to describe what happens when people pay attention to and process information. Processing information is a kind of learning in itself, but it is often important that the information learned also be retained. Retaining information over long periods of time involves memory. For the teacher this becomes a practical question: How do students remember and what can the teacher do to help them remember?

Over many years of research cognitive psychologists have made a distinction between short-term and long-term memory.[29] Short-term memory, as the term implies, doesn't last very long, and it doesn't hold very much. It is used to keep information temporarily "in mind" in order to act on it. In looking up a phone number, a person uses short-term memory to keep the numbers in mind long enough to dial them; and, alas, even then it is often necessary to take a second peek at the phone book, especially if there has been an interruption. How short is short-term memory? Estimates vary on the exact length of storage time. Visual images last in the sensory register for less than one-half second and sounds last only one-fourth second, but their features can be extracted and retained in short-term memory for somewhere between 15 and 30 seconds. The decay rate was established through experiments designed to eliminate the subjects' ability to rehearse the material continuously.[30] In other words, unless the information is rehearsed (repeated over and over mentally) or unless something else is done with the information to fix it in long-term memory, rapid decay sets in. Hence the name "short-term."

Short-term memory is also limited in capacity, that is, it doesn't hold very much. In a now famous and influential paper entitled "The

Magical Number Seven, Plus or Minus Two: Some Limits on our Capacity for Processing Information," G.A. Miller established that most people are limited to retaining between five and nine bits of information in their short-term memory.[31] In the experiments that he did, and in those done subsequently by others, the magical number seven kept popping up. In testing the number of sounds, digits, or words people could remember, the results were always about the same—somewhere around seven, plus or minus two—unless people did something with the information to establish it in long-term memory. Usually this meant taking a longer string of information and grouping it into a smaller number of "chunks." It would be difficult, for example, to remember the number

1776149219181941

as a single number, but it can be "chunked", as shown below, into the dates for the American Revolution, Columbus's discovery of America, the armistice ending World War I, and the bombing of Pearl Harbor.[32]

1776 1492 1918 1941

It is more likely that these four chunks will be retained, but this is no longer short-term memory! The material has, in fact, been transformed, encoded, and sent on its way to long-term memory.

What is the purpose, then, of short-term memory, with its demonstrated lack of staying-power and capacity? Some psychologists have even referred to it as the great bottleneck in information processing. (Others say that attention is the bottleneck.) Bottleneck or not, short-term memory plays an important function in holding information temporarily "in mind" while other monitors and control mechanisms get to act on it. It is like hanging a picture. One person holds the picture in place, while another takes a look and tries to decide whether to move it up or down, left or right or whether to hang it, put it in another room, or put it in storage. In hanging pictures it is not wise to go too fast or to look at too many pictures all at once. Similarly, short-term memory provides a necessarily limited mechanism for holding up words, images, ideas, and sounds to look at briefly while a decision is made about what to do with them next.

Long-term memory, not short-term memory as described above, is what most people mean when they refer to memory, and it is this kind of memory that is usually the concern of students and teachers. It picks up where short-term memory leaves off—after a few seconds—and goes on for weeks, months, and years.

Cognitive psychologists make distinctions among various types of long-term memory and recognize that somewhat different processes are at work for remembering different kinds of things.[33] A memory for events is called episodic memory and a memory for information is called semantic memory. Remembering the event of walking to school as a child is different from remembering what was learned about the Pilgrims in sixth grade. Iconic memory is a memory for images, auditory memory is for sounds, while psycho-motor memory is for movement, such as skiing or riding a bicycle. Most postsecondary teachers deal primarily with semantic memory, the memory for information and ideas, for concepts mediated by words.

How does long-term memory work and what can be done to assist it in its work? One commonly expressed view is that the mind records everything perfectly, like a human video recorder, but the trouble comes in play-back. When individuals representative of the general populace are surveyed and asked how they think their memory works, three-fourths believe that all the information is there in long-term memory; they just can't retrieve it.[34] This idea of a complete but inaccessible memory, while widely held, does not bear the scrutiny of research. Research suggests that the mind does not record everything, and that what is recorded is subject to inaccuracy, distortion, and serious decay.[35] Recent attempts to unlock the memory with hypnosis, "truth" drugs, and electrical stimulation result in as many false reports, fragments, and distortions as accurate memories. If long-term memory is not a video tape of experience, how does it work?

Again, until research and theory focused on human memory advances further, a model drawn from computer science provides some useful beginnings. There are four points of similarity between what a computer does and how long-term memory functions. This is what a computer needs:

> First, there must be a place to store the information. This may be on magnetic tape, on magnetic disk or in a variety of other forms. Second, there has to be a way to know what is stored where. This function is served by a file structure and by one of several indexes. Third, there must be a method to get information back out. This function is served by retrieval programs and subroutines. Fourth, there must be a method for aggregating raw data into meaningful concepts. This is

accomplished by analysis programs and other subroutines. Any memory system, biological or mechanical, must be designed to do these four things.[36]

The computer analogy is useful, but how is information stored, indexed, retrieved, and analyzed by humans?

Further attempts to elaborate memory processes have drawn on the study of verbal behavior, particularly semantics.[37] Research suggests that people employ hierarchical associations among concepts and use these hierarchies to retrieve the desired information. For example, "animal," "bird," "feathers," "wing," and "fly" are arranged in special places in memory according to their meaning. A bird is a kind of animal that has feathers and its wings enable it to fly. Knowledge is stored in hierarchical networks and is retrieved by drawing upon logical semantic associations. The structure of these networks can be mapped and tested. Further research has revealed that the rate at which words are called up is related to the frequency with which they are drawn on in language, the recency with which a word has been used,[38] and the age at which the word was originally learned.[39] Retrieval time is also influenced by how hard it is to give the concept a memorable code; for example, "justice" is probably harder to code than "zebra."[40] This relationship among words as reflected in their rate of retrievability is sometimes called "category dominance," "production frequency," or "typicality," but more often "semantic distance."[41]

All of this suggests that memory involves a complex network filing system. This becomes the crucial point that unlocks the key to understanding memory: Putting things into long-term memory and retrieving them involves *associations* among words, concepts, and ideas, usually, but not always, semantic associations. In other words, the best models of long-term memory currently available focus on the importance of word associations, hooking up one word with another word (or image or sound) to produce meaningful and memorable connections within the networked filing system. The human computer, with its potentially enormous and verifiably complex storage and retrieval system, relies heavily on language and the associations of meaning conveyed by language for its smooth functioning.

If it is known that memory depends on building associations between and among words, concepts, and ideas, what are some of the ways that an individual might go about storing information with the hope that it might be retrieved as needed? Four categories of "techniques" are especially useful for enhancing the storage and retrieval of information in long-term memory: rehearsal, encoding, imagery, and semantic association.

The most frequently used and least effective memory technique is rehearsal, sometimes referred to by educators as "rote learning." Rehearsal involves repeating information over and over again (out loud or to one's self) until it "sinks in." It is possible, for example, to memorize a difficult list of words if sufficient time is allowed between the presentation of the words for rehearsal.[42] Rehearsal, however, is not very efficient, and when it does work there is often another technique being used (perhaps unwittingly) besides pure repetition.

Far more efficient and productive is the memory technique known as encoding. At its simplest level, encoding means associating a key word with a to-be-remembered word; at its more complex levels it means transforming the information to be remembered into a new semantic unit or form. Using a synonym is a form of encoding; so is placing a word in a meaningful and memorable sentence. More complex encoding involves developing mnemonic devices known as acronyms, such as "HOMES" to remember the Great Lakes (Huron, Ontario, Michigan, Erie, Superior), or catchy sentences, such as "Every good boy does fine," to remember the lines on the treble clef (E,G,B,D,F). Research on encoding suggests, oddly enough, that more elaborate and distinctive devices work best.[43] One of the more useful forms of encoding is "chunking." Long strings of information can be subdivided or transformed into chunks, so that the number of individual units to be remembered is smaller and more manageable.

Another memory technique involves the use of imagery. Images are mental pictures. Research has shown that people generally find it easier to remember pictures than words.[44] When subjects were shown 1,000 vivid pictures, 1,000 ordinary pictures, and 1,000 words, on the average they remembered (identified correctly from test-pairs) 830 vivid pictures, 770 ordinary pictures, and 615 words.[45] One picture may not be worth 1,000 words, but vivid images may be useful in storing information in long-term memory. Associating words with vivid images is the main technique set forth in a popular best-seller of some years back by Lorayne and Lucas entitled *The Memory Book*.[46] Unlike some popular psychology books, this one advocates techniques that are in harmony with research. The authors explain step by step how to remember a new piece of information by associating it with vivid, preferably ridiculous and even bizarre images. Suppose, for example, that a person is asked to learn a list of words that begins with "airplane," "tree," and "envelope." Here is the authors' advice:

> First you need a ridiculous—impossible, crazy, illogical, absurd—picture or image to associate the two items. What you don't want is a logical or sensible picture. . . . A ridiculous or impossible picture might be: a gigantic tree is flying instead of an airplane, or an airplane is growing instead of a tree, or airplanes are growing on trees, or millions of trees (as passengers) are boarding airplanes. . . . Choose a ridiculous association between airplane and tree and see it in your mind's eye, right now. . . . The next item on the list is envelope. We'll assume that you already know, or remember, tree. The new thing to remember is envelope. Simply form a ridiculous picture, or association in your mind between tree and envelope. You might see millions of envelopes growing on a tree, or a tree is sealing a gigantic envelope, or you're trying to seal a tree in an envelope.

Apparently bizarre and elaborate visual associations work well as memory devices.

Another memory technique involving the use of imagery is known as the "method of loci." The object is to place items to be learned into a pattern of familiar locations, such as the rooms of a house, the corners of a classroom, or the shops along a familiar street. A grocery list, for example, might be learned, by placing each item on the list mentally at a different place in the kitchen: the milk in the refrigerator, the paper towels on their rack, a can of soup on the counter, etc. While shopping, one mentally walks through the kitchen and retrieves the items to be purchased.[47]

Another technique used to facilitate long-term memory is semantic association. Information that has meaning is more easily remembered than nonsense. Language has both what linguists call "surface structure," properties of the words themselves, and "deep structure," the underlying meaning the words convey.[48] What people do when they read a passage or listen to a lecture is look for the underlying meaning of the information, the gist of the content, or what students might call "the message." What people often put into long-term memory is not the exact words, but the message, and the message, in turn, is also what they recall. When subjects were given a passage to read about the performance of exploratory surgery, they later recalled a host of words, such as "doctor," "nurse," and "scalpel," that weren't in the passage at all. Apparently they remembered the general theme of the passage and made decisions on the basis of what words should have appeared in such a passage.[49] Other studies show that people remember exact wording in sentences only when the sentence itself is particularly noteworthy; otherwise they have trouble distinguishing the actual sentence from a paraphrase. Long-term memory is facilitated by associations derived from the underlying meaning of the information.

If this is how people remember, why do they forget? There are many explanations for forgetting. Sometimes forgetting involves interference from previously learned material; some involves motivated forgetting, such as the classical Freudian idea of repression; some involves failure in the retrieval system, as with tip-of-the-tongue forgetting; and some forgetting involves actual memory decay, as with aging.[50] More likely than not, however, what is called "forgetting" is really a matter of not learning the information in the first place. People don't "forget" names; more likely they don't learn them initially. Memory usually involves active processing that requires intentional effort. When subjects were asked to recall the head of a penny, most could not describe what was on it or where and couldn't distinguish real pennies from fake pennies that were presented, even though they dealt with them every day.[51] Did the subjects forget? Unlikely! One must learn something before it can be forgotten. When students say "I forgot," a more accurate admission would usually be "I didn't learn it."

The work of cognitive psychologists on memory has important implications for teachers. Teachers should know that however stimulating and interesting their classes, the excitement of the moment soon fades—maybe within 30 seconds—if students don't do something to remember the information they have encountered. Processing information is not the same as remembering it. Memory takes work, and students need some assistance with it.

How can a teacher assist students in the work of remembering? First, a teacher can help students realize that what sits on the shoulders is a mind, not a videocassette recorder. Students won't remember just by being present in class. It is important for teachers to explode the myth of "automatic memory—faulty recall." Furthermore, teachers can be much clearer in their own minds about what they want students to remember and to share those expectations "up front" with students. (Unfortunately, many teachers tell students what they want them to remember and then test them on other things.) But most of all, teachers can help students use one or more of the memory techniques needed for putting information into long-term memory. Teachers can show students how to use rehearsal, encoding, imagery, and semantic association by presenting information in forms that fit these devices. Consider once again the examples.

At the end of the lecture on the elements of visual design, Pierre de Chardin reminds students that the things he wants them to remember appear on the outline that they picked up at the beginning of class. "Yes, yes, of course you should remember 'Seurat-the-Dot' and 'Rembrandt von Line.' But what I really want you to remember is the six basic elements of design. What are they again?" The class recites in unison: dot, line, shape, movement, tone, and color. "Before you can start to use them, you have to remember them. Here, maybe this will help." He sketches on the pad at the easel a simple visual reminder of the six elements:

$$\cdot - \triangle \rightarrow \boxtimes \; C$$

Pierre holds up a copy of the art institute's catalogue and says, "When you look at anything, for example, the cover of the catalogue for our art institute, don't just look at it once; look at it six times. Look at it first for dots, then again for line, look again for shape, then for movement, again for tone, and finally for color. That's what I want you to remember, the six elements, so that every time you look at something they come popping into your head and you start looking for them."

Pierre turns on the slides again, which have been reset from the beginning. "For the last five minutes of class, look at the slides one more time and go over your notes. Use the images from the slides to help you fix in your mind the supporting information for each section of the lecture." The students sit forward, reviewing each slide intently, trying to find the best way to place the important bits of information in the right mental files.

When the last slide appears, the music of Debussy comes on again, floating across the room, signaling the end of class. Pierre leans against the desk at the front of the room, stroking his chin, deep in thought, wondering if he has done enough to make his lectures "unforgettable."

Professor Meade closes his lecture on demographics with a brief reminder of the assignment: "If you haven't done so already, be sure to read the assigned chapter in the textbook on 'World Population

Trends.' Learn the most important terminology, because the terminology provides you with the basic concepts for analyzing the population data. Don't bother with the actual numbers. The numbers are always changing; even as I speak here now, someone dies or is born. On the mid-term and the final I'll provide you with the data. What I want you to remember are the concepts you will need for analyzing the data." He pauses, then asks, "Any questions?"

A hand goes up timidly and an undergraduate asks how to tell which of the terms are most important. Professor Meade grimaces, then regains his composure. He points out that the key terminology is set in boldface type in the text and that there is a glossary in the back of the book where the most important terms are listed. "Don't try to memorize the words in the glossary by just repeating them over and over to yourself, though. It's much better if you understand what the concepts mean." He pauses and then turns to the empty screen and points, "Get the images of the line graphs and the pie diagrams fixed in your mind. Remember what we were doing with them. Think about what I did on the computer. Examine how the concepts are related. Draw yourself a little mental network of which concepts go together. It's all really quite logical. It's understanding we're after, and if you understand what the concepts mean, then, of course, you will remember them."

After a lively interchange of questions and answers about the origins of the universe, Professor Newton distributes one of his now famous information sheets. He has established quite a reputation for his cartoons, and students are always eager to see what he has drawn on the sheet to help them remember what took place in class. At the top left corner of the page, not surprisingly, is the small outline of a hand. In the center of the page at the top is a little stick figure climbing a ladder up to the stars with a banner on the left that reads "Pre-Scientific Literary Myths" and another on the right that reads "Scientific Cosmologies." At the bottom of the page is a drawing of a hydraulic press with the Milky Way compressed into one cubic foot, and on the back of the page at the top is a drawing of an explosion labeled "Big Bang." The rest of the sheet is filled, front and back, with lists of key words, new terminology with brief definitions, and the names of important scientists and the titles of their papers or books and the dates of their discoveries. The information is chunked into categories that correspond to the main ideas of the lecture. Under "Expanding Universe" are the names of Lemaitre and Fred Hoyle, and terms like "singularity" and "big bang." Under "Evolution of the Elements" is a general principle that reads succinctly: "The more abundant the element, the older it is." Below that is a small chart of some of the basic elements, with data about their abundance and estimated age of formation. At the bottom of the sheet on the back can be found the page numbers of the text that correspond to the material covered that day.

"Those of you who have talked to students who took this course last year," Professor Newton notes with a twinkle in his eye, "are aware that I have been known to include a question on the final exam that asks you to describe the big bang theory and give the evidence for it. So you might ask yourself what you would need to remember from all of this to give a full and complete answer to a question like that. Take your lecture notes, and the information from the text and use this sheet to try to pull it all together. What would you include if you wanted to tell a friend about this theory? What would you want them to know?"

Notebooks are closed and slipped into backpacks, feet shuffle, chatter begins. "Oh, one more thing," Professor Newton shouts above the din. There is a momentary hush. "This is a theory, you know, and like all scientific theories, it is subject to correction. Just recently astronomers have discovered some huge bubbles in the universe where there is nothing—nothing at all, just big bubbles of void. Their existence contradicts the idea of even and steady expansion since the time of the big bang. If you can explain those bubbles you can probably win the Nobel Prize."

CONCLUSIONS

Teachers who employ a lecturing and explaining strategy can become more effective by understanding and applying the research and theories of cognitive psychologists. Cognitive psychology does not have the luxury of direct observation usually associated with behavioral learning theory. Its research, although rigorous and scientific, relies more on inference and convergent validation. But its conclusions and models of information processing are very useful for postsecondary teachers who lecture. When we lecture we can be more effective if we understand how students attend to, process, and remember information. We will realize that students can focus their attention when directed to do so, that they can learn to identify the main features of the information being presented, and that they can learn how to remember what is important when given appropriate memory devices. Teachers who find it important to transmit information, the conceptual material that provides the intellectual substance for a sound education, usually like to employ the lecturing and explaining strategy.

NOTES

1. Ernest Boyer, *College: The Undergraduate Experience* (New York: Harper & Row, 1987), pp. 149-50.

2. John Brubacher and Willis Rudy, *Higher Education in Transition* (New York: Harper & Row, 1958), Chapter 9, "The Influences of the German University."

3. Donis A. Donis, *A Primer of Visual Literacy* (Cambridge, MA: The MIT Press, 1973). This work is used for a general reference on the subject of visual communication taught by the fictional Pierre de Chardin.

4. David Yaukey, *Demography: The Study of Human Population* (New York: St. Martin's Press, 1985). This work is used for a general reference on the subject of demography taught by the fictional Roscoe Meade.

5. Timothy Ferris, *Coming of Age in the Milky Way* (New York: William Morrow, 1988). This work is used for a general reference on the subject of astronomy taught by the fictional John Newton.

6. R. E. Mayer, *The Promise of Cognitive Psychology* (San Francisco: W. H. Freeman, 1981); William James, *The Principles of Psychology* (New York: Holt, 1890); F. C. Bartlett, *Remembering: A Study in Experimental and Social Psychology* (New York: Macmillan, 1932).

7. For a brief history of how cognitive psychology came into being as a field of study, see Ulrich Neisser, *Cognitive Psychology* (New York: Appleton-Century-Crofts, 1967). For more detail, see also Howard Gardner, *The Mind's New Science: A History of the Cognitive Revolution* (New York: Basic Books, 1985).

8. In an interesting twist of fate, Noam Chomsky, a young linguist, was asked to review B.F. Skinner's *Verbal Behavior*. The result was more than a book review. Chomsky emerged as a leading psycholinguist. See Noam Chomsky, "A Review of Skinner's Verbal Behavior," *Language*, 1959, 35, pp. 26-58.

9. R. Lachman, J. L. Lachman, and E. C. Butterfield, *Cognitive Psychology and Information Processing: An Introduction* (Hillsdale, NJ: Lawrence Erlbaum Associates, 1979).

10. A. Newell, J. C. Shaw, and H. A. Simon, "Elements of a Theory of Human Problem Solving," *Psychological Review*, 1958, 65, pp. 151-66. Other landmark works are D. E. Broadbent, *Perception and Communication* (London: Pergamon Press, 1958); G. A. Miller, E. Galanter, and K. H. Pribram, *Plans and the Structure of Behavior* (New York: Henry Holt & Co., Inc., 1960); N. Chomsky, *Aspects of the Theory of Syntax* (Cambridge: Cambridge University Press, 1965); and Ulrich Neisser's classic textbook, *Cognitive Psychology*.

11. The idea of observing the factory is adapted from R. Lachman, J. L. Lachman, and E. C. Butterfield, *Cognitive Psychology and Information Processing*, pp. 123-24. The concept of "convergent validation" is also drawn from this source.

12. Many of the models of cognitive processing are based on a classic chapter by Atkinson and Shiffran that sets forth the basic concepts of

"sensory register," "short-term store," and "long-term memory." See R. C. Atkinson and R. M. Shiffran, "Human Memory: A Proposed System and Its Control Processes" in K. W. Spence and T. W. Spence, eds., *The Psychology of Learning and Motivation*, vol. 2, (New York: Academic Press, 1968).

13. C. Cherry, *On Human Communication* (New York: Wiley, 1957).

14. D. E. Broadbent, *Perception and Communication* (London: Pergamon Press, 1958).

15. P. Lindsey and D. Norman, *Human Information Processing: An Introduction to Psychology* (New York: Academic Press, 1972).

16. A. M. Triesman, "Contextual Cues in Encoding Listening," *Quarterly Journal of Experimental Psychology*, 1960, 12, pp. 242-48. Anthony J. Sanford, *Cognition and Cognitive Psychology* (New York: Basic Books, 1985), p. 79. This work is also used frequently throughout the remainder of this chapter as a general reference on cognitive psychology.

17. R. M. Shiffran and N. Schneider, "Controlled and Automatic Human Information Processing II. Perceptual Learning, Automatic Attending and a General Theory," *Psychological Review*, 1977, 84, pp. 127-90.

18. The idea of examining the hand through increasing powers of magnification is drawn from Ferris, *Coming of Age*, p. 338.

19. The description of the human "scanning process," including the "template theory" and Selfridge's "Pandemonium theory," are drawn from Sanford, *Cognition and Cognitive Psychology*, pp. 39-43. The original references are O. Selfridge and U. Neisser, "Pattern Recognition by Machine," *Scientific American* (1960) 203, pp. 60-68 and O. Selfridge, "Pandemonium: A Paradigm of Learning" in *The Mechanization of Thought Processes* (H. M. Stationery Office).

20. The discussion of "top-down processing" draws heavily on the excellent summary of research in Sanford, *Cognition and Cognitive Psychology*, p. 51 ff. Some of the illustrations from Gestalt psychology are also drawn from Phillip Zimbardo, *Psychology and Life* (Glenview, IL: Scott, Foresman and Company, 1985), p.196 ff.

21. See Sanford, *Cognition and Cognitive Psychology*, p. 203 ff. for schema theory. The story is adapted from E. Charniak, "Toward a Model of Children's Story Comprehension," Technical Report 266, Artificial Intelligence Laboratory, MIT, 1972.

22. The source on "scripts" is R. Schank and R. Ableson, *Scripts, Plans, Goals and Understanding: An Enquiry into Human Knowledge Structure* (Hillsdale, NJ: Lawrence Erlbaum, 1977). The concept of "frames" is elaborated in M. Minsky, "A Framework for Representing Knowledge" in *The Psychology of Computer Vision* (New York: McGraw-Hill, 1975).

23. This widely used illustration is originally drawn from J. D. Bransford and M. K. Johnson, "Consideration of Some Problems of Comprehension" in W. G. Chase, ed., Visual Information Processing (New York: Academic Press, 1973).

24. See Sanford, *Cognition and Cognitive Psychology*, p. 195.

25. See Sanford, *Cognition and Cognitive Psychology*, pp. 55-61 for the "blackboard model." The original sources are R. H. Lindsay and D. A. Norman, *Human Information Processing* (New York: Academic Press, 1977) and D. E. Rummelhart, *Introduction to Human Information Processing* (New York: Wiley, 1977).

26. The "content" for the lecture is based on Donis, *Primer of Visual Literacy*, Chapter 3, "The Basic Elements of Visual Communication."

27. The concepts for the lecture on demographics and ideas for the charts and graphs are taken from the chapter on "World Population Growth" in Yaukey, *Demography*.

28. The ideas for the lecture on the "big bang" theory are taken from Ferris, *Coming of Age*. The pre-scientific myths of the earth's creation in different cultures are found on p. 350. The idea for the hydraulic press for "crushing" the universe is on pp. 272-73. LeMaitre's concept of the expanding universe is explained on p. 210 ff.

29. Sanford, *Cognition and Cognitive Psychology*, p.104 ff. William James (1890) called the two forms of memory "primary" and "secondary."

30. L. R. Peterson, "Short-Term Retention of Individual Verbal Items," *Journal of Experimental Psychology*, 1959, 58, pp. 193-98.

31. G. A. Miller, "The Magical Number Seven, Plus or Minus Two: Some Limits on our Capacity for Processing Information," *Psychological Review*, 1956, 63, pp. 81-97.

32. Lachman, Lachman, and Butterfield, *Cognitive Psychology and Information Processing*, p. 52.

33. E. Tulving, "Episodic and Semantic Memory" in E. Tulving and W. Donaldson, eds., *Organization of Memory* (New York: Academic Press, 1972).

34. E. F. Loftus and G. R. Loftus, "On the Permanence of Stored Information in the Human Brain," *American Psychologist*, 1980, 35, pp. 409-20.

35. E. Loftus, *Memory* (Reading, MA: Addison-Wesley, 1980).

36. Ibid., p. 172.

37. M. R. Quillan, "The Teachable Language Comprehender: Assimilation Program and Theory of Language," *Communications of the ACM*, 1969, 12, pp. 459-76.

38. R. C. Oldfield and A. Wingfield, "Response Latencies in Naming Objects," *Quarterly Journal of Experimental Psychology*, 1965, 17, pp. 273-81.

39. J. B. Carroll and M. N. White, "Word Frequency and Age of Acquisition as Determinants of Picture Naming Latency," *Quarterly Journal of Experimental Psychology*, 1973, 25, pp. 85-95.

40. R. Lachman, "Uncertainty Effects on Time to Access the Internal Lexicon," *Journal of Experimental Psychology*, 1973, 99, pp. 199-208.

41. Lachman, Lachman, and Butterfield, *Cognitive Psychology and Information Processing*.

42. A. Sanford, *Cognition and Cognitive Psychology*, p.107 ff.

43. S. K. Reed, *Cognition: Theory and Applications* (Monterrey, CA: Brooks-Cole, 1982).

44. R. N. Shepherd, "Recognition Memory for Words, Sentences and Pictures," *Journal of Verbal Learning and Verbal Behavior*, 1967, 6, pp. 156-63.

45. L. Standing, "Learning 10,000 Pictures," *Quarterly Journal of Experimental Psychology*, 1973, 25, pp. 207-22.

46. H. Lorayne and J. Lucas, *The Memory Book* (New York: Stein & Day, 1974). The quotation is from pp. 25-27.

47. Loftus, *Memory*, p.181.

48. N. Chomsky, *Aspects of a Theory of Syntax* (Cambridge, MA: MIT Press, 1965).

49. K. F. Pompi and R. Lachman, "Surrogate Processes in the Short-Term Retention of Connected Discourse," *Journal of Experimental Psychology*, 1967, 75, pp. 143-50.

50. Zimbardo, *Psychology and Life*, p.327 ff.

51. R. S. Nickerson and M. J. Adams, "Long-Term Memory for a Common Object," *Cognitive Psychology*, 1979, 11, pp. 287-307.

Inquiry and Discovery

"I'm too old," he thought, "for clear thinking. I'm too old and I've seen too much."
—Toni Morrison, *Beloved*

ENCOURAGING STUDENTS TO THINK

Teachers want their students to be able to think. We identify "teaching students to think" as one of the most important goals of our teaching, but we often lament that we don't have enough time or enough background to do a better job of it. Teaching is more than dispensing information; students also need to develop the ability to sort through and make sense of the deluge of information they encounter. But what is this process called "thinking," and why is it important that students be able to think?

One of the consistent recommendations coming from reports calling for educational reform is for the enhancement of students' thinking skills. Shocking examples underscore the urgency of the need. An analysis of results from nationwide tests given to high school students through the National Assessment of Educational Progress (NAEP) includes this example:

When students were asked to estimate the answer to 3.04 x 5.3 and were given these responses

    a. 1.6   b. 16   c. 160   d. 1,600   e. don't know

only 20 percent of the 13-year olds and 40 percent of the 17-year olds got the right answer. When asked actually to compute the problem, however, 60 percent of the 13-year olds and 80 percent of the 17-year olds got it right.[1]

In a study of the use of "formal operations" involving abstract reasoning skills (as defined by Piaget and Inhelder) it was found that many college freshmen performed concretely on formal tasks, instead of using abstract reasoning skills.[2] In a study of 300 students, ranging from tenth grade to fourth-year doctoral students, it was found that yearly gains were very low on six scales measuring reasoning skills in making arguments, and that overall gains across educational levels were only modest.[3] In a recent monograph on teaching critical thinking at the college level, Joanne Kurfiss noted that research provides "compelling evidence of serious deficiencies in the ability to reason among college students and the limited influence of college education on critical thinking skills. Depth of argument on controversial topics is minimal and increases marginally as a result of college instruction."[4] Although college teachers are eager to have their students become "good thinkers," and although college students have a demonstrated need to develop their thinking skills, somewhere, something goes wrong.

Why are thinking skills so important and why is there so much concern today about the way they are being taught? The classic argument for teaching people to think is that clear thinking is necessary for effective citizenship in a democracy.[5] Thinking has also been seen as a liberating force, freeing the individual from the ignorance that characterizes chauvinism and ethnocentrism, from narrow self-interest and "small-mindedness." One of the main purposes of a "liberal education" is to free students from "their biases, stereotypes, distortions, illusions and misconceptions."[6] It has also been argued that good thinkers are often better adjusted and happier individuals, who find life more interesting and rewarding. On the other hand, teaching people to think may increase the possibility of conflict within the self and conflict with society. As Raymond Nickerson points out, "people who do acquire the habit of thinking critically will, by definition, think uncommon thoughts."[7] Some of the world's best thinkers have pushed themselves to the edge of personal despair.

It has also been argued that thinking is a unique human function and represents the *telos* of humanness: "While we share much with the rest of the animal kingdom, we are unique in the degree to which our behavior is cognitively, as opposed to instinctively, controlled. . . . We want students to become good thinkers because thinking is at the heart of what it means to be human."[8] Perhaps the best, most down-to-earth argument is that people must be able to think if they are going to function. Thinking is necessary, just to get through the day. At that level, thinking is utilitarian and practical. Thinking is also necessary for the development of values and a sense of the meaning and purpose of life. In this sense, then, thinking is necessary not only for getting through the day, but for getting through the years, for addressing the fundamental questions of human existence.[9]

The reasons for teaching thinking are diverse and operate at many levels. To function in any society, one must learn to think; in the information age, thinking may be the key survival skill. It is not surprising that postsecondary teachers teach thinking for quite different reasons. Consider the following examples.

Jacques LaMer teaches a course called "Ocean Life Forms" at Pacific Coast Community College. Some of his students are transfer students who have an interest in science, but others are adults who want to learn more about the ocean because they live near the beach. As a prerequisite for the course, students must demonstrate that they have their Open Water Certification for SCUBA, because Jacques LaMer takes his classes out to sea. He knows that his students are highly motivated to understand what they observe on their dives, and he is an expert diver and Certified Dive Instructor himself. But Jacques LaMer is also a marine biologist and a well-trained scientist, and he hopes to teach his students the ways of thinking associated with the scientific method. "It just happens that I am interested in ocean life forms, but my deeper interest is in science. Students come to me very excited about the fantastic things they have seen on their dives. Some of them expect a dive guide who will explain everything to them. They are a little shocked when I ask them to figure it out for themselves. I want them to grapple with what they see as if they were the first ones to discover it."

Maynard Smith teaches a graduate seminar in the MBA program at Mid-West University. For his seminars he uses case studies almost exclusively because he believes that business students today must be able to engage in problem solving and decision making about "real-life" situations. By the time students come to him they have some fairly sophisticated skills in accounting, marketing, finance, and management. "They have the theories, but they don't always know what to do with them. They've been plugging along, course by course, writing papers on selected topics, doing assigned problems, and looking up the answers in the back of the book. Now, all of a sudden, here comes a case! They don't even know what the problems are, let alone the relevant data. So we have to get them engaged in some serious thinking. The students have to find the problems, define them, propose solutions, evaluate them, make a decision, and project the probable outcomes. It's a new way of thinking for them."

Edna Wolf teaches in the core curriculum humanities program at Elm Grove College. The class meets for lectures twice a week, but there are also smaller "break-out" sections for discussion that meet each week for two-hour sessions as well. In the colloquium sections the focus is on text—a particular poem or essay or a section of a novel. Students are responsible for having read the text assigned for the day, and when they come to class they are expected to have ideas—not just opinions—that can be set forth clearly and defended with appropriate examples. "The emphasis is on interpretation, but, of course, there are various levels of interpretation. We look closely at the language of the text, trying first to establish what the author was saying or describing. From there, the inquiry can go off in many directions, looking at the craft more deeply, or looking at various levels of interpretations. This involves a special kind of thinking that employs analogical uses of language. Naturally, I want my students to appreciate the works they are reading—there are good reasons why these works have become classics—but ultimately I want them to test the author's vision against their own experience. The 'magic' comes when a student reads a poem and discovers a different way of looking at the world."

There are many ways to engage in thinking and many reasons for doing so. Professors LaMer, Smith, and Wolf all teach thinking, but their objectives in doing so are somewhat different. Each will employ, in slightly different ways, an inquiry and discovery strategy in their classes.

THINKING ABOUT THINKING

Unlike the behaviorist tradition, with its roots in the work of identifiable research psychologists such as Watson, Thorndike, and Skinner, and unlike the field of cognitive psychology, which suddenly erupted on the scene in the 1950s, the people who have been thinking about thinking have been doing so for many centuries and in different fields. The tradition of the inquiry paradigm, yet another view of how people learn, is far more diffuse and ancient than the others. The primary roots are in psychology and philosophy, more specifically in what Matthew Lipman calls "cognitive psychology and philosophy of mind."[10]

Thinking has been perceived differently in every age, and one of the great contributions of philosophers through the centuries has been their effort to clarify for their age what is meant by thinking. "Thinking" was not the same at the time of Aristotle as it was at the time of Bacon or Descartes, and philosophy, as a way of thinking about thinking, preceded science by nearly 2,000 years. Yet many of the rules and distinctions that philosophers continue to make today about thinking—the difference between inductive and deductive reasoning, the basic rules of categorization, the procedures for examining syllogisms, the technique of dialogue—have their roots in Plato or Aristotle. The spirit of inquiry runs through the entire history of philosophy and many of the great philosophers have developed a "method" to carry on their critical inquiry. Philosophers tend to focus on products of thought and the analysis of these products, and today they continue to make this contribution by examining language, the meaning of assertions, and the rules of reasoning.

Psychologists, on the other hand, tend to focus on thinking *processes* as opposed to products.[11] They are interested in what goes on when people think, not only how rules and plans are developed and followed, but also how and why they are broken and disrupted. They study what takes place when thinking occurs, but also how thinking processes break down and fail. Some of these psychologists work very much in the manner of the cognitive psychologists who study attention, information processing, and memory; they just study thinking processes. They give their subjects various kinds of problems that require thought and examine what happens when their subjects engage in thinking. They then attempt to make generalizations about these processes.[12]

Then, of course, there is John Dewey, part-philosopher, part-psychologist, and creative educator. In the laboratory school at the University of Chicago, Dewey tried to develop in children "a habit of considering problems."[13] Dewey believed that problem solving was more suited to societal needs than acquiring information through memorization. For Dewey thinking was stimulated by problem solving, and disciplined inquiry was regarded as the route to social progress. Although John Dewey is best known as the father of the Progressive Education Movement, he is surely also the "grandfather" of the inquiry and discovery teaching strategy.

The more one thinks about thinking, the greater the variety of types of thinking that come to mind. There are, of course, the random thoughts that pass in and out of people's heads as they shower, eat their meals, or drive down the highway. Some authors designate this as "nondirected thinking," and differentiate it sharply from "directed thinking," which is goal-oriented and purposeful.[14] Most teachers want their students to think, not just have thoughts. Directed thinking, though, can take many forms and involve very different kinds of skills and abilities, including asking questions, analyzing arguments, identifying reasons, formulating hypotheses, seeking and weighing evidence, distinguishing facts from opinions, judging the credibility of sources, classifying data, making interpretations of observations, making inferences, using analogies, evaluating claims, establishing criteria, making value judgments, defining and operationalizing, considering alternatives, noting assumptions, and selecting courses of action.[15] Directed thinking also involves certain dispositions, personal habits of mind or attitudes, such as trying to be well-informed, being open-minded, being willing to consider opposing viewpoints, respecting evidence, suspending judgement, tolerating ambiguity, being curious and skeptical, and revering "the truth."[16]

Sometimes different kinds of directed thinking are contrasted, such as closed vs. adventurous thinking, convergent vs. divergent thinking, problem solving vs. problem finding, or vertical vs. lateral thinking.[17] Thinking, as a more general concept, is also often contrasted with reasoning, as a kind of thinking guided by or expressed through rules, often taking on the forms of scientific, mathematical, symbolic, geometrical, or linguistic reasoning.[18] Thinking is also understood to have a special relationship to knowledge; different kinds of knowledge are generated by different kinds of thinking. Likewise, to think within a particular area, one must have "domain-specific knowledge."[19] Some say that thinking is "discipline specific," and that a large part of what one learns in postsecondary education is how to think *within* different disciplines and professional fields.[20] On the other hand, others say that in spite of inherent differences among fields of knowledge, there are commonalities that undergird thinking in all fields.

Although thinking takes on many forms across many fields, there are three types of thinking that are especially important to those who teach in higher education settings—critical thinking, creative thinking, and dialogical thinking.

Critical thinking has been defined broadly as "judging the authenticity, worth or accuracy of something, such as a piece of information, a claim or assertion or sources of data."[21] Critical thinking usually refers to both a conclusion (a product) and the justification for that conclusion (a process). The justification is usually set forth in some manner of argument.[22] The emphasis in critical thinking, whether on criticizing the assertions of others or on building one's own arguments, is on a linear, step-wise, sequence of operations and procedures. Each operation involves "taking data apart to find evidence related to certain criteria and, then, judging the extent to which what has been found meet the criteria. . . ."[23] Crucial to most critical thinking is analyzing and making arguments. Critical thinking involves making a claim or assertion and supporting it with evidence, or examining the claims or assertions that others make.[24] There are rules for this, and the rules need to be followed.

Creative thinking, on the other hand, is "thinking guided—indeed driven—by a desire to seek the original. It values mobility; it revels in exploration; it requires flexibility; and it honors diversity."[25] Instead of following the rules, creative thinkers break them. They have "the ability to look at things in new and unconventional ways, often emphasizing arational or even non-rational styles of thinking."[26] Creative thinking usually results in creative products—works of art, music, dance; unique scientific theories or inventions; or unusual approaches to research. The key criteria linked in tandem are "appropriate" and "original." Creative products stretch or break boundaries, but they are also well-suited and valuable.[27] Creative thinking has several characteristics, such as "ideational fluency," the ability to generate large numbers of appropriate ideas easily and quickly; "remote association," the ability to call forth and link together ideas that would not ordinarily be associated; and "intuition," the ability to generate sound conclusions from minimal evidence.[28] Creative thinking also appears to take place under slightly different conditions from other kinds of thinking. There is usually a long and ardent period of preparation, a time for getting fully acquainted with the turf, followed by periods of new insight. Creativity involves working at the edge of one's capacities, being willing to take risks, being persistent in finding something that works better. Creative people are usually driven by internal rather than external standards of evaluation and are usually intrinsically, rather than extrinsically motivated. Creativity involves a process of reframing ideas, seeing the usual in an unusual light. Sometimes the process involves working intensely for a while and then getting away from things for a period of time, allowing the "unconscious" creative forces to work, letting go of rational, critical approaches, and waiting for the "aha" insight to come.[29]

Dialogical thinking is somewhat different. Some problems can be "settled within one frame of reference and with a definite set of logical moves"; for such problems there is usually a "right" answer.[30] These problems can be called "monological." For other problems "precise identification and definition depend upon some arguable choice among alternative frames of reference"; so that one must test not only the "evidence," but the whole frame of reference within which the problem is being considered. Such problems usually have more than one "right answer," and may be designated "multilogical." To deal with multilogical problems, one must either enter into a dialogue with another thinker, or in the absence of informed proponents of another point of view, must frame the dialogical exchange as if an opponent was present. Dialogical thinking is based on the assumption that "different questions require different modes of thinking." A further assumption is that there is a human tendency to resist this kind of thinking, because our primary nature is "spontaneous, egocentric, and strongly prone to irrational belief," and that it is only through "extensive and systematic practice that (people) recognize the tendencies they have to irrational belief." To put the matter bluntly, people tend to think that they are always right and fail to recognize that "even with an overwhelming sense of the correctness of one's views (one can) still be wrong." The result of this is that "people from different ethnic groups, religions, social classes, and cultural allegiances tend to form different but equally egocentric belief systems and use them equally unmindfully." It is through dialogical thinking, a kind of role-playing of the thinking of others, that one enters empathetically into opposing arguments and viewpoints, thereby examining one's own egocentric thinking and recognizing its strengths and weaknesses.

Some writers stress, however, that sharp distinctions between "critical," "creative," and "dialogical" thinking are inappropriate. These are not separate categories, they note, and probably shouldn't be regarded as opposite ends of a continuum. These are overlapping constructs used to identify a particular emphasis in what are highly complex and interrelated thinking processes. Various forms of thinking are complementary.[31] As one writer has put it: "When reason fails, imagination saves you! When intuition fails, reason saves you!"[32] Because there are many ways of engaging in thinking, it is not surprising that different teachers will stress different types of thinking. Consider again the teachers mentioned earlier.

Jacques LaMer takes his students down into the ocean, 30 or 40 feet, sometimes as much as 65 feet, usually by day, but sometimes at night. He knows his dive sites, and he knows what students are likely to encounter at each site. There are certain questions he likes to pose, certain set problems that he knows will stimulate an intense line of inquiry. And sometimes a certain kind of apparatus will set off a line of inquiry. "I like to introduce them to a piece of equipment and see if they can figure out what they could learn with it." One of his favorite lines of inquiry has to do with the way light behaves underwater. "I like to get them thinking about what happens to light when it goes into the sea. What happens to colors and how far down do the light rays go? What does it mean for the various life forms if light behaves in a certain way? And, of course, there's my favorite question about what makes the ocean blue." It's not long before the class is generating questions and from the questions they learn to form operationalized, testable hypotheses. "Then we need some evidence, so we go back out to the ocean again to make some more dives to look for the evidence." It's not always easy to know what to do with the evidence, how to analyze it, how to interpret it. So some time is spent back in the classroom again analyzing the data. "It's a way of thinking. If I can get my students started on this way of thinking, they can continue to pursue their own interests in the ocean. If they want a tour, let them hire a guide from a dive shop. I look at this as a course in underwater thinking, quite a contrast from the old stereotype about underwater basket weaving."

Maynard Smith uses case studies in business to cultivate problem-solving and decision-making skills. He spends time at the beginning of each case to get students to define the problem, generate alternative courses of action, and make lists of criteria for evaluating solutions. Although he realizes that there are times when a good thinker wants to suspend judgement, he points out to his students that there are few occasions in the business world where one has that luxury. "Most of the time you will face decisions where there is a high level of ambiguity, that is, no clear-cut choice between the right decision and the wrong decision. Top management knows that there aren't many perfect decisions; they only want to make sure you have included all of the important considerations and have given them the proper weight before you make a recommendation. Sometimes it's a matter of finding the best way out of a real mess." Professor Smith also knows that managers want the recommendations that they are given to be accompanied by projections of probable outcomes. "They want to know what the probabilities of success will be." Professor Smith has found that his students aren't accustomed to thinking in terms of probability. "When they arrive at a solution they think of it as either right or wrong, and they get in some fierce arguments about who is right. I tell them to think about the *chances* of being right and to cast their projections as probabilities. Hey, the weathercasters, even when they're fairly sure, tell you there will be an 80 percent chance of rain."

Edna Wolf begins with a poem, story, or essay that naturally stimulates thought. She wants her students to generate a profusion of ideas, to get their interpretations out on the table, and then to step back and examine those interpretations. "It's one thing to react; it is quite another matter to develop interpretations that hold up under scrutiny and can be defended." Because literature uses the vehicle of language, Professor Wolf devotes most of her energies to getting students to understand how language functions in the thinking process. She is interested in helping students reason about the text at many levels of interpretation simultaneously and to make arguments to support their interpretations based on evidence in the text. She also wants students to examine critically the interpretations that other students make, and eventually the interpretations that the best critics have made. "I'm not so much interested in creative interpretations as I am defensible interpretations. Many of the divergent ideas about how to interpret a piece of writing end up being indefensible. Much of the work of criticism involves reading very carefully, trudging through the text word by word. Then it is time to step back and examine what the author has created, to respond to the metaphors and images. I always tell my students that the creative part comes *after* you have arrived at a sound interpretation, at the point when you ask yourself how the author's vision affects the way you see life when you get up tomorrow morning."

TEACHING THINKING

If there are many types of thinking and many reasons for engaging in thinking, it is not surprising that people ask if such an important activity can be taught. The prospects for teaching thinking depend, once again, on what is meant by "thinking," and how thinking is related to intelligence.

As Raymond Nickerson points out, "intelligence" and "thinking ability" are not necessarily synonymous. "Intelligence relates more to the 'raw power' of one's mental equipment. Raw power is one thing and skilled use of it something else."[33] Thinking involves not only the raw power of intelligence, but tactics and knowledge of content (the subject one is thinking about) as well.[34] Or put still another way, thinking involves operations, knowledge, and dispositions.[35] If a distinction can be made among the various elements of thinking, it would appear that even if nothing (or very little) can be done to improve the raw power of intelligence, perhaps something (or very much) can be done to improve operations, use of relevant knowledge, and dispositions. If thinking is seen as a complex skill or set of skills, it is reasonable to assume that "thinking is something that may be done well or poorly, efficiently or inefficiently, and also to assume that how to do it better is something that one can learn."[36] Nickerson compares learning to think to learning a complex athletic skill, i.e., enlarging "the number of precoded motor programs that the player can call upon to meet the demands of the moment. . . . If thinking skills are really learned behavior patterns, we might expect an analogous effect of training, namely an enlarging of one's repertoire of precoded intellectual performance patterns that function relatively automatically in appropriate contexts."[37] Seen this way, thinking skills appear to be something that can be learned and, therefore, taught.

If thinking skills can be learned, it may be instructive to examine what differentiates skilled thinkers from novice thinkers. What do good thinkers do? A significant amount of research compares what novice and expert thinkers do. Citing many of these studies as evidence, Joanne Kurfiss summarizes the findings as follows:

> Novice-expert studies reveal striking differences between the two groups and striking similarities within groups, regardless of discipline. For example, experts work at the level of principles and plans before plunging into the intricate details of a solution. They may explore a number of possible representations of a problem before they commit to a particular solution. . . . Experts treat a solution plan as a hypothesis, checking their progress frequently to avoid a "wild goose chase." Experts also use heuristics to advance understanding of the problem. Successful problem solvers aggressively seek connections between the present problem and what they already know. Novices, in contrast, exhibit tendencies that preclude success, such as categorizing the problem on the basis of superficial features, failing to

include all elements of the problem in their representation, using trial and error instead of analysis and quitting.[38]

Two concepts embedded in this summary of findings deserve further elaboration—"heuristics" and (though not mentioned specifically) "metacognition." Heuristics are general "rules of thumb" that can be used for guiding the thinking process.[39] For example, "try to find out first what kind of problem this is, before seeking a solution," may be regarded as a heuristic, a rule of thumb that usually works. Expert thinkers use heuristics. Furthermore, expert thinkers become aware of their own thinking through an overall monitoring process known as metacognition, which has been defined as "the use of strategies to monitor and control attention and memory and to make decisions about how to proceed on a task."[40] Stated more simply, metacognition is "being aware of our thinking as we perform specific tasks and then using this awareness to control what we are doing."[41] Examples of metacognition include "planning, predicting, checking, reality testing, and monitoring and control of one's own deliberate attempts to perform intellectually demanding tasks."[42] Expert thinkers, as opposed to novices, have learned to be effective in using heuristics and in employing metacognitive skills.

In recent years, a number of formal "thinking skills programs" have been developed and employed, mostly in school settings, but also in postsecondary settings.[43] Some of these programs emphasize thinking skills in general (such as employing heuristics or using metacognition skills), whereas others emphasize thinking within a particular discipline or field of study. Can thinking skills be taught without using a formal program? Although formal programs provide a specific, well-thought-out structure and often include carefully developed and well-tested materials, surely any teacher who is determined to teach thinking skills can begin to do so by using inquiry and discovery strategies. To do so, however, one must begin by arranging classroom settings so that thinking can occur.

CLASSROOM SETTINGS FOR TEACHING THINKING

What kinds of classroom settings work best for the teaching of thinking? What does the teacher do that is different, for example, from lecturing and explaining, that fosters in the classroom the development of thinking skills through inquiry and discovery? It has been suggested that the shifting of educational priorities to emphasize thinking "requires a redefinition of the function of the class-room," a transforming of the setting for teaching into an "association of thinking" or a "community of inquiry."[44] Sometimes this requires a rearrangement of the physical space of the classroom, such as drawing chairs into a circle, gathering around a seminar table, or setting up "learning centers" where stimulating materials are assembled for investigation, as in a laboratory setting. Usually, however, the "redefinition of the classroom" has more to do with the psychological climate and the changed roles of teachers and students than with physical space. For thinking to take place, students need to get engaged in it, and that often requires some new roles for them and their teachers.

In a classic work on the inquiry strategy in teaching, Neil Postman and Charles Weingartner suggest that teachers who use an inquiry strategy rarely tell students what they should know and use questioning as the primary mode of discourse. These teachers are reluctant to accept a single statement as an answer to a question; they encourage student-student interaction, rarely summarize "conclusions," and usually let the "lesson" develop from the responses of students to a problem that has been posed.[45]

One useful list of what teachers do to create a classroom climate for thinking includes the following:

- **Listening to Students**—taking time to listen to what students are really saying.
- **Appreciating Individuality and Openness**—accepting each student's contribution as a precious thing and emphasizing the process, as opposed to finding the right answer.
- **Encouraging Open Discussion**—providing a climate where students can discuss their ideas and viewpoints with the teacher and each other.
- **Promoting Active Learning**—getting students involved in activities that require solving real problems, as opposed to telling about and showing how.
- **Accepting Students' Ideas**—providing an atmosphere where students' ideas are prized and it is safe to make mistakes.
- **Allowing Time to Think**—taking sufficient time to make guesses, try ideas out, see if they work and assimilate them.
- **Nurturing Confidence**—providing opportunities for students to be successful at thinking so that they develop the self-assurance to "dare" to think.

- **Giving Facilitative Feedback**—raising additional questions and challenging students to think further, but without quizzing students or chastising them for shallow thinking.
- **Appreciating Students' Ideas**—truly valuing what students say by admitting a mistake (as teacher) or acknowledging something you have never thought of before.[46]

Although these are excellent guidelines for what teachers often do when they use an inquiry strategy, it is important to remember that there are many kinds of inquiry lessons and that within these there will be additional (often subtle) shifts in the teacher's behavior. Sometimes the inquiry is open-ended, and there is no right answer or conclusion. At other times, there may, in fact, be a right answer; but it may be hard to find. Sometimes the task involves deducing or reasoning out the answer; whereas at other times the goal is to build up the best answer from the available evidence. At still other times, the teacher is trying to foster a unique insight or creative output.[47] The teacher's role may take on a slightly different emphasis as the goal of the inquiry shifts.

Students also take on different roles when an inquiry strategy is used; and if they have not had much previous experience with inquiry strategies, they can be puzzled or resistant. It may take a considerable amount of explaining and labeling to help students understand that their role is to become actively involved as thinkers and problem solvers. Once they "catch on" to their role, most students become highly motivated; in fact, "high arousal and as a result, maximal attention" has been identified as one of the key benefits of an inquiry strategy for students.[48] In some cases, high arousal is coupled with high expectations; and when anticipated successes don't come (or arrive only after great difficulty), frustration can set in. A teacher who is effective in using inquiry strategies is sensitive to the potential for frustration for students and walks the fine line between challenge and support.

How do teachers evaluate student learning when an inquiry strategy is employed? In classrooms where thinking is valued, teachers often take a unique route to the evaluation of student outcomes. Because "memory of the facts" or "performance of a skill" are not usually the objective, teachers have to develop other approaches to student evaluation. If the goal is to develop thinking processes, how does the teacher evaluate such a process? This is not easy, but Postman and Weingartner provide some provocative suggestions.[49] They urge teachers to look for the following things in their students:

The frequency with which they ask questions; the increase in the relevance and cogency of their questions; the frequency and conviction of their challenges to assertions made by other students or teachers or textbooks; the relevance and clarity of the standards on which they base their challenges; their willingness to suspend judgments when they have insufficient data; their willingness to modify or otherwise change their position when data warrant such change; the increase in their skill in observing, classifying, generalizing, etc; the increase in their tolerance for diverse answers; their ability to apply generalizations, attitudes and information to novel situations.

This is a difficult list to implement and hardly lends itself to standardized, multiple-choice tests, but it does suggest some of the important kinds of behaviors that teachers might seek in their students. Some of these behaviors will "appear before the teacher's eyes," but others, if operationalized carefully, lend themselves to more extended paper and pencil tests, such as "essay questions" and "term papers" where "thinking" is specifically required and formally displayed."[50]

What takes place in classrooms when teachers use inquiry strategies is often quite different from what goes on in "conventional classrooms." Barry Beyer sums it up well:[51]

The most supportive environment for the teaching and learning of thinking exists where student and teacher thinking can occur continuously, where learning activities regularly require thinking, and where students and teachers frequently reflect on and discuss their thinking. In such classrooms the active search for knowledge constitutes the focus of learning.

In the following sections of this chapter, three different types of thinking skills are explored in greater detail and examples of how to teach these skills are provided in the classrooms of Professors Jacques LaMer, Maynard Smith, and Edna Wolf.

THINKING AND REASONING

At the heart of the educational experience, whatever the setting, is an encounter with knowledge. The building blocks of knowledge are assertions—statements that something is so. In a course in ocean studies, for example, a professor might make one of the following four statements:

Most fish are very responsive to sunlight.

Most fish are not very responsive to sunlight.

Fish that dwell at the ocean bottoms are not very responsive to sunlight.

Even fish that dwell at the ocean bottoms are very responsive to sunlight.

Once an assertion has been made, reason can be used to examine it.

Assertions are part of a larger framework of arguments and beliefs. A series of assertions can be put together to make an argument that supports a belief. The word "belief" is slippery because in popular usage it is often confused with opinion, and sometimes refers to religious beliefs that are understood to be a matter of faith. But when philosophers use the word "belief," they are referring to ideas that can be supported by logical or empirical evidence.[52] In other words, for philosophers, beliefs are to be understood as expressions of knowledge. To say "I believe . . . " is to say "I know. . . ." Some beliefs are well supported, and are, therefore, more credible. Conversely, beliefs that are less well supported are less credible. Beliefs are expressed, therefore, in degrees of confidence. People generally try to use reasoning in framing the assertions that make up the arguments that support their beliefs. Beliefs that are well supported get acknowledged as "knowledge." Beliefs that are unsupported, or supported by only very little evidence, are sometimes called "irrational beliefs." Beliefs are important because people act on them. People who act on well-supported beliefs are said to be acting rationally, reasonably, or on the basis of knowledge. This is why knowledge is so important—having it, knowing what it is, and knowing where it comes from. Knowledge depends heavily on reasoning.

For centuries philosophers have divided the reasoning processes that support beliefs into two general categories: deductive and inductive reasoning. Deductive reasoning refers to the pattern of reasoning used in arguments such as the following:

All fish fly.
All guppies are fish.
All guppies fly.

Deductive reasoning usually involves several assertions and has to do with the rules that govern the relationships among the assertions. The formal name given to a set of assertions, such as those above about guppies, is "syllogism."[53] Now it is true that students don't sit around the residence hall lounge examining syllogisms. But some-times, buried within the statements that students make in a class discussion, are assertions that take on the pattern of a syllogism. Consider the following:

> Do all fish see? Well, how can you tell if a fish sees? I'd say if they have eyes. That's what eyes are for, for seeing. So I would say that if we are trying to figure out whether fish see, then lets look to see if they have eyes. Sure, the eyes will differ, but if they all have eyes, then in some sense, they all see. I don't know of any fish that don't have eyes, so I would say all fish see.

If that wandering argument is reduced to its bare essentials and searched for its basic assertions, and if the assertions are arranged in order, they appear as follows:

> All eyes are used for seeing.
> All fish have eyes.
> All fish see.

Here we have a syllogism, a set of assertions governed by rules that regulate the logic of the argument. It is not easy (as a teacher) to spot the syllogisms buried in the rapid-fire exchanges among students engaged in a hot classroom debate. It is even harder to get students to spot their syllogisms. But the elements of deductive reasoning are often there, and as such, they become a useful medium for examining thinking. In general, the premises (content of the statements) of a deductive argument need to be true, and the premises need to be arranged in such a way that the conclusions follow logically from the premises.

There are some things that can go wrong with the deductive reasoning used in syllogisms.[54] The first thing that can go wrong is that students will confuse the validity of the *form* of the argument with the truth of the conclusions. In both of the syllogisms about fish cited above, the syllogism is valid with regard to the *form* of the argument, but the conclusions are not true, in either case, because one of the premises is false. In the first syllogism, the first premise, "All fish fly," is not true; and in the second syllogism, "All fish have eyes" is not true. (There are some fish with no eyes that dwell in dark caves.) The logic of the syllogisms is valid, but the content of the premises is wrong. The nature of this content is sometimes referred to as "ecological validity," the truth of the statement in a real life context.[55]

Another thing that can go wrong with a syllogism is the way that the premises are linked. There are many ways to pair premises, and the number of possible combinations of premises is extensive.[56] Further complication comes from the use of "qualifiers," such as "all," "no," "some," and "not" in the premises.

The psychological processes for dealing with syllogisms have been studied extensively, and not surprisingly, common recurring patterns of error have been identified.[57] Not only do the sheer number of possibilities tend to overwhelm, but certain qualifiers apparently predispose people to positive conclusions. Without going into the many opportunities for error, it is safe to say that there is no general formula for evaluating syllogisms. It is necessary to examine each one, not only for logical structure but for the ecological validity of the premises. The idea that syllogisms are "simple proofs" is misleading.

Other forms of deductive reasoning also "go by the rules," and these, too, can be complicated.[58] One of these involves linear ordering problems such as:

Dolphins are bigger than tuna
but not as big as whales

These are fairly straightforward as long as the comparisons are positive and of the same order. What most people do is to use spatial imagery to make a mental diagram, such as the following:

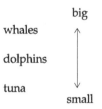

These problems get complicated, however, when the terms, in this case the sea dwellers, are rearranged and negative superlatives are used for comparison. For example, with regard to the ability to communicate, one might state:

Whales are worse than dolphins.
Tuna are worse than dolphins.
Which is the worst? Dolphins, whales, tuna or don't know?

The answer is "don't know." Tuna and whales are worse than dolphins, but between tuna and whales there is no evidence to label one "worst."

Still another form of deductive reasoning involves "if, then" statements. Known formally as *modus ponens* and *modus tollens* statements, these involve an "if clause," called the "antecedent," and a "then clause," called the "consequent."[59] For example:

> If there is a higher concentration of plankton in the water, then there will be more whales.

The statement must be "true" or "supportable" in itself to begin with. If it is, then there are various ways to reason about it, some being valid, others not. The first invalid argument is called "denying the antecedent" and the second is called "affirming the consequent."[60] There are conditions where the "then" follows logically and conditions where it does not.

The interesting thing about deductive reasoning from a psychological standpoint is that as the problems get more complex, they demand more of the thinker—more complex mental images, more "translations" of terms to make them equivalent, more concepts to "keep in mind," more alternatives to consider, and more operations (such as comparisons) to perform. As the complexity increases, the opportunity for error increases. The temptation to quit thinking also increases. The need for good monitoring (metacognitive) skills is greater, of course, as the opportunity for error increases. Deductive reasoning is surely not a matter of "simple ironclad proofs."

The other general category used by philosophers in describing reasoning processes is called "inductive reasoning." It is generally distinguished as a process of "building up" conclusions from empirical evidence. Whereas deductive reasoning involves reaching "necessary" conclusions derived by a "top-down" process of following the rules to make valid arguments, inductive reasoning involves building up the evidence until there is enough to draw a conclusion. The strength of an inductive argument is based on the amount and quality of evidence available. In the strict sense, then, inductive reasoning is always "invalid" because the conclusions are not necessary but only probable.[61] Inductive reasoning is what people do most frequently in everyday contexts, and it is the kind of reasoning found most frequently in academic classrooms and laboratories.

Although a sharp formal distinction is made between deductive and inductive reasoning, they are actually quite closely related.

In the deductive argument in the syllogism that begins "No fish fly," the ecological validity (content) of the first premise must be established. How is that to be done? By building an *inductive* argument based on the systematic study of the flying abilities of fish. The *processes* involved in the two forms of reasoning are quite different, however.

Inductive reasoning involves primarily a generalization process, "reasoning from parts to wholes, from few to all, from the particular to the general."[62] The process involves looking at specific instances and making generalizations about what one has observed in these instances that applies to other similar instances. As Nickerson notes, this process of being able to generalize depends on the assumption of regularity, that is, "on confidence in the lawfulness and noncapriciousness of the world. . . ." Regularity, in this sense, is the foundation of knowledge. How does one reason in such a world?

In postsecondary settings teachers encounter two kinds of inductive reasoning, formal and informal. Many college teachers, especially in the social and physical sciences and the professions that depend on them, have received training in the formal processes of inductive reasoning, usually through research methods courses and by conducting their own research. In formal research methods, a great deal of emphasis is put on framing a question, identifying a population for study, selecting a sample, making hypotheses, gathering data to test the hypotheses, making inferences to the larger population (sometimes with complex statistical procedures), and drawing conclusions. These formal procedures can break down at every step throughout the process. Although specific methods vary from field to field, the results of formal research studies are, of course, the basis of "knowledge" in the various academic disciplines and professions. Side by side with these formal methods, however, are the informal inductive methods students and teachers use all the time to "think aloud" in class discussions. When students (or teachers) are making assertions in a discussion, they are using inductive methods that follow similar, but slightly different, processes from those used in research. In making an assertion, they are really advancing a conclusion (a hypothesis based on evidence), and in drawing up the evidence they are sampling from a pool of already available knowledge or experience in memory to defend their assertion. The problems of sampling from that pool of knowledge and experience, making inferences and drawing conclusions, are similar to the problems encountered in more formal research processes. A better understanding of formal and informal inductive reasoning can be gained by examining some of the places where that reasoning commonly "goes wrong," that is, in typical errors in reasoning.[63]

One of the places where inductive reasoning breaks down is at the very beginning in the failure to define and operationalize terminology. If assertions are to be made about whether fish can see, it is necessary to define what is meant by "see." Because no person can ever get inside a fish and know for sure what they "see," it becomes necessary to operationalize the construct "see" in terms of behavioral responses to light and absence of light. Likewise, many informal discussions involving inductive reasoning flounder because constructs have not been operationalized in a way that the participants can tell what is being discussed.

Inductive reasoning also breaks down when sampling procedures are inadequate. In most formal research—because time and resources are limited—a sample must be drawn to undertake the study. Trained researchers know that there are guidelines to follow in determining both the composition and size of the sample. In informal inductive reasoning, a similar "sampling" problem exists when people are called upon to examine the evidence that supports their assertions. There is a strong tendency not to consider enough evidence; that is, to look at some of the evidence (a small biased sample) and then jump to a conclusion. There is also a tendency in informal reasoning to latch on to the most readily available evidence. When subjects were asked to estimate which is more frequent in English, words that start with the letter "k" or words that have "k" as a third letter, most subjects chose initial "k." In fact, there are more "third-letter-k" words, but the memory is not set up as well to retrieve them as to retrieve "initial k" words. The mind tends to use the sample of information most readily available and easily retrieved.

Inductive reasoning also breaks down in the forming and testing of hypotheses. For a hypothesis to be a true hypothesis, it must be set up in such a way that it can be tested, that is, supported or *not* supported. In formal research, this means wording the hypothesis carefully and gathering evidence in an unbiased way, so that the hypothesis has an equal chance of succeeding or failing. In informal reasoning this means being open to the evidence against one's assertions as well as the evidence for them. Unfortunately, when humans "reason," they tend to neglect the evidence *against* their assertions. Research studies have established what has come to be known as "the confirmation bias," the all-too-human tendency to seek evidence that confirms an assertion (or hypothesis) to the neglect of information that would disconfirm it. For example, when subjects are given a set of numbers (such as 8, 10, 12), and are asked to generate the rule governing the numbers, they will hypothesize the rule to be "successive even numbers." Then they will offer other sets of successive even numbers (16, 18, 20) to *confirm* the hypothesis. Rarely will subjects test the adequacy of their hypothesis by offering numbers that will *disconfirm* their initial hypothesis and suggest another series, such as 9, 11, 12 or 8, 9, 10. The rule could be, of course, "successive numbers," and disconfirming evidence from "odd numbers" would lead to that rule. The evidence from psychological studies on "confirmation bias" is overwhelming. Unfortunately, many people "reason" like the neurotic Bostonian who kept snapping his fingers to keep elephants out of his room because it had worked so well in the past.[64] Before a hypothesis can be established, counter-hypotheses should be offered and *disconfirming* evidence should be sought.

Unfortunately, however, the problems with hypotheses don't end there. Even when people do seek disconfirming evidence, when that evidence comes in, they tend to ignore it and keep their original hypothesis. Research shows that even when contradicting data has been received in abundance, the original hypothesis (because I made it?) is not easily discarded. Furthermore, when new hypotheses must be generated (after reluctantly giving up the old), too few hypotheses are generated. In fact, there is a strong human tendency to oversimplify and cast most situations as dichotomous—if it isn't this, it must be that—when a far more productive approach would be to generate several hypotheses.[65] People become attached to the hypotheses they make; they don't like to have them disproved and are reluctant to make new ones. Good thinkers are aware of these human tendencies and guard against them.

Inductive reasoning also breaks down when evidence is interpreted. Once the relevant data have been collected and analyzed, their meaning is not always self-evident. An interpretation needs to be made; and once again, human error enters into interpretation. One of the most common problems of interpretation involves correlations. Many hypotheses are set up to examine the relationship of two or more events or variables. When two events occur together, they may be said to co-relate or "correlate." But what does it mean that two events correlate and when does that actually happen? If the hypothesis, for example, states that a higher grade point average is related to living on campus in a residence hall, what would it mean to say that those occurrences are correlated? In formal research, after the actual data have been collected, there are sophisticated ways of analyzing the data to compute what is called a correlation coefficient, that is, a measure of how frequently these events are related as reflected in the data. In doing so, the formula takes into account not only all of the times that the events are related, but also how often they are *not* related. In less formal reasoning, the same process takes place, but there is a greater tendency to give importance to the instances of being related than to the instances of *not* being related.[66] If people see examples of two things being related, they tend to give undue importance to those instances, while failing to look for (or even consider) that there may be numerous instances where the events may not be related. Even worse, when a genuine relationship does exist, there is a tendency to leap from the idea of "correlation" to "causation." Just because two events are related, does not mean that one is causing the other. One might tend to leap to the conclusion that living in a campus residence hall causes students to earn higher grades. The reasoning fallacy in this leap is evident when the direction of supposed causality is reversed. Do high grades cause students to go live in residence halls?

In summing up the psychological research on reasoning, Nickerson notes that "many people reason as though they were trying to minimize cognitive load, rather than to make sound inferences." Careless reasoners will "casually elevate correlation to causation, affirm the consequent, persevere with hypotheses, and do whatever else keeps cognitive load down, so long as the conclusion does not conflict with . . . intuitions."[67] For most teachers this becomes a shocking affirmation of their deepest fear: "students are too lazy to think." On the other hand, deductive and inductive reasoning are hard work, not only for students but for all people, and it is only with great expenditure of effort that these forms of reasoning can be employed with any degree of success. Teachers can play an important role in helping students to understand where reasoning breaks down by letting their students know what to watch out for and do when the cognitive load gets too heavy.

When we want to have our students become familiar with the thinking processes involved in deductive and inductive reasoning we must give our students the opportunity to engage in those processes. Although it may be useful to explain to students much more about how these processes work than is usually done, learning "how to think" results from *doing* thinking under the critical guidance of a teacher. Consider what Jacques LaMer does with his class in Ocean Life Forms.

The students in Jacques LaMer's course at Pacific Coast Community College have gathered for their first class on a warm Friday evening, and they are excited about their all-day dive trip on Saturday.[68] But they are a little nervous, too. They have heard that Jacques LaMer has a reputation for making students think and nobody wants to look dumb.

"Take out a little piece of paper and a pencil."

"Not a test already, you haven't taught us anything." The class laughs nervously.

LaMer smiles. "In this class you have to teach yourselves." He pauses and returns to the instructions. "On your paper, I want you to write one or more answers to the question: Why is the ocean blue?"

Students look at each other and frown. It sounds simple enough; and it seems like they should know the answer, but most of them look baffled. "The ocean is blue because . . . " LaMer encourages them to write some reasons. After a few minutes he asks, "How many of you wrote one reason?" Most of the hands go up. "How about writing one or two more?"

"But isn't there only one reason that's right?" one student asks.

LaMer shrugs. "Maybe there is, but won't we want to check some other reasons, too, to see if they could be right or wrong?"

The students start writing more reasons. After a few minutes LaMer asks them to put their reasons in a safe place, so that they can come back to them in a couple of weeks. Then he asks, "What is the name that scientists give to those reasons you just wrote out?"

A hand shoots up. "Hypothesis, hypotheses?"

"Right—singular and plural." He writes it on the board. "Hypotheses. We like to have several." He sits on the edge of the desk. "Tomorrow we go on our first dive. You're all certified, right? And you've got your gear reserved? Some of you are more experienced than others, so most of this will be at no more than 35 feet, but I want two teams to go to 65 feet with me. We're going to be looking for something."

"Sharks?"

"No sharks. That's an irrational belief, anyway. Sharks probably wouldn't bother you. No . . . what we are looking for is light. The light that comes down on the ocean from the sun. What happens to it? If you can understand what happens to light, you can unlock a lot of secrets about what goes on down there. What do you think we'll find? Let's make some hypotheses."

"I think it will get darker as we go deeper."

"That's a good one. Here," he gives the chalk to a student, "write that on the board for us. Anything else?"

There is silence.

"One hypothesis. That's all we're going to look for? You could at least give me its opposite."

"You mean it won't get darker?"

"Exactly. We better check that out, too. We call it disconfirming evidence. What else?"

"Well, if it does get darker the deeper you go, there ought to be some rate, so like is it a uniform rate, or all at once at a certain depth or what?"

"That's good. Very good."

"And what about the colors. I've noticed that the colors are different. So maybe you don't lose it all at once, you just lose some of it."

"Those are great. We can work on getting those into just the right words, to operationalize them, but in general I'd say you've got the idea of hypotheses. Now . . . how could we test these hypotheses? What could we do tomorrow to . . ."

"We could look to see how things actually are at different depths."

"Good. And how could we be very systematic about that?"

"Well, we're in buddy pairs already, so we could use our depth indicators and check things out at various levels, like 10 feet, 15 feet, and so on."

"That's great. What you're suggesting is that we take a sample. We can't check out the whole ocean. So let's take a sample reading at 5 feet, 10 feet, 15 feet, and so on. How could we do that besides just looking?"

"Well, I've got a camera," one student offers.

"Good, and I've got some cameras for you too," LaMer answers. "Now, let's see, do we want to use the flash or what?"

A hand is waving wildly in the back. "I've got it. Let's get different groups. We'll have some just looking through our masks with the naked eye. Some will take pictures with no flash, and some with flash. And we'll do it like he said, every five feet."

"Sounds great. I'll organize a team of advanced divers and we'll do the same at 35 feet, 50 feet, and 65 feet. What do you think we'll see?"

The rest of the evening was spent in getting acquainted, forming teams, making transportation arrangements, and solving equipment problems.

Saturday was a perfect day, a clear sky and lots of bright sunlight pouring down on the blue ocean. The class boarded the two dive boats with their gear, their cameras, and lunch, and set out across the bay for the dive sites. After the routine buddy checking and rechecking of gear, the dive was underway. Everything went like clockwork. One by one the students entered the water and gathered at the anchor line to make their controlled descent. Those observing with their eyes had their underwater writing slates; those with cameras had agreed on high speed film, and the deep divers were set with their special plans for rendezvousing at 35, 50, and 65 feet. They gathered the data as planned at high noon, and then came up for lunch. After checking out their dive charts for a sufficient wait, they made a second pleasure dive. Many of the students were commenting at the end of the day that they were already seeing things they hadn't seen before, and they were fascinated by the differences they were observing in the light. Everyone agreed to have their reports written, the film developed, and the pictures labeled by depth for class next Friday.

Jacques LaMer had rearranged the classroom into work stations designated by depth at 5 feet, 10 feet, etc. "Let's get the data organized at each table. Drop off your reports and pictures at the stations, and then we'll assign teams by depth to analyze what we got."

The students were excited to see how the pictures turned out and how the information from the different sets of data compared. Not all the pictures were usable, but there was enough data to indicate a trend. LaMer asked the teams at each table to report on their data by depth, while a recorder put notes on the board.

"At five feet, everything is still pretty clear. The picture without the flash is a little darker, but we're still getting good light. The observers' reports fit the pictures."

"At 25 feet you can begin to see some real differences, especially in color. You still get vivid colors with the flash, but the camera alone is pooping out. The red is gone, and everything red using the flash is brown to the naked eye."

Each of the groups reported for each depth. After LaMer gave the students a chance to walk around to each station to look at all the pictures and reports, he asked them to take their seats. "O.K., now comes the tough part. We've really got to do some thinking. What does it all mean? What patterns do we see?"

There was silence. LaMer waited it out. He'd ask them to think, so give them a chance, right?

"Well, it gets darker, like our hypothesis said it would."

"So the evidence is accumulating in support of that hypothesis. Now we can make an assertion. We can say, the deeper we go the darker it gets. And if a lot of other scientists agreed with us, we would say we have good evidence for that belief. What else?"

"The light gets stopped. And it seems like there is a pattern to it the deeper you go, a regular pattern."

"But it's not all at once," another student adds, "because of the colors. It seems that the reds go out first, and then I can't quite tell, yellow disappears, and at 65 feet everything seems to just look blue, like one flat color of blue."

"Great observations. You are confirming some of the great experiments in oceanography. There is a lot of evidence for that belief. But now . . . why? If that's what's happening, why?"

More puzzled looks. Then a student asks, "you mean why does the light get stopped?"

"Exactly. What would be your inference?"

"Inference?"

"Yes, like your conclusion."

"Well, I don't know for sure but . . . maybe it's like when you jump off of a 50 feet diving board . . ."

"Not me . . ."

"Well, if one were to . . . one would go through the air faster than water, and when you hit the water. . . ."

"Splat," a student in the back row shouts.

"Right," LaMer notes with a chuckle. "Splat, because why?"

"Because water is more dense. It slows things up."

"Even light?" a student asks.

"Actually," LaMer adds, "the light slows down from 186,000 miles a second to 140,000 miles per second. Water is eight times more dense than air. So, yes, splat! What else?"

"Isn't there something about the light getting bent, too. I remember those pictures of the stick getting bent in water."

"And as the rays get bent what happens?"

"Oh, I've got it, I've got it. It's like a prism. So certain rays get stopped more than others, and that's why the red gets knocked out, and then the yellow, and at 65 feet everything's just blue? Could that be it?

"Well, if we had a spectrophotometer, and we could take it down in the ocean with us, that's exactly what we would find; different light frequencies are lost at different depths."

"But doesn't some of it get stopped by all the crud that's in the water. I mean, the algae and . . ."

"Sure, some of the light is actually absorbed by what it hits and some of it gets bounced around—we say, 'dispersed.'" LaMer pauses.

"Say, you are really terrific at this. Let's take a little break for snacks and when we come back we'll talk about what all this means for making food in the ocean."

When the students return to class, LaMer asks them if they have ever heard of photosynthesis. Most of the hands go up. "What's needed for photosynthesis?"

"Chlorophyll."

"And . . ."

"Sunlight."

"Bingo. So what are your hypotheses about where you will find algae, photoplankton, and other plant life in the ocean?"

"Where there's light."

LaMer thinks he can actually see the light bulbs popping on in his students' heads.

"If it takes light for photosynthesis, then . . ." the student pauses to think.

"If, then. That's good," LaMer encourages her. "If, then . . . what?" LaMer asks.

"Well, most of the food is near the top. I mean, how far down is there still enough light for photosynthesis?"

"Great question, what's your hunch?"

"Sixty-five feet?"

"Actually a little more than that. But we could have designed a dive to check it out, couldn't we? What we would find is that it's somewhere between 200 and 300 feet. So if that's where the food is, at the first 300 feet, then . . . If, then?"

"That's where the fish will be?"

"That's right."

"But don't some fish just eat other fish?"

"Yes, and those fish eat smaller fish, and those fish eat smaller fish, but eventually we get down to the vegetarians at the bottom of the food chain. So . . ."

"But surely there are fish that swim below 300 feet."

"Actually the ocean is very sparsely populated between 300 feet and 1500 feet. Then below 1500 there are the deep dwellers, those that live in the abyss. And what do you think they do?"

There is a long pause. "Well, they must catch other fish down there, or if not, I guess they come up, and . . ."

LaMer is pleased at how much has been accomplished already, how much good thinking is going on. "Is anyone interested in a night dive? What do you think we might see on a night dive? Any hypotheses?"

"Oh, no, not more hypotheses!"

"More fish or fewer fish at night?" LaMer asks. "What's your guess? Any hypotheses? Bring me your hunches about what we might see on a night dive when you come to class next Friday. Oh, yes, and by the way, can anyone tell me now why the ocean is blue? Take out that piece of paper and check out the reasons you wrote down."

The class is over. Students gather up their pictures. A student stops by at LaMer's desk on the way out and grins sheepishly: "I said the ocean was blue because of the reflection of the sky."

"Don't feel bad. That's what most people think. Now you know ..."

"The other light rays get absorbed, and there are a lot of blue ones left so they get reflected back. Is that it?"

"Bingo."

THINKING, PROBLEM SOLVING, AND DECISION MAKING

Life is full of problems calling out for solutions. Some of these problems are the "real" problems that people face in their daily lives at home, in the community, or on the job. Solving these problems is important and may be a significant step on the road to success and happiness. Other problems are of a more abstract and "impractical" nature, such as certain mathematical and logic problems, and are used mainly to "stretch the mind" or even entertain. Solving these problems is a challenge, but their resolution won't bring a pay raise or a more satisfying community or family life. Classroom settings are often used to practice solving both impractical and real life problems, and most postsecondary teachers are eager to have their students expand and sharpen their problem-solving abilities. Are there special techniques that students can learn to use in solving problems?

The term "problem solving" is used to indicate those processes directed toward an intellectually demanding task, the completion of which leads to an important or satisfying solution. Diane Halpern cites a classic example of a problem:

> Suppose you're driving alone at night on a long, dark stretch of freeway that is infrequently traveled when you suddenly hear the familiar "thump-thump" of a flat tire. You pull on to the shoulder of the road to begin the unpleasant task of changing a tire, illuminated only with the light of the moon and a small flashlight. Carefully, you remove the lug nuts and place them in a hubcap by the roadside. A

speeding motorist whizzes past you, hitting the hubcap and scatter-
ing the lug nuts across the dark freeway and out of sight. Here you
sit, a spare tire in one hand, a flat tire propped against the car and no
lug nuts, on a dark night on a lonely stretch of freeway. To make
matters worse, a cold rain is beginning to fall. What would you do?[69]

How is the problem to be solved? What kind of a problem is it and
what strategies might be brought to bear in solving it?

Halpern reports that one of her students claimed to have had
this problem occur in another setting, during daytime, with the
following resolution:

> . . . the flat tire occurred alongside a large mental institution near our
> college. While the hapless motorist sat pondering his problem, he
> attracted the attention of several "residents" of the institution, who
> gathered near the motorist along the chain link fence that separated
> them. One resident offered this solution to the motorist's problem:
> Remove one lug nut from each of the other tires and use them to attach
> the spare. Each tire should hold securely with three lug nuts until the
> motorist reaches a gas station. The grateful motorist thanked the
> institution resident and then asked, "How'd you think of such a good
> solution to this problem?" The resident replied, "I'm not dumb, I'm
> just crazy!"[70]

There are, of course, many different types of problems. A cross-
word puzzle presents challenges that are very different from a jigsaw
puzzle. Some problems are well-defined and some are ill-defined.[71]
Problems also vary in the nature of the skills required, in the appropriate approach to be taken, and in the level of difficulty, that is, both
in the kinds and numbers of cognitive processes involved. An effective approach for solving one problem may not be effective for
solving another.[72] In studies of novice and expert problem solvers, it
was discovered that experts have more domain specific knowledge—they know the subject area better—and they manage their
intellectual resources better. Which is more important? Both are
important, but it is precisely when one runs out of domain-specific
knowledge that one needs even better skills at managing intellectual
resources.

Is there a general way to approach a problem, even though
many problems are quite different? The classic study of problem
solving is Newell and Simon's *Human Problem Solving*, first published in 1972.[73] These authors provide a general scheme, now represented in many texts, for thinking about the problem-solving
process. Most problems call for an answer or resolution, which might

be called the "goal state"—what things will be like when the problem is solved. A problem also has an "initial state," the conditions that are given along with the statement of the problem. The distance (gap) between the initial state and goal state is the "problem space," the area within which the problem can be worked out. Within this problem space a variety of "solution paths" can be generated. This simple, but very useful, model for thinking about a problem can be diagrammed as follows:

PROBLEM SPACE

INITIAL STATE ⟹ Solution Paths ⟹ GOAL STATE

A short and efficient solution path is highly desirable in reaching the goal state.[74]

Given this model, the problem-solving process can be divided into steps or stages as follows: understand the problem, devise a plan or strategy, carry out the plan with revisions as necessary, and check the results.[75] The first step is extremely important and involves thinking carefully not only about the goal state (what outcome is called for) but also the initial state (what information, givens, and constraints are embedded in the problem). As the problem gradually comes to be understood, it is represented as a particular kind of problem. This representation is extremely important because it influences the strategies to be used and the various solution paths that will be considered.[76] Very often a "mental model" is used to represent the problem. In the instance of the flat tire presented above, it would have been useful to think of the problem as "get enough lug nuts to attach the tire." Expert problem solvers have a repertory of "mental models" so that when they confront a problem, they are able to represent it as a mental model and compare it with other mental models stored in memory. Research has shown that expert problem solvers can represent and classify problems correctly even when they have only one-fifth of the problem, long before they have enough data to actually formulate a solution.[77] Thus, problems can be grouped by type.

Some problems, for example, are problems of arrangement, as with anagrams where the task is to take a series of letters, CAISTSSIT, for instance, and rearrange them into a word, STATISTICS. Other problems require the discovery of a structure or relationship, as with analogy problems such a "Listen is to hear as look is to . . ."

Still other problems may be classified as transformation problems, when objects must be rearranged within a set of fixed rules, as in "move the three coins to a new position without . . ."[78] Once the type of problem has been identified (assuming a correct identification), the problem itself restricts what is possible and determines which strategies are suitable.

Devising a plan usually involves a search process—looking for various solution paths that fit the type of problem. Some search strategies are more efficient than others. An "exhaustive search" involves examining every possible alternative in some order; a "random search" involves no systematic order and no memory for previous paths tried; and a "trial and error" search involves trying some alternatives until a desirable one is found. These methods work best when the range of alternatives (solution paths) is very small. For example, in working with the anagram THA, there are only six possible solution paths for rearranging these letters, THA, TAH, HTA, HAT, ATH, AHT. The problem solver will arrive at a solution through trial and error when HAT is discovered, and even when HAT is the last option considered, it will be discovered eventually through both random and exhaustive search techniques. But when there are many solution paths and the solution paths themselves are complex and branching, these search methods become highly inefficient.[79] In fact, one might say that an exhaustive search is not "intelligent." It is at this point that effective problem solvers turn to heuristics, rules of thumb that will narrow down the search process so that fewer solution paths can be considered and the "right" solution paths can be discovered more rapidly. Although many complex heuristics are available, only a few of the more useful ones are presented here.

One useful heuristic is called "means-ends analysis." If the goal is the "end," and the "means" for getting there are not clear, it is sometimes useful to find subgoals, and then to devise means of reaching these. In plain language this is called dividing the problem into subproblems. In a frequently cited example known as the Tower of Hanoi Problem, the object is to move three coins from one stack (quarter, nickel, penny) and restack them in the same size order at another site using only one intermediary site and moving only one coin at a time. The mental model looks like this:

INITIAL STATE   GOAL STATE

Defining and developing a model of the problem is not difficult, but as one begins to search for a solution, a state of confusion begins to set in as the variety of solution paths present themselves. One thing to do with this problem is to seek an intermediary goal, a subgoal, which is a step along the way toward the ultimate goal state. One subgoal is to get the quarter on the third site. That can be done by freeing the quarter of the penny and nickel, by moving the penny to the third site, the nickel to the second site, and the penny back to the nickel. At this point the third site is vacant, ready for the quarter. The subgoal has been achieved. The next subgoal is to get the nickel back on the quarter. This can be achieved by moving the penny back to the first site, thus freeing the nickel so that it can be moved to the quarter at the third site. And so on.[80] The point, of course, is that the mental operations required for solving the problem can be managed better by working on subgoals, one at a time.

Another heuristic is to work backwards, the reverse of the means-ends analysis. The paper and pencil mazes that children enjoy working are usually more easily solved (is it cheating?) by starting at the goal and working backwards. This strategy works because there are fewer paths leading back from the goal than from the start. Working forward, each turn in the maze is a decision point; but working backward, the decision points turn into inevitabilities. Some problems are solved best by working from the goal state back to the initial state.[81]

Another heuristic involves the split-half method. Diane Halpern illustrates this with a game she invented. She is able to guess the age of anyone under 100 in seven guesses by using the split-half method. First, one asks the subject if they are under 50. If the answer is yes, the next inquiry is whether they are older than 25. And so on. The next question always splits the remaining amount in half until the answer is found.[82] In a sense, the old parlor game "Twenty Questions" can be played effectively by using variations of the split-half method. When the question is asked, "Is it bigger than a bread box" (assuming that people today know what a bread box is), the questioner is working on the dimension of "space" and has used the "bread box question" to categorize smaller and larger objects.

Whatever the answer, one can follow the question with another, which again divides the remaining space in some way. Although this technique works best with spatial dimensions, a variation of the method is used by asking if something designated "animal" is a "land-animal" or "mammal" or "four-legged," because these questions also seek to split up the territory, if not into halves, at least into definable dimensions. The split-half method and its variations can be used to narrow down the solution paths in a very efficient manner. There are other heuristics, including simplifying the problem, using an analogous problem for which the answer is known, inserting actual numbers for the variables in order to test what happens, and others.[83] The more complex the array of possible solution paths, the greater the need for a heuristic.

Once a solution has been derived, it is important to re-examine the problem in light of the solution. There is a tendency, once having found a solution, to stop thinking. But is this really the solution *to the problem*, or is it just another attractive idea? Effective problem solvers will examine the solution carefully to see if it matches the problem. They will also seek to solve the problem in another way and will even seek ways to disconfirm the solution.[84] In short, the solution may not be the only solution, the best solution, or (for that matter) even the solution.

Like other ways of thinking, problem solving has its hazards, its ways of going wrong. There is a temptation in the beginning to misread the problem and rush into solutions before a clear understanding of both the goal state and initial state have been obtained. Furthermore, in reading the problem (or otherwise confronting it), there is a strong tendency to bring to the problem one's personal presuppositions. Presuppositions are dangerous and ubiquitous; they are the constraints imported to the problem from general knowledge (or lack thereof), usually without the individual's being aware of them. One well-known example illustrates how presuppositions function:

> A man and his son were away for a trip. They were driving down the motorway when they had a terrible accident. The man was killed outright, but his son was alive, though badly injured. The son was rushed to the hospital and was to have an emergency operation. In entering the operating theater, the surgeon looked at the boy, and said, "I can't do this operation. This boy is my son." How can this be?

The boy can be the son if one sheds the presupposition that a surgeon must be a male. The female surgeon could, indeed, be the boy's mother.[85]

In addition, human problem solvers get locked into "mental sets," certain fixed ways of looking at things. Certain objects, such as spoons, hammers, and needles, have specific functions; it is natural to get stuck in their "functional fixedness" without giving due consideration to other ways these objects might be used in solving a problem. Furthermore, problem solvers are easily misled by irrelevant information. Consider the following illustration:

> If you have black socks and brown socks in you drawer mixed in a ratio of 4 to 5, how many socks will you have to take out to make sure of having a pair of the same color?

It is easy to be drawn to the irrelevant information about the 4/5 ratio. With some luck one may draw two socks of the same color in two picks, but "to be sure" (as the problem states) one need only make a third pick, for surely then two socks of the same color will have been drawn. The *relevant* information is that there are only two colors of socks in the drawer.[86]

Like other forms of thinking, problem solving can put a heavy strain on the cognitive apparatus, and as the problems become more complex and the system gets overloaded, there are human tendencies to break down. Effective problem solvers learn to use problem-solving strategies and then monitor very carefully what they are doing.

It is only a short step from problem solving to decision making, although the thinking processes involved are rather different. People are faced with decisions all the time: where to live, what career path to pursue, whether to get married, etc. In the business world, managers are called upon frequently to make decisions about hiring and firing personnel, whether to develop a new product, what size inventory to maintain, or how to launch a new marketing campaign. What kind of thinking is involved in decision making?

Decision making is different from problem solving in several ways.[87] Whereas problem solving requires moving through various solution paths to get to the one desired goal state, decision making involves weighing various pros and cons and selecting the better (or best) of two or more alternatives. Decision making differs from traditional problem solving in that there is usually no *one correct* solution; there are several options, and the task is to select the best.

Furthermore, in problem solving the solution is usually known to be good or bad, right or wrong at the time it is discovered; whereas in decision making the choice is known to have been good or bad only after some time has passed. The "right" decision is one that results ultimately in the best outcomes, hence, there is a strong element of prediction in decision making.

What should be taken into account in making decisions? Most decisions are multidimensional, a number of variables come into play. In admitting students to college, for example, one might do so on the basis of SAT scores alone. In doing so, a "unidimensional comparison" is made. If the admissions officer were to examine also, grade point average, class standing, activities, and perhaps some measure of effort and persistence, "multidimensional comparison" would be undertaken and the decision-making process would become much more complex and sophisticated. The central problem in decision making, therefore, is to decide which and how many factors (dimensions) to take into consideration and how to weigh them.[88]

As with problem solving there are some useful ways of conceptualizing the process of decision making and going about it in a systematic way. Expert decision makers advocate using a worksheet where the dimensions (variables) under consideration are laid out and given weights.[89] The task is to identify all of the relevant considerations and to determine their relative importance. For example, if a personnel decision to hire a new employee were to be made, one would want to identify and list the considerations (characteristics) that are important. These considerations will vary, of course, depending on the nature of the job responsibilities. Not all of the considerations are of equal importance, however, so a weighting system is used. A simple worksheet can be utilized to assure that all considerations are taken into account systematically and assigned a weight of importance. A weighted score by item and category and an overall assessment score are generated. This approach to decision making is employed to reduce personal bias and arbitrary attraction to only certain considerations. One problem with using a worksheet like this is that it is possible that none of the candidates under consideration will score very well. To deal with this problem, it is possible to establish a priori, an "ideal rule" that determines an ideal score successful candidates must approximate to be given consideration.[90] The worksheet, of course, can be applied to a variety of decision-making situations where there are many considerations of relative weight and identifiable pros and cons. The effectiveness of the worksheet process can be validated by returning to the decisions after some time has passed to see whether the decision made (in this case the candidate selected) "worked out" as anticipated. If not, other considerations can be added to the worksheet and the weighting system revised.

Like other thinking processes, decision making is subject to human failure. There are two pitfalls to which decision makers must be especially alert. One of these is what has been called the "Polly-anna Principle," or more simply "wishful thinking."[91] This is the tendency to overestimate the chances of being successful, to see the wonderful things that could happen as opposed to the risks. Expert decision makers evaluate risk; they ask what the consequences will be if the decision proves to be wrong.[92] They also know that there is more than one way to be wrong. It is possible to be wrong in choosing a certain direction, but it is also possible to be wrong in not choosing it. Risks show up both as "opportunities missed" as well as "blunders made." Effective decision makers walk the fine line between these consequences, but often they take the conservative course, choosing to err on the side of opportunity missed rather than taking on great risk with potentially disastrous consequences.

The second pitfall is called "entrapment."[93] Most decisions exist within a context of previous decisions. Sometimes these previous decisions have already cost a great deal in time, money, and effort. If a person or, collectively, the persons in an organization, have already made a big investment, it is easy to become "trapped" in those previous decisions, so that a free, fresh, and rational choice becomes difficult in the decision at hand. If time and money have been poured into a previous decision that proved to be less than successful, it is very difficult to say that it was a bad decision. Admitting a bad decision often means accepting responsibility, which in itself can carry consequences. So to avoid responsibility, another bad decision is often made. Expert decision makers try to make good decisions in the first place, and they are especially wary of getting trapped by previous bad decisions.

Once a decision has been made, it is usually set forth as a recommendation projecting the likely outcomes. In the business world, for example, managers want to know about the likelihood of success that accompanies a recommendation. Because decision making is usually multidimensional, and because many considerations are taken into account, the outcomes of a decision are usually cast as probabilities. Unfortunately, the projected outcomes of a decision are seldom clear cut, which is another way of saying that they are probabilistic. Even when a systematic approach is used in decision making, as with the use of a worksheet in a personnel decision, the predicted outcomes of the decision are at best probable. The most that can be said for a personnel decision, for example, is that there is a high probability that the individual who was selected will "work out" and become the kind of employee that was needed. There is (maybe) an 85 percent chance of success. Outcomes, therefore, are seldom stated in absolute numbers, not because problem solvers are afraid to take a stand; but because they have learned through experience that their recommendations (the results of their decisions) only have a probability of succeeding. Employment records may show, for example, that when the personnel worksheet is used conscientiously, successful hires will occur 80 percent of the time.

Although the newspapers and media are filled with reports of studies cast as probabilities, most postsecondary students have a very limited understanding of how to interpret this data. When undergraduate students are asked the meaning of the following statement of probability, "There will be an 80 percent chance of rain today," they produce some very interesting answers, such as:

- Of all the area (square miles) in the state, it will probably rain on 80 percent of it today.
- There will be a heavy storm today as opposed to scattered showers.
- It will probably rain 80 percent of the time today.
- Eighty percent of the weather forecasters agree that it will rain today.
- There is always a 50-50 chance of rain, so 80 percent means there's a better chance than that but not 100 percent sure.[94]

The actual meaning is as follows: Given many days in the past with conditions like those that exist today—with the same combination of atmospheric pressure, humidity, wind, and concentrations of clouds—it has rained on 80 percent of those days; therefore, there is an 80 percent chance that it will rain today, too.[95] Probability, in this sense, involves a prediction from a previous similar situation in which the variables (dimensions) have already been studied carefully.

Like most other forms of thinking, probabilistic thinking is subject to various forms of distortion and human error. For example, in Wheel of Fortune games, there is a tendency to say: "If number seven hasn't come up yet, it's about time for it" or "If number seven has come up twice already, it's unlikely to come up again." But in a truly random situation every number on the wheel has a chance of coming up on every spin; the wheel has no memory. Over a very large number of spins, the random distribution will play itself out, but in a finite period of time, there is no "memory" for what has been played and what hasn't. This tendency to impute memory has been called "Gambler's Fallacy."[96] Although highly irrational, it is used frequently.

Other errors in probabilistic thinking grow out of misunderstandings of the meaning of frequency.[97] "Frequency" is an important concept in probability because if an event is frequent, then its occurrence is highly probable. The error creeps in by confusing frequency with relative frequency. If a report suggests, for example, that there will be a need for more fraternity houses on college campuses because more men are joining fraternities than ever before, it is important to ask: What is the increase in fraternity memberships *relative to* the increase or decrease in college attendance by men? The preference for fraternities could increase while the number of men enrolling in college decreases. Problems in assessing frequency data also arise from subjective impressions about the frequency of events derived from the publicity or the inherent dramatic nature of these events. People tend to harbor greater fears of dying in an airplane crash than in an auto accident, although the frequencies (and probabilities) are quite different.

Probabilistic reasoning also can go astray when trends are being projected. Statisticians are wary of trends that have come out of relatively small samples. A trend toward 60 percent male births is much more likely to come out of a small hospital than a large hospital because of the small sample size at the small hospital. The data from a larger sample will tend to be more nearly like the overall data for the population. Statisticians are also wary of extrapolations—estimates based on present trends that are projected forward in time. Extrapolations are used with the assumption that present trends will continue, and, of course, they may not. Like many other thinking processes, probabilistic thinking can be side-tracked by human tendencies to be "unreasonable."

Problem solving and decision making involve their own special forms of thinking. There are unique ways to approach these tasks and there are useful techniques that can be learned. As with other forms of thinking, there are also unique ways for the thinking processes associated with problem solving and decision making to break down. The challenge for us, as postsecondary teachers, is to help students learn problem-solving and decision-making skills by actually engaging them in those thinking processes. Consider what Maynard Smith does when he uses the case study method in his business courses.

Maynard Smith has used case studies before, and he knows that his graduate students in the M.B.A. program at Mid-West University have encountered business cases as undergraduates. Fortunately, a large horseshoe-shaped tiered arrangement of curved desks and swivel chairs is available for this class, and he is able to maintain direct visual contact with each student as he wanders about in the center of the horseshoe. All of the students display printed namecards on the desktop where they sit, so Professor Smith can call them by name. He wants to introduce the case during the two-hour evening session tonight and engage the students in the "situation audit" with the hope that they will be able to define the main features of the problem embedded in the case. This will take some time and patience.

Professor Smith has done an extensive amount of consulting in the field of marketing, and over the years he has gathered some interesting material. Recently, after reading some books on case studies, he has written some of his own cases, and he is particularly pleased with the materials he has developed for this one, which include a databank available on computer and also a videotape.[98] He opens the case with a brief statement and a one-page handout as follows:

Ski International

Ski International is a retail network of ski shops that sells ski equipment and clothing in 34 stores in the U.S.A. and Canada. The President of the company has asked the Vice-President for Marketing to recommend a theme to coordinate the marketing program for the fiscal year that begins in approximately 15 months. The VP for Marketing has touched base with the Advertising Agency that currently holds the account and they have suggested several themes:

- **A Testimonial Campaign**—where credible "tellers" relate incidents where they had become involved in a crisis and their reliable equipment from Ski International pulled them through.
- **A Famous Figure Campaign**—where a well-known Olympic skier would endorse Ski International equipment.

- **A Beautiful-People Campaign**—where famous people from many walks of life would endorse Ski International.
- **A Quality-Comparison Campaign**—where comparisons of Ski International equipment are made to other brands and prices.
- **An Educational Campaign**—where brief mini-lessons are provided for beginners and intermediates.
- **A Youth Campaign**—where the appeal is to high school, college-age, and young adult workers.

The Vice-President likes most of these ideas. Can you help the Vice-President select one to recommend to the President?

Maynard Smith allows time for the students to read through the options and think about them; he then asks: "Which one do you like best?" The students know that someone will get called on. "What do you think, Bob?"

"I knew you'd ask me. I've never been on skis. I guess I like the educational campaign. Maybe if I learned something about skiing, I might consider trying it. I'd have to try it before I would buy one of the products."

"What do you think, Julie?"

"Well, are we just picking an ad campaign? Is this TV or what? A lot of those ideas sound fairly overworked. Do we have to stay with these options?"

"Do you have a better one?"

"Well, not now, but I'm not sure I like these."

"Susan?"

"It says that they sell equipment and clothing, so we would need to select a theme that would stress both."

Professor Smith nods. "That sounds important." During a brief silence he paces around the horseshoe and has a little conversation with himself. Are these really graduate students? Are they going to fall for this? Surely, they've had some marketing courses before. He counsels himself to be patient. Finally he asks, without calling on anyone, "What do you recommend?"

A hand shoots up in the upper tier. "I think I don't know enough to make a decision."

"Is that what you're going to tell the President, that you don't know enough?" There are a few snickers.

"No, but I hope I would have the guts to say that there are a lot of things to consider before we get to a decision about an ad campaign theme."

"Good! Such as?"

"Well, what was last year's theme, to start with. I would want a lot more information about how Ski International is performing right now."

"Such as?" Professor Smith turns to another part of the class. Hands are flying.

"Present sales volume."

"Profits. How are they doing now?"

"What do they sell the most of? And the least of?"

"Who is their competition?"

"What kind of people are their present customers?"

"What's their market niche?"

"What are their goals? Are they trying to grow or maximize return on investment?"

"What's the mission of this company?"

Maynard Smith is nodding his head up and down vigorously and smiling, "Now you are starting to sound like M.B.A. students. You're beginning to think. But before we try to get this information, let me ask you, what's the problem we are trying to solve here? Is it to come up with a theme for an ad campaign?"

"Well, that's what was called for, but . . ."

Smith smiles. "Yes, that was a little unfair, but in the business world you will be asked to do lots of things that aren't the right thing. So what's the right thing; what's the problem here? Bob?"

"It seems like the problem is to develop the right marketing strategy, of which an ad campaign is just a small part."

"Do you agree, Jane? Is that the problem?"

"Well, yes, if we define marketing strategy broadly, to include those things we were asking for information about. A company like this needs a marketing strategy, and coming up with one may be a big problem or a little problem, depending on what shape the company is in now."

"O.K.," Smith responds, "are we in general agreement on that?" He looks around the horseshoe at nodding heads. "If so, let's describe the goal state. What could we produce, what would the product be, at the goal state?"

"A marketing plan."

"That consists of what? Sally?"

"Objectives. A market target strategy. Certain specified program activities. A price strategy. A sales strategy. And an advertising theme, but that's just one piece."

"Good. These are the components of the outcome, the goal state when the problem is resolved. How do we get there?"

"We can work backwards now. Some of that information we were asking for is very important."

"I agree. I think we can chop this up into some pieces. Before we can recommend a market strategy, we need to know something about the company's niche. Before we can recommend a price strategy, we have to know about the company's finances."

"So you want some information on the initial state." Professor Smith draws a simple diagram of "goal state" and "initial state" on the board. "And in here, in the 'problem space,' we are going to come up with some solution paths, right?"

"So come on, Professor Smith, we need the rest of this case. Where do we get the data?" Laughter. "We know you've got something tucked away on your computer."

"Well, it just so happens that I do. But this is a relatively small company and its operations are widely dispersed. This company may not be able to come up with all the information you want, or even need. So I'll tell you what I'll do. I'll give you the MENU, and you will have to make some hard choices about which information you think is going to be most valuable to you."

Professor Smith projects the computer menu on a large screen at the front of the class. The items on the menu include:

CORPORATE MISSION AND OBJECTIVES
STORE BY STORE SALES UNIT ANALYSIS
CURRENT BUYER ANALYSIS
COMPETITOR ANALYSIS
MARKET TRENDS
AGGREGATE COMPANY FINANCIAL DATA
NEW PRODUCT TRENDS
BUSINESS ENVIRONMENT FACTORS

"You can read a brief description for each MENU category, then I'll let you choose four out of the eight. We don't have the resources to research more than that. Which four do you want?"

An agitated discussion ensues, with some fierce arguments between class members. Presuppositions and mental sets are challenged; critical information is identified and prioritized. Professor Smith referees and keeps asking for closure. When the students achieve consensus, he lets them take a break, during which he prints the requested data sheets and makes copies for the class. When the students return, the remainder of the evening is spent in pondering the data, raising questions about the meaning of the information, and trying to arrive at reasonable interpretations. During the course of the discussion, some students suggest ideas for further analyses that might be done on the data.

"For next week," Professor Smith concludes, "You are to bring in a 10-page analysis of this data. I don't want a summary. I want an analysis. You may go to the computer and run further analyses, use spread sheets, whatever. What are the trends? What are the insights you get from this data? What are the critical issues? This paper will become the first section of your case report, due in three weeks. Any questions?"

During class the following week, Professor Smith asks the students to draw on their written analysis of the data to begin to formulate alternatives. "What do you think this company should do? What kind of marketing strategy should it develop?"

After much discussion, two main alternatives emerge. One part of the class wants to market to the younger, high school and college-age market. Because they are still growing, and tend to get caught up in fads, it is argued, these end users represent a better market niche and market potential for repeat buyers. The stores are all successful in selling equipment, and equipment was what younger buyers are most interested in. The other part of the class wants to market to families. The stores are already selling primarily to families, and it is suggested that the stores should try to sell more to their proven customers than to go after a new market strata. A list of pros and cons is developed for each alternative, based on the data analysis. Toward the end of the evening, Professor Smith provides the students with a decision worksheet and asks them to identify all of the dimensions of the decision and then to weigh these dimensions in terms of their importance. Their homework is to complete the decision worksheet and to come in the following week with a decision—for one marketing strategy or the other—and the five most convincing arguments to support their choice.

When the students report the following week, there are, as one might expect, some heated arguments about which strategy is best. Eventually a binding majority vote is taken and the family marketing strategy is selected.

"Now we need to fill in the details. What comes next?"

"Well, now that we have an overall market target strategy, we will need a buying strategy, a sales strategy, a price strategy, and a promotion strategy."

"Good!" Professor Smith shows the students a brief videotape of a typical Ski International store. The students are taken on a brief tour and then watch an actual sales transaction. Then Professor Smith asks them how they can improve on what they have seen. Each student comes up with some remarkable ideas about opportunities. They decide that they will emphasize basic equipment—skis, boots, bindings—and reduce the clothing to three major recognized brand name suppliers. The goal is to cut clothing inventory, but to get families to buy everything at one store. A unique pricing incentive is established—the greater the total bill, the larger the percent of discount. The sales force is to be specially trained to sell every customer as much as possible to meet all their needs. Finally, the students suggest an advertising campaign, unlike any of those originally proposed, directed at families, that includes two catchy slogans: "Ski International—The One-Stop Ski Shop" and "The More You Buy, The More You Save."

Professor Smith thanks the class for their hard work and good thinking, and leaves them with a final assignment. "Go back over all of your work and write this up now as a case report. Attach any notes, analyses, spreadsheets, or computer runs that you have done as documentation of your thinking. Include your recommendation and supporting reasons. Outline briefly a marketing plan, such as the one we developed tonight. Then do one more thing. Cost this out, go back to the financial data and make a prediction about increased sales. You will cast your prediction in terms of probability. What is the range of gross sales increase and net profit increase that you expect, and what is the probability that this will occur? I want your best estimate of what will occur, not Polyanish wishful thinking. You will have to go back to some of your 'Quant' textbooks and your finance notes to review contribution margins, break-even points, and so forth. I want you to make a financial projection of what can be expected from this new marketing strategy. What is the likelihood that it will work; what are the risks that it won't? What can the President expect from this scheme? Is everyone clear on the report?" Professor Smith glances around the horseshoe. "Next week we will start another case."

Professor Smith is pleased with the final case reports when they come in. The problem is well-defined. Some of the data analyses are quite sophisticated. Students seem to be going well beyond a mere summary of the facts; the recommendations are well documented, and the projections are cast in terms of probabilities. The end products confirm his growing conviction in the efficacy of the case method for teaching students problem-solving and decision-making skills. He knows that employers today are looking for students who know how to think.

THINKING AND LANGUAGE

Language is the carrier of ideas, the conveyance of meaning, the indispensable vehicle of thinking. Thinking begins "inside" with what scholars in speech communication call "self-talk" and proceeds outward in speech and writing. Some psychologists would say that language strongly affects the way people think and that people in different cultures "think differently because of the language in which they are thinking." Known as the Sapir-Whorf Hypothesis, this classic idea—that forms of language determine the way people think—has been vigorously debated and researched by psychologists.[99] Although the stronger version of the hypothesis, that language *determines* thought processes, is not widely accepted today, the general principle, that thought and language are intimately related, is well established.

If language is the vehicle for thinking, the conveyance that carries meaning, it is also the source of much misunderstanding and many problems in thinking. For one thing, language is slippery; it doesn't convey the same meanings from one person to the next or even from sentence to sentence. Raymond Nickerson provides this humorous example of how the ambiguous use of language can spoil a deductive argument:[100]

- Nothing is better than eternal happiness.
- A ham sandwich is better than nothing.
- Therefore, a ham sandwich is better than eternal happiness.

The word "nothing," as it is used in these statements, becomes very "slippery," its meaning changing in important ways from the first statement to the second, thus leading to the ridiculous conclusion in the third. Or to push the point even further, what meanings might be conveyed in this example?[101]

He cooks carrots and peas in the same pot.

Does he cook two vegetables, or does he cook one vegetable and urinate? Good thinkers know that they should watch carefully to see how language is being used and misused, and they are aware of the various "tricks" that can be played with language to derail thinking.

Scholars who study the development and use of language—linguists, semanticists, psycholinguists—have been able to establish that language functions at many different levels and is used in diverse ways. The major findings of much of the early work in linguistics were presented in a classic text by S.I. Hayakawa (in his prepolitical days) entitled *Language in Thought and Action*.[102] According to Hayakawa, linguists have demonstrated that "meanings" do not reside permanently in words, and do not correspond to some immutable reality "out there." Rather, meanings reside in people, and people use words to give expression to their meanings. Although there is some agreement about the general meaning of words, words derive much of their meaning from contexts. The same words have different meanings in different contexts. Furthermore, the "truth" of various statements depends upon the ground rules about the way language is used in those statements. Moreover, this ambiguity, both with regard to meaning and to truth, cannot be cleared up easily by definitions, because definitions themselves are cast in words that are open to a variety of meanings and interpretations.

If language is open to many interpretations, depending on the meanings an individual wishes to convey, the context within which words are expressed, and the ground rules that govern "truth," how can there ever by any agreement about what is being said? Without agreement on truth and meaning, how is clear thinking to proceed? How is it possible to set forth one's thoughts so that others can examine, understand, and criticize them?

Philosophers have thought about this problem over the centuries, but in modern philosophy (in the early twentieth century) this concern about language became an intense preoccupation, so much so that some philosophers wanted to confine the scope of philosophy to the study of language and its meaning. One group of philosophers known as logical positivists (represented by the "Vienna Circle" in the 1920s and the work of Rudolph Carnap and A.J. Ayer) wanted to ensure that language was used only in the most precise way so that words would correspond as nearly as possible to the objects they signify.[103] Ayer set forth a strong argument in which he insisted that for any concept to have meaning it must be capable of being verified empirically (through the senses) and must have a direct correspondence to "reality."[104] Using this "empiricist criterion of meaning," the positivists threw out (boldly) all forms of discourse that could not be verified empirically, wiping out what were formerly important branches of philosophy, such as metaphysics and ethics, and branding them as meaningless nonsense.[105] There are still some radical empiricists today who insist that the use of language should be restricted to literal meanings, and that all statements, to be meaningful, should correspond to a reality that can be empirically verified. Empirical verification, of course, is the backbone of modern science, an endeavor that is not to be taken lightly for its achievements.

There are other philosophers, however, who argue that all language only "represents" reality; thus words and "reality" can never correspond exactly. All language is in some sense metaphorical and there is no such thing as a purely literal description. The position is summarized well by Marc Belth as follows:[106]

Even the simplest description, it has been shown, is couched in some language system that makes place for analogical perceptions or concepts. To look for nothing but exact "reprints" of events of the world asks too much, both of the world and of our language. . . . Even in the most precise account there would have to be some translation—onto paper, or clay or metal; into a sentence, a gesture, a visual expression. And merely to repeat precisely what is there would further oblige us to do something more if there is to be any use in that so-called replication.

Those who oppose the logical positivists insist that all language is analogical, and that the important thing to understand about thinking is not whether a description is "literal" or not, but what *kind* of analogy is being employed in the thought processes being used. All thinking involves comparisons (analogues), and the important thing is to be conscious of what models, analogies, and metaphors are being employed.[107] Thinking, therefore, involves the construction of metaphors—in the Aristotelian sense, "giving something a name that belongs to something else"—in order to "build a model, construct an analogy, fashion a metaphor, reflect some referent."[108] Thinking, in various fields of study, involves learning how to employ the metaphorical language used in that field according to established ground rules.

The debate about language, touched off by the logical positivists, is not easily settled, particularly with regard to the claims about "truth" made by the opposing sides. The metaphors that for some thinkers reveal a special kind of truth, for the positivists perform only what they call an "expressive function."[109] Much of the debate can be summed up in the familiar terms used by teachers of English composition to describe two different uses of language—"denotative" and "connotative." "Denotative" refers to words that carry "explicit references," and "connotative" refers to words that carry "suggestive, symbolic or associated references."[110] A "rose" may have a denotative reference to a specific kind of flower, but it may also have a connotative reference to a beautiful woman. Most English teachers would agree that language functions in *both* ways; that's why both terms exist. Perhaps it is best, then, to think of a continuum of positions with regard to language, and to realize that thinking becomes different things, and is practiced in different ways, depending on how one regards the language being used. The continuum can be represented as follows:

Use of Language

positivistic	_____	analogical
correspondence	_____	comparison
empirical verification	____	models, analogies, metaphors
literal	_____	figurative
denotative	_____	connotative

Some thinking involves using language in ways that will produce the most correspondence with empirically verifiable realities; other thinking involves using language in ways that are highly analogical and metaphorical. The important thing is to know the difference.

Assume that the goal, in a particular instance, is to engage in thinking processes where language is being dealt with in a more literal (denotative) way, that is, in a manner more compatible with the positivistic end of the continuum. Are there some ground rules to follow and some pitfalls to avoid?

First, it is important to be cautious about diction, the choice of particular words.[111] Clear thinkers are careful to avoid various distortions of language, such as *exaggeration* (words that augment reality), *euphemism* (less offensive words used to smooth over a bad situation), *bureaucratese* (formal stilted language intelligible only to the initiated), *propaganda* (emotionally charged words used to convert to a dogma or doctrine), and *stereotype* (words that classify on the basis of superficial characteristics and impute to the individual the characteristics of the class). Second, it is important to distinguish between the statements being made and the people who are referred to or addressed. Clear thinkers are aware of and are able to identify *ad hominem* arguments (which attack the opponent not the issue), arguments that *appeal to authority* (which cite experts as opposed to reason), arguments that *appeal to numbers* (which mystify with statistics), arguments that *appeal to tradition* (which affirm past practices), and arguments that *appeal either to pity or pride* (sympathy), to *popularity* (everyone does it), or to *guilt/virtue by association* (name-dropping). Third, it is important to listen for and analyze the way the argument is being constructed. Clear thinkers are aware of and are able to spot the *false dichotomy* (a complex situation set up as an either/or choice), *card stacking* (selective withholding of important information), *begging the question* (avoiding the issue), *leading questions* (inquiries based on false suppositions), *misinterpretation* (overstating or oversimplifying the opposition), *labeling* (naming without explaining), *quoting out of context* (providing selected phrases that distort the meaning), *irrelevant reasons* (arguments that carry little weight), and *deception* (misrepresentation or just plain lying). When the goal is to be exact and precise about what is being said, good thinkers not only look for these fallacies in what others say, but they monitor their own thinking processes so that they don't commit the same fallacies themselves.

Assume, however, that the goal is not to be exact and precise in the use of language, but rather to engage in analogical and metaphorical thinking, where the connotative functions of language are stressed. Are there some ground rules to follow and pitfalls to avoid? Are there ways of selecting, testing, and analyzing the metaphors used in analogical thinking?

Analogical thinking can employ many forms. Marc Belth makes distinctions among model, analogy, and metaphor. All three involve "acts of employing symbolic representations of familiar, understood events as the means for dealing with unfamiliar matters in order to endow them with descriptions, explanations and further exploratory conditions."[112] But all three are also different.

Models provide an image that helps pull together disparate pieces of information into some larger explanation. Without the model, the pieces are less well understood. Children play with "model" airplanes and "model" cars, and through such play learn about the larger world of airplanes and cars. Models are models *of* . . . something. Models provide "archetype idealizations" constructed out of specific images that facilitate further understanding or exploration. Scientists construct models of the atom or the DNA molecule to pull together individual observations of events and make consistent explanations. Physical scientists even seek out comprehensive models of the universe, such as Newton's model of the "perfect clock," and the current search by physicists for a "unified theory." Models are invented images used to interpret individual events that would otherwise have no similarities, correspondence, or relevances. Models give to the world qualities that would not otherwise be perceived. They are not totally subjective, because they are public and examinable. Members of various disciplines, using quite different models, can look at the models their colleagues use and either accept or reject them.[113] Models, themselves, can vary in the way the language is used, in the way the images correspond to the "realities" they describe. Belth makes the following distinction between "hard" and "soft" models:

> For example, a road map, drawn to scale and containing symbols for every feature of the road system between, say, Boston and Chicago,

including the different widths of road, alternative routes between intervening points, detours, roadblocks, rest stops, restaurants, waterways, mountain ranges of different heights, and so on, might be considered on one end of the spectrum as a Hard model. A model for reading a poem in order to be able to trace the meaning and connotations of all the metaphors used, the effects of the various rhythms and rhymes, the quality of the tension of feelings produced by the various techniques of writing poetry, and so on, might be on the other extreme end of the spectrum, the softest of the Soft models.[114]

Models are not only hard and soft, but they also vary from field to field. The models that physical scientists construct are different from those constructed by anthropologists or historians. And sometimes models used in one field, are borrowed from another, as when mathematical models are used to explain phenomena in the social sciences.

Are there any ground rules for developing and evaluating models? Is it possible to tell a "good" model from a "bad" model? Although the criteria are not of the kind that logical positivists would like to see, there are some guidelines. Models should be useful. To be useful, they should yield new insights, illuminate new features, and develop new understandings. Models should "fit" and account for the data, if not all of it, then most of it. Models should provide plausible explanations and valid interpretations. Models can also be examined for their internal consistency, how they hang together, the logic in the relationship of their component parts. Above all, models should be valuable as an aid to further investigation, providing new frameworks for further research and enabling the current model to be supported, or replaced with a better model. In other words, models are evaluated by the quality of the explanations they produce.[115] Without models, certain kinds of thinking simply don't take place.

Analogies are not as comprehensive as models. They are descriptions of phenomena on a lesser scale than whole systems. They are not so much descriptions *of*, as descriptions *as*, which is to say, a comparison is made. The analogy (comparison) may be made to things that are readily observable, hypothetical, or purely symbolic. The phenomena to be illuminated by the comparison may exist in the present, may have existed in the past, may someday exist, or may never exist in any sense that can be observed or measured. Hence, the need to describe not only what the "something" is, but what it is *like*.[116] Thus historians may compare the Kennedy years to "Camelot"

(Morison), sociologists may portray social relations as dramas played out on a stage (Goffman), and psychologists may compare the behavior of young children toward their parents to characters in the Greek drama *Oedipus Rex* (Freud).

What are the criteria for good analogies? There should be coherence and consistency within the analogy, that is, the things being compared should correspond. There should also be a purpose for the analogy, a reason for using the analogy for explanation. Furthermore, the analogy should clarify by making apparent obscure traits, relationships, features, and functions of the event for which the analogy is being constructed. The symbol system of the comparison should be generally understood and have enough warrant to be adequate to the task for which it is constructed. There should be a general set of rules that governs the symbol system so that it is possible to move from the event to the comparison in an orderly way.[117] Like models, analogies are also evaluated by the quality of the explanations they produce.

Metaphors are specific comparisons that allow a transfer of meaning from one element of the comparison to the other. Thus one may speak of a "flock of complaints" to imply that many complaints came all at once. As Marc Belth explains:

> metaphor deliberately makes use of both certain similarities . . . and . . . observable differences. This lends to every metaphor a quality of the absurd, for that difference is, in a sense, winked at. The "computer is like a brain" is an analogy. But, "In him one hears the clank of rust" is a metaphor. Inevitably, there is wit as well as absurdity in metaphor; the wit that stirs us when the familiar is violated.[118]

Thus, a metaphor becomes a kind of lens through which the familiar is seen in a new light. Metaphors serve to focus attention and are a cause for further reflection.

Metaphors can be classified by type.[119] Some metaphors involve using a part to stand for the whole, as in "Five beaks peeked out over the edge of the nest." Others use the whole to stand for a part, as in "The rooster's morning alarm sounded punctually." Sometimes metaphors involve using one name to apply to another name, as in "My colleague is a real strange bird." Or a metaphor may involve applying the name for one activity to another activity, as in, "Sometimes when you lecture, you have to wing it." Or with some metaphors, the quality of one event is applied to another, as in "During our last brainstorm session, the ideas were really flying." Each of these metaphors functions in a slightly different way, but all are used to make an illuminating comparison.

The unique function of metaphor is seen best in its artistic uses, in literature of many types, but especially poetry. In poetry, metaphor is used not only as a means to an end, to elucidate and describe, but as an end in itself to be contemplated and enjoyed. Thus the "meaning" of metaphors in poetry becomes a problem. While an image in a poem may have a referent (one level of meaning), the image takes on a life of its own as well, and may be the source of new meanings and interpretations brought to it by the reader. The same is true of the sounds and rhythms of poetry, which become an object of enjoyment in themselves. The reader then responds to these sounds and rhythms, much as one would listen to music.

Because metaphors have a "life of their own," they are often intentionally unclear. Metaphors are used to set up deliberate ambiguities, incongruities, and paradoxes, such as "surely the flame that burns in old age, is not the flame that was kindled in youth." It is not easy to tell exactly what is meant by that statement, but the image is provocative enough to engage the reader in further contemplation.

Are there ground rules for evaluating metaphors? Are some metaphors better than others? What is a "good metaphor"? Literary scholars speak of "fresh" metaphors and "dead" metaphors. A fresh, or live metaphor is one that appears to be newly created for the occasion. The dead metaphor has been parroted (to use a dead metaphor) over and over again. A live metaphor directs the attention in new ways to new attributes. A live metaphor provides new ways of seeing, new insights, and, to the extent that it does this, it can be said to have intensity of power. A live metaphor has the power to confront the reader, to create distance between the idea and the reader, or to put the idea in a new or larger context.[120]

In the artistic uses of metaphor, there is often deliberate intention to distort, and it is through distortion that the metaphor gains its power. In "bad poetry" the metaphors are used for didactic or moralistic purposes, to teach a lesson or preach a sermon. When fresh metaphors are used effectively in "good poetry," the reader is drawn into the contemplation of an event, or of self, in a new way. As Marc Belth notes:

> What really makes for good metaphors are images in which the familiar, perhaps even the ordinary, are suddenly shown in a new light, in which the ordinary is given a new form, new value; where dullness is stripped away and new excitement grows. We are brought

to pause, to wonder, and to contemplate them as if we had not observed them before. And, of course, we have not. That is the point of the poetic metaphor. It has created a new and vibrant form in its symbolism. . . . But because the events symbolized are not present, the symbol itself becomes the subject of our contemplation.[121]

Live metaphors are especially important, therefore, in art, particularly in poetry. The ultimate purpose of metaphors in poetry is to elicit a contemplative response in the reader. As Belth concludes:

In any art, the capacity of the artist to quicken in the reader this sense of his own identity marks the ultimate value of the symbols he has used, the metaphors he has created. For the artist enriches us within ourselves by this indirect revelation of his own inner world. It is not so much that we share his world, but that in the reading we are given new ways to create our own inner worlds.[122]

Matters of aesthetic theory are, of course, enormously complex, and not every artist or critic would agree with the above statement. Nonetheless, clear thinkers realize that thinking also takes place in the arts as well as the sciences, and that such thinking involves peculiar uses of language, particularly the skillful employment of models, analogies, and metaphors.

Teachers who want to have their students become familiar with thinking processes that draw on different uses of language will set up their classrooms in such a way that students can engage directly in those processes. The initial choice of text—the scientific report, historical essay, novel, or poem—is crucial, of course, but the way in which the teacher guides the discussion of the text is also extremely important. The focus of the inquiry and discovery process is in this instance on language. Students can sharpen their thinking skills as they discover that the way one goes about thinking in a particular subject depends heavily on how language is being used in that subject. Consider what Edna Wolf does when she presents a short poem to her colloquium section.

The students at Elm Grove College come to Edna Wolf's colloquium prepared to discuss an assigned text. Two oblong oak tables sit side-by-side, forming one large square table, around which 20 students sit face-to-face. Their professor is part of their group, but they know that she is there to guide them in an inquiry that is essentially theirs. The text is an untitled poem in eight lines:

A Route of Evanescence
With a revolving Wheel—

A Resonance of Emerald—
A Rush of Cochineal—
And every Blossom on the Bush
Adjusts its tumbled Head—
The mail from Tunis, probably
An easy Morning's ride —[123]

Edna Wolf outlines the purpose of the inquiry and sets some ground rules: "I want you to arrive at an interpretation of this poem. What is the subject? What is it about? What does it mean? And then, what evidence do you have for the interpretation you are making? To do this you will need to listen carefully to each other. You communicate respect by the way you listen." The students are staring at the poem, deep furrows, like plowed fields, cut across their foreheads. "Before we begin there may be a few troublesome words. What are they?"

"Evanescence?"

"Yes, who has looked it up? Anyone?"

"Fleeting? Here today and gone tomorrow?"

"Yes, and also vanishing," Professor Wolf adds.

"Anything else?"

"Cochineal?"

"Anyone?"

"A seashell but also a color, a reddish color."

"Good. And Tunis, of course is . . ."

"The capital of Tunisia."

"A city in North Africa."

"All right, let's begin with first impressions. What are they? What do you see?"

After a long pause, one young women raises her hand shyly.

"You don't need to raise your hand; just speak when there appears to be a chance to take a turn."

"I see a stream . . . and, maybe a waterwheel? Something set in nature, with lots of flowers and trees. And the sounds of the stream; I hear the stream."

"All right, a stream, a waterwheel, something in nature. Good. Someone else?"

After more silence, a young man sits forward and says, "I see a mail truck. It's bouncing along this dirt road to some rural location. And when it goes by, it blows all the flowers, and they adjust to get back in place again. It's bringing the author a special letter from far away."

"All right, so we have a stream and mail truck. You're beginning to pick up on some of the images, such as the blossoms adjusting. Someone else?"

Another young man speaks: "I see the sun. Maybe a sunrise or sunset, I'm not sure which, but the route is the sun's route across the sky. The sun is a revolving wheel, or could appear to be. And for the sun to get here—wherever here is—would be an easy morning's ride from Tunis."

"Good. You are trying to account for several images with one explanation."

Another young woman speaks up, somewhat agitated, "It's not that specific—not a stream or road or anything. It's life. It's the passage of life, like this revolving wheel and everything is just rushing by with no purpose or meaning. Just this endless flow."

Edna Wolf leans back in her chair and adjusts her glasses on her nose. "Well, you have some interesting images out on the table here—a stream, a mail truck, the sun, life. And you are raising some important questions that you might want to pursue. I hear you asking about the language, whether to take it literally or more figuratively. Is this something specific being described here—a little scene—or is this an abstract idea? And if it is a little scene, where is it? Who's looking at it and from what point of view?"

There is more silence and then the inquiry continues. Each of the images is elaborated and defended, and a few new ideas emerge. Many of the students believe that a specific scene is being described, some momentary event, but they also hold out the possibility of an abstract idea, too. Maybe both, a specific something with a larger meaning.

Edna Wolf summarizes where they have come, noting that they are all in their own way trying to account for the words and images in the poem, and she urges them to look more closely at the individual words of the poem. "What is a route of evanescence? And why a rush of cochineal?"

"A route that's changing, and then vanishing?"

"So not a fixed route. That argues against the sun or a mail truck."

"Not necessarily."

"Maybe something that flies. Maybe a bee or a bird."

"Oh sure, a poem about the birds and the bees."

Everyone enjoys a little comic relief and they look at their professor to see if she minds; then they come back to their work.

"Resonance is a sound word applied to color, and . . . so is rush. A rushing something that makes a noise . . . and disturbs things."

The students examine the individual words of the poem for a while this way and then Edna Wolf asks them, "Now what about the overall poem itself, its form, its rhyme, its meter. You studied that in high school."

The students pick up the challenge, noting that "Wheel" rhymes with "Cochineal" and that if you stretch it a little, "Head" rhymes a little bit with "ride," or at least sounds like it. And the poem has beat, but it is not always perfect. And the students notice all these words with "r's."

"The last two lines are a problem, though," one young man insists. "They just don't fit. Here's this scene, and then . . . I don't know what, maybe a comment on the scene. But I don't see how they go together yet."

The analysis proceeds, moving along on its own until that line of thought seems exhausted. Sensing this, Professor Wolf starts the class off in a new direction with her question, "Does anyone want to know who wrote this poem?"

A chorus of students reply, "Yes, tell us." Some others say, "What difference does it make?" A lively discussion develops around the issue of "author's intent"; is it important to know what the author meant? Finally, Professor Wolf asks whether anyone would object to knowing the author. And since no one objects, she tells them that the author is Emily Dickinson.

"Oh, I remember her. We studied her in high school. Didn't she live in New England somewhere? Amherst?"

"And she stayed to herself. What do you call it—recluse—and wouldn't see anybody. Lived in this little room in the family house."

"That lady was crazy," a young man who hadn't spoken before jumps in.

"Wait a minute now. That's not fair. And so what if she was, it's her poetry that . . ."

"A mad woman's ravings? Nobody sane would write a poem like this!"

"Wait a minute—no name calling. You don't like the poem so you attack the poet?"

"Well, is it a poem or isn't it? If she's crazy . . ."

Edna Wolf lets this tempest continue until it blows itself out, then asks what it might do for them if they knew more about the author and the author's intent.

"It's not what the author meant; it's what the reader makes of it."

"What do you think about that?" Edna Wolf asks. The class appears to be sharply divided between those who think the author's intent matters and those who don't. Several students argue that every individual has a right to his or her own interpretation. Professor Wolf asks them if that means that one interpretation is as good as another. That question really stirs the students up.

"Well, if it's your opinion and you're sincere about it, who can say?"

"Well, I can respect your opinion—tolerate it—but that doesn't mean mine is not a better interpretation."

"What do you mean, 'better'?"

"It fits the poem better, the images, what the author had in mind. You can't just go off on your own."

"Why not?"

The discussion bounces back and forth across the room; the students seem to forget that Edna Wolf is there or that this is a class. Finally, she leans forward, trying to get a turn. "You are dealing with some very difficult matters of aesthetic theory here. Let me try an interpretation for you, and you tell me if you think it is 'better' or 'worse' than some you have already offered. What if I were to tell you that I think this is a basketball game—say, the Boston Celtics and the Los Angeles Lakers. The 'route of evanescence' is the path of the basketball down the court. One team is in red uniforms and the other is in green."

"Oh, come on."

"No, listen to her, that's the rule."

"And as the player dribbles down the court," Professor Wolf continues, "the crowd watches, their heads bouncing up and down with the ball. The player with the ball slam dunks it—don't they call that delivering the mail? An 'easy morning's ride' for him. What do you think?" asks Professor Wolf, straining to keep a look of seriousness on her face.

"Oh, that's terrible, Dr. Wolf. How could you do that? You've ruined it."

"Hold on. Why not? She has accounted for every line."

"But the language, it's just not basketball language."

"It's better than the stuff you guys were coming up with."

"Oh, no, it's terrible."

A small brush fire rages and Edna Wolf sits back to watch it burn. "See what you started," the student next to her points out.

Finally someone asks, "Does this poem have a title?"

"Oh, we're back to author's intent?"

"No, seriously, does it have a title? If it does, I'd sure like to know what it is."

"No, hold on. I think we can get this on our own. We're almost there." The student who mentioned the birds and the bees earlier tries to put it all together. "You have to look at the first line: 'A Route of Evanescence.' That sets the limits right there. Something that goes on an impermanent, changing path and then vanishes. That has to be something that flies. When did she live?"

"Before the Celtics."

"That's for sure, and that's another thing that's wrong with the basketball interpretation."

"Mid-nineteenth century, right, Dr. Wolf?"

She nods affirmatively.

"O.K., so it's not an airplane. What flies that would be in her world? Birds, bees. She looks out into the garden from her room. She sees this creature come winging through; it stops at the flowers, and in a flash it's gone."

There is a moment of silence. The students ponder the interpretation. Some like it. Some are skeptical.

Edna Wolf sits forward. "For some time this poem was a mystery, and if you come on it cold, as we did this afternoon, it can be quite a puzzle. But scholars have discovered that it was a poem that Emily Dickinson included in one of her many letters to friends. In thanking a friend for a small painting of some flowers known as Indian Pipes, Emily wrote back, 'I cannot make an Indian Pipe, but please accept a Hummingbird,' and included this poem."

Another silence. The students are busy reading the poem one more time.

"A resonance of green, a rush of red."

"What are the revolving wheels?"

"The wings, the little wings whirring."

"And the sounds, I can hear it."

"I still don't get the mail from Tunis."

A student points out that hummingbirds can fly 125 miles per hour. And they migrate—maybe to North Africa?

"Maybe," Edna Wolf stands up. "But let's take a break, we've been at this for more than an hour. Let's come back and see if we can push this a little deeper. Maybe we can get to some deeper level of meaning."

The students go after soft drinks. A few go outside for some fresh air. Some sit on the grass in clusters, still carrying on their little disagreements.

When the students return from their break, Edna Wolf begins. "We don't always know the subject of a poem, and it is important, therefore, to learn to do what we did this morning. In this case, scholars happened to discover this letter with the reference to the hummingbird. So we can continue now with the assumption about the author's intent. Some of you saw some other things as well, and if we didn't have that letter, perhaps we would look at the poem differently. But let's assume, for the rest of the discussion, that the subject is a hummingbird. We don't stop there. The author has created this set of images for us to respond to, this metaphor for . . . for what?

What is the hummingbird like? Or what is it that is like this hummingbird?"

More silence, deep pondering this time.

"Certain things in nature, most everything in nature comes and
goes. It's here and then it vanishes. The leaves, the blossoms, the birds
all die."

"To me it seems like, well . . . certain things enter our lives . . .
maybe only for a brief time . . . but they can make a difference. Maybe
she's saying, or the poem is saying, something like that."

"It's a very sad poem now all of a sudden for me. I see this
disturbed lady, looking out on her garden. And this hummingbird
comes, and it's the big event of her day, and it vanishes in an instant."

"But is that sad? Look what she made out of that moment. I think
it's beautiful."

"Didn't she write a lot of letters; she wouldn't see people directly, but she wrote to them? So here comes this little creature,
bringing her another letter from some exotic city. Some message, some
news about the world."

"It seems like bad news to me, if everything is . . . vanishing."

There is a pause, then Edna Wolf asks, "What do you think of
this metaphor of the hummingbird, then? Is it fresh and provocative?
Does it turn you in upon yourself to ponder life?"

"Well, yes, once you comprehend its meaning, it gives you all
kinds of things to think about. The hummingbird stands for, as
someone suggested earlier, life itself. We are all the hummingbird, all
is evanescence."

There is a lively exchange about whether life is just fleeting and
meaningless, or whether the meaning of life comes from the knowledge humans have of its impermanence. One student suggests that
maybe the purpose of poetry and other forms of art is to provide that
meaning, or at least to raise questions.

At the close of the second hour, Edna Wolf thanks the students
for working so hard and doing so much good thinking. "During our
inquiry we raised the question about whether one interpretation of a
poem can be better than another. For next time I want you to think
about whether one *poem* can be better than another. What makes a
poem a good poem or a bad poem? I'm going to pass out to you an
earlier version of this poem, from Emily's own pen, some 20 years
before. She made two attempts to capture this bird in verse, and I want
you to think about whether it is possible to say that one poem is better
than the other. Here it is."

Edna Wolf passes out a single sheet of paper with these lines
on it:

Within my garden rides a Bird
Upon a single Wheel
Whose spokes a dizzy Music make
as 'twere a traveling Mill—

He never stops, but slackens
Above the ripest rose
Partakes without alighting
And praises as he goes,

Till every spice is tasted—
And then his fairy Gig
Reels in remoter atmospheres—
And I rejoin my dog—.

"What do you think about the metaphors here? Can you compare the language in the two poems?"

The students slip the poem into their notebooks, pack up their things, and wander out into the hall. Edna Wolf sits alone for a moment at the table. All of her hummingbirds have vanished. She ponders the discussion for a moment. It was good, but could there be a way to make it better? She remembers going to a conference recently where she saw a demonstration of a videodisc accessed by computer. The material was on the classic poem "Ulysses" by Tennyson. It was impressive, laser access to a choice of professional actors reading the poem, a brief film clip on Ulysses, another on the context of the Peloponnesian Wars, and a choice of interviews with critics. Would it be possible to find such a resource on Emily Dickinson, or better yet to make one of her own with one of the new authoring languages? Something that would bring Emily Dickinson to the classroom—her home, Amherst, a manuscript in her own handwriting. Not for a lecture—no, not for that—but to bring in just the right resource as it came up naturally in the inquiry. The video would have to aid the thinking process, not interrupt; it would need to provide an even stronger stimulus for debate. My goodness, could such an old traditionalist as herself be having such "hi-tech" thoughts?

CONCLUSIONS

Teachers who use inquiry and discovery strategies are hoping to teach their students to think. But "learning to think" can mean many things. Thinking is no simple, unidimensional activity. It can take a critical or creative turn; it may be carried on through an interior monologue or exterior dialogue. It may involve inductive or deductive reasoning, problem solving, or decision making. It will take on various forms depending on the way language is engaged in the process. Thinking is no simple matter and clear thinking is difficult to achieve, because thinking processes break down so easily and at so many points. Nonetheless, learning to think is not impossible; it involves learning the rules, the patterns, the techniques, and the pitfalls of different kinds of thinking within various subject areas. Good thinking also involves learning to monitor the activity of one's own mind. All of this is learned by practice—by thinking—under the guidance and criticism of an effective mentor, presumably a teacher who is also a "good thinker" and who understands thinking processes. Above all, thinking involves asking questions—sometimes new questions about old questions in the search for new answers. Teachers who want to help their students become better at thinking usually enjoy using some adaptation of the inquiry and discovery strategy.

NOTES

1. M. Burns, "Teaching 'What To Do' in Arithmetic vs. Teaching 'What To Do and Why,'" *Educational Leadership*, 43, 34-38. Cited in Robert Marzano and Associates, *Dimensions of Thinking* (Alexandria, VA: Association for Supervision and Curriculum Development, 1988).

2. A.E. Lawson and J.W. Renner, "A Quantitative Analysis of Responses to Piagetian Tasks and Its Implications for Education," *Science Education*, 58, pp. 545-59. Cited in Joanne Kurfiss, *Critical Thinking* (Washington, DC: Association for the Study of Higher Education, 1988).

3. D.N. Perkins, R. Allen, and J. Hafner, "Difficulties in Everyday Reasoning" in W. Maxwell (Ed.) *Thinking* (Philadelphia: The Franklin Institute Press, 1983). Cited in Raymond Nickerson, David Perkins, and Edward Smith, *The Teaching of Thinking* (Hillsdale, NJ: Lawrence Erlbaum, 1985), pp. 136-37. The variables included length of the argument made, lines of argument included, awareness of objections to positions taken, being "off track," relationship of reasons to conclusions, and overall rating of the argument.

4. Joanne Kurfiss, *Critical Thinking* (Washington, DC: Association for the Study of Higher Education, 1988), p. 1.

5. Matthew Lipman, "Some Thoughts on the Foundations of Reflective Education" in Joan Baron and Robert Sternberg, *Teaching Thinking Skills: Theory and Practice* (New York: W.H. Freeman, 1987), p. 153.

6. Richard Paul, "Dialogical Thinking: Critical Thoughts Essential to the Acquisition of Rational Knowledge and Passions" in Baron and Sternberg, *Teaching Thinking Skills*, p. 139.

7. Raymond Nickerson, "Why Teach Thinking?" in Baron and Sternberg, *Teaching Thinking Skills*, p. 31.

8. Ibid., pp. 31-32.

9. Richard Paul, "Dialogical Thinking: Critical Thought Essential to the Acquisition of Rational Knowledge and Passions" in Baron and Sternberg, *Teaching Thinking Skills*, p. 129.

10. Matthew Lipman, "Some Thoughts on the Foundations of Reflective Education" in Baron and Sternberg, *Teaching Thinking Skills*, p. 156. See also Marzano, et al., *Dimensions of Thinking*, p. 680.

11. Edys Quellmalz, "Developing Reasoning Skills" in Baron and Sternberg, *Teaching Thinking Skills*, p. 87. Quellmalz makes interesting comparisons of the relative contributions of philosophy and psychology to the field of thinking.

12. See Anthony Sanford, *Cognition and Cognitive Psychology* (New York: Basic Books, 1985), Chapters 12-14, for a review of the research on thinking processes that has been done by cognitive psychologists.

13. See Daniel Tanner and Laurel Tanner, *Curriculum Development* (New York: Macmillan, 1980), p. 399, for a discussion of Dewey's interest in cultivating thinking skills. John Dewey, *How We Think* (Lexington, MA: Heath, 1910) and *How We Think: A Restatement of the Relation of Reflective Thinking to the Educative Process* (Boston: Heath, 1933).

14. Diane Halpern, *Thought and Knowledge* (Hillsdale, NJ: Lawrence Erlbaum, 1984), p. 3.

15. For a chart that lists various goals for a critical thinking curriculum see Robert Ennis, "A Taxonomy of Critical Thinking Dispositions and Abilities" in Baron and Sternberg, *Teaching Thinking Skills*, p. 12 ff.

16. Ennis, "Taxonomy of Critical Thinking," p. 12. See also Barry Beyer, *Practical Strategies for the Teaching of Thinking* (Boston: Allyn & Bacon, 1987), p. 19.

17. Raymond Nickerson, David Perkins, and Edward Smith, *The Teaching of Thinking*, p. 50.

18. Matthew Lipman, "Some Thoughts on the Foundations of Reflective Education," in Baron and Sternberg, *Teaching Thinking Skills*, p. 157.

19. Beyer, *Practical Strategies*, p. 19.

20. Chet Meyers, *Teaching Students to Think Critically* (San Francisco, Jossey-Bass, 1988). Meyers's thesis is that "critical thinking should . . . be developed in different ways by teachers in different disciplines" (p. xi).

21. Beyer, *Practical Strategies*, p. 33.

22. Kurfiss, *Critical Thinking*, p. 2.

23. Beyer, *Practical Strategies*, p. 33.

24. Ibid., p. 34.

25. Ibid., p. 35.

26. Nickerson, Perkins, and Smith, *Teaching of Thinking*, p. 86.

27. Ibid., p. 87

28. Ibid., pp. 90-92. Nickerson discusses each of these abilities in greater detail than is done here.

29. Marzano, et al., *Dimensions of Thinking*, pp. 23-28.

30. Richard Paul, "Dialogical Thinking: Critical Thought Essential to the Acquisition of Rational Knowledge and Passions" in Baron and Sternberg, *Teaching Thinking Skills*, p. 128. The observations about dialogical thinking made in the rest of this paragraph draw freely on this excellent chapter. The quotations are from pp. 130 and 132.

31. Marzano, et al., *Dimensions of Thinking*, p. 17, 28.

32. Loren Crane, "Unlocking the Brain's Two Powerful Learning Systems," *Human Intelligence Newsletter*, Winter 1983, 4(4), p. 7, cited in Barry Beyer, *Practical Strategies*, p. 36.

33. Nickerson, Perkins, and Smith, *Teaching of Thinking*, p. 44.

34. D.N. Perkins, "Thinking Frames: An Integrative Perspective on Teaching Cognitive Skills" in Baron and Sternberg, *Teaching Thinking Skills*, p. 57.

35. Barry Beyer, *Practical Strategies*, p. 20, 25.

36. Nickerson, Perkins, and Smith, *Teaching of Thinking*, p. 45.

37. Ibid., p. 46.

38. For a detailed listing of the studies from which this summary of findings is drawn, see Kurfiss, *Critical Thinking*, pp. 30-31.

39. Beyer, *Practical Strategies*, p. 19.

40. Kurfiss, *Critical Thinking*, p. 42.

41. Marzano, et al., *Dimensions of Thinking*, p. 9.

42. Nickerson, Perkins, and Smith, *Teaching of Thinking*, p. 103.

43. Some of these thinking skills programs include Feuerstein's "Instrumental Enrichment" Program, the "Structure of Intellect" Program based on the work of Guilford, "Science...A Process Approach," "BASICS," "ThinkAbout," the "CoRT" Program, "ADAPT," "DOORS," "COMPAS," "LOGO," "Philosophy for Children," and many others. Among those programs specifically designed for higher education settings are "Project Intelligence," a collaborative project involving a company, Harvard University, and the Venezuelan Ministry of Education; "Patterns of Problem Solving," developed by Rubenstein at UCLA; Schoenfeld's "Mathematical Problem Solving," developed at the University of California, Berkeley; "A Practicum in Thinking," developed by the Psychology Department at the University of Cincinnati; the "Cognitive Studies Project" at Manhattan Community College; the "Portable Patient Problem Pack" (P4), developed by Barrows and Tamblyn for medical students; "ADAPT," developed by a group of professors at the University of Nebraska, Lincoln; "DOORS," patterned after ADAPT; "COMPAS," a cooperative project of a consortium of seven community colleges; "SOAR," developed for the sciences at Xavier University; "DORIS," used with freshman at California State University, Fullerton; and a number of programs that deal with written and spoken

language. For a useful brief description of these and other thinking skills programs, see Nickerson, Perkins, and Smith, *Teaching of Thinking*, Part II, Chapters 6-10. See also Paul Chance, *Thinking in the Classroom: A Survey of Programs* (New York: Teachers College Press, 1986).

44. Matthew Lipman, "Some Thoughts on the Foundations of Reflective Education" in Baron and Sternberg, *Teaching Thinking Skills*, p. 153.

45. Niel Postman and Charles Weingartner, *Teaching as a Subversive Activity* (New York: Delacorte Press, 1969), pp. 34-37.

46. Louis Raths, et al., *Teaching for Thinking*, 2nd ed., (New York: Teachers College Press, 1986), pp. 164-67. The headings are direct quotes, the elaborations are a paraphrase of the more extensive elaborations made by the authors under each heading. See also Meyers, *Teaching Students to Think Critically*, Chapter 5, "Structuring Classes to Promote Critical Thought," for similar ideas.

47. See Harold Morine and Greta Morine, *Discovery: A Challenge to Teachers* (Englewood Cliffs, NJ: Prentice-Hall, 1973). The authors outline and discuss various types of discovery lessons in Chapter 6, "Modes of Discovery," p. 80ff.

48. Jerome Kagan, "Learning, Attention and the Issue of Discovery" in Lee Shulman and Evan Keislar, *Learning by Discovery: A Critical Appraisal* (Chicago: Rand McNally, 1966), p. 158ff.

49. Postman and Weingartner, *Teaching as a Subversive Activity*, pp. 36-37.

50. See Meyers, *Teaching Students to Think*, Chapter 6, "Designing Effective Written Assignments."

51. Beyer, *Practical Strategies*, p. 66.

52. Raymond Nickerson, *Reflections on Reasoning*, (Hillsdale, NJ: Lawrence Erlbaum, 1986). For a more complete discussion of assertions, arguments, and beliefs, see Chapters 3, 4, and 5.

53. Nickerson, *Reflections on Reasoning*, p. 112.

54. Ibid., p. 71.

55. Diane Halpern, *Thought and Knowledge: An Introduction to Critical Thinking* (Hillsdale, NJ: Lawrence Erlbaum, 1984), p. 63.

56. Anthony Sanford, *Cognition and Cognitive Psychology* (New York: Basic Books, 1985), p. 357ff.

57. Sanford, *Cognition and Cognitive Psychology*, p. 70ff.

58. Halpern, *Thought and Knowledge*, p. 70ff. The examples and diagrams are adapted.

59. Nickerson, Perkins, and Smith, *Teaching of Thinking*, p. 113ff.

60. Halpern, *Thought and Knowledge*, p. 74ff. The chart is adapted from a similar chart by Halpern, p. 76.

61. Ibid., p. 78.

62. Raymond Nickerson, *Reflections on Reasoning*, The quotations are from pp. 70 and 71, respectively.

63. The discussion that follows is based on a similar but much more detailed discussion in Nickerson, Perkins, and Smith, *Teaching of Thinking*, pp. 118-30 and on Diane Halpern, *Thought and Knowledge*, Chapter 4, "Thinking as Hypothesis Testing," pp. 93-112.

64. Research evidence is cited in Nickerson, Perkins, and Smith, *Teaching of Thinking*, pp. 121-23. The "elephant story" is from p. 121. See also Anthony Sanford, *Cognition and Cognitive Psychology*, p. 336ff, for research on "overconfidence."

65. Nickerson, Perkins, and Smith, *Teaching of Thinking*, pp. 126-27.

66. Ibid., pp. 127-28.

67. Ibid., p. 30.

68. The background information for this section is based on Jacques Cousteau, *The Ocean World* (New York: Avondale Press/Harry N. Abrams, 1979), "The Lessons of Light," pp. 61-77.

69. Halpern, *Thought and Knowledge*, p. 160.

70. Ibid., p. 160.

71. Ibid., p. 165.

72. Nickerson, Perkins, and Smith, *Teaching of Thinking*, pp. 66-68.

73. A. Newell and H.A. Simon, *Human Problem Solving* (Englewood Cliffs, NJ: Prentice-Hall, 1972).

74. Nickerson, Perkins, and Smith, *Teaching of Thinking*, pp. 71-72. Nickerson summarizes the model set forth by Newell and Simon. The diagram is my own work.

75. The stages are outlined in another classic work on problem solving: G. Polya, *How to Solve It*, 2nd ed., (Princeton, NJ: Princeton University Press and New York: Doubleday, 1957). Cited in Nickerson, Perkins, and Smith, *Teaching of Thinking*, p. 75.

76. Nickerson, Perkins, and Smith, *Teaching of Thinking*, p. 71.

77. Sanford, *Cognition and Cognitive Psychology*, p. 309, cites a study by D.A. Hinsley, J.R. Hayes, and H.A. Simon, "From Words to Equations: Meaning and Representation in Algebra Word Problems" in P.A. Carpenter and M.A. Just, eds., *Cognitive Processes in Comprehension* (Hillsdale, NJ: Erlbaum, 1977).

78. For a discussion of problem types, see Sanford, *Cognition and Cognitive Psychology*, p. 286ff.

79. Halpern, *Thought and Knowledge*, p. 189.

80. The Tower of Hanoi problem is cited and explained in Halpern, *Thought and Knowledge*, p. 183, and by Sanford, *Cognition and Cognitive Psychology*, p. 297.

81. Halpern, *Thought and Knowledge*, p. 184-85.

82. Ibid., pp. 192-93.

83. Nickerson, Perkins, and Smith, *Teaching of Thinking*, pp. 74-81.

84. Ibid., pp. 78-89.

85. Sanford, *Cognition and Cognitive Psychology*, pp. 310-11.

86. Halpern, *Thought and Knowledge*, pp. 199-201. The problem about socks comes originally from J.F. Fixx, *Solve It* (New York: Doubleday, 1978).

87. The material for this section is drawn from and relies heavily on Halpern, *Thought and Knowledge*, Chapter 7, "Decision Making," p. 209ff.

88. Ibid., pp. 225-26.

89. The idea of the worksheet is presented in Halpern, *Thought and Knowledge*, p. 228ff. The personnel example is my own development.

90. Halpern, *Thought and Knowledge*, p. 234. For the concept of "ideal rule," Halpern cites R.R. Carkhuff, *The Art of Problem Solving* (Amherst, MA: Human Resource Development Press, 1973).

91. Ibid., pp. 221-22.

92. Nickerson, *Reflections on Reasoning*, p. 32.

93. Halpern, *Thought and Knowledge*, p. 222ff.

94. A colleague of the author, Dr. William Dorn, asks his freshman students in mathematics courses this question and gets answers such as these.

95. Halpern, *Thought and Knowledge*, p. 123.

96. Ibid., p. 137.

97. Ibid., pp. 137-52. The material presented below on relative frequency, subjective interpretations of frequency, and small sample size is based on this more detailed discussion in Halpern.

98. The material for this case is adapted from a case entitled "Alpen Ski Shoppes Incorporated: Selecting Advertising Appeals," written by Ron Gist, Professor of Marketing at the University of Denver. Marketing concepts were drawn from David W. Cravens and Charles W. Lamb, *Strategic Marketing: Cases and Applications* (Homewood, IL: Irwin, 1986), Chapter 3, "Guide to Case Analysis." A general book on using the case method is C. Roland Christensen, *Teaching and the Case Method* (Boston: Harvard Business School, 1987). Teachers interested in writing cases may wish to refer to Michiel Leenders and James Erskine, *Case Research: The Case Writing Method* (London, Ontario, Canada: School of Business Administration, The University of Western Ontario, 1978). The Harvard Business School has been a leader in the use of the case method and in developing cases. For listings of cases and for their newsletter, write Harvard Business School, Publishing Division, Operations Department, Boston, MA 02163. There is also a *Case Research Journal* published by the Case Research Association, Ohio State University, 1775 College Road, Columbus, OH 43210.

99. Halpern, *Thought and Knowledge*, p. 27. The original reference is to E. Sapir, *Culture, Language and Personality* (Berkeley, CA: University of California Press, 1960) and B. Whorf, *Language, Thought and Reality* (Cambridge, MA: MIT Press, 1958).

100. Nickerson, *Reflections on Reasoning*, p. 4.

101. Halpern, *Thought and Knowledge*, p. 27.

102. S.I. Hayakawa, *Language in Thought and Action* (New York: Harcourt-Brace and World, 1964), cited in Nickerson, *The Teaching of Thinking*, p. 248-50.

103. Morton White, *The Age of Analysis* (New York: George Brazilier, 1957), Chapter 13, "Logical Positivism: Rudolph Carnap," p. 203ff.

104. For a summary of Ayer's argument, see John Foster, *Ayer*, (Boston: Routledge and Kegan, 1985).

105. White, *Age of Analysis*, p. 203ff.

106. Marc Belth, *The Process of Thinking* (New York: David McKay, 1977), p. 32.

107. Ibid., p. 26.

108. Ibid., p. 34.

109. White, *Age of Analysis*, p. 220.

110. Eric Gould, *Reading into Writing: A Rhetoric, Reader, and Handbook* (Boston: Houghton Mifflin, 1983), p. 69.

111. The examples for this section are drawn from Halpern, *Thought and Knowledge*, Chapter 2, "The Relationship Between Thought and Language," and Nickerson, *Reflections on Reasoning*, Chapter 6, "Stratagems," and Chapter 7, "Some Common Reasoning Fallacies," pp. 102ff. The arrangement and classification of the material is the author's own synthesis.

112. Belth, *The Process of Thinking*, p. 7.

113. Ibid., pp. 56-59.

114. Ibid., p. 67.

115. Ibid., pp. 67-73.

116. Ibid., pp. 29-33.

117. Ibid., pp. 35-36. The author has paraphrased freely from five criteria provided by Belth.

118. Ibid., pp. 75-76.

119. Ibid., The types of metaphors are listed p. 79. The examples are my own.

120. Ibid., Chapter 5, "Poetic Thinking," p. 95ff.

121. Ibid., p. 119.

122. Ibid., p. 121.

123. The text of the poem is taken from Charles R. Anderson, *Emily Dickinson's Poetry: Stairway of Surprise* (Garden City, NY: Doubleday & Co., 1966). The letter identifying the subject of the poem is mentioned (and documented) on p. 132. The earlier version of the poem is also presented on pp. 132-33. The poem is discussed in detail in Chapter 7, "Evanescence." Details about Dickinson's life can be found in the biography by Richard B. Sewell, *The Life of Emily Dickinson*, vols. I and II (New York: Farrar, Straus, Giroux, 1974). Biographical material and a valuable introduction to interpretation of form and content can be found in Thomas H. Johnson, *Emily Dickinson, An Interpretative Biography* (Cambridge, MA: The Belknap Press, 1960). A psychobiography of Dickinson, which stresses the pathological

nature of her maladjustments, is John Cody's *After Great Pain: The Inner Life of Emily Dickinson* (Cambridge, MA: Belknap Press, 1971). For critical work by several recognized scholars, see Richard B. Sewall, *A Collection of Critical Essays* (Englewood Cliffs, NJ: Prentice-Hall, 1963). Obviously, there is a huge corpus of biographical and critical work on Emily Dickinson. For a comprehensive bibliography, see Willis J. Buckingham, *Emily Dickinson: An Annotated Bibliography* (Bloomington, IN: Indiana University Press, 1970). For a brief overview of Dickinson's life and work, see Christopher Benfey, "The Riddles of Emily Dickinson," *The New York Times Book Review*, May 18, 1986, p. 1ff.

Groups and Teams

I had three chairs in my house; one for solitude, two for friendship, three for society. —Henry David Thoreau, *Walden*

LIVING AND LEARNING IN GROUPS

It has been said that "from the family of our birth to our funeral entourage, groups have a significant impact on our development and behavior."[1] As Malcolm and Hulda Knowles have noted: "First in the family, then the clan, the tribe, the guild, the community, and the state, groups have been used as instruments of government, work, fighting, worship, recreation and education."[2] Like the social insects, bees and ants, humans organize for collective survival.

In the information age, groups pervade every aspect of human life: executives work through committees, scientists conduct research in teams, church workers hold conferences, citizens serve on political action groups, and psychologists conduct group therapy. Indeed, so much time is spent in groups today, that they have become a source of much joking.[3] A committee has been defined as "a group of people who can do nothing individually but, as a group, can meet and decide that nothing can be done."

Whatever the feeling (or reality) that society is oversupplied with unproductive groups, there is no question that educated persons today must know how to participate effectively in groups and on teams. Teachers are increasingly turning to groups and teams, not only to achieve the desired educational outcomes of some aspect of their subject, but also to ensure that their students will know how to work well together in groups. But what is a "group," and how can groups be used in educational settings?

Defining "group" would appear to be relatively simple, but scholars have struggled for years to agree about the essential components of an appropriate definition. Different definitions stress different things. *Relational definitions* stress the interpersonal exchange that takes place; *structural definitions* stress the norms, roles, and patterns of power within the group; and *psychological definitions* stress the motivations and perceptions of group members.[4] Because it is not easy to arrive at one universally applicable definition of "group," it may be more useful to think about the elements of a satisfactory definition, in order to arrive at a better understanding of the characteristics of a group.[5] Malcolm and Hulda Knowles offer some helpful criteria. A collection of people is likely to be a "group" when it possesses the following characteristics:

- **A Definable Membership**—collection of two or more people identifiable by name and type.
- **Consciousness of Membership**—the members think of themselves as a group, have a "collective perception of unity," and a conscious identification with each other.
- **A Sense of Shared Purpose**—the members have the same "object model" or goal or ideals.
- **Interaction**—the members communicate with one another, influence one another, react to one another.
- **Ability to Act in a Unitary Manner**—the group can behave as a single organism.[6]

Although each group will have its own particular qualities, most groups have these general characteristics.

When is a group too small or too big to be a group? Can the interaction of two people (commonly referred to as a "dyad") be considered a "group"? Although dyads are widely used in classrooms and are generally treated in the literature on group processes as "groups," it should be noted that the interaction of two people has some characteristics that are quite different from the interaction of three people.[7] When two people interact, there is only one channel to connect the two; when a third party is present, there are multiple channels, an opportunity for a "network" or "system," and, most important, the opportunity for the third party to observe and comment on the communication of the other two. The upper limit to size depends on the purpose of the group. Although some "magic numbers" have been proposed, the upward limit depends on the task to be accomplished. Depending on the purpose, adding to the group size can make an important difference—sometimes positive, sometimes negative. One useful rule for size is as follows: "A group needs to contain a number of people sufficiently small for each to be aware of and have some relation to the other."[8] If some members have no opportunity to interact because the group is too large, their contribution to the goal will be minimal or insignificant. On the other hand, a group needs to be large enough to accomplish its task. Size depends on purpose.

Over the years, different types of groups have developed to serve various purposes, including (with some overlapping of functions) task groups, t-groups, focus groups, encounter groups, sensory awareness groups, quality circles, leaderless groups, organizational development groups, synanon groups, sociodrama groups, creativity groups, and so on.[9] Not all group methods are relevant to college classroom settings, but many, with some adaptation, can be very useful. College teachers who want to use groups as a teaching strategy begin by asking what type of group might be best suited to the kind of learning outcomes desired.

WHEN GROUPS ARE USED

What is it, then, that groups are good for, and what are some of their limitations? Many faculty members have spent all too many hours on academic committees—sometimes their only experience of group processes in an educational setting—and it is not surprising that the suggestion that groups can be useful in instruction is sometimes met with blatant skepticism. For what educational outcomes are groups especially useful? What are the likely hazards and shortcomings involved in employing group processes?

One useful test of whether or not to use a group process is to examine whether the task itself is anything more than "summative," that is, does the task require anything more than the sum of the outputs of each individual member? In tasks where the output transcends the total of individual outputs, there is an "assembly effect."

> An assembly effect occurs when the group is able to achieve collectively something which could not have been achieved by any member working alone or by a combination of individual efforts. The assembly effect bonus is productivity which exceeds the potential of the most capable member and also exceeds the sum of the efforts of the group members working separately.[10]

Therefore, if a group were to perform a task that could be performed just as well (or better) by an individual or as merely the sum of individual efforts, a group process probably is not appropriate.[11]

What kind of collective activities are groups able to perform best and what are the benefits of using a group? First, research has established that there is simply a higher level of ideation (the having of ideas) in groups. People not only pool their ideas, but there is something about the process that generates more ideas. In an early review of studies of group problem solving, it was found that ideation is 60 to 90 percent higher for groups than for individuals.[12] The same review revealed that in general groups produce better products than individuals. Consider this classic problem:

> A man bought a horse for $60 and sold it for $70. Then he bought it again for $80 and sold it one more time for $90. How much money did he make in the horse-trading business.[13]

For this problem, individuals tend to present far fewer options (they close down on a single solution), and their solutions are far less creative than when the same individuals discuss the options in a group. There is no guarantee that groups will come up with the best solutions to problems, but they will usually generate more ideas and alternatives.

Second, groups are useful in the change process, particularly with regard to opinions, attitudes, and beliefs, what social scientists label OABs. A great amount of research on OABs was done following World War II, and the findings are among those fundamental principles of the social sciences summarized and reported by Bernard Berelson and Gary Steiner in *Human Behavior: An Inventory of Scientific Findings*.[14] In brief, "people hold opinions, attitudes and beliefs (OABs) that are in harmony with their group memberships and identifications." OABs are rooted in group behavior and grow out of social contacts and group affiliations. In other words, opinions, attitudes, and beliefs are not simply the product of individual thinking but are rooted in social relationships. It is not surprising to learn, therefore, that OABs are not easily changed. In fact, "the more a person is emotionally involved in his beliefs, the harder it is to change him by argument or propaganda—that is, through an appeal to intelligence—to the point of virtual impossibility." Again, not surprisingly, "when OABs do change, it is through the influence of a reference group, perhaps a new affiliation."[15] More recently, and supporting these same principles, the literature on persuasion suggests that the best persuasive technique is listening—helping people to "talk through" their objections. Groups, therefore, are especially useful for examining "matters of the heart," what educators refer to as "affective learning."

Third, some of the early work by Kurt Lewin demonstrated that there is a higher acceptance of outcomes when they are arrived at through a group process.[16] Members are more likely to accept an outcome (even if they don't agree with it fully) if they have had the opportunity to discuss it in a group. In recent years an outpouring of literature on management, leadership, and organizational change has stressed the importance of involvement (participation and inclusion) in bringing about acceptance of new ideas and change.[17] Groups produce in the participants a sense of ownership over outcomes.

These are good reasons for using groups, and teachers who are especially interested in affective learning outcomes will want to consider the use of group processes, but there are also some drawbacks. Research has shown that some negative things can also happen in groups. For one thing, individuals, in general, tend not to work as hard in groups as they do as individuals. Known as "The Ringlemann Effect," from the researcher by that name who conducted crude tug-of-war experiments in the 1880s, it has been established that two people don't pull twice as hard as one and three don't pull three times as hard as one, and so forth, as group size increases. More recent studies by social psychologists have established clearly a similar idea called "social loafing." It appears that the most social loafing occurs when it is not possible to distinguish the individual's contribution to the group output.[18] As teachers, we need to be aware of and deal with "social loafing" when we use groups.

Second, groups tend to be unwieldy, inefficient, and slow. Although the quality of group decisions may in the end be higher, it takes a long time to get results. One reason for this is that groups tend to have a short attention span. One study revealed that the average length of time used by a group to discuss a single theme was 58 seconds. Groups tend to jump quickly from topic to topic.[19] If we are aware that groups can be very inefficient, we can help students working in groups to budget their time and stay on task.

A third hazard is known as "groupthink." The term was coined by social psychologist Irving Janis in 1972 to apply to "a mode of thinking that people engage in when they are deeply involved in a cohesive in-group, when the members' striving for unanimity override their motivation to realistically appraise alternative courses of action."[20] Janis studied the decision-making groups of United States presidents and concluded that there was a common pattern: a lack of healthy disagreement led to such major fiascoes as Pearl Harbor (1941), the Bay of Pigs invasion (1962), and the escalation of the Vietnam War (1964-72). Janis includes the following among his list of symptoms of groupthink: an illusion of invulnerability and morality, the rationalization of criticism, and shared stereotypes of opposing groups.[21] What happens is that the group develops an illusion of unanimity, and individual members either buckle under group pressure or engage in self-censorship of their opposing views. If we are aware of the groupthink phenomenon, we can help our students avoid it.

A fourth hazard is known as "the risky shift" phenomenon. Simply stated, "the risky shift refers to the fact that groups tend to gamble more than their individual members do if each were making the decision alone. That is, a group tends to select an alternative that has a bigger payoff but a lower probability of attainment." Although not true of all groups, some groups have a tendency to take more risks and act less conservatively than individuals. The apparent reason for the risky shift (the shifting of risk to the group) is a diffusion of responsibility; if everyone is responsible, then no one is.[22] If we are aware of this phenomena, we can point it out when it seems to be occurring in a group. Consider the following teachers who are using group processes.

Vicki Hastings teaches courses in the Wellness Program at Pacific Coast Community College. The program is part of the community outreach mission of the College and draws males and females of all ages, from every walk of life, and from every ethnic background and social class, who have, nevertheless, one thing in common: the desire to lead healthier, happier lives. Although their motivations for joining the classes are often quite different, they share a common desire to improve the way they look and feel. Vicki has taught physical fitness courses long enough to know that making lasting changes in the body—real changes that will produce long-term improvements in personal appearance and physical health—is not easy.

Such changes require fundamental alterations in attitudes about a whole host of things: diet, exercise patterns, mental dispositions, work, leisure, and way of life. "Changes in the body require changes in the heart," she points out. Vicki knows, for example, that some of her students have to do some real soul-searching about their orientations to food. Others have to work on self-concept, basic attitudes toward their body, issues of self-control, and a reworking of life goals and priorities. "I know that I can't do it all, that some of these problems, for some people, require counseling or medical attention; but I know that if I don't begin to address these issues, I will just be leading another exercise class, where half of the students drop out after a few weeks." She also knows that the class needs to be fun, that the students want to enjoy each other, be active, and "get a lift" from the class. Lately, Vicki has begun to use more and more group activities. She has noticed how groups give people a feeling of belonging, a sense of support, and a medium for interaction. She has observed, with pleasant surprise, that when the climate is right, people aren't afraid to share some of their fears and insecurities, some of their quirky attitudes and secret hang-ups.

Nancy Green teaches interior design at the Art Institute of the South. She and her colleagues have developed a carefully worked out curriculum designed to develop in their students the "real-world" competencies needed to be successful in the interior design business. Nancy teaches an integrative seminar, the final, capstone course in the curriculum. The goal of that course is to provide an opportunity for students to pull together and apply their learning from all of the previous courses in the curriculum. Nancy has noticed from her own interior design business, that when she develops a proposal to make a bid on a project, she and the other employees in her business have to work together as a team. "There are five of them now," she notes, "and each employee has some specialized skills and plays a unique role on the team." Her chief assistant is good with creative ideas and renderings for the layout; one long-time associate has become an expert on materials and furnishings and where to find them. Nancy knows she is lucky to have a trustworthy financial person who is excellent on costing out projects, and the newly hired Art Institute graduate is a whiz on computer-assisted design layout. Nancy's role, increasingly, is to help them function as a team.

Nancy believes the integrative seminar ought to simulate, as nearly as possible, what it is like to put together a real bid on a project. So she has decided to break the class of 20 into four teams of five students each, just about the right size for breaking the job into its component parts. Each of the four teams works on the same project. By working together as a team, the students will have more ideas than if they were to work alone. She knows the hazards, e.g., some social loafing by a couple of students who tend to be a little lazy. She knows also that there will be a tendency for groups to propose solutions that have higher risk of not working out, either from a design standpoint or financially. But, all in all, she believes that the quality of the projects will be higher if she uses a group strategy. Among other things, the students will learn what it takes to work effectively as a team.

Jonathan Wesley teaches the class in social transformations at New England Theological Seminary. Having a background in psychology as well as social ethics, Professor Wesley is deeply concerned about individual attitudes and contemporary social issues. He has worked at the denomination level on the Task Force on Social Action and with several local churches in developing viable programs for their congregations. During the summers he is in demand as a leader for workshops at camps and retreats. From all of this experience, Professor Wesley has become certain of one thing: People's social attitudes are deeply rooted in their group memberships and their personal experiences. Furthermore, these attitudes are not easily transformed. He knows what won't work: lectures, sermons, and social action seminars that simply present information. "There was a time," he reminisces, "when we thought that if people were just better informed, they would change their attitudes. The Church saw its role as an information provider. Today, we know that information is important, but not enough." Professor Wesley has come to believe that for society to change, people must change, and that these personal transformations come about best through participation in small groups, which he likes to call "Transformation Groups." Not quite t-groups, not quite group therapy, but drawing heavily on the principles of both, Professor Wesley's Transformation Groups provide an open and accepting climate where people can examine their opinions, attitudes, and beliefs.

All of these teachers are exploring the use of groups in their teaching. All are using groups in rather different ways and for different purposes. It will be useful for them to know something about the research that has been done on groups to better understand what to look for and how to facilitate the groups they are using with their students.

ORIGINS OF THE FORMAL USE AND STUDY OF GROUPS

Although much attention has been given in recent years to the importance of groups in modern social structure—as if to suggest that the prevalence of groups is a new phenomenon—human beings for centuries have assembled themselves into groups for a variety of purposes and have given their groups special names, such as "guilds," "councils," "tribunes," "communes," "congregations," "troupes," "teams," and "companies."[23] Groups have also been used for educational purposes, from the small "bands" who followed such wandering scholars as Confucius or Plato, to the "guilds" of students in the Middle Ages who hired faculty, paid their salaries, evaluated their performance, and called them to task for not covering material they agreed to teach. How far the "student union" has strayed from its original purposes!

In modern times, groups have been used in more explicit and self-conscious ways: for educational purposes to bring about change, for therapy, and for achieving goals through team efforts. What are the origins of this more deliberate use of groups? When did the "group movement" start, and who were the key leaders in exploring, identifying, and employing the educative potential that resides in group processes?

The self-conscious use of groups for educational and therapeutic purposes has its historical origin not in one movement or key thinker, but in several. One important historical source has been the use and study of groups in employment settings. A classic set of research studies conducted by Elton Mayo and his colleagues at Western Electric in the 1930s revealed the importance of "human factors" in the productivity of workers.[24] Although the variables being studied had to do with better working conditions, such as lighting, it turned out that the personal attention being given to the workers as a group by the researchers proved to be the most important consideration. Now known for the classic "Hawthorne Effect" in research methods, the study set in motion further explorations of the importance of human factors in work environments where people work in groups. Expanded efforts to train workers in group processes gave birth to the Human Relations Movement.

The "movement" was advanced, somewhat by accident, in 1946 when Kurt Lewin and his associates were conducting group training for community leaders responsible for enforcing the Connecticut Fair Employment Practices Act. Lewin, an immigrant from Germany and a professor at MIT, was well known for his work in "group dynamics" and his research on the effects of authoritarian and democratic leadership styles on group behavior.[25] The group leaders held evening meetings to discuss the processes that were taking place in the groups each day. Some of the workshop participants began attending these meetings, in which their behavior and its effect on the group was discussed and analyzed openly. It was discovered that when group members were confronted objectively with data about their behavior and were encouraged to think about that data in a nondefensive way, meaningful learning could occur. The staff began to theorize about what they were observing and began planning ways in which group experiences could be structured to heighten this kind of learning.[26] In the summer of 1947, shortly after Lewin's death, his associates met in Bethel, Maine, to sponsor the first formal group training programs, in which "trainers" assisted the group in discussing its behavior.[27] This kind of group became known as a "T-group" or "basic skill training group." In 1949, Lewin's former associates formed the National Training Laboratory for Group Development (NTL) under the auspices of the National Education Association with offices in Washington, DC.[28] From such inauspicious beginnings, the "t-group" took on many forms and has become widely used in diverse settings.

Another important historical source is the work of Carl Rogers and his advocacy of client-centered therapy. In 1946 and 1947—the same years that Lewin and his associates were working in the East—Rogers and his associates at the Counseling Center at the University of Chicago became involved in training personal counselors at the Veteran's Administration. The goal was to train counselors to become effective in working with GIs returning from World War II. In Rogers's own words: "Our staff felt that no amount of cognitive training would prepare them, so we experimented with an intensive group experience in which the trainees met for several hours each day in order better to understand themselves, to become aware of attitudes which might be self-defeating in the counseling relationship, and to relate to each other in ways that would be helpful and could carry over into the counseling work."[29] The Chicago groups led by Rogers focused explicitly on personal growth and differed somewhat from the "training groups" developed by Lewin and NTL. Eventually, Rogers moved to California and became involved with the encounter group movement there. In California, another "strand" of the group movement developed under the banner of "humanistic psychology," drawing eclectically on the work of Maslow, Reich, Jung, and various eastern religious traditions. In the 1960s an independent training center, The Esalen Institute, was established in northern California, where the "encounter group" reached its fullest expression.[30]

Another important historical source is the work of J.L. Moreno, an Austrian immigrant known chiefly for his work with role playing and psychodrama. Moreno, himself a colorful and spontaneous figure, developed the idea for a "spontaneity theater" while he was a medical student in Vienna. During his lunch hour he would sit in the park and tell stories to children who would spontaneously act them out. He loved to direct these little dramas from his favorite spot in the crotch of a tree. Later, when he came to New York during the Great Depression, he earned his living by engaging actors to dramatize daily news events. His methods for recreating social events led to the development and practice of psychodrama, which was later used widely in Veterans' hospitals to help patients reenact certain crisis events in order to gain a better understanding of the personal meaning of these events.[31] The work of Moreno showed that members of groups don't always sit and talk; sometimes they get up and act.

Another historical source is group therapy. Although the idea of therapy conducted in groups dates back as far as Freud and his followers, and although the term "group therapy" seems to have been coined by J.L. Moreno in the 1920s[32], the widespread use of groups for explicitly therapeutic purposes is also a post-World War II phenomenon. Confronted with numbers of disruptive patients at a Veterans' hospital and inadequate resources to treat each of these patients, a group of psychiatrists and psychologists led by W.R. Bion developed a theory for treating patients in groups. Bion's work at the Tavistock Institute in London became the basis for modern group therapy techniques.[33]

As groups began to be used widely in the 1960s and 1970s, they also came to be studied more seriously by academics, and a vast literature on group processes eventually emerged.[34] Groups have been studied from many vantage points, but most of the literature that is valuable to teachers—insights about group processes—comes from the field of speech communication.

What is known today about groups and teams? Have the years of studying group processes yielded consistent observable patterns of behavior, general principles, and theories about what takes place in groups? College teachers who use groups as a teaching strategy need to become effective "group-watchers." What can we expect to see?

WHAT SCHOLARS HAVE NOTICED ABOUT GROUPS

Most groups, whatever the type, go through various phases or *stages*. It takes a while for a group to become a group, to develop an identity and become productive. The life-cycle of groups has been the object of much research, and although scholars who study group behavior disagree on what to call these phases, most agree that groups pass through them. One classic formulation of these stages uses four catchy rhyming words:

- **Forming**—a stage of testing and member independence, with emphasis on defining the task.
- **Storming**—a stage of intragroup conflict and emotional expression.
- **Norming**—a stage of development of group cohesion and establishing the "rules."
- **Performing**—a stage of functional role relatedness and emergence of solutions.[35]

Most groups go through some stages.

Of particular interest to teachers is the way that ideas emerge in groups over time. In one useful theory a spiral model is set forth, whereby ideas appear to grow until they become "anchored" in the group's thinking. These anchors are then used as a base for additional ideas. This spiral process is described as follows:

One member introduces an idea, and other members respond with agreement or disagreement, extension or revision. The idea is the object of discussion, and it develops over time to reflect the group's viewpoint. When an idea is developed to the point that it is an object of agreement by all group members, the group anchors its position on that idea and introduces new preliminary ideas progressing from that anchor point of agreement.[36]

The group then reaches out from its anchor point, considers the new ideas, and tests these through a similar process.

Another thing to look for in groups is the nature of the communication at a very fundamental level of description. Who talks? How often do they talk? Who do people talk to? Who do they look at when they talk—one person, the group, the floor or ceiling? Who talks after whom and who interrupts whom? And what types of statements are being made—assertions, questions, responses?[37] And what is all this talk about?

Many scholars who have studied groups have noted that communication seems to be taking place at two levels, often simultaneously.[38] At one level, members are communicating about the *task* to be completed; at another level they are dealing with the *process* needs (sometimes referred to as "social" or "maintenance" needs) of the group members. The "task" is the activity that a group is required, either by someone or by itself, to perform. It is what people do, what they work on, or what they produce in and through groups.[39] If a group of students is asked to choreograph a brief aerobic exercise routine, or if another group is asked to produce a proposal for an interior design contract, that is their task. Some of the communication that takes place in groups is about the task, but not all of it.

Other communication is about the process. "If a group is composed of living, breathing members, then something is always happening. A group is a dynamic organism, always awake, never really still; group dynamics and interpersonal dynamics and intrapersonal dynamics are operating all the time."[40] When people participate in groups, they bring with them their individual needs for recognition, identity, status, and inclusion. Some of the key variables that researchers have identified as being important in the "process" or "social" dimension of group communication are "members' credibility, personal attraction, power or status, degree of similarity, conformity pressures, degree of trust among members, level of competition, language usage and communication strategies."[41] All of these variables can influence the social and emotional climate of the group. Process variables, in turn, affect the way in which the task is undertaken and completed. One may separate task and process dimensions of group behavior in theory, but the *in vivo* interaction of task and process behaviors in groups makes them virtually inseparable in practice.[42]

When the social or process needs of the group are being met in satisfactory ways the group becomes *cohesive*. Cohesiveness refers to the ability of the group members to get along, their loyalty, pride, and commitment to the group. Or, more simply, cohesiveness is the degree of liking that members have for each other.[43] When there is a high level of bickering in a group, when members express boredom or search for excuses to avoid group meetings or drop out, the group usually lacks cohesiveness. Something is "going wrong" at the process level. Cohesiveness is an output of an effective group process, but once established, it is an input to subsequent group activities.[44]

Furthermore, the outputs at the process level and task level are intertwined. If the output at the process level may be called "cohesiveness," and the output at the task level may be called "productivity," clearly, there must be a relationship. As might be expected, cohesive groups are more productive, but only up to a point. As cohesiveness increases, productivity increases until cohesiveness reaches such a high level that productivity falls off. How is this curvilinear relation explained? When group members become too fond of each other, they spend too much time socializing and too little time on the task. They may have a "reserve productivity" that could be much higher than their actual productivity, because they enjoy, perhaps too much, the process behaviors that make the group cohesive.[45]

As teachers who use group processes we will realize that communication is almost always taking place at two levels. It is natural and expected, then, that students aren't always focusing their activity exclusively on the task. Students have other (process) needs as well, and these will surface as a natural part of being in a group. One hopes that social needs will be met in such a way that the group will become cohesive, but an observant teacher knows when a group has become so cohesive that it no longer puts forth its best efforts on the task.

As groups mature, passing through various stages, they eventually develop a *structure*.[46] Just as a building has a structure—foundation, walls, roof, doors, windows—so a group also has a structure, where members "take their places" and serve particular functions. The group's structure is not always immediately obvious. Some people, because they have more to contribute, or because they have more initial status, take a more central place in the group's structure, while others end up on the periphery. Furthermore, different groups develop different kinds of communication networks, which also give the group structure. In some groups the communication moves back and forth from the members to one leader, like spokes of a wheel; in other groups, communication moves in a chain or hierarchy; in still others, communication is open and free-flowing with every member communicating with every other member. These networks of communication help to determine the group structure, and *vice versa*. The location of a member within a group's structure can have important consequences for morale, leadership, and friendship opportunities within the group.

The structure of a group becomes clearer as one examines the *roles* that various group members begin to play. The idea of roles was elaborated in some detail by sociologist Erving Goffman, who described the social system as a stage where human beings act out their parts in roles, like actors on a theater stage. Goffman believed that roles are "the basic unit of socialization . . . ," where the important "tasks in society are allocated and arrangements made to enforce their performance."[47] In groups, roles are the "set of expectations which group members share concerning the behavior of a person who occupies a given position in the group."[48] There are many different kinds of roles that members can act out in a group. The classic delineation of these roles was worked out by Kenneth Benne and Paul Sheets during the initial National Training Laboratory meetings in 1947.[49] These role descriptions, classified into "task," "maintenance," and "individual" roles, continue to be useful and are quoted widely in books on group communication. The roles are listed and their descriptions paraphrased below:

Task Roles

Initiator-Contributor suggests new ideas or procedures.

Information Seeker asks for clarification of ideas, facts or evidence.

Opinion Seeker asks for agreement or disagreement by other group members.

Information Giver offers facts or relates own experience.

Elaborator clarifies and further explains.

Coordinator shows relationships among ideas and pulls things together.

Orientor defines where the group is, summarizes, keeps things on track.

Evaluator-Critic evaluates the group's information and accomplishments according to some criteria.

Energizer prods the group to a decision or action.

Procedural Technician does routine tasks to support the group's work.

Recorder writes down suggestions, takes minutes.

Maintenance Roles

Encourager agrees with, praises, or accepts the ideas of others.

Harmonizer resolves conflict, mediates differences, and reduces tension, often with humor.

Gate-Keeper keeps channels of communication open, encourages others to participate and be heard.

Standard Setter expresses standards for the group to reach.

Group Observer evaluates the mood of the group.

Follower goes along with the group trend, passively accepts the ideas
of others, serves as audience.

Individual Roles

Aggressor attacks others, or the group, in various ways to promote
own status.

Blocker opposes others' ideas beyond reason and refuses to cooperate.

Recognition Seeker calls attention to self by boasting, acting in unusual
ways.

Self-Confessor engages in irrelevant discussion, uses the group audience for expressing personal problems.

Playboy displays lack of involvement in group through humor, cyni-
cism, or horseplay.

Dominator monopolizes the group for personal ends by asserting
authority, interrupting, giving directions.

Help Seeker calls forth sympathy from the group through unreasonable expressions of insecurity or inadequacy.

Special Interest Pleader speaks for a group outside the group.

Not all groups will contain members who play out all of these roles,
but this classic description can be used as a valuable checklist of what
to look for in most groups.

Eventually, when the roles that people play within a group
become well-established, and when the structure of the group becomes set, the group can be said to have established group *norms*.[50]
As certain behavior patterns are repeated, they become endowed
with "normalcy." It becomes "expected" that a certain member will
come into the room, take the same seat, play the same role, and
participate in the same way each time. Norms will differ, of course,
from group to group, and what may appear to be a bold and abrasive
confrontation in one group may be viewed simply as open and direct
self-disclosure in another. Eventually, however, the behavior is established as a norm (or rule), and individual members will "inter-
nalize" these norms and play by the group's rules. As teachers who
use group processes, it is important for us to be aware of the structure
of the group, the roles that members play within a group, and the
norms that get established. Some of the roles that people play in
groups are useful in helping the group to reach its goals; others are
clearly detrimental. The skillful facilitator of a group learns how to
help people play productive roles and how to assist the group in
establishing positive norms.

Teachers who use group processes will also become effective
observers of what happens to *individuals* within the group. All indi-

viduals who become members of a group struggle to some extent with their place in the group.[51] Not everyone feels immediately comfortable in a group, and it is not unusual for individuals to express some initial anxiety about their involvement. One important factor that influences the "comfort level" of individual members is the extent and quality of the *listening* that takes place. When a person interacts with another person in a group, a "communication event" takes place that involves self-disclosure and feedback. Self-disclosure occurs when a person lets someone know something about them that the listener wouldn't ordinarily know.[52] This need not be a deep, dark secret (though it may be), but can refer to any idea or feeling a person is expressing. The second half of the communication event occurs when someone else in the group or several members of the group make a response in return. Usually this response, if it is truly a response to what has been said, and is perceived by the sender as a response, rather than simply as a new disclosure, is called "feedback."[53]

In order for this transaction of self-disclosure and feedback to take place in an effective way, *active listening* needs to take place. People engage in many types of listening all the time—social listening, courteous listening, critical and discriminating listening, to name a few—but members of groups are usually striving for some form of active listening.[54] "Active listening implies that the person listens with the total self, including attitudes, beliefs, feelings and intuitions," and in group communication, active listening is regarded as essential. Active listening is sometimes further differentiated as "deliberative listening" and "empathic listening."[55] The deliberative listener is actively engaged in trying to understand ideas, standing ready to agree or disagree, criticize, summarize or conclude. The empathic listener is focusing on feelings, trying to understand the speaker's comments and feelings from the speaker's point of view and environment. In either case, when active listening is taking place the feedback is likely to be more appropriate and useful than when the quality of listening is poor. Poor listening occurs when the listener gets prematurely involved emotionally (losing objectivity), when the listener is busy preparing answers (before fully understanding the disclosure), when the listener is distracted, when the listener is "set off" by emotionally laden words, or when the listener allows personal prejudices to interfere with understanding. Good listeners try to concentrate on listening, avoid interrupting the speaker if possible, demonstrate interest and alertness, seek areas of agreement, search for meanings and avoid getting stuck on specific words, and demonstrate patience. They also try to provide clear and unambiguous feedback, repress the tendency to respond emotionally to what is said, ask questions, and withhold evaluation of the message until the speaker is finished.[56] Sometimes we need to assist group members in becoming more skilled as active listeners.

Not all of the communication that takes place in a group occurs at the verbal level. In recent years, new importance has been given to *nonverbal communication* and the role it plays in the total communication process. Nonverbal communication occurs in a variety of ways in groups, and sophisticated "group-watchers" will look for the following:

- **Proxemics**—the way group members arrange themselves in space, through seating arrangements, physical distance, and general body orientation.
- **Appearance**—overall physical appearance, dress, attractiveness, style, and mood.
- **Kinesics**—body movement, postures, gestures, and movements of the head, limbs, hands, and feet.
- **Facial Expressions**—facial features, movement of eyes and mouth.[57]

All of these ways are used by group members to further communicate their ideas, attitudes, and feelings within a group. How does nonverbal communication relate to verbal communication? Sometimes directly, by repeating or elaborating a verbal message, or by accenting its important points. At other times, however, a nonverbal message may contradict the verbal message, sending a visible clue throughout the group that what is being said is not what is being felt.[58] In a sense, then, group members are always communicating, whether they speak or not, through gestures, facial expressions, or the place taken in the group. It is not possible to *not* communicate because people are always sending messages and making meaning, whether they are responding overtly or not.[59]

Teachers who use group processes also know how to look for, spot, and deal with the twin bugaboos of group dynamics—*conflict* and *apathy*. What can be worse than working with a group where the members fight all the time? Perhaps leading a group where nobody does anything! What can teachers do to deal with conflict and apathy in groups?

First, it is important to realize that some conflict is normal and even necessary. A distinction can be made between conflict and tension, and between primary tension and secondary tension.[60] Primary tension is almost always present when a group has just been formed. It can be likened to "stage fright" and its symptoms are nervous laughter, long uncomfortable pauses, rare interruptions, profuse apologies, and excessive politeness. Secondary tension comes when the group members have become well enough acquainted to generate true disagreement. Tension, at a low level, can be a centripetal force that holds the group together. Activity marked by a certain level of disagreement will create some cohesion. But when tension exceeds an acceptable threshold, and open conflict breaks out, tension becomes a centrifugal force that can pull the group apart.

What are the signs of group conflict? Below are some of the ways "fighting behavior" is expressed in groups:

- Members are impatient with one another
- Ideas are attacked before they are completely expressed
- Members take sides and refuse to compromise
- Members disagree on plans or suggestions
- Comments or suggestions are made with a great deal of vehemence
- Members attack one another on a personal level in subtle ways
- Members insist that the group doesn't have the know-how or experience to get anywhere
- Members feel the group can't get ahead because it is too large or too small
- Members disagree with the leader's suggestions
- Members accuse one another of not understanding the real point
- Members hear distorted fragments of other members' contributions[61]

When does conflict become destructive and what causes it? Sometimes it is caused by the behavior of particular individuals in the group, but not always. Individuals can disagree about outcomes, which produces genuine conflict; but individuals can also generate conflict in a cooperative context as well, where they agree on outcomes, but disagree about the means of getting there.[62] Group watchers also look beyond individuals for the sources of conflict. Sometimes conflict arises because the group is unable to meet the demands made of them—they don't have enough resources or time, or their task is not well-defined. Sometimes conflict results when the group behavior of members is being influenced by outside interests. In other words, conflict also can be generated by structural problems of the group.[63]

What are some strategies for dealing with and resolving conflict in groups? If there are structural problems in the group, if the task is ambiguous or the resources or time allotted too thin, then these issues should be resolved, if possible. If the conflict is growing out of genuine differences of opinion, standard procedures for resolving the conflict include taking a vote, compromise, mediation, arbitration or determined efforts to reach a consensus. The key to the successful resolution of conflict within a group is to face it, identify it, and meet it head-on. Understandably, this may take some courage; but in the end, the group will usually be better off for it. Hopefully, "the group that fights, unites!"[64]

The other, but no less troublesome problem that can arise in groups is apathy. In some groups, the members don't appear to care enough about the group to get excited about anything. Members may do what they are told, but they have little commitment to the group's activity.[65] Apathy can be expressed through low level of participation, a dragging conversation, frequent lateness and absenteeism, restlessness, overquick decisions, failure to follow through on decisions, and reluctance to assume any further responsibility.[66]

What can be done about apathy? Apathetic groups can be made up of apathetic individuals; but more likely, apathy is the result of structural problems in the group. Often the task the group is working on is perceived as unimportant, or is not as important as something else they could be working on. The group has not "bought in" to the problem sufficiently to arouse feelings of involvement. In other instances, the task may appear to be important, but the group is afraid to take it on. The task may seem overwhelming, requiring too much effort or risk. The climate within the group may not foster risk-taking, so that members are unwilling to expose themselves to attack, ridicule, or failure. Or in other instances the group does not know how to go about the task, sensing that they lack essential knowledge, skills, resources, or leadership. In still other instances, the group may feel that its efforts won't be appreciated, that its recommendations won't be received, that the task is merely an exercise, a sham effort at democracy, because the "real" decisions are being made elsewhere. Sometimes a prolonged fight or unresolved conflict causes a group to become discouraged or individual members to withdraw.[67] All of these conditions, alone or together, can produce apathy. Almost always some major restructuring of the group—some new definition of the task and the conditions for achieving it—must be undertaken to counter apathy.

After years of research, scholars have come to at least some tentative agreement about the principles that guide group processes. It is known that groups go through stages and phases, that there is a task level and process level in group communication, that groups exhibit or lack cohesiveness, and that they have a structure that involves roles and norms for its members. It is known that group members engage in self-disclosure and feedback, a process that works best when there is active listening. It is also known that tension will develop in groups, and that conflict and apathy are natural occurrences within groups and that the reasons for such behavior can be identified and resolved.

USING GROUPS IN CLASSROOM SETTINGS

What are the different ways that the group teaching strategy can be used in classroom settings? How can groups be structured, and what will different structures achieve?

Sometimes it appears that a group strategy is being used when, in fact, something quite different is taking place. In traditional classrooms a lecture is often followed by a "discussion" in which students are in a sense "quizzed," either on the lecture material or on the assigned textbook reading. When students are asked "to verbalize until they hit upon a formula that pleases the teacher: or to regurgitate the main points of a lecture or text, what is taking place is a 'recitation,' not a group process."[68] Furthermore, group strategies should be distinguished from the "inquiry and discovery" strategy presented in the previous chapter, although there is, in fact, some overlap. Sometimes students are arranged in the form of "groups" to engage in problem solving, decision making, or other forms of thinking. When the emphasis is on the *thinking* being done, it is more appropriate to consider this to be an employment of an inquiry and discovery strategy. Of course, thinking also takes place when group strategies are being used. But when the emphasis is more on the group interaction and the communication exchange taking place among group members, particularly at the affective (feeling) level, it is more appropriate to think of this use of a group as a "group strategy." What, then, are some examples of the ways group strategies are employed?[69]

Get-Acquainted Activities. Sometimes groups are used for helping students get acquainted. Before students can engage in any significant discussion of a serious subject, it is important for them to get acquainted with at least some other members of the group. The best way to go about this is to break the group into dyads. The general principle is to provide an excuse for students to talk about themselves in ways that they wouldn't ordinarily. Once they have the excuse—they have been given directions that include the excuse—they are usually quite willing to engage in beginning levels of self-disclosure and feedback. For example, students might be asked to share with each other the ways they would complete the following sentences:

> I'm best at . . .
> I'm not very good at . . .
> Basically, I'm the kind of person, who . . .
> I need to . . .
> The thing I enjoy most is . . .

Or students might be asked to rank the following words as values that are most important to them, and then discuss why they have ordered them in the way they did:

freedom	self-respect	excitement
order	pleasure	recognition
compassion	accomplishment	security

Students use these words as a "jumping-off point" for some interesting sharing. A device that proves useful in helping students to talk about their past, is the following:

> Sketch the floor plan of the house where you spent most of your childhood. Describe who was in that house, where you fit in, and where the most important communication took place.

In groups, people will often compliantly engage in behavior that breaks a social norm because everyone has been asked to do so.

Working as Partners or Triads. Many teachers say they can't use groups because their class is held in a large lecture hall with fixed seating. But a large class can be broken easily into partners or triads by having students talk to the person directly in front of, behind, or beside them. There is no rule either that states that students have to *sit* in their chairs, so it may be possible to have students stand up, wander around, find a partner or two, and talk to them just "standing around." Or classes may be structured to use partners or triads as with lab partners in biology, reading "critics" in a writing class, or for working on "listening and speaking" in a foreign language. One of the favorite instruments used with partners and triads is the Agree/Disagree List. The list is simply a collection of assertions— potentially about anything. In front of each assertion is a space to be marked A (agree) or D (disagree). For example:

A   D

——— ——— People who are physically fit may feel better but are not necessarily healthier.

——— ——— Personal appearance is an important factor in job success.

——— ——— People who exercise more can eat more without gaining weight.

After responding initially to each statement, students working in dyads or triads can discuss why they agreed or disagreed with the statement, and then go on to discuss why they agree or disagree with each other. Agree/Disagree lists can be developed for almost any topic and employed to stimulate a lively discussion as a follow-up.

Brainstorming. Although the term "brainstorming" is widely used and misused today to apply to a general method of generating ideas, brainstorming has its roots in a special technique developed in 1957 by Alex F. Osborn to increase the number of ideas listed during a group's deliberation.[70] Osborn, a successful advertising executive with a special interest in creativity, was interested in how to train his associates in generating more and better ideas through groups of 10 to 12 people. Osborn's rules for brainstorming are fairly simple: adverse criticism is taboo, "free-wheeling" is welcomed, quantity of ideas is desired, and combination and improvement of ideas are sought. When ideas are presented initially, no one is allowed to say "That won't work, we've tried it, or it's too expensive." Ideas are not to be evaluated concurrently with their presentation. Wild, implausible fanciful ideas are encouraged, as many as possible. Among the large outpouring of ideas there may be some good ones. Members are encouraged to "hitch-hike" on ideas presented earlier, expanding and developing them. The criticism of ideas is suspended until a later, post-brainstorming session designed for the evaluation and categorizing of the ideas. Almost any classroom subject, where the goal is to generate new outlooks and alternative viewpoints, is a natural for the use of brainstorming. Because groups are generally useful for increasing the level of ideation, a specific technique for doing so will augment that natural strength.

Participants and Observers. Some students tend to dominate a discussion; others seem to hang back. This natural tendency can be formalized by arranging the group so that part of the class members are formally designated "participants," with others designated "observers." The observers may be arranged as an outer circle around an inner circle of participants; or in a lecture hall, participant and observer groups can be composed by dividing the room front and back or left and right. Participants may engage the task; observers may be asked to monitor the process, reserving their comments for later. Sometimes, after the participants have worked for a while on the task, the roles may be reversed.

Group Presentations. There are a number of ways in which groups can be used to make presentations to a larger group.[71] Students often enjoy making presentations to their peers through one or more of the following arrangements.

- **Panel**—a pre-arranged, yet informal, discussion of a specified topic. Usually led by a moderator, the discussion is spontaneous and may deviate from its planned direction.
- **Symposium**—a series of brief, but formal presentations on a central theme, after which the participants may receive questions from the audience or may engage in a discussion themselves.
- **Colloquium**—an expert or group of experts being questioned by the audience or by an information gathering group. The experts know the topic, but not the specific questions, ahead of time.
- **Round Table**—individuals are called upon to discuss a problem, face-to-face, while others look on.
- **Buzz Group**—a larger group (the class or audience) is broken down into small face-to-face groups to discuss some aspect of the topic that has been presented by a panel or in a lecture. Sometimes a spokesperson is appointed to report back to the larger group.

Each method sets up a slightly different way in which group members interact with each other and with the class as a whole.

Cooperative and Competitive Groups. Research has shown that competition between groups tends to increase within-group cohesion, but within-group competition decreases cohesion.[72] Put another way, when appropriate levels of competition are established *between* groups, members will pull together more *within* each group. If the situation is structured so that there is competition within the group—for example, for grades awarded for individual performance—the group will not experience as much cohesiveness. There is one interesting by-product of within-group competition: If the competition is not overwhelming, sometimes individual members will isolate and work harder on their part of the task, thus raising the quality of the group product through their contribution. Most college students enjoy team activities, not only for the camaraderie that develops within the group, but for the satisfaction that comes from competing well against another team. Competitive teams usually experience a slight increase in motivation and, in turn, a heightened sense of cohesiveness. Some projects can be structured in such a way that competition becomes natural—being on the team that finds the best solution or most creative idea or gets the task done first. Usually this builds internal cooperation. Other projects can be structured so that completion of the task itself requires high levels of internal cooperation. One classic group "game" asks 10 to 12 participants to join one hand with a member across the circle; then, with all members having done so simultaneously, to escape from the circle without releasing their handclasp. To extricate all members from the complex web of handclasps as intact partners requires a great amount of within-group cooperation. Whatever the task, the variable of cooperation and competition can be manipulated to affect various outcomes.

Role Play and Dramatization. Groups can also be used for role playing or acting out a typical situation from daily life. In an effective role play, the roles are clearly defined, usually through a thumb-nail sketch of the characters or the situation provided initially to the players in writing. Sometimes the outline for the initial dialogue, or the scenario for action, will be rehearsed or thought out in advance so that the players will have a chance to project how they will get into their parts. Role playing works well in a number of situations: Where professionals such as nurses, teachers, attorneys, pastors, or counselors are asked to play out a particular professional role; where people are in fact in opposite roles, such as boss/employee, parent/child, salesperson/customer, and in situations where ethnic, religious, or social class differences make human relationships challenging. Role playing allows the participants to get into a situation that may be new or different, and through the action experience dimensions of a problem that may have been overlooked or seen from a rather different point of view.[73] When the role play has been completed, it often serves as a stimulus for the group to talk about. Sometimes the action is replayed another way by other players, and sometimes the roles are reversed, allowing the players to gain the perspective of the opposite role. When role plays are expanded to include several players and a more complex scenario, the event becomes a dramatization. If the drama being played out is used for therapeutic purposes, the activity is sometimes referred to as "psychodrama." In the words of J.L. Moreno, the founding father of psychodrama, "Psychodrama consists of two roots—drama means action, and psycho means mind. It is really mind in action."[74] In a true therapeutic psychodrama, the players act out some situation in their own life to discover or recapture their feelings about a particular event.

Games. The idea of "serious games" has its roots in a branch of mathematics dating back to the 1920s known as "game theory." In general, games involve two or more persons, specific information, rules, opposing interests or conflicts, finite materials or settings, and goals or conclusions. Serious games can be purchased "off-the-shelf" as a commercial product, or developed by a teacher for a specific instructional situation. Games are a more elaborate and formal instrument for organizing group behavior.

Perhaps this brief list of types of activities will serve as a stimulus for thinking about some of the ways that groups can be used with different subjects, to achieve different objectives. The most important principle is, "Be inventive."

THE TEACHER'S ROLE IN USING GROUPS

The question naturally arises: What is the role of the leader in working with groups? In particular, what is the role that the college teacher plays when a group strategy is being employed?

There is a vast literature in the social sciences on leadership,[75] only some of which is about leadership roles in groups. The earliest research on leadership focused on traits, on trying to discover the characteristics of great leaders.[76] As the studies accumulated, the list of traits grew longer, until the list became nearly meaningless. More recent research has demonstrated that leadership effectiveness depends heavily on the context—what leadership skills a particular situation requires. The situation is shaped by the task and by the group's desires. Thus, what has emerged more recently as the dominant leadership theory has come to be known as the "functional approach." Instead of focusing on the characteristics of the leader, as if these were permanent and universal qualities, the functional approach stresses the group (or organization) and its needs. What tasks are to be performed by the group and what does the group need to fulfill these tasks? Surely there is no one best leader or one best leadership style that will be appropriate for all groups. Different groups will require different kinds of leadership depending on the task and the composition of the group. Thus, teachers need to ask: What is this particular group trying to achieve and how can I best help them? Even more important perhaps: How can I cultivate and draw on the leadership that will naturally emerge in the group?

One way to think about leadership in groups is to return to the now familiar distinction between task and process. A teacher who uses group strategies will provide leadership on *task* functions by making certain that the goal is clear, reasonable, and achievable; by interpreting the purpose, importance, and relevance of the task to the group; and then by helping the group to stay on the task. The teacher can provide useful feedback to the group by diagnosing the group's situation and letting the members know what their condition is at the present moment, how they are progressing, what quality of work they are producing, and how they are using their time. The teacher watches for confusion and tries to help the group clarify its goals and establish priorities for the sequencing of its activities. Sometimes the teacher plays an important role in helping to draw out of the group information that members already possess; at other times, the teacher seeks out and provides new information on behalf of the group. Sometimes the teacher needs to motivate the group to get it started, to help the group organize itself, and to guide the group to closure. Often this means helping the group to take action. Occasionally, the teacher will need to help a group through a task crisis, such as when the group wants to give up or start over, or when some members want to go off in their own direction.

A teacher will also want to help the group, when appropriate, with its *process* functions as well. The teacher plays a very important role in establishing the emotional climate within which the group will work, both by verbalizing the ground rules and modeling appropriate behavior. The teacher is honest, yet tactful, in dealing with ideas and warm, yet objective, in dealing with feelings. The teacher can also provide emotional support to individual members who need to "save face" or who are being rejected. The teacher often plays an important role in regulating the discussion, encouraging silent members to participate, slowing down aggressive members who overparticipate, and stimulating appropriate kinds of individual contributions. The teacher sometimes paraphrases and summarizes the content of discussion, reflects back to the group what members are saying or feeling, and helps members distinguish how they agree or disagree with one another. The teacher can play an important part in helping individual members find and play their role, and in helping the group establish and remember group norms. Occasionally, a teacher will need to keep a healthy exchange of ideas and feelings from turning into an ugly scene by resolving group conflict through mediation or compromise.

These may be new kinds of classroom roles for teachers who have only used a lecturing and explaining strategy heretofore, but these are leadership behaviors that can be learned, practiced, and perfected.

The teacher who uses a group strategy, however, is not always the leader of the group. Sometimes leaders emerge *from* the group. Researchers have studied a phenomena known as the Leaderless Group Discussion (LGD), a situation in which no formal leader has been appointed by outside authorities.[77] The Leaderless Group Discussion is probably a misnomer, because, in reality, almost all groups generate leaders. The LGD simply has a broader capacity to determine for *itself* what its goals, norms, and roles will be and what kind of leadership it will provide. Sometimes teachers function with the class as a whole serving as the group and with the teacher as the leader; at other times, however, teachers will organize the class (especially if it is a large one) into several smaller groups. A teacher may appoint a leader for each group, or the teacher may let "natural" leaders emerge, in which case, the conditions of the LGD prevail.

The popular wisdom is that leaders emerge because they want to be leaders, and that they excel over all others in the struggle for leadership. Actually, this is about the reverse of what actually happens. Not all of the people who end up being leaders want to be leaders and some who do want to be leaders quit trying to be. Leadership emergence is primarily a process of elimination; some people get rejected or drop out, and the one who is left is recognized by the group as its leader.[78] Emergent leaders tend to participate more and are more verbal; they express their thoughts articulately and are forceful and dynamic. They are informed and are willing to express strong opinions, but they are rarely argumentative. They also frequently seek the comments of others. They do not come on too strong, especially in the early phases of the group's life. Teachers who prefer to let leaders emerge will keep in mind that the leaders who do emerge will have some of the characteristics described above, but will also be uniquely qualified to provide leadership in the functional areas where the group perceives that it needs leadership. It is important for teachers to recognize that a group's leader must be "legitimate," that is, the group will need to feel that the leader has the approval of the group.[79] If a group perceives that it is working with a leader who is not legitimate, or if the group is somehow unable to let a leader emerge naturally, there are likely to be problems in the group.

When there are several groups with several leaders, the teacher's role changes from leader of the group to "leader of the leaders." What the teacher does in that situation is to work *through* the leaders on task and process functions within the groups, serving as a resource to leaders in the various functions they carry out for their groups.

If one were to prioritize the many things that college teachers do as leaders of groups in classroom settings, two functions surface immediately as being of primary importance. The first is *setting the task*. This means selecting the goal for learning, defining the task clearly, and devising the appropriate instrument or stimulus to set the group in motion. The second most important function is *composing the groups and establishing the ground rules* for the way they will function. How many groups will there be? What size will they be? Will the emphasis be on cooperation or competition? How will leadership be handled? How long will the groups continue to function? These are all important questions that the teacher needs to resolve, for the most part, "up front." Setting the task and composing the groups with their ground rules are extremely important functions for the teacher who is using a group strategy because almost everything else follows out of these early decisions. Sometimes teachers who use group strategies feel like they "aren't doing anything" in the classroom. Perhaps the most important thing they *do* is in the plans they make and the instruments they develop before they enter the classroom. Consider how Vicki Hastings uses group strategies in her classroom.

Vicki Hastings was beginning to note that the efforts she had made to use groups with her wellness classes had met with a good response from her students. One day, before the beginning of a new term, she decided to meet with three other faculty in the Wellness Program to "brainstorm" ways they could use more group strategies. Then Vicki spent another day deciding which of these ideas she would employ in her class, and most of the rest of the week developing instruments for her files.

Because she usually had such a variety of people of all ages, ethnic backgrounds, and walks of life in her classes, she wanted to take some time in the beginning to help people get acquainted. She developed a humorous instrument that people could use in dyads. She would ask people to switch partners, three times, as they worked their way through the items of the instrument, so that they could get acquainted with at least three other members of the class. Students would be asked to circle *one* of the pairs, after the lead instruction, "I'm more like:"

> A tortoise or a hare
> A sea gull or a koala bear
> A bicycle or an airplane
> A collector or a salesperson
> A file cabinet or a liquor cabinet
> Red or pastel blue
> City or country
> Etc.

Then the students would be asked to share why they had circled what they had and to elaborate. The items would give the students an excuse to disclose some things about themselves that they wouldn't ordinarily, and to begin to think about issues related to the kind of person they are and the way they live. So much for opening class on the first day.

Vicki also developed several other dyad instruments for her files. One, which she was especially eager to use, was an Agree/Disagree list on the advantages of being physically fit. She gathered up a number of assertions from her wellness newsletters from Harvard and Berkeley. In addition to the documented assertions, she included some more dubious claims to give the instrument some variety and controversy. She could use this instrument fairly early in the course when people were still assessing their motivations for getting involved seriously in a wellness program.

Vicki also developed some instruments to be used with groups of five to six people to teach nutrition concepts. After giving a brief explanation of the three basic nutrient groups—proteins, carbohydrates, and fats—she would break the class into groups and give each group a fairly long list of foods to classify, based on the dominant kind of nutrient in that food.

Vicki also knew that she would spend some time during the term trying to teach her students the importance of examining the percent of fat per total calories in various foods in order to be able to plan more systematically how to control the percent of fat in their daily diet. To be successful at this, the students would need to develop skill in reading the labels on cans and packages and then share some of their attitudes about these foods. She had made a practice of collecting various labels, so it wasn't hard for her to generate a "list of labels" the students could use in their groups to try to calculate what the percent of fat was in that item. She also knew that this instrument would generate a lively discussion on "truth in advertising."

Vicki also knew that one of the keys to success in changing eating habits is to be aware of alternatives. When confronted with a particular food, or situation, that is certain to produce an undesirable result, what is the way out? Vicki put together a list of such "challenges" that she could use with groups of eight for "brainstorming." Without evaluating, for the time being, the suggestions that were surfacing, students would be asked to generate as many alternative actions as possible to such items as the following:

- late night snack of cookies and milk
- five-course dinner party with good friends
- a quick stop at a fast-food outlet
- half-time refreshments at the football game
- breakfast committee meeting
- cocktail party, open bar

If students were to confront these challenges in small groups, perhaps they would feel more ownership over the solutions they would generate. She would also have them share their ideas with the group as a whole.

Vicki was also a strong believer in the importance of getting her students to engage in and enjoy a variety of exercise activities, and she knew that people would not persist in their exercise program if they didn't like it. She usually shared with the class a chart that showed the amount of exercise derived—calories expended per minute—for various types of activities, such as walking, golf, running, swimming, racquetball, bicycling, etc. Using the chart, it would be possible to lay out a program of so many minutes of selected activities per week. The task would be to have each student devise a program that best suited them and then to share that program with a group of four other students. The five then would agree to pursue their own programs that week, and check back with the group to see how well it was adhered to and how much it was enjoyed. This might be a good activity for near the end of the term.

Equipped with a new set of ideas and a file cabinet of stimulating instruments, Vicki made this her term to experiment with group strategies. By the middle of the term Vicki was feeling more confident in her use of groups, mostly because so many of her activities had met with such an enthusiastic response from her students. They had come to expect that they would be involved in a variety of stimulating activities during the evening, and they had become comfortable enough with each other to share what they were thinking and feeling. So Vicki walked into class—a large, carpeted exercise space with good sound equipment and video recorder—with a bag full of instruments and a bundle of enthusiasm.

"Let's begin with Sharing Time." In anticipation, the students had arranged themselves in a tight circle on the floor. "Sharing Time" had grown out of the get-acquainted activities that Vicki had introduced in the first classes. Students had requested that they be able to continue to take a few minutes at the beginning of class each week to share things that they were experiencing in their lives or discovering about themselves. One student shared that her uncle had a heart attack that week. "Age 43, supposedly in good health, but apparently not 'well' in the way we talk about 'well' in this class. It was a real shocker to me, visiting him in the hospital. He's going to be O.K., and they'll do some by-pass work on him, but . . ."

"Was he someone you were close to?" a student asked.

"Not all that much. That's not how it hit me. It was more—Wow!—this stuff we're talking about in here is real. It really could be *me*—same inherited body type, similar work habits. It's making me think. And my motivation—I wouldn't miss this class for anything now."

"So all of this wellness business has taken on a different kind of personal reality and urgency for you this week," Vicki reflected back to her.

"You hit it, yeah. That's it."

After a couple more "sharings," Vicki introduced the first activity of the night. She usually didn't assign much reading, and there were no formal quizzes, but she had a few articles she liked to use with the class. In one of her favorites, the author compares the benefits and drawbacks of various forms of aerobic exercise—running, cycling, cross-country skiing, swimming—and lists some of the physical side-effects that could occur as well as the logistic problems, equipment needs, and sheer inconveniences. Vicki had passed the article out to the class last week and had solicited five volunteers to serve on a panel, each to summarize and present the benefits and drawbacks of their assigned activity. Vicki served as moderator of the panel and raised questions about how to decide on which activities were best.

Eventually the idea of alternating a variety of activities emerged, and Vicki was able to introduce the idea of "cross-training," doing several different activities in moderation and alternation, thus getting the aerobic benefits of each. The panel members were very conscientious in summarizing their views, and soon the rest of the class was involved in a lively discussion about which forms of exercise they preferred and why.

When the discussion seemed to have run its course, Vicki shifted to another activity. "Remember how we have talked about how eating patterns are established in our childhood and how almost all eating occurs in a social context? I want you to do a role play tonight, and I need some volunteers. What we are going to do is a short dramatization of a dinner table scene. We might call it 'All my Meals' or something like that. I have a brief description here for each of the characters—Grandma, Mother, Father, Teenage Son, Elementary School Age Daughter, and Baby. Any volunteers? And, I forgot to mention, I want to videotape this so that we can replay it and see if there is anything we can do to help this poor family." The students fell into a stony silence, eyes darting around the room, looking for the first volunteer. Finally, the oldest member of the class raised her hand, "O.K., I might as well volunteer for Grandma." Soon others volunteered and the cast was complete. What followed was an exaggerated, but credible portrayal of the typical familial mingling of food and affection, the way each member of the family is loved—especially the children—through the piling on of food. The dialogue was interspersed with admonitions about being a "good eater," a member of the "clean plate club," etc. As the videotape was being rewound, students commented on how funny, but how realistic, the scene had been for them. "It was spooky; as if these people had been in my house when I was growing up. I couldn't believe it, the same words, same phrases."

Vicki smiled. She had written the "script"; that was *her* family, too. She let the class members chatter among themselves, then drew them back to attention for more instructions. "O.K., I'm going to divide you into three groups. I will replay this tape and stop it at three critical points. Group one takes the first stopping point, group two the second, and group three the third. Your task is to come up with how the situation could be handled differently. What could one of these players have done or said that might have changed the course of that scene?"

After sharing their proposed solutions, the students had a great time discussing whether the situation was redeemable or hopeless, but they all agreed that they had been there as children and that many of them felt they were still perpetuating those patterns in their own home.

Vicki usually saved the second part of the class for some strenuous aerobic activity. Often she just led the class though a series of routines, but tonight, after some warm-up activities and a review of typical movements, she told the class that she was going to divide them into groups of five and have them choreograph a brief aerobic dance routine using some of the movements they had just reviewed. She showed them a brief video tape of the routines done by the national aerobic dance champions. "Now it doesn't need to be this good or this difficult, but this will give you an idea of what can be done." She gave them a handout that listed many of the movements, just as a reminder. Then she gave them time to get into their groups and begin to get some ideas. "When you are ready, I'll put the music on. You'll all work with the same music. I'll just keep playing it over and over so you can practice. When you are ready, we'll have you show what you have created to the other groups. And as a little incentive to work hard, we'll vote on our own champions. O.K. Go for it."

Vicki circulated among the groups, helping them to be creative, resolve differences, and refine their product. She was pleased at what they had produced. And they were incredibly proud of themselves, especially the winners!

Vicki had noticed that in previous weeks at the end of class, the students would hang around after class to talk; or on her way out she would spot some of them having a fruit drink in the student union snack bar. So that night Vicki had brought a treat—a couple of carved out watermelons filled with cut-up fruit. "No obligation to stay," she noted, " but if you want to hang around and chat, here's something you might enjoy."

It's interesting to watch what happens, Vicki thought, when a group really becomes a group. Amazing! They don't want it to end.

As Vicki was turning out the lights—the only way to get the stragglers to leave—one of the students came up to her and said, "I hope you know how much this class means to me; it's the high point of my week. Sorry for staying so late; I don't have much of a home to go home to."

Vicki knew that she could be there until morning if she asked why. Instead she thought quickly of the strength and support of the group. "If you feel comfortable, maybe you would want to bring that up at sharing time next week. The group might like to know how they have become your family."

The last light went out and Vicki locked the door on a good class.

USING TEAMS FOR PROJECTS

There are two types of groups that are of special interest to teachers. The first are "teams," where the emphasis is on the achievement of a specific goal. The second type is the "growth group" or "transformation group," where the emphasis is on the personal development of the members. In teams the emphasis is on task, and in growth groups the emphasis is on process. Naturally, both task and process elements are present in both types of groups, but the difference in emphasis is distinct and strong. In the remainder of this chapter, these two special types of groups will be explored, along with their classroom uses in postsecondary settings.

It is not easy to distinguish teams from groups in general. All teams are groups, but not all groups are teams. The study of teams, a specialized kind of group, is a more recent phenomena in the field of speech communication. In a stimulating new study of teams by Carl Larson and Frank LaFasto entitled *TeamWork: What Must Go Right/What Can Go Wrong*,[80] teams are defined as two or more people with a "specific performance objective or recognizable goal to be attained; and (wherein) coordination of activity among the members of the team is required for the attainment of the team goal or objective."[81] The authors were troubled by what appeared to them to be a widespread inability in our society for people to collaborate effectively. At the same time they saw the growing complexity of problems as well as solutions and the necessity for "teamwork" in addressing most problems of greater magnitude. They decided to study "high-performance teams" to see what made them effective and what went wrong when they weren't effective. They identified for study, teams representative of many different types of functions from all walks of life: sports teams (Notre Dame and Navy football teams), investigative teams (the Challenger spacecraft disaster), heart surgery teams (DeBakey, Cooley), mountain climbing teams (Everest), new product teams (Chicken McNuggets, IBM/PC), epidemiology teams, management teams, and many others. Then they interviewed team members to gather data about the teams and built up a theory of "team effectiveness" from the data. They found that effective, high-performance teams consistently exhibited the following eight characteristics:

- Clear, elevating goal
- Results-driven structure
- Competent members

- Unified commitment
- Collaborative climate
- Standards of excellence
- External support and recognition
- Principled leadership

Each of these characteristics deserves further examination.

Clear, Elevating Goal. Effective teams have performance objectives that are stated clearly so that everyone can tell unequivocally what the goal is and whether (or to what degree) it has been attained. The goal also needs to be "elevating" in the sense of being personally challenging to individual team members or the teams as a whole, or "elevating" in the sense that achieving the goal really makes a difference to someone else, as in performing heart surgery, stopping an epidemic, or developing a new product. When teams became ineffective, their goals were ambiguous and members uncertain, or the original goal had been lost. This loss of focus or confusion of priorities usually came through organizational politics or personal power agendas of team members.

Results-Driven Structure. Although the same performance objective can be reached with teams that are structured in different ways, the structure must always move the team toward getting results. Not all teams have the same kinds of objectives. Three basic types of teams were identified: problem-resolution teams, creative teams, and tactical teams. Each needs a slightly different structure. Problem-solving teams need *trust*. All the members must work together, share everything, and sincerely trust each other. Creative teams need *autonomy*; they need to be free from organizational pressures and constraints; they need what might be called "breathing room." Tactical teams, on the other hand, need *clarity*, everyone knowing what they are supposed to do and how and when to do it. In addition, all teams, to have a results-driven structure, need clear roles, an effective communication system, methods of monitoring performance and giving feedback, and a means for recording and making fact-based judgments.

Competent Team Members. Successful teams are composed of the right people selected for the right reasons. In general, team members need the right balance of technical skills and abilities and personal qualifications for working well with others. But not all teams need the same skills; the skills needed depend on the goal. Problem-resolution teams need members who are intelligent and analytical, but sensitive enough to interpersonal needs to build trust.

Creative teams need members whose cognitive approach might appear to be a bit unusual on a day-to-day basis; these are the "what if" independent thinkers, who are tenacious and patient. Tactical teams, on the other hand, need members who are highly responsive, quick to execute, and able to work with precision, within small margins for error. Tactical teams also need people who have a sense of urgency, can identify strongly with the team, and who enjoy winning or being successful. All teams need members who have the essential skills and abilities, a strong desire to contribute, and a capacity for collaboration. Teams need the right "mix" of qualified members.

Unified Commitment. Effective teams also have developed a unified commitment, that elusive, hard-to-define quality of "team spirit." What is it? It is the willingness to do what needs to be done to help the team succeed. It is manifest in huge amounts of mental and physical energy to achieve the goal. It involves a strong team identity. How does it come about? It develops as a natural extension of the enthusiasm for the clear, elevating goal, but it is also nurtured by involvement, participation, and refining the goal and establishing the means of getting there. Commitment involves striking a balance between giving oneself over to the group (integration) and using one's own individual talents to best help the group (differentiation). Although it is difficult to say what unified commitment is, ineffective teams clearly lack it.

Collaborative Climate. If the essence of teams is "teamwork," then teams need to function within a climate that fosters teamwork. The word most often used to characterize this climate was "trust," and trust was characterized as having four elements: honesty, openness, consistency, and respect. When trust exists, team members will stay focused on the goal, will communicate more effectively, will compensate for each other's shortcomings, and will be more open to criticism and risk, thus improving the overall quality of outcomes. When a collaborative climate exists, team members are more likely to share information, admit problems, help overcome obstacles, and find new ways of succeeding. Such a climate is not easy to build, but appears to be related to the involvement that team members have and the autonomy the team has to do its job.

Standards of Excellence. Standards define the expectations for performance. Pressures to perform can come from many places— from the members themselves, from the team as a whole, from the anticipation of success or risk of failure, from sources outside the team, or from the team leader. Standards have to be de-intellectual-ized and made concrete, so that everyone knows what they are. Standards are not achieved, however, just by setting them. Because standards are easy to ignore, teams have to use a great deal of discipline and hard work to achieve their standards of excellence and must remain vigilant in enforcing them. Standards are only attained through performance.

External Support and Recognition. The performance of teams is affected in peculiar ways by the presence or absence of external support and recognition. Such support may come in the form of praise, allocation of resources, or rewards to individual team members. Oddly enough, teams that are doing well may be able to function without it, though they believe that their achievement warrants more. Teams that are doing poorly may do even worse without it. Lack of external support, for a team that is struggling, may lead to lower morale, erosion of confidence, and feelings of frustration and futility. While external support and recognition may not be a significant factor in ensuring team success, lack thereof can contribute to failure. External support can have an especially positive effect when that support rewards the team for behaving as a team.

Principled Leadership. The leaders of effective teams see themselves as being involved in transformation—leadership that involves change. They have a vision of the future—some idea of the way things could be and should be, a desire to move beyond the status quo, and a peculiar ability to unleash the energy and talents of contributing members. Effective team leaders are "principled," in that they govern their own leadership behavior by such principles as being fair and impartial, being willing to confront and resolve issues, and being open to new ideas and information. In turn, they expect group members to be guided by principles, such as trying to collaborate effectively with others, making the team goal higher than individual goals, and standing behind team decisions. Effective team leaders create a decision-making climate that encourages members to take risks and to act, so that the goal can be achieved. Effective team leaders are able to suppress their own ego needs and create a contagion among group members that unlocks their own leadership abilities.

If these are the characteristics of effective teams, what happens when teamwork breaks down? What are the causes of malfunctioning teams? Most frequently mentioned in the study was lack of unified commitment, when team members, in one way or another, put their own interest above the team interest in attaining the goal. The next most frequently mentioned problem is lack of external support and recognition—the sense of not having what is needed to get the job done. With regard to leadership, the most frequent complaint is about leaders who are unwilling to confront and resolve the issue of inadequate performance of team members, i.e., letting a team member get away with poor performance. The next most frequently mentioned problem with leaders is with those who willingly take on too many goals, thus upsetting the priorities and diluting the team's efforts to achieve high standards in pursuing the goal.

Is there anything that college teachers can learn from this fascinating study of teamwork? If we are going to organize a class into teams to work on projects, what do we need to attend to in order to assure that the teams will be reasonably successful? Consider how Nancy Green uses teams to work on interior design projects at the Art Institute of the South.

As Nancy Green thought about the Integrative Seminar in interior design, she asked herself: How far shall I go with these projects? It started out as a final paper, then grew each year into something more complex. What would happen if I let the project become the seminar and the seminar the project? How would I handle that? What if I put all of my energy, and the students' energy, into project teams?

Nancy went back over the findings about successful, high-performance teams. She knew that she had to begin with a *clear, elevating goal*. She would provide the four teams an interview report from a potential client with all the detailed information they would need, including budget range, to make a bid on an interior design contract. All four groups would work on the same project within the same parameters, and the object would be to see who could come up with the best solution within the givens. That could be made clear, but how could the goal be elevating? She would try to make this as "realistic" as possible, but even so the students would be inclined to treat it as just another "make believe" class project. Was there any way she could make it "the real thing"? After thinking about it for a while she came up with a terrific idea. Sometimes her firm would take on projects for nonprofit institutions and do them on a break-even basis for the experience and publicity. She had received a request for a bid last week from the State Board for Occupational, Technical and Proprietary Education. They were planning to move into some new office space near the Capitol and wanted to make the offices as functional and attractive as possible. She thought the students would like that—a real project—and the team that prepared the best presentation would win the bid.

Nancy knew that she played an important role in helping the teams to establish *standards of excellence*. She interviewed the State Board Space Committee herself and assembled a complete report, full of interesting data about their needs and desires. After sharing the interview data with the students, she asked the whole class to discuss what would have to go into the process to produce high quality projects. They agreed that all teams would need to develop charts of the organizational hierarchy of the department, a people to people and people to services matrix, and adjacency diagrams. From these they could begin to generate design solutions. The class also agreed that the final product would include an attractive presentation notebook, with pleasing graphic qualities in itself, which contained a reduced fold-out copy of the floor plan, macros for each department, micros of four or five typical offices and work stations, some charts and graphs to illustrate communication flow, a list of all furnishings with detailed "specs," and a budget that included costs for all furnishings, shipping, and installation. In addition to the notebook, each team would produce some pictorials, two perspective renderings and one axonometric (a cut-away looking in from the ceiling), as well as a finish materials board with wall paints, swatches of fabric, furniture surfaces, and hardware samples.

Nancy knew that the teams would need to be composed of *competent team members*. "I knew it was important for the teams to have the right mix of members, so I decided *not* to let the groups form naturally, but to take a strong hand in composing the teams." She needed each team to have members who had space planning skills, creative design skills, financial expertise, graphic presentation skills, writing ability, and artistic ability to do renderings, axos, and the finish materials board. She knew the students fairly well from other classes they had taken from her, and so she tried to compose the teams in a way to maximize their chances of being successful in reaching the goal. On the first night she had each class member fill out a skill card on which they checked off their special skills and interests. She used these cards and some brief interviews with the students when she collected the cards to gain some sense of the total pool of skills available. Then she composed the groups so that they would have a good mix of talents, skills, and personalities.

Nancy decided to compose the teams but *not* to pick the leaders; she would let the project manager emerge from the team. But she insisted that each team have a designated project manager at the end of the first week, and she decided to meet with the managers every week to monitor progress and to serve as their mentor on their leadership roles. She asked the project managers to come up with a set of principles that they would adhere to as managers, and she asked them to share those with their teams. Then she asked the leaders to have their team members generate a few rules that they also would be willing to live by. "I encouraged the project managers to think of themselves really as leaders, not just monitors of time and resources." To do so, they would need to get their groups to be creative, to keep in mind the standards of excellence, and to act to get the job done well and on time. Above all, the managers would need to suppress their own ego needs and would need to help other members of the group unleash their own creativity. She told them that one of the worst things a project manager can do, from the point of view of the team members, is to let some members of the team get away with poor performance, or no performance at all. "I told the project managers that they would have to deal with that, on their own preferably, but if not, to come to see me and I would stand ready to help them deal with an ineffective team member."

Nancy believed that she could play an important role in *providing external support and recognition* for the teams. Certainly she could be responsive in locating and allocating resources. She made sure that times were available at the Art Institute on a regular basis for studios, workspace, and computer design equipment. She made catalogs, fabric swatches, and price lists available from her office. "I even offered my own home for one meeting at the middle of the term." She made it clear to the students that she would do whatever she could to provide the resources they needed and would be "standing by" as a consultant on any problems they wanted to check out with her. Above all, she provided encouragement, assuring them that the best project would get the contract.

What really happened? Consider two of the groups, Group A, that won the contract, and Group D that had the poorest performance of the four groups. Group D had trouble doing their initial homework: They didn't read the interview report carefully, and they tried to skip over making their people to people matrix and adjacency diagrams. They plunged into design solutions prematurely and then had to back up and do their preliminary planning again, thus losing time. One member consistently failed to contribute, and even after being reprimanded by the project manager, failed to get work in on time. Two other team members always seemed to be going in opposite directions with design solutions, so that the team never developed a unified commitment. The final project appeared to be a compromise, rather than an expression of conviction; and the notebook and supporting renderings were hastily compiled and were of poor quality. The project manager blamed the team members, and they, in turn, blamed the project manager. Nancy had done what she could to help this team be effective, mentoring their leader and warning them of consequences, but she also gave them room to fail. On the other hand, Group A realized that they needed to divide up the work carefully among the members and establish a timeline of due dates. They selected a strong project manager and developed a results-oriented structure. Each member of the team was in touch with every other member of the team daily, and the whole team met once a week just to touch base. They realized that long meetings involving long arguments would waste time, so they delegated most of the work and spent their time doing it. They spent one long meeting hammering out the overall design solution but from there on it was "get it done." Their notebook was superb in its written and graphic presentations, and their supporting art work was of professional quality. They were able to provide the cleverest, most satisfying solutions—both for the use of space and artistically—and they did so with a bid that was below the budget minimum. In the end, the team wanted to give credit to the superb "people skills" of the project manager, but he said that it was really the team members who did the work.

Nancy Green was pleased with the generally high quality of three of the four projects. "Anyone of them could have won the bid, but the winner had a slight edge on price and creativity. In the real world, that's how it works, and that's what the students learned."

USING GROUPS FOR PERSONAL GROWTH

The second type of group of special interest to teachers is the "personal growth group" or "transformation group." As noted earlier, people *change* in groups, sometimes only in superficial ways, but at other times in ways that affect the self more deeply. Teachers who are interested in providing a climate for personal development at some deeper level often turn to group experiences that emphasize "process." Very few teachers would think of themselves today as leading anything like what were once called "encounter groups" or facilitating what is known in a more formal setting as "group therapy," nor would they be qualified to do so. Knowing something about the methods and processes of these groups, however, can be valuable to teachers who are interested in creating an educational environment where personal growth can occur.

Personal growth groups in educational settings have their roots in what were earlier described as "t-groups," "encounter groups," "sensitivity training," or "laboratories in human relations."[82] Developed more than four decades ago, these groups were designed to provide a setting in which "participants work together in a small group over an extended period of time, learning through analysis of their own experiences, including feelings, reactions, perceptions and behavior."[83] It was discovered that groups such as these could provide a laboratory for learning what the real world often denies. What are the outcomes of learning in the classic encounter group? These will surely vary, depending on the purposes and composition of the group, but in the words of Carl Rogers:

> In such a group the individual comes to know himself and each of the others more completely than is possible in the usual social or working relationships. He becomes deeply acquainted with the other members and with his own inner self, the self that otherwise tends to be hidden behind his facade. Hence he relates better to others, both in the group and later in the everyday life situation.[84]

Learning about one's self is the basic, fundamental goal of the classic encounter group. In addition to these learnings, there are some "meta-goals," some larger side-benefits, which include learning to recognize that what one thought were "givens" are actually choices, learning to heighten and develop one's sense of inquiry and hypothetical spirit, learning to develop greater authenticity in the expression of feelings, and learning to develop a collaborative (as opposed to a hierarchical) sense of authority.[85]

How does this occur? Like other kinds of groups, encounter groups have their stages. In describing these stages, Carl Rogers also suggests why these groups work.[86] Briefly summarized, the stages are as follows:

- **Milling Around.** When the facilitator makes it clear that the group must take responsibility for their own goals and direction, the members don't know what to do. There is a lot of polite, surface interaction.
- **Resistance to Personal Expression or Exploration.** People begin to share their public self but resist showing much of their private self.
- **Description of Past Feelings.** People gradually express feelings about how they have behaved or once behaved, but not much about what they are feeling at the moment.

- **Expression of Negative Feelings.** The first "here and now" feelings are usually negative, something critical that one member of the group says about another.
- **Expression and Exploration of Personally Meaningful Material.** If negative feelings have been expressed and assimilated without catastrophic results, other group members realize that it may be possible to share something deeper, some personally important feelings.
- **Expression of Immediate Interpersonal Feelings.** Participants may now be able to engage in an exchange of personally meaningful feelings occurring in the here and now.
- **Development of a Healing Capacity of the Group.** Some group members begin to show a natural and spontaneous capacity for dealing with others in a helpful and therapeutic fashion.
- **Self-Acceptance and the Beginning of Change.** Some group members begin to accept who they really are and what they are like, which lays the foundation for change.
- **Cracking of Facades.** Participants begin to drop their defenses and discard their cover-ups.
- **Individuals Receive Feedback.** Participants get a stronger sense of how they appear to others.
- **Confrontation.** Sometimes a stronger kind of feedback is provided, a "leveling" of one person with another, often quite negative.
- **Helping Relationships Develop Outside the Group Sessions.** Group members find ways of assisting each other between group sessions in their "real" lives.
- **Expression of Positive Feeling and Closeness.** Increasing feelings of warmth, positive attitudes, and a group spirit often emerge as a sense of trust is built up.
- **Behavior Changes Occur in the Group.** Changes in gestures, tone of voice, and helpfulness reveal behavioral changes growing out of deeper emotional changes within individuals.

Although these stages are often overlapping and may not always become manifest in this particular order, something like this process can be observed in many types of classic encounter groups.

Teachers who use personal growth groups (or other types of groups that emphasize process) can also learn something valuable from the literature on group therapy. Although therapy groups tend to emphasize mental health—from the Greek *therapia*, meaning "healing"—the processes employed in group therapy can be used for the more modest educational goal of personal growth. Irvin D. Yalom, the author of a definitive text on group therapy, *The Theory and Practice of Group Psychotherapy*, notes 11 therapeutic factors that have been identified as important in bringing about change.[87] Although the factors may vary in their differential importance and in their interplay from group to group, the presence of these factors seems to be related to bringing about growth:

- **Instillation of Hope.** Groups contain people who are at some point along the coping-collapse continuum. The therapy group holds forth hope that help can be found. Belief in the efficacy of the group and its leader is itself a therapeutic factor.
- **Universality.** Many people enter a therapy group feeling that they are "unique in their wretchedness." Often caught in their own social isolation, without much opportunity for consensual validation, they usually experience a great sense of relief that they are not alone and that there are certain "common denominators" in human problems.
- **Imparting Information.** Sometimes members are helped through the information that they gather either from the therapist or other group members. When therapy groups have a special topic or the members have a common interest, such as alcoholism, divorce, eating disorders, or how to cope with a chronic disease, information about the condition may be a particularly valuable part of the therapeutic process.
- **Altruism.** Sometimes group members experience growth through the act of giving itself. Many people come into a group so demoralized that they think they have nothing to contribute. When they find that others listen to their ideas and suggestions and take them seriously, it is often a boost to their self-esteem.
- **The Corrective Recapitulation of the Primary Family Group.** Therapy groups resemble families in that many of the interactions that can take place—dependence, defiance, rivalry, self-efface-ment—are potentially like the interactions of family members. Many people who are involved in group therapy discover and reveal that they have had some unsatisfactory experiences in their primary families, and find in the group the opportunity to reca-pitulate and rework these experiences.
- **Development of Socializing Techniques.** Some group members come to a group lacking certain interpersonal skills, not knowing that they are perceived as overly shy, regal, tactless, or aggressive.

People are often able to learn through accurate interpersonal feedback how to discard old habits and learn new social skills.

- **Imitative Behavior.** Members of groups tend to sit, walk, talk, and even think like the therapist or other members of the group. When members see other members relating effectively and making changes that help to solve their problems, imitation becomes a positive therapeutic force.
- **Interpersonal Learning.** Because people's perceptions of their experiences are often subject to distortion, it is often necessary for people to re-evaluate or re-learn some of their perceptions. This interpersonal learning is at the heart of all therapy, including group therapy, and is sometimes referred to as a "corrective emotional experience." When members experience the group as a safe place for sharing and there is accurate and honest feedback sufficient for reality testing, then a corrective emotional experience can occur. This usually comes through the review of some critical incident in the individual's life, either in the past or in the here and now.
- **Group Cohesiveness.** In group therapy, growth depends not only on the relationship to the therapist, but to other members of the group as well. Although cohesiveness in itself is not a therapeutic factor, it provides the conditions for the sharing of feelings and the sense of membership, acceptance, and approval that may be instrumental in building self-esteem. Group cohesiveness allows other growth-promoting factors to work.
- **Catharsis.** Sometimes members of the group are able to use the group to "get things off their chest," and from "getting feelings out" there is a certain catharsis. It is usually recognized, however, that catharsis, while important, is not enough. Without catharsis, therapy could turn into an intellectual discussion. Catharsis works best, however, later in the life of the group, when the group has developed cohesiveness, and when other therapeutic factors are also operating.
- **Existential Factors.** In group therapy, participants sometimes gain a new appreciation of what "life is all about." They learn that existence is lonely, full of pain, and not always fair. They learn to live life more honestly and to take ultimate responsibility for life's decisions. Recognition of mortality, the capriciousness of existence, and the need for responsible choice are sometimes referred to as "existential factors" in therapy.

These are the conditions that enable growth within a group therapy setting. How do they get established and what is the role of the therapist in facilitating the emergence of these conditions within the group?

The facilitator plays certain roles that are similar to those of the leader in other groups. The facilitator, as "gate-keeper," helps to compose the groups and tries to ensure continuity and avoid attrition. The facilitator also establishes procedural rules and helps the group to establish desirable norms about communication, such as active involvement, nonjudgmental acceptance of others, extensive self-disclosure, desire for understanding, and motivation for change. The facilitator may give explicit instructions, comment on something that has taken place, provide an instrument or activity, raise questions, or reward members with praise for positive behavior. The facilitator may also model the behavior that is appropriate to the norms through nonjudgmental acceptance, interpersonal honesty, and spontaneity. The reason for establishing these norms, of course, is to provide a climate that encourages growth.

One of the most important things the facilitator does is to encourage group members to talk about and deal with the "here and now." Although many forms of psychotherapy are noted for "dredging up the past"—due in part to Freud's original emphasis on understanding the formative experiences of early childhood—one of the unique aspects of group therapy is its emphasis on the present. Members are expected to deal with the real problems of their present lives, but perhaps even more important, with the real communication events taking place within the group at the moment. Especially in the early part of the life of the group, it is important for the facilitator to move the group from the abstract to the specific, from outside to inside, and from the general to the personal. As the group experience develops, the group itself will realize that its task is to focus on the here and now.

The facilitator also monitors the process that is ongoing in the group and provides for the group an "illumination" of what is taking place through "process commentary." The commentary will focus on recurring themes, deeper meanings, and the relationship between outside problems that members may be having and the "here and now" problems they are having within the group. The facilitator, without being judgmental, points out how a member's behavior makes others feel, and how the behavior brings about reactions from others, and in the end influences that member's own self-esteem.

Sometimes the facilitator will give a "mass process commentary," that is, feedback to the group as a whole about its behavior.

Although there is not always immediate and direct transfer of the principles of encounter groups and the techniques of group therapy to postsecondary classrooms—some adaptation is always necessary—there is a value that arises from the study of these principles and techniques for teachers who wish to create educational environments where personal growth can take place. Consider, for example, how Jonathan Wesley uses a group strategy in his course on social transformations.

The 12 students in Jonathan Wesley's class on social transformations come from many different religious persuasions. Some came to New England Theological Seminary after successful careers in another walk of life, and most have strong, or at least well-shaped, political views. The purpose of the course is to provide a context where social attitudes can be re-examined, and the roots of those attitudes rediscovered. Jonathan Wesley provides a group setting to examine selected social issues and allows about five weeks for a particular issue and then moves on to another. The purpose is not to "cover" all the current issues, but to experience the process of transformation as it applies to a few issues, such as criminal justice, abortion, and euthanasia.

In the first session, after laying out a few brief ground rules about listening, feedback, and support, Jonathan asks the group to share what experiences they have had, if any, with crime, either with committing a crime or being the victim of a crime, themselves personally or through a family member or friend. There is a silence, then some jokes about traffic violations, then more silence. Eventually one woman tells a story about how her parents ran a small grocery store, and how it had been robbed a few times. She shares how they felt and admits that she grew up within an environment where there was a lot of hard feeling about stealing and not much sympathy for law-breakers. Other members of the group begin to relate examples of crimes that they have heard about, and eventually one member shares a somewhat terrifying experience of having been "mugged" and robbed while waiting for a subway. Jonathan Wesley helps the group members to identify some of their feelings of outrage and injustice, their sense of personal affront, and their frustration in knowing that in most cases the perpetrator was not even apprehended. Then he points out that the examples the group has provided are all of being victimized, and he asks if anyone has had any experience on the other end, with committing crimes. There is a long silence, some nervous laughter and joking, but eventually one member tells a story about an uncle who was a gun-runner, a trader in illegal military weapons, and how he got caught and is serving time in prison. The other class members, encouraged by Wesley, explore with her what the family's feelings were about the uncle and how they related to him. "He's sort of a black sheep. Nobody wants to admit he's really part of our family." It became clear, and Jonathan Wesley pointed this out, that most class members had some experience with being a victim, but little acquaintance with people who commit crimes, even white collar crimes.

At the next session Jonathan Wesley asked the students what they thought about the "criminal justice" system and in particular about capital punishment. A lively discussion ensued. Except for one young woman, who admitted that she was raised in a "pretty conservative environment," most of the students had serious concerns about capital punishment. As might be expected from seminary students, there were strong opinions expressed about justice, forgiveness, redemption, and the possibility and limits of rehabilitation. After the students had a chance to pursue this, Wesley gave them a handout that contained a detailed diagram showing for a major U.S. city how many crimes were committed; how many arrests made; how many cases were dismissed, plea-bargained, and taken to court; how many were convicted and serving time; and the percent of those serving who would become repeat offenders. The students were quite surprised at the figures, especially the numbers who went unpunished, and they began to raise some questions about the "system." It seemed unfair, to many of them, that so many crimes went unpunished, but to others it seemed unfair that so little was done in the way of rehabilitation to prevent repeated offenses. A middle-aged African-American student named George said that he thought that most of the attitudes in the group were based on the members' experience with being victimized and he criticized the group for not being more sympathetic to the criminal. "Nobody seems to even be raising the question as to why people get into this kind of trouble in the first place." He spoke his piece and then sat back. The group agreed that they had been ignoring this issue and had better begin to discuss it next time.

The next session was spent on trying to understand some of the conditions that give rise to crime, but most of the group members admitted that they didn't have much empathy for this. "We can list circumstances, but we don't really feel it because we haven't been there." George then pointed out that the conditions of society created a situation where crime was the only real alternative for the disenfranchised, and the "justice system" was really an "injustice system" because it only dealt with consequences and not causes. A young Puerto Rican woman joined in, pointing out that this was why so many prison inmates were members of minority groups. "You have to look at the causes—unemployment, frustration, alienation!" Others disagreed. As the discussion of this issue grew more heated, Jonathan Wesley pointed out that the tensions in the group, here and now, were very much like the tensions in the society generally, that many people see the issue through the eyes of the victim and forget, almost entirely, the social causes and the point of view of the offender. Several members of the class said that they had never talked with an offender, and they wondered if it would be valuable to bring to class (or go visit) some—what should you call them?—convicts.

Jonathan Wesley arranged to have the class visit the Center for Adolescent Treatment, known affectionately by the inmates as the CAT House, and to hear two convicted murderers, aged 19 and 21, tell their stories. Here were two articulate, now nearly rehabilitated, murderers telling in a matter-of-fact way how they grew up, how they first got into trouble, and how they committed the murder. Most impressive, however, was their ability to talk about what had occurred to them psychologically, and how they were learning about the cycle of feelings that led to the crime. The students asked them a lot of questions about their rehabilitation program: "What is your therapy? Are you making progress? Will you ever get paroled? Do you have future plans? Do you ever think about the victim and the victim's family?"

Back in the class the next week, the students shared their reactions to the visit to the CAT House and began to talk much more freely about their feelings about victims and criminals. "I realized how isolated I have been from this whole issue. I mean, that's what we do in our society, we put these people AWAY, out of sight out of mind."

A young woman who hadn't said much before spoke up, "For me it was, there but for the grace of God, go I. I mean, I wasn't going to spill it all in here on the first day, but I got into some trouble as a teenager—some shoplifting, some minor stuff with possession. I could have ended up like that. It was scary. So I was really impressed with the help these kids were getting."

George, the African-American, spoke up again, "Oh, I was impressed, too. But remember what you were seeing was a very special, highly subsidized, nationally recognized treatment center. This is not, my friends, what you see in the average prison. No, I'm sorry . . . ," he broke off, choked with emotion.

Jonathan Wesley reflected back to George that he seemed to have very strong feelings about this issue and asked if there was something more he could share with the group at a more personal level.

There was a long silence, then a startling self-disclosure: His brother had been convicted, first of minor crimes, sentenced, then back on the streets, and finally shot and killed by a police officer in a hold-up. It was a wrenching revelation for him to make to the group.

They floundered for a minute, all turning to Jonathan Wesley for a response. His response was not what they expected. "Uh, huh, you're turning this over to the authority in the group. That's what we do about this, turn it over to the authorities. Come on, you are training to be clergy. What's your human response?"

One by one, the members of the group found a way to help George to tell more of his story, to support him in his grief and rage, to let him know that they understood him better now. They showed him that they were sorry about what had happened, and they let him know that they were better able now to share some of his anger with the system.

At the next class, the students were asked to summarize briefly where they had come on this issue—both intellectually and emotionally—and what impact the group experience had for them. Most of the students said that they were surprised to discover how "one-sided" their thinking had been. They were still very concerned about victims and the rights of victims, but they realized that their attitudes about offenders had grown up in isolation from any feelings about them as real people. One student said that hearing the kids from the CAT House stirred her up emotionally in a way that made her . . . "a different person." She admitted, "I just never came face to face with this before. I've always thought of it as something for the newspapers or T.V. But here they were . . . they could have been *my* kids." Most of the students said that George's story about his brother really ripped them up, and George, himself, admitted that he had never talked about it, not even in his own family circle. He thanked the group for giving him a chance to relive something that had been bothering him for a long time, and he hoped that maybe they had grown some, too, from hearing his story and helping him to work it out.

Jonathan Wesley never knows exactly where his transformation groups will go. He knows that the class environment he creates enables growth for those who wish to grow. He believes that society will be transformed when people are transformed, and he knows that whatever else religion may be about, it is about sharing the human condition and finding ways to ameliorate it.

CONCLUSIONS

Groups play a very important place in society, and no educated person can function well today without knowing how to participate effectively in the dynamic life of groups and teams. Furthermore, certain kinds of learning take place best only in groups. Effective teachers know when to use groups, how to compose them, how large to make them, and how to monitor them. Group members will always engage in both task-oriented and process-oriented behavior. Groups will evolve a structure, a history, a degree of cohesiveness, and some pattern of leadership. Teachers who use groups encourage active listening, know how to resolve conflict, and discourage social loafing or a groupthink mentality. Various types of activities and instruments can be employed with groups, and sometimes teams are composed for group projects. Teachers who value affective learning and a deeper exchange of feelings in the classroom enjoy using groups and teams.

NOTES

1. Jerry Wofford, Edwin Gerloff, and Robert Cummins, "Group Behavior and the Communication Process," in Robert Cathcart and Larry A. Samovar, *Small Group Communication: A Reader*, 3rd ed., (Dubuque, IA: Wm. C. Brown, 1979), p. 33.

2. Malcolm Knowles and Hulda Knowles, *Introduction to Group Dynamics* (New York: Association Press, 1959), p. 15.

3. B. Aubrey Fisher, *Small Group Decision Making*, 2nd ed., (New York: McGraw-Hill, 1980), p. 1. As a professor who studied group communication, Fisher had collected a number of jokes about groups.

4. Charles Pavitt and Ellen Curtis, *Small Group Discussion: A Theoretical Approach* (Scottsdale, AZ: Gorsuch Scarisbrick, 1990), pp. 12-18.

5. Fisher, *Small Group Decision Making*, p. 17. Fisher draws the concept of "groupness" from John K. Brilhart, *Effective Group Discussion*, 3rd ed., (Dubuque, IA: Wm. C. Brown, 1978), p. 17.

6. Knowles and Knowles, *Introduction to Group Dynamics*, pp. 39-40.

7. Fisher, *Small Group Decision Making*, pp. 24-26 for information on group size.

8. John K. Brilhart, *Effective Group Discussion*, pp. 20-21.

9. Carl Rogers, *On Encounter Groups* (New York: Harper & Row, 1970) and Alton Barbour and Alvin Goldberg, *Interpersonal Communication: Teaching Strategies and Resources* (New York: Speech Communication Association, 1974).

10. Barry E. Collins and Harold Guetzkow, *A Social Psychology of Group Processes for Decision-Making* (New York: Wiley, 1964), p. 58. Quoted in Fisher, *Small Group Decision-Making*, p. 65.

11. For more detail on types of group tasks (additive, conjunctive, disjunctive, complementary, etc.), see Pavitt and Curtis, *Small Group Discussion*, pp. 26-29.

12. Irving Lorge, "A Survey of the Studies Contrasting the Quality of Group Performance and Individual Performance, 1920-1957," *Psychological Bulletin*, 1958, 55, pp. 337-72.

13. The example was used originally in research performed by H.H. Johnson and M.M. Torcivia and is referred to in Pavitt and Curtis, *Small Group Discussion*, p. 43.

14. Bernard Berelson and Gary Steiner, *Human Behavior: An Inventory of Scientific Findings* (New York: Harcourt, Brace & World, 1964).

15. Ibid., p. 557ff.

16. Kurt Lewin, "Forces Behind Food Habits and Methods of Change," *Bulletin of the National Research Council*, 1943, 108, pp. 35-65.

17. Paul Hersey and Kenneth H. Blanchard, *Management of Organizational Behavior* (Englewood Cliffs, NJ: Prentice-Hall, 1988), p. 18ff. See especially Chapter 2, "Motivation and Behavior."

18. Pavitt and Curtis, *Small Group Discussion*, pp. 38-40.

19. Fisher, *Small Group Decision Making*, p. 63. The study referred to is David M. Berg, "A Descriptive Analysis of the Distribution and Duration of Themes Discussed by Task-Oriented Small Groups," *Speech Monographs*, 34, pp. 172-75.

20. Irving Janis, *Victims of Groupthink: A Psychological Study of Policy Decisions and Fiascos* (Boston: Houghton Mifflin Co., 1972); quoted in Larry L. Barker, Kathy J. Wahlers, Kittie W. Watson, and Robert J. Kibler, *Groups in Process: An Introduction to Small Group Communication*, 3rd ed., (Englewood Cliffs, NJ: Prentice-Hall, 1987), p. 68.

21. Ibid., p. 69, reporting on Irving Janis, *Groupthink*, 2nd ed., 1983.

22. Fisher, *Small Group Decision Making*, p. 61.

23. Alvin Zander, *The Purposes of Groups and Organizations* (San Francisco: Jossey-Bass, 1985). The examples presented below are drawn from Chapter 2, "Functions Served by Groups," p. 14ff.

24. A. Paul Hare, *Handbook of Small Group Research* (New York: Free Press, 1976), Appendix 2, "The History and Present State of Small Group Research," pp. 388, 392.

25. Robert T. Golembiewski and Arthur Blumberg, *Sensitivity Training and the Laboratory Approach* (Itasca, IL: Peacock Publishers, 1970), p. 4.

26. Alvin Goldberg and Carl Larson, *Group Communication* (Englewood Cliffs, NJ: Prentice-Hall, 1975), pp. 162-63. For more detail, see Kenneth Benne, "History of the T-Group in the Laboratory Setting" in Leland

Bradford, Jack Gibb, and Kenneth Benne, *T-Group Theory and Laboratory Method* (New York: Wiley, 1964).

27. Goldberg and Larson, *Group Communication*, p. 163.

28. Thomas R. Verny, *Inside Groups* (New York: McGraw-Hill, 1974).

29. Rogers, *Carl Rogers on Encounter Groups*, pp. 3-4.

30. Hare, *Handbook of Small Group Research*, "Sensitivity Training," pp. 413-14.

31. A. Paul Hare, *Handbook on Small Group Research*, "The History and Present State of Small Groups Research," p. 392.

32. Verny, *Inside Groups*.

33. W.R. Bion, *Experiences in Groups* (New York: Basic Books, 1959).

34. For an overview of the research on group processes, see Alvin Goldberg and Carl Larson, *Group Communication* (Englewood Cliffs, NJ: Prentice Hall, 1975). One of the early classics in the field is James H. McBurney and Kenneth G. Hance, *Discussion in Human Affairs* (New York: Harper Brothers, 1939). A well-known study of groups from a sociological viewpoint is George C. Homans, *The Human Group* (New York: Harcourt, Brace & World, 1950).

35. Bruce W. Tuckman, "Development Sequence in Small Groups," *Psychological Bulletin*, 63, pp. 384-99. Described in Fisher, *Small Group Decision Making*, p. 140.

36. The quotation is from Fisher, *Small Group Decision Making*, p. 142, where the theory is summarized. The spiral theory comes from Thomas Scheidel and Laura Crowell, "Idea Development in Small Discussion Groups," *Quarterly Journal of Speech*, 50, pp. 140-45.

37. Golembiewski and Blumberg, *Sensitivity Training*, p. 87. The questions are borrowed from a larger checklist for observing group communication.

38. Goldberg and Larson, *Group Communication*, p. 46. The distinction goes back to some of the earlier work of Homans. See also Fisher, *Small Group Decision Making*, p. 37ff.

39. Barber, Wahlers, Watson and Kibler, *Groups in Process*, p. 37.

40. Patrick R. Penland and Sara Fine, "Group Dynamics" in Cathcart and Samovar, *Small Group Communication*, p. 26.

41. Michael Burgoon, Judee K. Heston, and James McCroskey, *Small Group Communication: A Functional Approach* (New York: Holt, Rinehart & Winston, 1974), p. 10.

42. Fisher, *Small Group Decision Making*, pp. 38-39.

43. Ibid., pp. 39-43.

44. Pavitt and Curtis, *Small Group Discussion*, p. 64.

45. Fisher, *Small Group Decision Making*, p. 42.

46. Barker, Wahlers, Watson, and Kibler, *Groups in Process*, p. 53ff, provides a good discussion of group structure from which I have drawn extensively.

47. Erving Goffman, *Encounters* (New York: Bobbs-Merrill, 1961), p. 87. Quoted in Fisher, *Small Group Decision Making*, p. 167.

48. Hare, *Handbook of Small Group Research*, p. 131.

49. Kenneth D. Benne and Paul Sheets, "Functional Roles of Group Members," *Journal of Social Issues*, Spring 1948, pp. 4, 41-49.

50. Fisher, *Small Group Decision Making*, pp. 183-84, contains a good discussion of group norms.

51. Eric Berne, "The Individual and the Group" in Cathcart and Samovar, *Small Group Communication*, p. 61.

52. Fisher, *Small Group Decision Making*, p. 29.

53. Ibid., p. 70.

54. Barker, Wahlers, Watson, and Kibler, *Groups in Process*, p. 83.

55. Charles M. Kelley, "Empathic Listening" in Cathcart and Samovar, *Small Group Communication*, pp. 350-51.

56. Barker, Walhers, Watson, and Kibler, *Groups in Process*, pp. 82-87. The list below is quoted directly on p. 87.

57. John E. Baird, Jr., and Sanford Weinberg, "Elements of Group Communication" in Cathcart and Samovar, *Small Group Communication*, p. 296. The list is shortened, adapted, and paraphrased.

58. Ibid., p. 297.

59. Lawrence Rosenfeld, "Nonverbal Communication in the Small Group" in Cathcart and Samovar, *Small Group Communication*, p. 306.

60. Fisher, *Small Group Decision Making*, pp. 50-55.

61. Leland Bradford, Dorothy Stock, and Murray Horowitz, "How to Diagnose Group Problems" in Golembiewski and Blumberg, *Sensitivity Training*, p. 142. Quoted directly.

62. Pavitt and Curtis, *Sensitivity Training*, pp. 100-01.

63. Leland Bradford, Dorothy Stock, and Murray Horowitz, "How to Diagnose Group Problems" in Golembiewski and Blumberg, *Sensitivity Training*, pp. 142-43.

64. Fisher, *Small Group Decision Making*, pp. 57-59.

65. Ibid., p. 54.

66. Leland P. Bradford, Dorothy Stock, and Murray Horowitz, "How to Diagnose Group Problems" in Golembiewski and Blumberg, *Sensitivity Training*, p. 145.

67. Ibid., pp. 146-47.

68. Gerald M. Phillips, *Communication and the Small Group* (Indianapolis, IN: Bobbs-Merrill, 1973), pp. 75-76.

69. Many of the examples presented below are drawn from my own teaching experience and from my previous book, *Teaching Strategies for the College Classroom* (Boulder, CO: Westview Press, 1976), p. 93ff.

70. Alex F. Osborn, *Applied Imagination* (New York: Scribner's, 1957). Cited in Alvin Zander, *Making Groups Effective* (San Francisco: Jossey-Bass, 1982), p. 21. The exposition of Osborn's ideas is drawn from Arthur M.

Coon, "Brainstorming—A Creative Problem-Solving Technique" in Cathcart and Samovar, *Small Group Communications*, p. 135ff.

71. Goldberg and Larson, *Group Communication*, p. 72ff. Not all of the categories listed in this text are presented here.

72. James H. Davis, "The Effects of Task Performance on Cohesiveness," in Cathcart and Samovar, *Small Group Communication*, pp. 151-52.

73. Barker, Wahlers, Watson, and Kibler, *Groups in Process*, p. 212.

74. J.L. Moreno, "The Psychodrama" in J.E. Fairchild, *Personal Problems and Psychological Frontiers* (New York: Sheridan House, 1957); quoted in Michael Burgoon, Judee K. Heston, and James McCroskey, *Small Group Communication: A Functional Approach* (New York: Holt, Rinehart and Winston, 1974), p. 90.

75. See, for example, Hersey and Blanchard, *Management of Organizational Behavior*, especially Chapters 4 and 5. See also Warren Bennis and Burt Nanus, *Leaders: The Strategies for Taking Charge* (New York: Harper & Row, 1985); James MacGregor Burns, *Leadership* (New York: Harper & Row, 1978); N.M. Tichy and M.A. Devanna, *The Transformational Leader* (New York: John Wiley, 1986); and Robert Waterman, *The Renewal Factor* (New York: Bantam, 1987).

76. This brief historical review of the general research on leadership is drawn from Pavitt and Curtis, *Small Group Discussion*, Chapter 9, "Leadership: Early Views," p. 245ff, and Chapter 10, "Leadership: Contemporary Views." These chapters provide a detailed discussion of the theories as well as the key research studies supporting the theories. A similar summary of the trends in research can be found in Fisher, *Small Group Decision Making*, pp. 203-07.

77. Ibid., p. 22ff.

78. Ibid., p. 207ff, for a discussion of Leaderless Group Discussion and the emergence of leaders in groups.

79. Ibid., p. 219.

80. Carl E. Larson and Frank M.J. LaFasto, *TeamWork: What Must Go Right/What Can Go Wrong* (Newbury Park, CA: Sage Publications, 1989). The ideas for the rest of this section are drawn exclusively from this work and are found as would be appropriate in each chapter.

81. Ibid., p. 19

82. Rogers, *On Encounter Groups*, p. 1.

83. Charles Seashore, "What is Sensitivity Training?" in Golembiewski and Blumberg, *Sensitivity Training*, p. 14.

84. Rogers, *On Encounter Groups*, p.9.

85. Warren G. Bennis, "Goals and Meta-Goals of Laboratory Training" in Golembiewski and Blumberg, *Sensitivity Training*, pp. 19-23.

86. Rogers, *On Encounter Groups*, pp. 16-40.

87. Irvin D. Yalom, *The Theory and Practice of Group Psychotherapy*, 3rd ed., (New York: Basic Books, 1985). The listing of therapeutic factors and their

paraphrased descriptions are drawn from Chapters 1-3, pp. 3-69. Each factor corresponds to a section heading in those chapters, except for the discussion of catharsis, which is found on p. 84ff, and the discussion of existential factors, found on p. 92ff.

Experience and Reflection

Learning
is finding out
what you already know
Doing is demonstrating that
you know it

—Richard Bach, *Illusions*

LEARNING THROUGH EXPERIENCE

Not all teaching takes place in classrooms. Increasingly, as postsecondary teachers, we find ourselves involved in various kinds of structured learning arrangements that occur outside of classrooms and frequently off campus. In many institutions, students are provided with formal experiences—internships, practicums, work experience, overseas study, and various forms of clinical education—designed to provide an opportunity for significant learning. It is this base of experience that triggers the learning, hence the term "experience-based learning." What a teacher does to facilitate this learning is often quite different from what is done in the typical classroom.

Experience-based learning is not easy to define. Many terms are being used today, often interchangeably, to refer to rather different out-of-the classroom learning experiences. Almost everyone, of course, learns from experience (and, alas, we all know people who never seem to), and sometimes this experience is quite painful. Sometimes people seek out educational institutions to obtain credit or otherwise certify their informal learning as "life experience" or "prior learning." Often these experiences and the arrangements to acknowledge them are referred to as "experiential learning" (not to be confused with "experimental learning"), and many institutions have discovered how to employ some rather sophisticated devices for evaluating the learning that has occurred. The term "experiential learning" is slippery, however, because in a sense all learning, even classroom learning, is "experiential." In this chapter, the narrower and more precise term, "experience-based learning," is used to refer to "sponsored" or "guided" experiences from which significant learning occurs. In most colleges and universities experience-based learning also involves a pre-established procedure for selecting or assigning the experience, planning for it, and reflecting on it, especially if some form of credit or certification is involved.[1]

Perhaps the best way to define "experience-based learning" is to give positive examples of the kinds of learning situations that illustrate what is meant by the term. In 1977 a carefully designed survey was administered by the Council for the Advancement of Experiential Learning (CAEL), and in developing the questionnaire it became necessary to define the types of programs that institutions sponsored. The following nine categories emerged:[2]

- **Career Exploration.** Placement in business, service, or professional settings to explore career possibilities and develop job-related skills.
- **Career or Occupational Development.** Placement designed to facilitate development of skills and experience related to a specific career.
- **Cooperative Education.** Alternation and integration of work and study periods on campus and in industrial, business, government, or service settings.
- **Professional Training.** Service in assigned responsibilities under supervision of a professional, in such areas as education, medicine, law, social work, nursing, or ministry.
- **Public Service Internship.** Service in an institutional setting, usually unremunerated, often to assist in some aspect of community development.
- **Social or Political Action through Service Learning Internships.** Working for change through community organization, political activity, or research and action projects.
- **Personal Growth and Development.** Projects designed for personal growth such as wilderness survival experience, apprentice-

ship to an artist or craftsman, or participation in a human relations group.

- **Cross-Cultural Experience.** Significant involvement in another culture or subculture, in one's home country or in a foreign country, as a temporary family member, worker, volunteer, or student.
- **Field Research.** Group project in which concepts and methods of a discipline (anthropology, biology, geology, archeology, sociology) are applied in a field environment.

All of these categories of experienced-based learning have one thing in common: They use a significant, potentially enriching experience as the basis or primary stimulus for learning. Out of this experience, many kinds of learning can arise.

Most institutions, and most teachers who get involved with experience-based learning programs, realize that simply "having" the experience is not enough. For the fullest educational potential to be realized, a reflection process is also necessary, some means to help the student glean from the experience its meaning and particular kinds of learning. Helping students to learn through reflection on experience brings us to the last and final teaching strategy, which is based on still another paradigm of how people learn. Consider three teachers and their students, each involved in a quite different setting, where there is a high potential for learning through experience and reflection.

Betsy Warner, a professor of sociology at Elm Grove College, wears two hats. During the fall term she team-teaches in an interdisciplinary core course in the social sciences and an advanced course for majors on community organization; during the winter term she goes to Brazil with a group of 10 students from Elm Grove to supervise their Overseas Service Term. Elm Grove provides a wide range of experience-based learning options, including overseas study and service in several countries, a Washington-based internship in political science, an urban studies internship in Chicago, various cooperative education work placements, and an "own plans" independent field experience that students design and implement along with their major advisor. All students are required to engage in at least one off-campus experience, but they have many opportunities to do so and often, after one experience, they voluntarily elect another. Elm Grove has a major commitment to experience-based learning and over the years has developed a high level of sophistication in providing logistical support structures and organizational procedures to enhance the quality of these experiences.

Students begin the process by stopping in at the Off-Campus Learning Center to learn about the range of available opportunities. The Center houses a small library of information on placement opportunities, including notebooks of "reports" by students. Greg Adams, a first-term sophomore, with an eye on graduate study in international relations, knows that he needs to begin making serious plans about his off-campus experience. He begins browsing through materials and in a few minutes finds himself engaged in a lively discussion with one of the Center counselors about a community action project in Brazil. "It looks interesting, but what do you do?" Greg asks impatiently.

"It changes from year to year. *Centro de Aprendizagem do Trabalho* started out as an artisan's craft center for adults in a very poor neighborhood, to bring them in from the streets, give them some reasonable employment, teach them a skill, and help them to improve their life. But Dona Flora, the woman who founded it, couldn't be content with just the craft center. She saw other needs and opportunities, particularly with the children of the workers, so she started a school. Anyway, every year *Centro* has some new project because Dona Flora is so successful; she sells the crafts to expensive hotels and clubs in Rio and São Paulo and saves enough profit for some carefully managed expansion. This year, Professor Warner told me, they are building facilities for an upper elementary school."

"What about the language?"

"No problem. Professor Warner has excellent Portuguese. What they need is good workers. She provides a crash course on survival Portuguese as part of the orientation."

"I'm still trying to picture what I would do."

"Why don't you talk to Professor Warner. That's the next step anyway. I can sign off on your application form here, but she's the one who picks the project participants and she's tough."

"I know. I've had her in class."

The next week Greg has an interview with Professor Warner. He finds out more about the placement—much more.

"Crude living conditions. No hot water. A wider community that is safe physically, if you stick together, but a very poor neighborhood, in some ways very depressing. But *Centro* is a little oasis of culture and creativity. The school has a unique philosophy about what education is, about what life is for that matter, and just being there is an experience in itself. This year, mornings will be spent volunteering as an aid with the teachers, so that you get to try your hand at teaching; the afternoons are spent on the construction project."

"I know that you go there as a volunteer, to serve," Greg notes, "but what have you noticed that students get out of the experience?"

"Different things. An awareness of how hard life is for some people in other parts of the world. A sense of the dilemma of serving. How to help without being condescending. A more realistic sense of what it's like to survive in another culture. But what I want to know is what *you* want to learn. As part of your application I require a brief essay that includes a statement of what you want to get out of this. We have some fairly extensive orientation sessions before we leave, and while you are there I'll expect that you keep a journal, participate in weekly reflection meetings with our group, and have three or four personal conferences with me. When we get back to campus, I'll want a reaction paper from you and an exit interview. Any problems with that? It's 15 hours of credit, you know."

"No. Sounds fine. I hope I get accepted."

Hiroshi Ikeda is the Director of the Small Business Management Center at Pacific Coast Community College (PCCC). For five years he ran his own specialty food shop and studied business at night school. Now he is a partner in a small accounting firm, but what he enjoys most is his full-time faculty appointment at the Center. Two years ago PCCC ventured into what has now become its fastest growing area of service to the community: customized training. As an alternative to listing courses in the class schedule and hoping that enough students would show up, Pacific Coast began sending program developers into the community to find out what educational needs might best be served. Meetings with business leaders turned up an astounding array of opportunities, but many of the companies said that they needed on-site, hands-on training, customized to the needs of their workers. Three new programs were begun in local businesses where PCCC became a talent broker for faculty who had just the right skills to address the training needs of that business. It was Hiroshi Ikeda, however, who brought the plight of the small business manager to the attention of the dean of instruction. "These are the people who really need customized training. Each situation is unique, and they have nowhere to turn. Why can't we devise a way to help them one-on-one, to learn from their own experience in their own setting?" And so the Center for Small Business Management was born, with Hiroshi as the director.

Today the Center serves approximately 45 small businesses in the district with Hiroshi and a staff of three. The program is now well-known, and it is not unusual for Hiroshi to get a desperate phone call for assistance.

"How can we help you, Mrs. Martinez?"

"I don't know. That's why I am calling."

"What's your business?"

"My daughter and I run a small candy store. It *was* small, anyway. We operated out of our home for several years, but this fall we moved into a store in the mall. Things went fine at first, but ever since the holidays there's been no business. I'm really worried!"

"What do you know about our program?"

"Not very much, but I've heard you have some good ideas."

"Would you like me to stop by, so that we could talk about your concerns."

"You would come here?"

"Yes."

"How soon?"

The following week Mr. Ikeda stops in at The Sweet Tooth in the Beachfront Mall. He brings a brochure on the work of the Center and goes over it with Maria Martinez and her daughter, Dolores.

"It's a course that you register for and pay for like any course, and you can earn 18 credits toward your associate's degree in Small Business Management, if you wish. But beyond that, it's unlike any course you have ever encountered. You sign up for a year; then you are entitled to 12, on-site, three-hour visits by Center personnel. We will sit down with you and help you analyze what's happening in your own business—not some other business or some hypothetical business—but *your own business.*"

"Good. I need some help."

"I understand that. In this course the textbook is your business and your experience is the teacher. My role is to help you learn from that experience. There are a series of lectures and seminars over at the campus, and we will plug you into some of those as needed, but the place to begin is with your own situation. You need to complete this survey before my visit with you next week. It's not hard, it just asks you to think about what you are doing. Do the best you can."

Sue Best is director of Field Studies at New England Theological Seminary. All students, sooner or later, come through her office, because they are required to have at least one term of assigned field experience in a setting related to their special interests. Most students talk with her the term before they plan to engage in field work in order to do some planning. She has a lot of questions that she fires at them to try to get a sense of their interests and needs. She keeps a list of good placement settings posted on the huge bulletin board outside her office. Ralph Graham stands outside her office pondering the board, 10 minutes early for his appointment. Ralph is always early, a norm of punctuality he has carried over from his years of experience in selling insurance. He doesn't like to be caught off guard, so he plans ahead.

"Tell me about yourself." Sue prompts some self-disclosure, which she senses is not always easy for Ralph.

"What would you like to know?"

"Whatever you think might be valuable so that we can make a good placement for you."

"Well, as you can tell, I'm a little older than some of the students. I've sold shoes, encyclopedias, real estate, and I finally thought I had found it in insurance. But after 15 years I woke up one morning asking myself 'why?'"

"And you ended up here . . ."

"That's a long story, but, yes, and I'm hoping to use what's left of my life to serve the Church."

"As . . ."

"I'm not sure, but probably as a pastor in a small parish. Maybe in a small town. Maybe in a congregation that has a fair number of older people. I don't mind working with the old folks; I'm getting to be one myself."

Sue is already thinking through a number of options, but she wants to do some more checking first. Obviously this is no candidate for the Methodist Center for the Homeless or for the Social Services Addiction Program downtown. "Have you had any pastoral counseling?"

"The basic course in the required core, but nothing more than that yet. It seems like it might be better to learn that on the job, walking beside a strong pastor. I guess that's why I'm planning ahead on my field placement. I love my studies, but to tell the truth, I don't have much sense of how to carry on a ministry out there in a local congregation. I'm not afraid to meet people and make calls; I've done enough of that. I'm just not sure what to do with or for the people I'll be meeting."

Sue Best is watching him closely, her light blue eyes searching him to size up his needs. There's something she likes about him in spite of his stodginess. He's very rigid, and a bit naive for all his years of "experience," but he's being honest and he's asking for a new experience, not easy in middle age. She searches her mental bulletin board of jobs, and one pops out at her as being nearly perfect. Working with Pastor Dwight out at Pleasantville would be great for Ralph Graham. Pastor Dwight is a wise, old pastor with lots of practical experience. "O.K. I think I have a good idea for you." She shares it with him, describes the church, the pastor, and offers to call to check on availability and set the process in motion. "You'll like Pastor

Dwight once you get to know him. It will be a good experience for you . . . if you are ready for a little challenge."

Ralph Graham isn't quite sure what Sue Best means by "ready for a little challenge." The way she says it has something of an ominous ring.

REFLECTION-IN-ACTION

Although "experience-based learning" came to be widely institutionalized in American higher education only after World War II, precursors and forerunners abound: Cooperative Education was established at the University of Cincinnati in 1903 and at Antioch College in the Great Depression; studying at a foreign (particularly German) university has roots in the nineteenth century. How did educators come to believe that the experience of work, service, and travel could be educational? Surely it is possible to work, serve, or travel without learning much. How is it that raw experience becomes "educative"? What must be done to or with that experience to glean an educational harvest?

Some answers to these questions are found in the work of David Kolb, a contemporary theorist of experiential learning.[3] Drawing on the earlier work of Lewin, Dewey, and Piaget, Kolb sets forth a cyclical model of experiential learning:

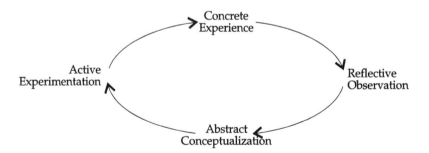

Experiential learning begins in concrete experience. The learner *has* some experience to begin with and then begins to reflect on what that experience means. As the reflection deepens, the learner formulates abstract conceptualizations about what has taken place, that is, how experience works. As the abstract conceptualizations are developed, they must be tested to see if they do indeed work. This is done through a process of active experimentation, which of necessity returns the learner once again to concrete experience.

For Kolb, "the impulse of experience gives ideas their moving force, and ideas give direction to impulse." Learning, therefore, "is best conceived as a process, not in terms of outcomes." Learning that is an accumulation of facts, ideas, or behaviors will not serve the learner long, because the accumulated facts, ideas, and behaviors will soon be outdated. For Kolb, "ideas are not fixed and immutable elements of thought but are formed and reformed through experience." Understanding is a process of continuous construction, built on the interaction of ideas and experience. "Failure to modify ideas and habits as a result of experience is maladaptive. Therefore, one must engage in a continuous cycle of experience, reflection, abstraction and testing, finally returning to experience once again."

Kolb's work shows that "experienced-based learning" involves some steps, some phases, a going out and coming back, and, above all, a process of reflection. But what is the learning that takes place from experience? Is it a mere application of classroom knowledge to a practical setting, or is there a new, perhaps qualitatively different, kind of learning that grows up out of experience? This is a difficult issue, but there are those who would argue, "yes," and who would say that "professional knowledge," in particular, is of a different order from knowledge of a discipline gained in classrooms.

A strong case for the qualitative difference of knowledge gleaned from experience has been made by Donald Schön in a stimulating book entitled *The Reflective Practitioner: How Professionals Think in Action.*[4] His argument is as follows: Professional education—the education of practitioners in law, medicine, theology, social work, engineering, and business—has been dominated by a model for training known as Technical Rationality. Based on a set of positivist assumptions about empirical methods for gaining knowledge, the model of Technical Rationality stresses the development of a standardized body of knowledge—information, principles, theories—that can be applied consistently to recurring professional problems. Most professional training, therefore, involves an early disciplinary or basic science phase, an applied science (skill) or applications phase, and a professional attitudes phase. The model has dominated professional education so completely that almost no one questions it. Furthermore, the distinction between basic science and its applications in the professions has led to a status hierarchy (pecking order) within higher education, with those engaged in the work of the "pure" sciences and the disciplines perceived as making a more valued contribution than those engaged in the less-demanding work of "application." Although all of the professions have made their way into the university and rely heavily on the knowledge generated by the disciplines, the "schools of useful knowledge" have paid a price, consistently having to pay homage to the "higher learning," the fundamental theory that professionals and technicians apply to practice.

Schön goes on to argue, however, that the world of professional practice today is not as neat and tidy as the model of Technical Rationality would suggest. There is, in fact, a crisis of confidence in the professions, and a growing realization of the mismatch of traditional patterns of practice and knowledge with the actual professional problems encountered. Today, professional practice is increasingly characterized by "complexity, uncertainty, instability and value conflict," and it is widely recognized that "professional practice has at least as much to do with finding the problem as solving the problem." In Schön's words:

> In real-world practice, problems do not present themselves to the practitioner as givens. They must be constructed from the materials of problematic situations which are puzzling, troubling, and uncertain. In order to convert a problematic situation to a problem, a practitioner must do a certain kind of work. He must make sense of an uncertain situation that initially makes no sense . . . . When we set the problem, we select what we will treat as the "things" of the situation, we set the boundaries of our attention to it, and we impose upon it a coherence which allows us to say what is wrong and in what directions the situation needs to be changed. Problem setting is a process in which, interactively, we *name* the things to which we will attend and *frame* the context in which we will attend to them.

This view of professional life suggest that the older model of more or less routine problems of practice to which standardized knowledge applies is no longer functional. There are too many cases that are not in the books, too many unique and unpredictable elements, too many unstable contexts, for the old formulas to work. What is needed today, Schön argues, is a new way of preparing professionals that goes beyond the incomplete model of Technical Rationality, a new way of knowing, which he calls "reflection-in-action."

Reflection-in-action, it turns out, is a way of knowing that grows out of experience. It is a kind of knowing that is *in* our action, and the workaday life of the professional depends heavily on this tacit knowing-in-action. Professional practitioners must think about what they are doing while they are doing it, and it is in this way that they learn from experience.

> Stimulated by surprise, they turn thought back on action and on the knowing which is implicit in action. They may ask themselves, for example, "What features do I notice when I recognize this thing? What are the criteria by which I make this judgement? What procedures am I enacting when I perform this skill? How am I framing the problem that I am trying to solve? Usually reflection on knowing-in-action goes together with reflection on the stuff at hand. There is some puzzling, or troubling, or interesting phenomenon with which the individual is trying to deal. As he tries to make sense of it, he also reflects on the understandings which have been implicit in his action, understandings which he surfaces, criticizes, restructures, and embodies in further action.

If we put aside the model of Technical Rationality, and its assumption that intelligent practice is always some application of a prior-learned knowledge, there is a common-sense resonance to the idea that we do learn from experience, and there is a kind of knowing that grows up rather naturally from action. The tight rope walker, for example, "learns" to walk the wire from walking the wire. Baseball pitchers speak of "finding the groove," a process of getting a feel for the ball and adjusting to the mound, the stadium, and the succession of batters. While they are out on the mound, they get feedback on pitching to the batters, adjusting, noticing what is right, and then they repeat what has been successful. Similarly, the jazz musician who improvises with others gets a feel for the music and the other musicians, varying the theme, making new combinations and contributions, evolving with the others a way of playing together. Schön suggests that this is what the professional does through reflection-in-action. It is a matter of getting a "feel for the ball," "thinking on your feet," "learning by doing," and "keeping your wits about you." Knowing-in-action is the foundation of professional know-how.

Although Schön may be accused of overstating the case, particularly in his criticism of the usefulness of previously acquired disciplinary knowledge, his task was to "shake up" some rather firmly entrenched ways of thinking about the training of professionals. This he has done well, and in the process has provided an interesting description of how people in general learn from experience. He has begun to articulate still another paradigm of how people learn—by reflection on immediate experience.

EXPERIENCED-BASED EDUCATION AS HOLISTIC LEARNING

Is there any support for a learning paradigm that suggests that people learn through "reflection-in-action"? How might such a paradigm be further described and elaborated, and what evidence is there to suggest that experience-based learning is valid? What kind of learning is it, and how is it different from the all-too-familiar model of "muddling through"?

Experience-based learning might best be described as holistic. Of all the paradigms set forth in this book, experience-based learning involves more of the person—eyes, ears, touch, taste, smell, mind, emotions, intuition. It is as if the learner were put into a situation and then asked to survive by doing anything that human beings are capable of doing to learn from experience. Do people actually learn in this holistic way, that is, as an entire organism? One of the earliest thinkers to describe this kind of learning was Sigmund Freud.

As the founder of psychoanalysis, Freud is well known for his description of the human psyche as consisting of the id, superego, and ego, but perhaps his greater contribution is in his assertion of the inseparability of the warring components of the tri-partite self.[5] Freud saw that human action is the manifestation of a complex but unitary self, the total accumulation of all past experiences, those which we comprehend in our awareness, and those which are hidden from our consciousness. He understood that holding the self together is essential, but not easy.

Freud's theories have, of course, been criticized vigorously, and there have been good reasons put forth to suggest that certain of his ideas are either wrong, obsolete, or in need of serious modification.[6] But Freud's overall concept of a complex, layered self, functioning as a totality, often beyond conscious grasp, is still a valuable insight that drives much of the thought in clinical psychology and psychiatry today. Much of Freud's language, however, was abstract and full of neologisms, appearing to float above empirical reality. Is there other evidence, apart from Freud's theorizing, that humans are perhaps made up of many selves that function as one self, many brains that function as one mind?

In recent years there has been an outpouring of research on the human brain—how it has evolved, what it consists of, and how it functions. Classic summaries of that work are found in Paul D. Maclean's *A Triune Concept of the Brain and Behavior* and in the more popular work by Carl Sagan, *The Dragons of Eden.*[7] Oddly enough, recent brain research also suggests a tripartite brain, with three components functioning as a whole, but not always in complete harmony. The evolution of the human brain, according to the most recent theories, is a story of "successive accretion and specialization of three further layers surmounting the spinal cord . . . after each evolutionary step, the older portions of the brain still exist and must still be accommodated. But a new layer with new functions has been added."[8] It is as if we look at ourselves and the world through three different mentalities, two of which have no speech. The three brains can be distinguished anatomically, functionally, and neurochemically.[9] Although the subject is very complex, it appears to be possible to distinguish the three areas as *reptilian*, the kind of minimal brain possessed by reptiles who evolved over 200 million years ago; the *old mammalian* kind of brain that flourished in other, nonhuman, mammals about 60 million years ago; and the *new-mammalian* cerebral cortex that evolved in humans as something rather new and different.[10] As with other aspects of anatomy, the human brain recapitulates its evolutionary development in the growth of the human fetus, which also develops "three brains" in sequence.[11] Although not the largest overall, the human brain, which is roughly three pounds and a quart in size (1,500 grams and a liter) is the most developed and highly complex of animal brains, particularly in its new mammalian portion. If a giraffe might be thought of as a "neck-freak," and an elephant as a "nose-freak," human beings are "brain-freaks."[12] Human brains are on the average six times larger, relative to body weight, than other living mammals. (Dolphins are notable big-brain exceptions.) This process of brain enlargement, apart from the expected increase in size related to body size, is known as encephalization. The function related to encephalization was language, and ultimately the development of the capacity for intelligent behavior, not only the ability to communicate but to use linguistic images to map the territory of human experience.[13]

What are the functions of these three layers of brain and how are they specialized? Again, the subject is complex, but it appears that the reptilian brain plays an important role in aggressive behavior, territoriality, ritual, and social hierarchies, the more "instinctual" behavior related to our life in social organizations. The old mammalian brain appears to have more to do with emotions. The "master gland," the pituitary, is an important part of this limbic region of the brain and plays an important role with feelings. Not only rage and anger have their seat here, but perhaps also the beginnings of altru-ism. The new mammalian brain, or neocortex is the site of most cognitive functions. In size it represents 85 percent of the human brain, and is differentiated into various lobes with separate func-tions.[14]

If the human brain is made up of different layers with special-ized functions, in what ways are these "three brains" compatible and incompatible? It should be noted, of course, that the three compo-nents of the brain are not really three separate brains. The brain is "well wired" and the components are intricately connected. At the same time, understandably, the relationship of the parts is not always smooth. Leslie Hart has created an intriguing metaphor for describ-ing this relationship:

> If we visualize a grandfather, father and son (or equivalent females) with these personalities forced to live and work together—all being partners in a business, let us say—it is obvious there will be constant conflict and contention . . . *Our brain as a whole is not harmonious, but works through a precarious, constantly changing balance of these three partners*.[15]

Thus modern brain research provides intriguing parallels with Freud's original concept of the tripartite self. Although it would be incorrect to relate the id, superego, and ego to the three layers of the brain—Sagan concludes that the psychoanalytic tripartite mind is only weakly in accord with the biological triune brain model—there was in the basic thrust of Freud's thought some truth, an awareness of something in the construct of the human psyche that made it function in a holistic way, yet with tension among the component parts.

The "bad news" about brain function, therefore, is that the three parts of the brain don't always get along together. The "good news" is that the human brain has great flexibility, many specialized places designated to conduct a multitude of functions, and an enormous capacity of 10 to 12 billion neurons (maybe as many as 30 billion), tiny switches comparable to the circuits of an electronic computer, all standing ready to make connections. Humans have a tripartite, highly interconnected, well-wired neurological system for dealing with experience. How does this awesome mechanism work?

Leslie Hart, in his fascinating book, *Human Brain and Human Learning*, attempts to spell out the implications of brain research for human learning.[16] Hart believes that most theories of learning are not based on a sound understanding of the brain, and that most research on learning has been conducted on animals that don't have a brain that is anything like the human brain. Using the physical evidence and modern theories of brain evolution as a starting point, Hart speculates on how the brain was used in the earlier life of *homo sapiens*, before the relatively recent development of "civilization." As hunter-gatherers, humans evolved as nonspecialists (compared to most animals), willing to eat almost anything, and able to spread across the globe and survive in almost any climate or habitat. As "brain freaks" humans developed a capacity for an unprecedented amount of learning, which resulted in being able to breed, live, survive, and dominate where less-developed animals could not. The way humans learn, Hart contends, is not, however, in a logical, rational, linear mode, the staple of most schooling. Rather, the human brain operates in a multilinear way all at once, using all of the sensibilities, employing its many layers, going down many paths simultaneously.

> We identify an object, for example, by gathering information—often in less than a second—on size, color, shape, surface texture, weight, smell, movement, any sound it may make, where it is found, what else is with it, any symbolic information within it (such as label or price sign), how other people are responding to it, and so on. All of these investigations by the brain to answer the question "What is this?" go forward along many different paths, and branching paths, among the brain's trillions of connections, at the same time. From the vast information stored, answers or tentative answers get pulled out, then assembled, compared and interpreted by, if possible, extracting a pattern. The whole miraculous procedure bears no relationship to linear processing.

Hart argues that "logic," conceived of as a step-by-step, linear, sequential way of thinking, did not appear for millions of years, and that most of what humans developed as the broad foundations of society and culture—clothing, tools, weapons, utensils, housing, dance, music, language, religion—did not require "logic," but this more multidimensional holistic kind of learning. Even many of the great scientific discoveries, later put forth in their logical form, were not *arrived at* logically. What the brain does, and is best at doing, is to write and retrieve "programs," to recognize, store, and utilize the patterns that emerge from experience. "The brain is, by nature's design, an amazingly subtle and sensitive *pattern*-detecting apparatus." It's strength is in its holistic, multipath ability to make sense of the world by generating, storing, and calling forth programs to deal with experience.

The implications for learning are clear, Hart argues. Instead of imprisoning students in classrooms, where they are forced to engage in linear, step-by-step learning (pre-determined subject fragments arranged in fixed sequences that seem logical to somebody), students should be given the opportunity to engage experience in their own personal, individual, mostly random way. To illustrate the point, Hart provides the example of young children learning to play baseball, a process not characterized at all by logical sequence.

> Watch Little Leaguers play baseball, and you can marvel at their skill and grasp of an intricate game, and related knowledge, picked up over years in random fashion, mostly by participation as opportunity offered. If the game were to be taught logically, there would be a unit on its origins and history, on terminology, on the playing-field geometry, on hitting, on fielding, on base-running, and so on down the list. Obviously, none of the players learned this way. They "picked-up" the game by exposure over many years, in an utterly random, unplanned way—perhaps with no formal teaching at all. If they do get coaching, it will likely be on a purely individual basis, as the need is seen.

Human beings, both children and adults, seem to "pick up" learning in a somewhat random, happenstance manner from all kinds of exposure to experience.

So much for the holistic side of the argument. What occurs when the parts of the brain don't cooperate well? Hart introduces the concept of "downshifting" to describe inter-component conflict. The highly subtle pattern-detecting capabilities are in the newest, neocortex tissue; the old more primitive schematic programs and the cruder emotions are in the older tissue. Usually the newer brain is capable of monitoring the whole in a kind of executive oversight, drawing on the functioning of all parts of the brain and keeping them in delicate balance. But sometimes the older brain takes over, particularly when the organism is under threat. Sometimes, the action of the new cerebral brain is suspended in favor of the faster-acting simpler brain resources of the older brain.

> It becomes plain that *absence of threat is utterly essential to effective instruction.* Under threat, the cerebrum downshifts—in effect, to greater or lesser extent, it simply ceases to operate. To experienced teachers, this shutting down of the newest brain is an old story and a familiar frustration. The threatened (student) ..."freezes," and seems

unable to think, stabs wildly at possible answers, breaks into tears, vomits, or acts up, perhaps to the point of violence. Since language exists almost wholly in the new brain, downshifting leaves us speechless, quite literally.

The triune brain seems to work fairly well in its natural environment, but under pressure, such as the pressure of classrooms, something can "snap."

Hart is not alone in this analysis of holistic learning. Frank Smith, a Harvard-educated psycholinguist, the author of many books on literacy and a well-known text on reading, sets forth a similar view of holistic learning in his recent book, *To Think*. One expects from the title and the chapter headings another book on the complexities of thinking processes and how to teach them; instead, one finds a sustained argument for viewing thinking as a natural, commonplace process, the normal business of the brain. Like Hart, Smith sees thinking as far more than reasoning and views it as a natural, not an esoteric or especially difficult, process.

> The brain is more like an artist than a mechanic. It constantly creates realities, actual and imaginary; it examines alternatives, spins stories, and thrives on experience. The brain picks up huge amounts of "information" on our journey through life, but only incidently, the way our shoes pick up mud when we walk through the woods. Knowledge is a byproduct of experience, and experience is what thinking makes possible.[17]

Smith notes that when children learn a language, for example, the process is very informal. Most children, by age four, have learned 8,000 words and add 20 words a day to their vocabulary, whether in school or not. They may have trouble learning *the teacher's* word lists, but they will learn the words they hear or see around them in relevant contexts. Even high school students, however distracted by other matters, continue to add about 3,000 words a year to their vocabulary. Most learning, Smith argues, grows up naturally from experience.

> If learning is normally so easy, why should it sometimes be so difficult? Learning is easy when it is part of the flow of events in which we are involved, when we can make sense of what we are doing, when the brain is in charge of its own affairs. Just like remembering and understanding, learning is easy when it is not a particular focus of attention, when it happens to us in the course of doing something else. We learn best when we are engaged in an activity that is interesting and meaningful to us, where our past experience is relevant.

On the other hand, learning is difficult when it is a deliberate intention, undertaken against the flow of events and made the specific focus of attention . . . learning is difficult when it is contrived.

What enables this natural learning from the flow of events and what is the brain doing to facilitate learning? As one might expect from a psycholinguist, the emphasis is placed on language. Smith argues that the primary function of language is not communication but thinking. Thinking involves the creation of realities, the interpretation of experience. This process of making meaning of experience occurs in many ways—through the fine arts and music, through the creation of scientific mathematical symbol systems, through the finding and making of patterns (as Hart also emphasized)—but especially in the creation of stories.

> Language enables us to put together and express the stories that make our lives meaningful, in whatever cultures we live. If we had no stories, we would not have the kind of thought we have . . . . Language enables us to create the stories we need to make sense of experience and to share experience. With language we can set the stage, paint backdrops, depict scenes, introduce characters, reflect on intentions and emotions, and understand conflicts and outcomes. This is not "information," except in the most trivial and incidental sense—this is the making of events . . . . Any meaningfulness that we find in our own experience is what we put there . . . . Most of the beliefs we have about the world and our place in it come in the form of stories. Most of the beliefs we have about other people, and the way we regard them and treat them, are in the form of stories. Stories are the mortar that holds thought together, the grist of all our explanations, rationales and values.

What Smith develops in his book is an image of thinking that is "a single continual, all-embracing operation of the mind, powered by an imagination that never rests, not a collection of disparate skills, some of which may be absent or deficient until taught." It is not surprising, therefore, that Smith sees learning "as less a matter of instruction than of experience and opportunity." The goal is not, therefore, to teach thinking, but to immerse students "in an environment that promotes and encourages thought."

What emerges from this discussion of brain research is a still different paradigm of human learning, one that stresses the holistic, multitrack, simultaneous processing capabilities of the triune brain while downplaying the more specialized linear, "logical" capabilities, which may not be the brain's "special talent." The brain seems best at making meaning of experience. The paradigm of holistic learning drawn from brain research brings us back, full-circle, to Schön's description of the reflective practitioner as one who learns from experience through reflection-in-action.

What are the implications of this paradigm for experience-based learning? What kinds of situations can be posed for students that call upon them to respond holistically to experience? Consider once again the three students described earlier as they enter their respective settings for experience-based learning.

Greg Adams enjoys the orientation sessions that Professor Warner conducts on Brazil to help students get into the customs, the life, and the people. He works hard at learning some Portuguese and gets a big laugh out of Professor Warner's presentation of the do's and don'ts of the nonverbal gestures that go with the language. What he can't believe, however, is the incredible shock of the first two weeks. Everything is different! First of all, even though it didn't seem to be all that hot, he notices he has less energy. The food is good, but very different—cheese rolls and cold ham for breakfast along with slices of mango or papaya; manioc, rice, and beans with chicken or rabbit for lunch; and great afternoon snacks of *pastel* with that wonderful soft drink, *Guaraná*. But it is all at the wrong time of day. He is hungry in the morning, but not for fruit; and the big meal at noon wastes two hours right in the middle of the day. And at 6:00 o'clock, rather, 18:00 hours, when he is starved, there's no food. Then more food and beer before bedtime! No wonder these people never get anything done.

The work is fascinating, but frustrating. The school really is a little gem of creativity. Every day he observes something new. The little kids are learning some of the same techniques that are used by the adults in the artisan center. The children are taught to spin yarn and weave, grind earth colors, make dyes, paint, and work with clay in the same ways that the adults do. But this isn't just a trade school. The dyes are used as a medium for learning the spoken and written words for colors. Scraps of wood left from the shop are used to learn measurement and gain an awareness of shapes. The crude environment of the classrooms—rude huts, no glass in the windows, everything open to the outdoors—is actually incredibly rich with art work, wall hangings, pictures, pottery; and everywhere outside there are flowering plants, strategically placed along dirt paths. There is a huge "jungle gym" made of logs. Everything is recycled; nothing is wasted. The cotton seed from the spinning of the thread is saved to put into the fodder for the cattle to enrich the milk for the children. "Weeds" from the organic farm are cut, not pulled, and used to feed the rabbits.

The rabbits provide a high protein diet, but when they are butchered, their blood is taken to a hospital and returned later as serum; their ears are ground into glue for the woodcrafts. Nothing is wasted. And the human relations—there is no fighting, the kids are treated as individuals and made to feel special, the teachers are there to help them. A wonderful sort of Albert Schweitzer-like atmosphere prevails. The incredible thing to Greg is that nobody talks about what is expected, or at least it didn't seem that way from his increasing ability to understand Portuguese. There is no lecture on how to behave at this place, no orientation book, no list of rules posted on the wall. Everyone seems to know what to do, because the whole community really has an integrated philosophy. You can sense that this is a relaxed atmosphere where people really count, where the children are the first priority, where the environment is respected. In many ways, it is a very special place.

On the other hand, maybe things are a little too relaxed. It is hard to tell what the children are really learning. There are no tests, no exams, and, apparently, no records. And the work project is *very* frustrating! The 10 students are available every afternoon to assist the contractor in speeding the project along, but nothing happens in the afternoon from noon until after 2:00, sometimes 2:30. And then, nobody seems to be in charge. The workers are terribly inefficient, and some people seem to be doing jobs that don't really contribute much to help build the building, like sweeping up the sawdust all day long with palm-leaf brooms, when sweeping could be done in 10 minutes at the end of the day. One day he tried to show the workers how to be more efficient by bringing a whole stack of boards to where they are nailing, instead of stopping after each board to walk across the site to get another one, but he could tell they weren't very pleased about his suggestion. It is as if there is this massive conspiracy to "chill out." Greg doesn't know what to think of all this except to know that he is more than mildly upset. He isn't quite sure what the problem is, for them or for himself. He knows that he feels a high degree of sympathy for the general low standard of living, the suffering, and he has an impulse to help. But it seems like the Brazilians don't see any problem or want any help. He feels this rumbling sensation in his intestines— more than just the beans—and he catches himself frequently with his teeth clenched.

Maria Martinez and her daughter, Dolores, sit down together in the back office of The Sweet Tooth one night after closing time to pour over Mr. Ikeda's questionnaire. The "Closed" sign is in the window and the night lights are on. It's a cute little store, narrow and long, with a spacious kitchen in the back. Dolores loved doing all the painting and decorating, including the candy cane stripes at the doorway and the white display case with all the different candies. The business was off to a good start, but now . . .

"You will have to help me with some of these terms, Dolores. I'm not sure I understand all this."

"Well, I don't know them either, Mom, but Mr. Ikeda said just to do the best we can."

"Do we have a cash flow problem?"

"I think that means are we out of money. For this month the answer is 'no,' because we still have a lot of money in the bank from the holidays, but February, March . . . maybe!"

"O.K., next question. Do we show a loss on our income statement even though we have a positive cash flow? Dolores, what's an income statement?"

"Maybe . . . like our books, income and expenses . . . you know where we write everything down."

"I think a statement is more than that, maybe a summary."

"I don't think we have one, Mom."

"O.K., look at this question. Who are your customers? Well, there's Mr. Gonzales and Mrs. De Silva who always come in when we had the shop in our house. But these people now, I don't know them. They just come in from the mall when they are buying shoes or underwear or something."

"I think it means more like what kind of people, like what age, where do they come from, how much money do they have to spend. . . ."

"And look at this it asks us who our potential customers might be? What does that mean?"

"Maybe who we could be selling to that we haven't thought about?"

"But that was the whole idea of moving to the mall, to get more customers. Do they mean other than the mall?"

"Maybe we need to think about that. Maybe we could be selling our candy somewhere else, too."

"Dolores, look at this. What are our fixed costs and unit costs? What is our break-even point? This is over my head. There's no way. . . ." She puts down her pencil and folds her arms.

"But, Mom, that's what Mr. Ikeda is for. He'll teach us. You don't have to know everything tonight, he just wants to know what we are doing now. If we were doing all this stuff, we wouldn't need him."

"Dolores, I'm just a cook. I make a good candy, right? People buy my candy. They say, this is good candy, Maria, very good. You should open up a store. So we open a store. Now look at us. I'm a nervous wreck. My mind goes blank. Maybe we'll be out of business soon, and I can go back to my kitchen at home."

"Mother, come on! We know candy. We just have to learn the candy business."

———

Ralph Graham meets with Sue Best two weeks before the starting date to double-check on the arrangements for his field placement with Pastor Dwight in the little church in Pleasantville. She assures him that everything is set and reminds him to come back at least twice during the term to let her know how things are going.

The first meeting with Pastor Dwight goes well. He appears eager to have some help with the pastoral calling, and Ralph is happy to take on some regular assigned duties.

"The real work of the Church," Pastor Dwight declares, "is out in the community, in hospitals, and in people's homes. The problem is you never get your work done. It's like the laundry: you just get a little cleaned up and there's more to do."

"I'll be happy to help in any way I can." Ralph assures him.

"Then why don't I assign you these three from out at the Ecumenical Home, and you can pick up two of the five folks we currently have in Mercy Hospital."

"It sounds fine to me. Do you want to introduce me to get started, or . . ."

"No, no, you just stop in and tell them who you are. We don't need to make a lot of work out of this. . . ."

"I didn't mean to make extra work, I just thought you might want to share with me how you go about things."

"I figured you'd know that. That's a good seminary out there. I'm sure they teach you . . ."

"Well if that's what you prefer, I'll just get started."

Ralph Graham is a little surprised, but he can see how a field placement should relieve the pastor not burden him with more to do. Ralph gets in his car and drives out to the Ecumenical Home. He can't remember when he was last in a nursing home, if ever, and he realizes immediately that he is in a different world. One old man guards the entryway, saying "Howdy" to everyone who passes through. The lobby is filled with two rows of chairs placed just too far apart for people with a little hearing loss to converse comfortably. The men, dressed in their terry cloth robes and cotton pajamas, sit on one side, the women, in the soft pink and blue gowns, on the other. The women knit and crochet; the men stare into space. The dog, a therapy pet, growls as Ralph walks between the two rows to check in at the desk. The first person on his list is being given a bath; the second is sound asleep; the third, he discovers, is sitting in one of the rows in the lobby, third one down on the men's side. How does he begin? What does he say? There must be some technique to this. Luckily, when he introduces himself, Mr. Smith invites him down to his room. It takes Mr. Smith a while just to stand up, and then several minutes to navigate the hall, stopping frequently to catch his breath. They have a good chat. Reverend Graham reads some passages from Scripture and prays with Mr. Smith. It seems like a good first visit, but is it what he is supposed to do? He's feeling his way.

He drives to Mercy Hospital, checks in with the candy stripe lady at Information, and proceeds up the elevator. His first call is a real shocker; he wonders if Pastor Dwight has set him up. Sam Jones was in an industrial accident, the kind that supposedly can't happen; he caught most of his lower right arm in a sheet metal press. He went through 10 hours of restorative surgery just yesterday. He is heavily sedated with morphine, but is still rocked about every 30 seconds with spasms of pain that jolt him upright and contort his face in agony. Good God, Ralph half curses, half prays, what am I supposed to do with this? In spite of his suffering, Sam Jones seems glad to see him, is pleased that Ralph has taken the time to visit him, and is grateful for Ralph's prayers.

Up two floors, out on the E wing, Ralph finds John Elwood, a man in his late 80s who was recently diagnosed with bone cancer. John is about to be dismissed, but he's very anxious about going home because there is no one there to take care of him. They have a long talk. Ralph is amazed at how much John is telling him. Is this just because Ralph is clergy? John is quite perplexed, and he wants Ralph to phone the Ecumenical Home for him and see if they'll take him. Ralph isn't sure what he's supposed to do, but he's fairly sure that it's not that. Ralph reads some Scripture with him and prays with him. That seems to calm John down. When Ralph starts to leave, Mr. Elwood takes his hand and holds on for dear life. Ralph wonders if he will ever get out of his grasp.

The next day, Ralph discusses his visits with Pastor Dwight. He goes over each one carefully, and Pastor Dwight listens closely, but he doesn't have much to say. It appears to Ralph that he has been doing the right things. Maybe Pastor Dwight has been at this for so long that he can't remember what it was like to do it for the first time. He assigns Ralph two more names.

A week later Pastor Dwight calls Ralph into his office. He has just received a call from the Elwood family. Old John is all in a dither about staying alone and wants to go into the Ecumenical Home. The family thinks it's too soon, that John can do well at home for a few weeks, maybe a few months, if he has some intermediary resources, like visiting nurses, "Meals on Wheels," and so forth.

"What do you think about the situation, Ralph. What did you find on your follow-up visit with John?"

"Follow-up visit? I'm sorry Pastor Dwight. I didn't realize I was supposed to make a follow-up visit. You gave me some more names and . . ."

"Usually when a patient goes home from the hospital, we . . ."

"I guess I should have realized that."

"Yes, and I guess I assumed. . . . Well, they can't teach you everything in seminary."

Ralph felt terrible. Of course he felt bad about Mr. Elwood, and he assured Reverend Dwight he would call on John at his house tomorrow. But Ralph also felt like he wasn't getting the help he needed from Pastor Dwight. How should he know what to do in every situation? That's what he came here to learn. It was a real sink or swim situation and right now he was sinking.

THE REFLECTION PROCESS

Each of these students certainly has plenty of "raw experience" from which learning might arise. What is the teacher's role in assisting these student's as they reflect on their experience? To draw once again on Kolb's model, where and how does the teacher intervene in the cycle that moves from concrete experience and reflective observation through abstract conceptualization and active experimentation back to concrete experience again?

Although the process of reflection is not called "counseling," because the goal is still teaching, and the resolution of more serious, ongoing personal problems goes beyond the domain of teaching, much of what takes place through the reflection process is *like* counseling. It is useful, therefore, to know something about theories of counseling and psychotherapy to engage students more effectively in the reflection processes associated with experience-based learning.

The whole idea of personal counseling and its more long-range and often more serious counterpart, psychotherapy, is so much a part of our present environment, that it is hard to think of a time when counseling didn't exist, when someone needed to discover (or invent) its basic principles. It was Freud and a close colleague named Breur who first discovered that by talking things through, their patients could reflect on their experience and actually reduce their level of anxiety and the overt expression of symptoms. One of

Breuer's patients, named Anna O. in the literature, referred to this as her "talking cure."[18] Although Freud was a good observer and could quickly sense what was "really happening" with many of his patients, he grew to respect the importance of letting his patients talk. "Listening became, for Freud, more than an art; it became a method, a privileged road to knowledge that his patients mapped out for him." He realized that the cure was in the talk. Freud compared this process to the technique of excavating a buried city.

Today there are many "schools" of counseling and psychotherapy, each having grown out of the creative clinical work of some pioneering thinker and each stressing something unique about human nature and the therapeutic process.[19] The followers of Alfred Adler, one of Freud's colleagues and originally a member of the Vienna Psychoanalytic Society, stress the embeddedness of the individual in family and social structure. Basic concepts that are taken for granted in popular psychology today—inferiority complex, self-concept, lifestyle, family birth order—have their roots in Adlerian theory. The followers of Carl Rogers stress the inherent self-actualizing tendency within the individual to express, maintain, and enhance the self, a tenacious inner motivation, almost an instinct, to grow and become. The therapeutic process is seen as providing a climate where the self can grow and emerge in the presence of another who provides positive regard, warmth, and respect. The followers of Rollo May stress the importance of such "existential issues" as birth, death, freedom, and meaning, the shared dilemmas of the human condition that produce feelings of isolation, estrangement, and alienation, in short, anxiety. Existential therapists stress individual freedom and personal choice; their goal is to help their clients experience existence as real, to function as responsible, autonomous individuals. The followers of Fritz Perls and what has come to be known as "gestalt therapy" stress the importance of living in the present, in the "now," and they hope to help their clients experience the moment fully, not explain it, rationalize it, repress it, or sematicize it, but live it. The followers of William Glasser and the movement known as "reality therapy" stress the importance of the human drive for success and for recognition of a job well done and a sense of worthiness. They hope to help clients focus on behavior, the present and the future, not the past, and to develop specific plans to change failure behavior to success behavior and eventually create a "success identity." The followers of Albert Ellis and the movement called "rational emotive therapy" stress the importance of what the individual *thinks* about experience, how the self "talks to the self" about reality. Their goal is to help clients through a disputational process to identify and alter "irrational beliefs" about the self and the world, to change ideas and attitudes, so that they can let go of self-defeating, ineffective, maladaptive behaviors.

Are there some "root concepts" that hold these diverse theories together, some "givens" that might serve as a foundation for the reflection process? There are significant disagreements among the schools of psychotherapy, and it is not accurate to suggest that they are "really saying the same thing." However, it is not unreasonable to suggest that there may be common principles from which the various schools proceed. The first of these principals is the familiar Freudian idea of internal conflict, a complex but unified self made up of body, mind, and emotion, with the various components pulling and tugging at each other, somehow searching for a more satisfying and effective functioning of the whole. The second principle is that therapy involves a precarious balance of support and challenge, empathy and probing, understanding and confrontation. As teachers who serve as facilitators of reflection, we need to recognize that students who engage in experience-based learning are usually involved holistically in a way that produces inner conflict, and they need both support and challenge for the process of reflection to produce significant growth.

It is useful for teachers to have in mind a framework for thinking about what transpires during the course of reflection. Just as lecturing is more than talking, reflection is more than listening. How can the listening be structured? The basic framework presented below, not so much a "school" as an overview of the process, was chosen primarily for its value as an *educational* resource, a framework within which a teacher can operate to become a better facilitator of reflection.

Gerard Egan sets forth a model of what typically takes place (or should take place) during the counseling process in his popular text, *The Skilled Helper: A Systematic Approach to Effective Helping*.[20] Egan notes that "helping" (his more generic and preferred term for counseling) provides a context not only for solving problems, "crises, troubles, doubts, difficulties, frustrations or concerns," but also for engaging "missed opportunities and unused potential," chances to deal more creatively with ourselves, our work, and others. This is an especially useful framework for the teacher who wants to think about "helping" in an *educational* context. With experience-based learning, students often discover themselves "in a jam," so that they must reflect on their situation as a "problem" that they need to do something about; but just as often (perhaps more often) they find themselves in situations where they fail to see what is happening and are at a loss to know what can be educational about their experience. In this context, the teacher, as a skilled helper, can help the student not only in solving problems but in capitalizing on missed opportunities and realizing unused potential.

To make this happen, Egan suggests that dividing the helping process into three stages can make it more effective. These three stages can then turn into three steps. In the first stage, designated "The Present Scenario," clients (or other persons to be helped) are urged to identify, explore, and clarify their problem situations and unused opportunities. In essence, this is a matter of *helping clients to tell their stories*, to clarify their situation, make an initial assessment of what is happening, and begin to identify resources. It is hoped that genuine self-disclosure can take place, even at this early stage; but it is not uncommon for clients to engage in resistance or reluctance, particularly if they lack trust in others, are uncomfortable with the intensity of the helping exchange, worry about the extent of what might be uncovered, or fear the process of change itself. Helpers can recognize this resistance as normal, a common technique of avoidance that they see in themselves as well, and as an opportunity for helping the client, through appropriate support and encouragement, to move through the resistance to a more preferred state of self-disclosure. Sometimes this involves *challenging the client* (within a climate of acceptance and understanding) to replace blind spots with new perspectives. If the counselor only sees the world as the client sees it, the counselor has little to offer.

What needs to be challenged? Egan lists "failure to own the problems; failure to define the problems in solvable terms; faulty interpretations of critical experiences, behaviors and feelings; evasions, distortions or game playing; failure to identify or understand the consequences of behavior, and hesitancy or unwillingness to act on new perspectives." Although challenging will often meet resistance, the challenge will usually gain more acceptance when it includes new information for the client (facts or insights), a deeper kind of empathy (real understanding), some appropriate self-disclosure from the counselor (I've been there, too), and more immediacy in the exchange (I notice that right now you and I . . .). Sometimes the counselor may even give a surprising or humorous response

(Maybe you never should have taken on this assignment, or You can't sleep? Maybe you should try staying up all night!). When challenging is necessary, it is important to keep in mind the overall goals of the challenge (not just to challenge for the sake of challenging), to do so in the context of a good overall working relationship with the client, and to keep the challenges tentative (maybe you are . . . perhaps you could . . . etc.).

Once the story has been told and the general issues have been presented, it is important, even at this initial stage, to assess the situation and decide what the client and counselor might do to make some progress. Egan calls this *gaining leverage*, helping the client get the most out of the helping. It is done by first assessing whether the problem or lost opportunity as presented is important enough to warrant some work or not, or whether the issues need to be reconceptualized. Once this is done, it is valuable to pick some aspects of the problem to focus on and then begin to consider some actions that might make a difference.

In the second stage, designated "The Preferred Scenario," the counselor and client try to arrive at a description of what the situation would look like if the problems and lost opportunities were managed successfully. The major goal of this stage is to *help the client construct the future* by becoming aware of more possible futures and picturing themselves as managing their problems as part of that future. This can be facilitated by getting the client to ask appropriate, future-oriented questions: What would I be doing differently with people? What current behavior would I need to eliminate? What would be happening that is not happening now? What accomplishments would be in place? When the number of future options has been increased, it is often useful to return to the original story to identify the gaps between the presented and preferred scenarios, to reconsider the blind spots and points of resistance, and to select points of leverage, the critical things to begin to do.

At this point it becomes possible to help clients *craft productive agendas*, a more formal process of setting goals. This works best when the agendas contain goals stated as accomplishments, clear and specific, measurable and verifiable, realistic, substantive, in keeping with the client's values, set within a reasonable time frame. With goals in place, the next step is to help the client actually *commit to the agenda*. The counselor can enhance the client's commitment by checking to see if the client owns the goals (making sure they are the client's goals not the counselor's or those of a third party), by ensuring that the client has considered all the options and set an appealing agenda (something to do as well as something to stop doing), by encouraging detailed and challenging agendas that will actually make the situation better, and by developing action plans (maybe even contracts) that reduce the obstacles and lead to success.

In the third stage, designated "Linking Preferred Scenarios to Action Strategies," the focus is on implementation. Sometimes, even when people have concrete goals and a strong commitment to them, they don't know how to achieve their goals. They know what they want, but they get stuck and don't know how to get there. The next step, therefore, is to *help clients develop action strategies*. Often this requires some additional creativity, some further brain-storming and the subtle use of probes and prompts: What people, places, or things could help you to . . . ? or Have you considered . . . ? It is important to *help clients choose best-fit strategies*, which are best for them and truly fit their situation. The strategies for "getting there" need to be capable of delivering (or approximating) the goal, need to reside within the client's available resources, and need to be effective and consistent with the client's own values. In selecting realistic strategies, it is important to strike a balance between risks and probabilities of success; not to engage in wishful thinking, playing it safe, or simply avoiding the worst. Action strategies get tested in the concrete by *helping clients formulate plans*. Here "planning" is used in the narrower sense of putting implementation strategies into a sequential order and assigning timetables for activities. In general, this simply means articulating goals and sub-goals in more detail, using time wisely and realistically, and developing contingency plans. The counselor at this step is helping the client to avoid entropy and to use follow-through to attain goals. When goals are achieved, it is time to terminate the helping relationship.

Although the overview of the counseling process as it was summarized here may appear to be somewhat oversimplified and have about it the air of a "cookbook," it is useful to have a fairly simple conceptual framework to use as a guide for engaging students in the process of reflection. Consider once again the three teachers introduced earlier and how they employ this framework with their students in three quite different settings for experience-based learning.

Betsy Warner notices that Greg Adams hasn't said much in the weekly reflection meetings, but she can see that he is listening carefully to the others and that he appears to have a lot going on inside. When it comes time for their first personal conference she decides to walk into town with him to the *Cantinho do Céu* where they can chat more informally and sip some *Guaraná*. They find a table out near the street.

"*Saúde*," she toasts his health with raised glass. "How has it been going for you?"

"Good. Quite good." Greg replies, fidgeting with the silverware on the blue and white checked tablecloth.

"Like Brazil?"

"What I've seen. I'm sure there are many Brazils, but here . . . it's very fascinating. The school is quite incredible."

"What have you noticed?" she asks.

"A caring atmosphere for kids. A philosophy that pervades everything, a lot of unwritten rules."

"Sociologists call them informal norms. Yes, good observation. Like what?"

"Don't waste anything. Learn by doing. Learn because there's a reason. Find a way to help every child learn. It's good." Greg feels more at ease with her, like it's O.K. to say what is on his mind.

"*Tudo bem*? Everything fine?" she uses the familiar greeting in a more literal way.

"Well, not everything. Sometimes it seems a little laid back, like nobody's keeping track of what these kids are learning. In fact, sometimes I wonder if they are learning much."

"And that seems like a problem to you?"

"Perhaps. It would be nice to know if . . ."

"To have someone checking?" she asks.

"Maybe not checking, but . . . I don't know, it seems like there really is a hang loose atmosphere here generally."

"*Otimo*! A very perceptive observation after three weeks, I'd say. Any other examples?"

"The workers. It's so disorganized. No one in charge. So much time wasted."

"You'd feel better if someone was in charge?"

Greg laughs. "Yeah, I might feel better, but I'm not sure anything would change. It's like there's this conspiracy of nonproductivity."

"In the school as well?"

"I hadn't made the connection, but now that you mention it, maybe that's it. I'm not sure the kids are learning, not sure the building will ever get built."

"So where's all this need for achievement coming from in you?"

Greg laughs. "Probably my New England upbringing. My parents. Yankee Puritanism."

"That's a good insight. Maybe you need to relax a little. On the other hand, it does bother you and you came here to make a contribution."

"Yes, but I'm beginning to think, well, so what if the building doesn't get built."

"It's not your problem right?" She brushes the backs of her fingers back and forth against each other in the familiar Brazilian sign of indifference.

Greg is truly puzzled about how to answer. There is a pregnant pause. "Actually, it's not my problem. It's theirs. And if they don't see it as a problem, who am I to . . ."

"To be judgmental, so intolerant," she finishes the sentence for him, not quite the way he had planned.

"But I guess the fact that it bothers me is a problem, at least to me."

"So what's this all about? Why does it bug you?"

Greg needs some more time to think. "Well, on the one hand, there's all this love, all this good intention, this ability really to enjoy the moment here. But on the other hand, there's so little output, so little productivity, such a scarcity of the attitudes and values required for achievement. I mean, I can see why there's no progress, why the economy is a disaster. There wouldn't be a need for this school if . . ."

"Say it! If these folks would just get their act together."

"Well. I wouldn't put it quite that way."

"And it's not your problem?"

"Except that this is supposed to be a *service* project, and I don't feel like I'm being very effective at serving."

"Perhaps that's a good way of defining the problem for you. How to be of service?"

"I guess that's it. Yes, and how to cope with all this inertia."

"Greg, this is a big problem. It's one that most of the other students are having, too; and in fact it's a problem that almost everyone has when they come to a developing country. The cultures—yours and this one—are vastly different. Have you talked to the other students about this?"

"We joke some, but we don't talk seriously like this."

"You might think about why. But then let's pick out some aspect of this that you could work on. Something manageable. What about with the kids? Anything you could do differently with them? Maybe something to help measure their progress?"

"That's not wrong? I mean, who am I to . . ."

"You said it bothered you. You also told me that you genuinely liked some of the things that were going on in the school. Maybe in the context of showing your appreciation for something the teachers are doing, you could introduce a new idea, something they might eventually appreciate from you."

"So it's like I'm only going to be here a little while, and maybe if I don't get *my* act together . . ."

"Aha, precisely what you accused them of. What harm can come of it, if you go about it with the right attitude? Maybe when we meet next week, you can tell me about what you have done at the school and perhaps we can talk some about what things would look like if you, and some of the other students, were better able to be of service here."

In their next meeting at the *Cantinho do Céu* Greg Adams and Professor Warner pick up the same theme—how to be of service—and it feels like they are on familiar territory. Greg knows she wants to help him, and he has grown accustomed to her little challenges.

"O.K., so I talked to the other students like you suggested, and we all agreed that we had better find a way to cut through this or we are all going to go home frustrated and disappointed."

"Good. Any bright ideas? What would be ideal; maybe we could start there."

"What would be ideal would be if all of us could identify at least two or three areas where we could make a contribution, without violating the general philosophy of *Centro*; because we all agreed that we have already learned something ourselves and that we really respect the concept of the school."

"For you that might mean . . ."

"Well, certainly the evaluation project. Developing some simple tests, beginning to keep records."

"Specifically, like what?"

"When the teachers teach the kids their colors, they just keep going over them; nobody stops to check to see what individual kids know. It wouldn't take much to develop a check list, and test each child informally on colors. Most of us know the names for the colors."

"You've passed preschool Portuguese?" Betsy adds with a wry smile.

"Give me a break! And we could use the results for more teaching or for moving the kids on to something else."

"So this might be one agenda item. Sounds good. What about the building project in the afternoon?"

"Well, I don't know how this will work, but maybe if we could get together with the workers and—there must be some kind of foreman—and set a more specific daily goal, like so many layers of brick, so may tiles on the roof."

"Do you think that's realistic?"

"Maybe not, but we've got to do something."

So Professor Warner and Greg sit there at the little table with the blue and white checked cloth brainstorming ideas and writing them on the back of a napkin. Eventually Greg selects three more ideas to work on. He will see if he can get some of the other students to buy in, and they will do what they can to get the project moving. Greg agrees to report back in two weeks on the progress he is making on the agenda.

When Greg and Professor Warner meet again, Greg isn't quite so full of enthusiasm. "I wouldn't say things blew up really; it was just that there was a lot of resistance. The workers weren't very excited about setting goals."

"It could have been a little frightening to them, having all these American kids around trying to make them more productive. Do you have any theories about what was going on?"

"Lots of them. First, it probably *was* frightening, I'm sure you're right about that. But also, there were no incentives. What's in it for them? Certainly no increase in their lousy pay. No bonus. Maybe some satisfaction. They seem to have pride in what gets built, but . . ."

"And your theory is?" Betsy probed.

"That unless there are some incentives, and throughout this society there aren't many, there's not much reason to . . ."

"Do anything. Unless you are rich. And if you are poor you will never be rich, so why bother."

"And in fact, many of the poor survive, because their needs are minimally met by make-do jobs," Betsy adds.

"Like sweeping sawdust with a palm-leaf broom," Greg observes, "so their incentive to be productive just isn't there."

"A good theory, perhaps, and one that fits here—maybe. But let's be careful. There are many parts of this society that are very productive. Many people who have a lot of drive. Many Brazilians who are just as frustrated as you are with their people, their government, their society."

"I know. I think I've seen them. In fact, I think I could name them at the *Centro*."

"Your allies, perhaps. So back to the drawing board. Maybe we need to build another agenda."

Greg and Professor Warner have several more conferences like these, and Greg becomes one of the more outspoken members of the weekly reflection groups. Back on campus he delves into the literature on developing countries and writes a stimulating summary of his reactions to his off-campus service term experience, which includes his own theory of how to be of assistance in developing countries. In the exit interview with Professor Warner he is able to identify a long list of specific things that he has learned in Brazil, and he has them neatly categorized into things he has learned about Brazil, about teaching, about cultures and societies, about economic development, and about his own growth.

"I guess what I've really been struggling with is the whole idea of service. I went there with a strong sense of cultural relativity and what I thought was a spirit of tolerance—maybe too much tolerance. I appreciate the differences even more now, but you can't be of service if you don't have something to offer. Having something to offer means having something a little better. If you don't believe in that, well, you're just going to be paralyzed."

"And you discovered that they have some things that are better, too?"

"Oh, yes, definitely. We could learn a lot from that school, and I did."

Professor Warner just sits there nodding her head affirmatively, over and over without saying anything, as Greg rattles on. He's got it now, she's thinking. He's getting this idea of service worked out. "So where are you going next year?" she asks.

Hiroshi Ikeda glances over the questionnaire that Maria Martinez and her daughter, Dolores, have prepared for him. He nods his head thoughtfully, noting that they have very few standard business practices in place. He is going to have to begin at the beginning, but on their turf, not laying some packaged course on them, but letting it grow up out of their experience.

"Tell me, in your own way, as simply as possible, how do you see it? What's happening?"

"We never should have moved to the mall. I'm just a simple housewife, a good cook. How did I get talked into this?"

"Mom, it was your dream. How can you say that?" Dolores asks, frowning. "Mr. Ikeda is here to help us."

"Only if you think help will help. You sound very discouraged, Mrs. Martinez. Is that the problem, to close down the store so that you can go back home?"

"Do you think it is that bad?" Mrs. Martinez asks, somewhat taken aback by the question.

"I'm asking you. Is that the problem? You'd like to be out of here by, say, March?"

Dolores is shocked. Can he be serious. "Mom, you know that's not the problem. Besides we have a lease until next September. We would lose our . . ."

"Well, no, of course I want the business to succeed, but right now it isn't."

"So let's define the problem. What's the story here?"

Mrs. Martinez sits forward on her chair and wrings her hands. "It's not the candy."

"Good product, right?" Mr. Ikeda notes. "And the first few months?"

"Good sales." Mrs. Martinez replies.

"How good?" He asks.

"That's one of our problems," Maria begins. "We have an accounting book, and at the end of the day we balance the register, and we enter the total sales in our book. But we don't know how to make a report."

"So, you need what?"

"A system for keeping track of income and expense."

"Good. That's easy. Every business has to have a way to monitor cash receipts and cash dispersements, and the Sweet Tooth is no exception. It's called a balance sheet."

"Can you show us how?"

"There is a seminar on this over at the College next week. What else?"

"We have one person in the kitchen and two people part-time at the counter. I'm not sure we are doing the payroll deductions right, and their checks, and . . ."

"For about $35 a week, you can get that done by a payroll processing company. Almost nobody does their own."

"Wait a minute," Mrs. Martinez sits straight up. "I'm not sure I want anybody knowing our business."

"You don't have to do it. It's just a suggestion. What bothers you? You don't trust them?"

"Mom. It's O.K. It's a service. What can they do?"

"Well, maybe."

Mr. Ikeda winks at Dolores. "O.K. what else?"

"Our business was great in December, but it's terrible now," Mrs. Martinez complains.

"How bad is terrible?" Mr. Ikeda asks.

"You mean maybe it's normal to be bad at certain times?" Dolores asks.

"The candy business has its ups and downs, the best of times and the worst of times. How do they balance out, that's the question."

"So the good months carry the bad months?" Dolores asks.

"If they can. What would it take?"

"Maybe our balance sheet would tell us if we had one."

"That's a start, because it's a record of costs and sales. What does it take to keep this place open?"

"Well, there's the lease," Mrs. Martinez chimes in, "and that's what's killing us."

"Is it? You have the lease, the utilities, and the payroll basically. That's before you even start making candy. Those are called fixed costs. When you buy the sugar and chocolate and nuts, those are called unit costs. What does it cost to make, say, five pounds of candy?"

Dolores looks puzzled, but she realizes it is something she can get the answer to if given some time. "So what we need to do is figure out what it takes to open the doors . . ."

"Break even."

". . . and how much we can make beyond that on the candy, once we pay for the ingredients."

"You've got it. O.K. enough for now. What's the first thing you want to do?"

"I'll come to the seminar and learn to make a balance sheet. Mom?"

"I'll contact the payroll processing company."

"Good start. And you do need some help fast, so I'll be back in a week, not next month, for your second visit. By that time I want to be able to talk to you about what you would like this store to be like in six months."

A week passes quickly, but Dolores and her Mom do a lot of thinking in the meantime. Almost every night they sit at the desk in the back room thinking about what they really want the Sweet Tooth to be. When Mr. Ikeda returns, they are ready for him.

"O.K. if you could have it just the way you wanted it, what would this business look like in six months?"

"Tell him, Dolores, you've got some good ideas."

"First. We know what our fixed costs and unit costs are now. We know that there will be good months and bad months, and we can predict what they will be. But . . . it's not as bad as we thought. December alone can almost carry three bad months. We can make it, but we won't make much money."

"So what are the options? Raise your price or find more customers."

"Maybe raise the price just a little, because a little adds up, but basically we need more steady customers every month. The good months all depend on some holiday."

"Therefore . . ."

"Can we sell the candy someplace besides the mall?"

"Why not?"

"Like where?"

"School fund raisers? Companies for Secretaries Day? Churches for women's groups and youth groups. Prizes. Free give-aways by businesses that also want to attract more customers."

"Those are great ideas, Mr. Ikeda. Then we don't have to sit here waiting for more people to come through the door? It's O.K. to go out and find them."

"You betcha!"

"And who is going to go out?" Mrs. Martinez asks. "And who pays them?"

"You're really catching on to how this works," Mr. Ikeda praises her. "You can figure out how much it costs and how much it will make and whether it's worth it. And I'll show you how. But let's back up. What are you going to look like in six months?"

"Good months carry bad months for six months, but after that there is a clear and strong overall profit on store sales. In six months we are doing enough special sales to double the profits."

"Nice goal. What will it take to get there?"

"Here, Dolores, here's a piece of paper. Make a list."

"On time balance sheets. Payroll service. Keeping books according to Generally Accepted Accounting Principles. Maybe put the accounting on a computer or get it done for us. More flyers. Samples of packages, baskets of our products. A half-time person at the counter to relieve me, so I can go market the special sales."

Mr. Ikeda helps Dolores and her mother put the list into an order of priority. Then he helps them cost it out, showing them how to compute more precisely the costs and profit margins on the special sales. After going over the details and building the action agenda, he promises a return visit in one month to see how much progress is being made on the achievement of the six-month goals.

Mr. Ikeda drives back to his office at PCCC and glances over his calendar. So far this month he has turned around a candy store, a boutique, a bookstore, a landscaping business, a fitness gym, two dentists, and even those stubborn M.D.s at the skin clinic. He is convinced now that most people are so busy working at a struggling business that they don't take time to reflect on what they are doing wrong, what they are doing right, or what they might be doing.

Sue Best comes out from behind her desk and sits down opposite Ralph Graham in one of the easy chairs by the round coffee table. He appears to have grown a little nervous waiting in her outer office.

"Tea or coffee?"

"No, thanks, I'm fine."

"How's it going?"

"Fine, I think. I'm certainly getting some exposure to older people, and that's what I asked for."

There is a brief silence, then Sue Best probes, "So everything's O.K.?"

"Yes, I think so. I have been making the calls I'm assigned at Mercy Hospital and at the Ecumenical Home. I can't say that I really know what I'm doing, but I'm catching on. I like the people I call on and they seem to enjoy my visits."

There is more silence, then she asks, "What do you do? Describe one of the visits."

"Well, we talk. Talk about whatever they want to talk about. And I usually read some Scripture and say a prayer, and they seem to appreciate that."

Sue notices that Ralph seems pretty tight, not able to share very much. "And Pastor Dwight, have you had a chance to talk with him about your calls?"

"Well, yes, we've talked. He didn't have much to say. To tell the truth, it's pretty much a sink or swim situation."

"How so?" Sue asks.

"Well, I don't get much guidance. I just do what I do. I sort of improvise and hope not to mess up too often."

"So you'd like some more direction."

Ralph thinks it over. "Well, yes, some ideas about how to deal with specifics."

"And what does Pastor Dwight say when you ask him for more guidance?"

"Ask him?" Ralph crosses and uncrosses his legs and shifts about in his chair. "I guess I haven't really asked him."

"Why not?"

"Well, I guess I thought that he would know that on a field assignment like this I would like more help."

"Love your neighbor and always know his needs? Pastor Dwight wants to help, but you probably need to be more specific about telling him what help you need."

"That's interesting. I guess I was thinking he would know I was green."

"You're a little old for green. You are, in fact, green at this, but Pastor Dwight knows you're a grown up and he isn't going to rush in unless you ask. Besides he's busy."

"I know. I feel like I'm imposing, like I'm creating a lot of work for him."

"And what does he say when you tell him that."

Ralph smiles. "Bang, you got me again. I guess I haven't been very frank with him. I find him hard to talk to. It seems like he has a chip on his shoulder about seminary students, and, well, about NTS for that matter."

"Because?"

"It seems like he expects they, you, whoever, should teach us more of the practical side, yet he knows you don't; so he's just waiting for me to screw up."

"And did you?"

Ralph wags his head from side to side, then wobbles a palm-down hand back and forth. "Well . . . yeah, I guess I did."

"And?"

"Well, it didn't have to happen. If I had more guidance . . ."

"If you had asked more directly for specific guidance."

"Perhaps. I see what you're saying. It didn't feel very good to screw up, though."

"First time ever in life?"

"Come on, that's not fair."

"You're right. But you're a person that doesn't like to fail if you can help it. You like to plan ahead and you hate to get caught, to get blind-sided."

"You're right on the money there. How do you know this stuff?"

"I didn't; it was just a hypothesis, but you agreed, right? Besides, Pastor Dwight called me."

"He called?"

"Sure. He wants to help you more, but he doesn't know how."

"Really?"

Sue Best smiles. "This feels a little like marriage counseling. Look, let's back up a little. What would this placement be like for you, and for Pastor Dwight, if everything was going great?"

Ralph thinks it over. "I'd like to do some things together, to watch him make some visits, and maybe have him watch me make some visits. And then I'd like to talk to him about what goes on. About specifics. For example, should you wake a patient up if they are sleeping? I don't even know that."

Sue smiles. "Old people sleep a lot. Chances are, if you want to talk to them, you're going to have to wake them up. Otherwise, you're going to spend a lot of time on the road and in waiting rooms. Do you think the doctor wakes them up?"

"Well, that's the doctor."

"Oh, yes, and he has something important to do, and you're just clergy right?"

"You got me again."

"O.K., so let's get a handle on this. How are you going to get from where you are now to where you'd like to be?"

"Sounds like Pastor Dwight and I need to clear the air. I have to tell him what I need."

"Very directly. Maybe a list of specifics. Do you have a regular time to meet to go over visits?"

"No, we need to set one. And I'll propose doing some visits together."

"Sounds good. I want to see you in two weeks to find out how it's going then. And I'll also want you to talk to me about this work as *ministry*. What are you really supposed to be doing in these encounters? Maybe put your thoughts down on a page or two. We can use that as a starting point next time."

The two weeks fly by. Ralph and Pastor Dwight have a serious conversation. It's not easy, but they both lay it out on the table. Ralph talks about his need for more guidance, his ignorance of how to proceed on even the most fundamental matters, his resentment over being blind-sided in the Elwood situation. Pastor Dwight talks about his general suspicion of seminary students, his frustration with the abstractness of the seminary curriculum, and his sense of being overworked, literally overwhelmed, at certain seasons of the year. It clears the air, and they begin to work together, to share, to like each other.

Ralph reports all of this to Sue Best on his next visit. She is pleased. "O.K.," she agrees, "now we can move on to reflecting on what this field experience is all about. These visits you make. How are they an expression of ministry."

"Well, I wrote that paper."

"Good, I don't want to see it. That was for you not me. Tell me what you are learning about ministry?"

"This is all changing for me, so it's going to sound confused, but there really are specific things a minister can do, and I don't mean just reading Scripture and saying prayers. I mean, I do that, too. What I really learned from the Elwood situation . . ."

"Where you screwed up?"

Ralph smiles. "Yeah. Pastor Dwight jumped back into that situation with me and it turns out that John Elwood went home without the first idea about what was going to happen to him. The nurse was supposed to have a patient care plan, and maybe she did, but it didn't get communicated to him. And the doctor, well, he'd done his diagnosis and there's no treatment in this case. The family was concerned, but they didn't know about resources or where to turn. I have to hand it to Pastor Dwight; he knows where everything is in that community. And in a couple of hours, he was putting things together that really made sense to the family and John."

"Good. You really saw something happen. Everything was falling through the cracks. No one was doing anything, and here was poor John sent home alone to die. How would you express that theologically as ministry?"

Ralph paused to think, and then to find the right words. "It's being there when no one else is. That's what it's all about, I guess. But I've never thought about it exactly that way before the Elwood situation. And it's not just being there, it's *doing* something, the appropriate thing."

Sue Best shook her head. "You're catching on."

"But how do you know what's the right thing?"

"Years of experience, I suppose." Sue Best leans back and beams at Ralph. "Maybe you can ask Pastor Dwight how he knows what he knows, now that you're such good friends."

CONCLUSIONS

Teachers who use the experience and reflection strategy are usually working with students outside the classroom in various forms of experience-based learning such as work, travel, or service. The experience serves as the base for a unique form of holistic learning characterized by reflection-in-action. Relying on their wits, students are alternately immersed in and drawn back from experience, using the multitrack simultaneous processing capabilities of their not-always harmonious triune brains to make meaning of their experience. By writing and retrieving programs to cope with experience, and by telling stories to interpret experience, students draw out of their activity the theories and abstractions needed to make sense of their concrete observations. The teacher becomes a skilled helper in this process of reflection by providing a framework of support and challenge, and by encouraging the student to describe opportunities and problems in a specific way, so that a plan of action can be formulated and implemented. To help students get the most out of their challenging experiences, to make those experiences educational, teachers learn to become skillful in employing the experience and reflection strategy.

NOTES

1. Arthur Chickering, *Experience and Learning: An Introduction to Experiential Learning* (New York: Change Magazine Press, 1977), Chapter 1, "Roots and Definitions," provides an excellent discussion of the various types of experiential learning.

2. The listing and description of the categories are adapted from Joan Knapp and Leta Davis, "Scope and Varieties of Experiential Learning" in

Morris Keeton and Pamela Tate, eds., *Learning by Experience—What, Why, How* (San Francisco: Jossey-Bass, 1978). The list is quoted directly; the descriptions are shortened. See also J. Duley, "Editor's Notes" in J. Duley, ed., *New Directions for Higher Education: Implementing Field Experience Education*, no. 6, (San Francisco: Jossey-Bass, 1974), pp. vii—viii.

3. David Kolb, *Experiential Learning: Experience Is the Source of Learning and Development* (Englewood Cliffs, NJ: Prentice-Hall, 1984). See especially Chapter 2, "The Process of Experiential Learning." The quotations are from pp. 22-23. Kolb goes on to develop a theory of learning styles (see "Perspective One: The Students") based on the four points in the learning cycle. Kolb contends that most students learn best through one or more of their four abilities: concrete experience, reflective observation, abstract conceptualization, and active experimentation.

4. The argument for a special kind of experience-based professional knowledge is made by Donald A. Schön in *The Reflective Practitioner* (New York: Basic Books, 1983). The essence of the argument is drawn from Part I of that volume, pp. 3-69. The quotations are from p. 40 and p. 50, respectively. See also Donald A. Schön, *Educating the Reflective Practitioner* (San Francisco: Jossey-Bass, 1987), Part I, Chapters 1 and 2, pp. 3-22.

5. An authoritative recent biography of Freud is Peter Gay, *Sigmund Freud: A Life for Our Time* (New York: Doubleday, 1988, Anchor Edition, published in cooperation with the publisher of the original hardcover edition, W.W. Norton & Co., 1988), pp. 403-16.

6. Freud's ideas of developmental stages, his overemphasis on the earlier years of life, his distorted emphasis on sexuality, and his Victorian views of women have come in for some especially strong criticism.

7. Paul D. MacLean, *A Triune Concept of the Brain and Behavior* (Toronto: University of Toronto Press, 1973) and Carl Sagan, *The Dragons of Eden: Speculations on the Evolution of Human Intelligence* (New York: Ballantine Books, 1977).

8. Sagan, *Dragons of Eden*, p. 53.

9. Ibid, p. 57.

10. See Leslie Hart, *Human Brain and Human Learning* (New York: Longman, 1983). This simplified description is drawn from Hart who bases it on the work of MacLean, *Triune Concept of the Brain*.

11. Sagan, *Dragons of Eden*, p. 60.

12. Hart, *Human Brain*, p. 35.

13. Harry J. Jerison, "Evolution of the Brain" in M.C. Wittrock, ed., *The Human Brain* (Englewood Cliffs, NJ: Prentice-Hall, 1977), p. 42 ff.

14. The description of the dominant functions of the three brain areas is drawn from Sagan, *Dragons of Eden*, p. 62 ff.

15. Hart, *Human Brain*, 37-38.

16. Ibid., Chapter 6, "Bad Fit: Old Brain in a New Setting," p. 46 ff. The quotations are from pp. 52, 53, 60, and 109.

17. Frank Smith, *To Think* (New York: Teachers College Press, 1990). The quotations are from pp. 12, 49, 112-114, 124, and 126, respectively.

18. Peter Gay, *Sigmund Freud*, p. 65. The ideas discussed here are drawn from pp. 65-72. The quotation is from p. 70.

19. The very brief presentations of various theories of counseling and psychotherapy that are presented here are based on selected chapters in William A. Wallace, *Theories of Counseling and Psychotherapy: A Basic Issues Approach* (Boston: Allyn and Bacon, 1986). For another perspective on these and other theorists, see also Raymond Corsini and Danny Wedding, *Current Psychotherapies*, 4th ed., (Itasca, IL: F.E. Peacock Publishers, 1989). Although most teachers (unless their specialty is in clinical psychology) will not have the appropriate background to discriminate among the theories or be able to apply them, the theories provide a sense of the rich diversity (and controversy) within the field and some insights into the variety of techniques that are employed.

20. Gerard Egan, *The Skilled Helper: A Systematic Approach to Effective Helping*, 4th ed., (Pacific Grove, CA: Brooks/Cole Publishing Company, 1990). The outline of stages presented here is found in Chapter 2, but the model is used as the organizing framework for the whole book. Information about various stages and steps are drawn especially from Chapters 7, 8, and 10-16. Material has been paraphrased and simplified, hopefully without doing violence to what is a detailed and carefully worked out model on a complex subject. Readers who are interested in Egan's model are strongly urged to read the entire work.

Choosing and Using the Teaching Strategies

We must all be cut out for what we do, he thought. However you make your living is where your talent lies.
                    —Ernest Hemingway, *The Snows of Kilimanjaro*

LEARNING PARADIGMS REVISITED

The teaching strategies presented in the previous chapters are based on different and sometimes conflicting paradigms of how people learn. But exactly *how* are they different, and what difference does the difference make in their choice and use? Furthermore, how does one deal with the "truth claims" of each of the learning paradigms?

In the Preface to his now classic *The Reforming of General Education*, Daniel Bell recounts the old story of a rabbi confronted with the conflicting accounts of two women in the midst of a heated controversy.[1] The rabbi listens intently to the story of the first woman and after having heard her through, responds: "You are absolutely right!" The rabbi's wife, who is listening in, says to her husband, "Wait a minute, you have only heard one side of the story. Listen to the other woman." The rabbi listens just as intently to the second woman, and when she has finished her story, the rabbi responds: "You are absolutely right!" The rabbi's wife, quite astonished, turns to him and says, "Just a moment, they can't both be absolutely right." The rabbi scratches his head and tugs on his beard, then turning to his wife says, "You are absolutely right!" The differences in the teaching strategies pose a problem for the teacher that is similar to that confronted by the rabbi: All of the strategies are different, but they all seem to be "true." How are we to think about these differences in the learning paradigms upon which the teaching strategies are based? Are they all "absolutely right?"

It is worthwhile to return to the work that gave birth to much of the popular talk today about paradigms and paradigm shifts, Thomas Kuhn's *The Structure of Scientific Revolutions*.[2] In Kuhn's use of the term, "paradigms" are prior to and more complete than the set of rules for conducting their investigations. These investigations are designed to elaborate the paradigm, not to produce novelty. Above all, the paradigms are limiting: their power derives from seeing the world in a certain way, but this vision is narrow, leaving out other perspectives. Kuhn provides this striking example:

> An investigator who hoped to learn something about what scientists took the atomic theory to be asked a distinguished physicist and an eminent chemist whether a single atom of helium was or was not a molecule. Both answered without hesitation, but their answers were not the same. For the chemist the atom of helium was a molecule because it behaved like one with respect to the kinetic theory of gases. For the physicist, on the other hand, the helium atom was not a molecule because it displayed no molecular spectrum. Presumably both men were talking of the same particle, but they were viewing it through their own research, training and practice.

In a similar way, advocates of different learning paradigms make different assumptions about what is important in learning, choose different phenomena to study, and suggest different applications for their results. They see learning through the lenses of their own research, training, and practice. Behaviorists and cognitive psychologists reach different conclusions about learning because they make different assumptions and choose to study and elaborate things differently to begin with. Thus there is always some disagreement and often some fierce battling among those who operate from within different paradigms. Committed advocates of experience-based learning will surely have a hard time understanding the behaviorist, who wants to build skills systematically and efficiently through shaping, task analysis, and reinforcement. As Kuhn notes;

> The proponents of competing paradigms are always at least slightly at cross-purposes. Neither side will grant all the non-empirical assumptions that the other needs in order to make its case . . . they are bound partly to talk through each other. Though each may hope to convert the other to his way of seeing his science and its problems,

neither may hope to prove his case. The competition between paradigms is not the sort of battle that can be resolved by proofs.

It is important to recognize, therefore, that the learning paradigms
are different, that they describe learning in different ways, that those
who use them to conduct research will go about their investigation
in unique ways, and that those who employ them as a basis for
teaching strategies will practice their art, at least to some extent, in
different worlds.

However, the learning paradigms are not *absolutely* different
and without relationship to each other. They are not totally enclosed
boxes; rather they are more like boxes with windows, so that one can
stand within one of the paradigms and look out at and see into the
others. It is possible, for example, to stand within the paradigm for
group learning and see the behavioral paradigm at work in the way
the facilitator reinforces the participation of group members in the
communication process. Likewise, it is possible to operate within the
inquiry strategy, using the paradigm that describes various thinking
skills, and to see "group dynamics" at work when a group is trying
to solve a problem. There are relationships, and perhaps even some
overlaps, but for the most part, the paradigms are separate and
distinct. They describe different approaches to different kinds of
learning.

If this is the case, how is the teacher to cope with the very real
differences in the learning paradigms? One avenue of resolution is
to settle on one that is regarded as "best." In this way the paradigms
are treated as mutually exclusive and hierarchical: one has to be
better than all the rest. But as we have seen "best" is always relative
to some set of criteria, what Kuhn calls "the non-empirical assumptions" on which they are based. Another avenue of resolution is to
use one of the paradigms to co-opt the others, to be able to take one
set of descriptions and reduce it to another set. What really takes
place with groups, the behaviorist might argue, is reinforcement
theory working in a social setting. Another avenue to solution, and
the one advocated here, is the eclectic approach: to recognize the
differences in the learning paradigms, but to draw upon all of them
selectively according to their strengths to achieve different purposes.
Each of the paradigms elucidates something important about learning and provides a different way of looking at the processes involved
in that kind of learning. Each is "true" in its description of learning,
yet is limited to a particular view of learning. As Joseph Schwab
noted years ago:[3]

> Nearly all theories in the behavioral sciences are marked by the coexistence of competing theories. There is not one theory of personality but many . . . There is not one theory of learning but half a dozen . . . It will remain the case, then, that a diversity of theories may tell us more than a single one . . . .

The diversity of learning paradigms provides an intellectual base for a diversity of teaching strategies. The array of teaching strategies available to us provides a richness of options from which to choose, but which strategy is to be used when? How do we go about choosing and using the teaching strategies?

AN INSTRUCTIONAL MODEL FOR EMPLOYING THE STRATEGIES

Having become acquainted with the five teaching strategies, and having explored carefully their differences, teachers naturally ask: How do I choose the "right strategy"? One way to deal with the problem is to say: I will employ the strategy with which I am most comfortable. The reference for the selection becomes the teacher's skill. "I'm a fairly good lecturer, and it is what I have seen the most of and am best at, so I will use the lecturing and explaining strategy." Although the problems with this approach are fairly obvious, it is, in fact, what most of us do. Early in our career—with or without a few years of genuine experimentation with different types of instruction—we fall into a "method" that appears to be most comfortable. Although there is something to be said for doing what we do well, and although the strategy may seem appropriate for us, it may not be at all appropriate for the students or for the anticipated learning outcomes, the goals of instruction.

Similarly, teachers may say: "I will employ the strategy with which my students are most comfortable. My students like working in groups, so I will use the 'Groups and Teams' strategy." Although it is important to take into account the nature of the students, and that means more than just their preferences—selecting a strategy solely on the basis of student preference may not be appropriate either. This is where the idea of "learning styles" breaks down; selecting a teaching strategy on the basis of a student's preferred learning style may or may not make sense, given the goals that have been established for learning outcomes. These are two quick, obvious answers to the question about the selection of teaching strategies: Choose what is comfortable for the teacher or choose what is comfortable for the student. Both of these answers seem to be wrong. What is really required in the selection of a teaching strategy is the matching of the strategy to some set of criteria. For the strategy to be "appropriate," it needs to fit with some concept of what one is hoping to achieve, some delineation of the goals and possibilities for instruction. Where are these criteria to be found and how are they to be used?

It is useful to return to the original model of teaching presented in the first chapter. There, teaching was described as a process of communication between a teacher and a student about a subject within a setting, illustrated as follows:

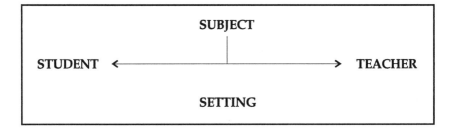

In subsequent chapters, ways for gaining insights about the subject, the student, and the setting were elaborated as three "perspectives," and ways to structure the communication between the teacher and student were elaborated as five teaching strategies. The pieces from this earlier model can be rearranged now into a new instructional model, one that speaks to the question of choosing and using the strategies.

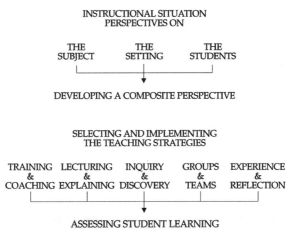

To select a teaching strategy, we begin by analyzing the instructional situation, our peculiar configuration of subject, setting, and students. We do so by revisiting each of the perspectives, asking the questions raised through those perspectives, and developing a composite perspective. The composite perspective contains the criteria for selecting teaching strategies and also sets the guidelines for implementing the strategies.

DEVELOPING A COMPOSITE PERSPECTIVE

To be effective teachers, we know that we need to raise serious questions about what we are trying to teach, where we are trying to teach it, and to whom this instruction is directed. The "perspectives" chapters in this book were designed not to produce absolute answers, but to help any teacher "ask the right questions" about the task of instruction. By asking appropriate questions, we can gain perspective on our instructional situation, and by putting all the answers to all the questions together, we can develop a composite perspective. The following lists of questions are provided as a useful review for each of the three perspectives:

The Subject

What knowledge is most worth having?

How do I define and describe my subject?

What do I hope to teach *through* the subject?

What decisions do I need to make about the learning outcomes that are most desired—cognitive, affective, and psycho-motor?

What decisions do I need to make about scope? depth and breadth? centrality and balance? flexibility and choice?

What is considered to be essential, foundational, or the essence of what I am trying to achieve?

What is the larger context of goals or framework of values within which this teaching is embedded?

What is the "philosophy" of education undergirding this teaching?

What issues and points of controversy are involved with these goals and how have these issues been debated in the past?

What do I most value as the outcomes of my instruction?

The Setting

What are the physical arrangements of classroom space and how may they be altered to accommodate the teaching I want to do?

How will people be arranged within the classroom and how will this arrangement affect communication?

What are the social roles to be played out by the teacher and the students in this classroom?

What is the larger institutional context within which this teaching will take place?

What type of institution is this with regard to comprehensiveness? selectivity? type of control (public, private)? orientation (proprietary, religious)? prestige? visibility?

What is the mission of the institution and what is its institutional saga?

How are the culture and climate of the institution expressed?

How are the traditions of the academic disciplines and fields of study represented at this institution?

How do the characteristics of the setting enhance or limit what I hope to achieve through my teaching?

To what extent is there a good fit or some adjustment to be made between what can be done here and the institution where I did my graduate work? the institution where I was an undergraduate? the institution where I hoped to teach?

The Student

To what student generation do these students belong?

To what student culture do these students belong?

With what campus subcultures are they affiliated?

How old are they and what social-emotional development tasks are they addressing?

How do they view their education?

At what stage of cognitive development are they and how do they view thinking processes?

What kinds and degrees of intelligence do they manifest?

What are their general and specific aptitudes and how do these relate to their levels of achievement?

What motivates them and to what degree and in what ways are they motivated or not motivated?

What learning styles do they appear to prefer and how do personality variables interact with preferred approaches to learning?

What are the strengths and weaknesses in their capacity for sensory processing and do they manifest any sensory disabilities?

What is their ethnic background and to what extent do they identify with their ethnicity?

What is their economic and social class background?

What sex are they and what is the nature of their gender socialization?

What we do as teachers, either formally and systematically, or informally and almost instinctively, is to build a composite picture of the instructional situation. We pick out the most important questions for that situation and seek the answers in the best way we can.

Sometimes we have data to provide the basis for reliable answers; sometimes our answers are more tentative, serving as hypotheses that we must test out during our teaching. Consider the following example of a composite perspective drawn from an illustration used earlier:

Edna Wolf believes that the knowledge most worth having comes from an understanding of the classics of literature, both in themselves, as artistic expression, but also as vehicles for exploring the meaning of life. She views literature not only as something she teaches about but also as a vehicle for exploring life's deeper issues. She knows that she is interested primarily in cognitive outcomes, the ability to use language in a metaphorical mode to think deeply about issues. She knows that she is more interested in depth (understanding complexity) than breadth (coverage) and she knows that she wants to strike a balance among historical periods and various genres. She has worked out these objectives with her colleagues at Elm Grove College who share her philosophy and her sense of the importance of selected classics in shaping the content of the curriculum. Elm Grove has a clearly delineated mission as a liberal arts college, and because it is small in size, selective in admissions, and has a culture that supports academic inquiry and a climate conducive to serious study, she knows that she can expect most of the students to work hard most of the time on their assignments. She knows that this student generation is more job-oriented than in the past, but she also senses that they are more confused, more willing to search for answers to the unanswerable questions.

Most of the students at Elm Grove are of the traditional college age group (18-24) and most seem to be working on the developmental tasks of that age. They seem to have a strong desire for interaction with each other and to explore more intimate acquaintances with each other. They are somewhat lacking in life experience. Most of the students are very bright, with high aptitudes for a challenging college experience, excelling in verbal intelligence, but most are still trying to discover how to make a good argument, how to use evidence, and how to evaluate arguments made by others. Edna knows that the student body is fairly homogenous, but that there is enough ethnic and social class difference and enough variety of outlook on gender socialization to make for interesting differences of opinion in class discussions.

Edna Wolf knows that the inquiry strategy fits well with what she is trying to achieve, and that it addresses the kinds of cognitive skills she aims for as outcomes. She also knows that the students have the ability and motivation to get engaged in the task, and that thinking deeply about the poem by Emily Dickinson will not only give them a chance to develop their ability to make and to deal with arguments supported by evidence, but will also provide a context for social interaction that they will find motivating.

The composite perspective sketched briefly here provides an illustration of what we as teachers might think about as we go about selecting and implementing the teaching strategies. In another instructional situation, a totally different composite perspective could be derived by asking the same questions. There are many factors to take into consideration, and, obviously, it is not possible to consider everything that one could consider in developing a composite perspective. It is useful, therefore, to think of some of the factors as *driving* factors that drive the selection of the strategy, such as goals, outcomes, philosophy, and the social, cognitive, and developmental level of students. Meanwhile, other factors can be thought of as *controlling* factors that control how the strategy will be implemented, such as institutional mission, culture and climate, student culture, and student aptitudes and motivation. Thus most of the factors eventually come into play, either driving the selection of the strategy or controlling its implementation, and different factors will take on different degrees of importance, depending on the situation.

SELECTING AND IMPLEMENTING THE TEACHING STRATEGIES

Once a composite perspective has been formed, it is necessary to return to the teaching strategies themselves and to think seriously about their characteristics, especially their strengths and weaknesses. Certain strategies are better than others for achieving certain things. It is necessary, therefore, to have a good grasp of the essence of each of the strategies. The concise summaries presented below provide an opportunity for comparing the teaching strategies on the basis of such things as their best use, the motivation they generate, the type of student participation they are likely to elicit, the teacher's role in implementing the strategy, and overall strengths and weaknesses.

Training and Coaching Strategy

Best Use: Beginning or advanced skill development, when a complex task needs to be learned as accurately and as efficiently as possible.

Learning Paradigm: Behavioral learning theory. Learning by moving from present performance level through successive approximations toward an operationalized goal.

Historical Roots: Research by Watson, Thorndike, and Skinner on operant conditioning during the first half of the twentieth century.

Applications: Behavioral objectives, task analysis, computer assisted instruction, criterion-referenced evaluation, mastery learning, and instructional design.

Student Participation: Involves students at cognitive and psychomotor levels in active exploration and practice of approximations while adjusting to feedback from consequences.

Nature of Motivation: Stimulates motivation extrinsically through consequences: reinforcement, feedback, knowledge of results, and success with the task.

Student Fit: Best for students who may lack intrinsic motivation, who need immediate success, and who like a step-wise, hands-on progression toward a concrete goal.

Teacher's Role: Emphasis is on setting clear and measurable objectives, analyzing the task, sequencing learning experiences, using technology, and providing well-timed and appropriate feedback.

Strengths: Clear and specific goals, high level of control of the process, efficient procedures, and observable outcomes. Complex tasks can be simplified and teaching can be extended through technology. Instruction can be individualized and students can proceed at their own pace. More students can reach higher levels of achievement.

Weaknesses: Lack of emphasis on thinking and other cognitive processes. Inattention to feelings and social needs of the learner. Reinforcement can become a preoccupation and structure can become rigid and confining. A powerful strategy with high potential for abuse.

Lecturing and Explaining Strategy

Best Use: Conveying important information and explaining how things work or came to be.

Learning Paradigm: Cognitive learning theory. Learning by attending to, processing, and remembering information.

Historical Roots: Research by verbal learning theorists, linguists, and systems analysts that gave birth after 1950 to the new subfield of cognitive psychology.

Applications: Transmitting information, stimulating interest in ideas, introducing new terminology, and explaining concepts and functions.

Student Participation: Involves students visually and auditorially in a highly individualized cognitive effort to attend to, process, and remember information.

Nature of Motivation: Derives from the internal need to find patterns in and make sense of verbal and visual stimuli so that they can be understood and remembered. Presupposes some background and internal disposition toward the subject.

Student Fit: Best for students who are intrinsically motivated and are skilled in listening, watching, and dealing with abstractions conveyed in words and visual symbols.

Teacher's Role: Emphasis on selecting, ordering, and presenting information with appropriate visual support, so that the essence of the subject can be attended to, grasped, and remembered.

Strengths: An efficient arrangement for presenting a body of information. Stresses cognitive activity in learning and acknowledges variation in processing across different individuals. Useful for conveying information to large groups. Outcomes can be readily tested.

Weaknesses: Lack of emphasis on thinking and problem solving. Inattentive to feelings and student needs for social interaction. Invites passivity. Tends to ignore present performance level and postpones evaluation of outcomes. Separates learning from real world experience.

Inquiry and Discovery Strategy

Best Use: Developing and refining critical, creative, and dialogical thinking skills.

Learning Paradigm: Philosophical and psychological models of different thinking processes. Learning by engaging directly in one or more types of thinking related to a particular field of inquiry.

Historical Roots: Ancient and modern philosophy and recent psychological investigations of thinking.

Applications: Deductive and inductive reasoning, problem solving, and decision making. Literal and figural uses of language, including the use of models, analogies, and metaphors.

Student Participation: Involves students primarily at the cognitive level in thinking and in metacognitive monitoring.

Nature of Motivation: Stems from the dilemma or problem posed, which draws upon students' intrinsic curiosity and desire to find satisfying or creative solutions.

Student Fit: Best for students who have high levels of natural curiosity, are good at verbal expression, and are able to engage in sustained investigations using linear reasoning or creative problem solving.

Teacher's Role: Emphasis on selecting appropriate tasks for inquiry and establishing a climate where students are encouraged to engage in thinking. Facilitating discussion by asking questions, probing assumptions, examining assertions, calling for hypotheses, and asking for evidence.

Strengths: Useful for engaging students directly in tasks that require thinking and employ open-ended questions. Spontaneous and free-flowing. Focuses on the processes whereby questions are framed, evidence is evaluated, and "knowledge" is established.

Weaknesses: Can be slow, cumbersome, and difficult. Discussion can bog down in digressions, and failure to find satisfying solutions can be frustrating. Presupposes in students some base of knowledge and a willingness to search for understanding.

Groups and Teams Strategy

Best Use: Exploring feelings, especially opinions, attitudes, and beliefs, and working on tasks that require the collective resources of group members.

Learning Paradigm: Group communication theory. Learning through group interaction or teamwork.

Historical Roots: Post-World War II research on groups, particularly the pioneering work of Lewin, Rogers, and Moreno.

Applications: Increasing the level of ideation, examining the emotional basis of commitments, building acceptance of outcomes, and engaging in activities and projects that require teamwork.

Student Participation: Involves students at emotional as well as cognitive level through group communication. Students engage in behavior related to process as well as task.

Nature of Motivation: Grows out of human need for inclusion and recognition, and is supported by peer interaction that builds group cohesion.

Student Fit: Best for students who enjoy social interaction, who have skills in speaking and listening, and who are willing to share feelings and perceptions.

Teacher's Role: Emphasis is on composing the groups, developing the instruments or tasks that set the group in motion, and monitoring the group at both task and process levels.

Strengths: Draws on collective contributions of total membership, involves participants at emotional level, fosters active participation and cooperation in learning. Provides for human social need for interaction and allows for flexibility and group ownership of the learning process.

Weaknesses: Can result in social loafing by some members, avoidance of individual responsibility, conflict, apathy, or "group think." Can be slow, inefficient, and subject to breakdown at the process level. Presupposes willingness for self-disclosure and a minimal level of listening skills.

Experience and Reflection Strategy

Best Use: Reflection on a potentially educative experience from which personal learning and self-discovery may derive.

Learning Paradigm: Holistic learning. Learning by reflection on what has occurred or is occurring in experience under the guidance of a mentor who provides challenge and support.

Historical Roots: Recent studies of brain evolution and function. Counseling theory with its roots in Freud's "talking cure."

Applications: Experience-based learning settings, such as service, work, travel, or cross-cultural encounter.

Student Participation: Involves students holistically in multichannel processing of experience and provides opportunities for verbal expression about the meaning of the experience.

Nature of Motivation: Grows out of the student's initial involvement in selecting the experience and wanting to succeed in it and make sense of it.

Student Fit: Best for students who learn by doing, have some ability to "size up" a situation, and possess an openness to self-examination.

Teacher's Role: Emphasis is on matching students to appropriate experiences, devising adequate orientation, providing useful mechanisms for reflection, and engaging in one-on-one interaction as a skilled helper who provides support and challenge.

Strengths: Puts students in "real-world" learning situations, which involve the total self and call for insight, action, and self-examination. Often a welcome relief from more-structured classroom learning. Spontaneous, "down-to-earth," and useful.

Weaknesses: Forgoes the benefits of more systematic input of new information and structured inquiry. Subject to the hazards of vague goals, loose structure, and ambiguous outcomes. Many factors in the learning situation may be beyond the control of the learner and the teacher.

The selection and implementation of the teaching strategies involves seeking a "goodness of fit" between what the composite perspective calls for and what the strategy has to offer. If we have a clear idea of what we are trying to do, what the setting allows, and what the students need, and if we understand the best uses and the strengths and weaknesses of each of the strategies, matching the most appropriate strategy to the instructional situation should not be a problem.

Can more than one strategy be selected for a particular class? Yes, serially, but not in a way that "mixes" strategies together. It is likely, in fact, that during a given bloc of instructional time, a teacher will use part of the time for lecture and explanation and part of the time for group activity. Sometimes a class might begin with inquiry and end with lecture, or open with an explanation to introduce the development of a set of skills through the training and coaching strategy. What will not work very well is to mix together indiscriminately the various strategies so that they become blurred and indistinct. If an outside observer, trained in the use of strategies, can't tell what the teacher is doing, trouble is probably on the horizon; chances are good that not much *learning* will take place.

Implementing the strategy involves making the strategy work in creative ways, for this subject, this setting, and these students. Ways to implement each of the strategies have been presented in the illustrations in each chapter. It is advisable to use these illustrations as models for generating new applications for different subjects in different settings. In doing so it is important to be creative. Implementing the strategies often involves a "creative leap" from the theory presented in the paradigm to the actual implementation in a particular setting. Sometimes creativity results in apparent failure, and it is important in implementing the strategies to take risks, to be patient, and to try new approaches more than once, that is, to practice the implementation. There are no limits to what can be invented to implement the strategies, ranging from the very complex and sophisticated to the clever and parsimonious, but it takes time, patience, and a lively imagination. In addition, it requires some feedback.

ASSESSING STUDENT LEARNING

Assessing student learning is the final step in the instructional model. When teaching strategies are employed creatively and the focus is on learning, the methods used to assess students will vary with the kind of learning that is taking place through that strategy. This appears to be a simple principle to grasp, but in reality it is not so easy to apply. What are the obstacles?

In the first place, assessment of student learning gets confused with grading in postsecondary settings. Indeed, they are often thought of as synonymous. Although we as teachers cannot turn our backs on the responsibility to produce grades—graduate schools, employers, honors committees, parents, and scholarship administrators need to examine students' grades occasionally—there is a difference between generating grades for a class list and establishing a comprehensive evaluation system that produces useful information about progress in learning both for the student and the teacher. It is hoped that grades will reflect progress in learning, but a comprehensive evaluation system should produce more than grades. What happens, ironically, is that in the scramble to produce grades, teachers may fail to gather information that provides knowledge about student learning. Typically, a teacher will spell out for students, usually in the syllabus, what the grade "depends on," and with some variation the following pattern is produced: Quizzes 20 percent, Mid-Term 25 percent, Final 30 percent, Discussion Group 15 percent, Attendance 10 percent. Once this is done, it is easy to turn off one's brain and conclude that an evaluation system has been established. But has it?

The second obstacle to developing a more comprehensive approach to the evaluation of student learning is the narrowness of the range of evaluation devices used by many teachers. The tendency in most postsecondary classrooms is to give quizzes, tests, or exams that require students to select right answers (multiple choice, true-false, matching) or to supply correct answers (completion, short answer, essay), and this handful of testing methods often exhausts the repertory of many teachers. Furthermore, most of these testing methods, though they have the potential for evaluating some fairly complex learning outcomes, are used to test factual recall. Studies have shown that most tests used in postsecondary settings require simple recall of information.[4] Even more alarming, one study showed that when faculty claimed that one-third of their test questions involved complex cognitive skills, independent judges found that 90 percent of the questions were recall tasks.[5] Although most tests can be devised in such a way as to examine more than recall, and although there are some useful suggestions available for how to develop such tests, there is a tendency to stay within the confines of the narrow range of options that most teachers use.[6] Can alternatives be developed?

Another obstacle to developing a more useful student evaluation system is the natural tendency to focus on end product evaluation as opposed to evaluation that takes place along the way, what measurement specialists refer to as "formative evaluation." Although it is important to know if students can reach the objectives of the course (or subunit within a course), it is also useful to know how many students are at what stages along the way. Students need evaluation information to know "how they are doing," and teachers need that information to make mid-course corrections. With the emphasis being placed today on "outcomes assessment," it may be important to be reminded that evaluation is most useful as an ongoing process, as opposed to a "terminal experience," about which one may or may not be able to do anything, if the feedback ever arrives. Are there ways to make evaluation continuous?

A final obstacle to designing a more comprehensive evaluation system is our own insecurity with receiving feedback about how students are actually progressing. Sometimes we don't ask, because we just don't want to know. It would be extremely useful, in most courses, to know the answers that students might give to the following questions:

- How is this course meeting (or not meeting) your expectations?
- What things do you perceive that you are learning in this course?
- What seems to be too difficult or too easy for you in this course?
- What could be done to make this course more stimulating for you?
- How do you think you are doing in this course?
- How much effort are you devoting to this course?

Knowing what we know about what students could say in response to these questions, it could be rather threatening to hear their answers; nonetheless, knowing what students feel about a course before it is over could be very useful to the teacher. Is there a way to do this?

Keeping these four concerns in mind—to think of evaluation as more than grading, to use a broader range of evaluation methods, to do more formative evaluation, and to find out from students how they are feeling about a course before it is over—we can return to the teaching strategies, and to the examples embedded in the presentation of each strategy, to think more carefully about how to align the system of student evaluation with the strategy being employed.

Training and Coaching

The behavioral learning paradigm requires the setting of operationalized, measurable objectives and the establishment of present performance levels. The learning that takes place occurs in the gap between present performance and objective; thus the scene is set very clearly for how to go about evaluation. Teachers know that one basis for giving a grade is whether the objective has been reached, and surely this is an important consideration in assigning a grade, but other factors, such as the initial performance level (starting point) and amount of genuine effort expended, may also come into consideration. The training and coaching strategy lends itself to observation, particularly where a psychomotor task is involved, so that sometimes all that the teacher needs to do is to ask the student to engage in the task and then observe the results. Formative evaluation is extremely important because it is tied closely to the incremental progress (successive approximations) of the student toward reaching the objective.

Beth Anderson requires completion of the task, swimming 100 meters, in order to obtain an "A" for the course, but she is willing to give "B's" to students who don't obtain the objective but who put forth strong effort and who may have begun the course as fearful nonswimmers. She is a frequent observer of each student's progress, and she will often ask individuals how they are feeling about their progress and if there is anything she might do differently to help them.

Tony Clementi realizes that teaching students to read music will give them a chance to improve their grade in the overall context of his music appreciation course, but he does not grade the special "remedial" sessions he provides. These tutoring sessions provide him with some special understandings of the students most "at risk" in his course, and every two weeks, throughout the rest of the course, he gives these students a brief survey, wherein they can describe how they are doing and whether they perceive the need for additional help.

Jolene Jefferson knows that her students in developmental math have a long and painful experience with failure, so she wants to emphasize "success" in her grading procedures. Jolene uses a mastery learning system wherein she sets certain levels of mastery (85 percent, 90 percent) and provides whatever help she can to facilitate success. She requires mastery level for an "A," but she also considers initial performance level and effort in giving grades lower than "A." She uses frequent paper and pencil "tests," but she makes it clear that the purpose of these tests is not always to establish a grade; she regards them as "practice tests" (of which she has many forms) for error analysis and letting students know about their progress. Because she knows her students well and has good rapport with them, she frequently asks them how it is going, and whether there is anything else she could be doing for them.

Lecturing and Explaining

The paradigm of human information processing drawn from cognitive psychology has built into it a special emphasis on attention, processing, and memory. Surely one basis for assigning grades in a course that uses the lecturing and explaining strategy is the amount of (quantity) of information recalled and the understanding (quality) the student demonstrates in using that information. Although paper and pencil tests are a standard method of testing, other methods can also be employed. It is important to check frequently on what students are retaining and understanding and not to save all evaluation for one "brainbuster" final exam. When this strategy is employed, special efforts often need to be made to get some feedback on how the course is working for individual students.

Pierre de Chardin has made it clear in his lecture on the elements of visual communication what he expects students to remember and has given them some techniques for attending to the visual elements of a picture. Sometimes he uses multiple choice exams, but in this case he wants to know if students can actually *use* the design concepts in analyzing a visual representation. He asks students to bring in interesting pictures and to work with a partner in analyzing those pictures in terms of "dot, line, shape, movement, tone, and color." Then he asks some of the students to come before the class to "explain" their examples by using the basic elements of design. In this way he is able to get some sense of how individual students are applying the concepts. The following week he projects three slides, allowing students up to 10 minutes per slide, to describe in short-answer format how the elements of design are employed in each slide.

Roscoe Meade has devised an item pool of carefully constructed questions on demographics. But the questions all require his students to reach far beyond factual recall. He poses questions that require students to employ concepts such as "natural increase, fertility, mortality, and density." Students can memorize the definitions to the terms, but if they don't understand how the concepts work together, they won't be able to do well with the questions. Professor Meade always includes a section at the end of his quizzes where students can indicate if and where they are having problems along with an opportunity to make a request for help. In response to these requests, individual office conferences will be scheduled, sometimes with groups of 3 to 4 students having problems in the same area.

John Newton distributes "information sheets" after most of his science lectures that serve to help students focus on the important information—figures, dates, and concepts in the lecture. But his tests are almost always essay exams in which he asks students to present the evidence, evaluate the evidence, weigh the conflicting evidence, or otherwise describe the support for a particular scientific theory. He will ask students, for example, to distinguish between scientific and literary descriptions of the origins of the universe and to present and weigh the evidence for the "big bang theory" by discussing the concepts of "expanding universe," "singularity," and "evolution of the elements." He does this with each of the major units as he moves through the course and evaluates the student essays more rigorously later in the course than in the beginning. Professor Newton keeps copies of the previous exams and actually compares earlier with later performance. Every three weeks Professor Newton picks three students to have lunch with him to discuss how the course is working out for them and what he could do to improve it.

Inquiry and Discovery

The paradigms of thinking upon which the Inquiry and Discovery Strategy is based are quite diverse, and many different kinds of evaluation can be used to measure the outcomes of these learnings. With this strategy it is especially easy to fall back into testing factual recall, when, in fact, what one hopes to examine are thinking processes. Because thinking is different things in different subjects and can involve a wide range of thinking skills, from inductive reasoning to dealing with metaphor, the evaluation methods need to be tailored to the kinds of thinking that the students have been doing. Because thinking processes are relatively covert, the challenge is to devise evaluation techniques that will make those processes overt, so that they can be examined.

Jacques La Mer engages students in deductive and inductive reasoning processes in his course on ocean life forms, and what he hopes to discover is whether students are beginning to develop some skill in scientific thinking. He has carefully embedded within his instruction numerous questions that call for a student response, and he monitors closely the answers students provide. His goal is not to see whether students can spit back to him the information they have learned about what happens to light when it enters the ocean; rather he wants to know if they have learned something about the reasoning processes used to derive that information. What he does with his evaluation— both orally in class discussion and on written exams—is to pose additional questions about the sea, and ask students to generate hypotheses and counter hypotheses and devise plans for making observations and gathering data about problems he provides for them. He looks closely at the answers students provide, not so much to see if they are right or wrong, but to evaluate the quality of thinking that seems to be taking place.

Maynard Smith uses case studies in the teaching of problem solving and decision making in marketing. He is involved with his students, both as a class and as individuals, as they work their way through the cases and develop their case study reports. He does not require separate quizzes and exams for purposes of grading; the case study reports provide ample information for that. He examines the reports carefully, not so much for the conclusions and recommendations, but for evidence of how the conclusions were drawn and the recommendations supported. At the conclusion of each case he asks for three volunteers to discuss with him how the case might be rewritten and how he might teach it differently.

Edna Wolf asks students to select a poem that they like from a list she provides and to go to the library and read what various critics have had to say about the work and the author in references she recommends. When students come to class the day of the "test," they are asked to respond to the poem by writing an interpretive essay. The emphasis, of course, is not on getting "correct" interpretations or even interpretations that are congruent with those made by critics, but on how the interpretation and criticism are shaped and set forth in writing. By the end of the term, Edna Wolf feels that she knows the student's minds and has a good sense of their capabilities in interpreting the classics of literature. She is also interested, of course, in gaining a sense of how her students relate the universal themes of literature to their own lives, and once each term she invites students over to her house for dessert for an off-the-record discussion of "life" that often lasts well past midnight.

Groups and Teams

The paradigm drawn from group communication theory elaborates how people learn as members of groups and teams. The learning that occurs results from the communication that takes place among group members, but will vary depending on the task and the nature of the process established by the group. In evaluating the learning that results when group processes are employed, sometimes the emphasis is on the product that has grown out of the task, while at other times the emphasis is on the personal change that has occurred for individuals through the group process. The teachers who use this strategy have learned to become good "group watchers," and they monitor closely the behavior of individuals within the group, and the group as a whole, to provide feedback on process as well as on progress toward completion of the task. Thus evaluation is easily incorporated as an ongoing activity when this strategy is employed.

Vicki Hastings uses a variety of group strategies in her wellness class and because students are constantly doing something as a member of a group, she has many opportunities to observe them in action, as participants on a panel, as actors in a role play or as "dancers" in an exercise routine. She knows who contributes and who puts forth extra effort. It is important to her to see how students change their attitudes and lifestyles, so toward the end of the course she asks students to get together in dyads to share with each other how they have changed and what they are doing to live healthier lives. She provides a tape recorder for each pair and asks them to record—off the record—how the course is impacting their lives and what activities in the course influenced them most.

Nancy Green uses teams to complete an interior design project and because the project *is* the course, it is important that she be able to evaluate what has taken place. She establishes two levels of evaluation for the course grade, one for the quality of the project and one for participation. She grades the final project, assigning it a letter grade, which is distributed to all members. To establish the participation grade she asks for a self-evaluation grade from each student, a grade which they would recommend for each of the other members of the team, a grade they would recommend for the project leader, and a grade from the project leader for each team member. She examines and weighs these recommendations, reserving her right to establish the final participation grade for each student. She stays in touch with the project leaders during the course, and at the end meets with them one more time to get their feedback on how to improve the process for the course the next time it is offered.

Jonathan Wesley is especially interested in the personal growth that takes place during his social transformations class. He can observe some of this change as he monitors the group process, but he also likes to have students think about what has occurred for them, so he asks each student to write a 1- to 3-page paper at the end of each issue focusing both on how they see the issue differently and on what they have learned about themselves. He finds it nearly impossible to assign a grade to these papers, or for the course, but he reminds himself that what he is looking for is not a brilliant social policy statement, but the student's honest and sincere grappling with the issue and his or her feelings about it.

Experience and Reflection

The paradigm drawn from brain research elaborates how people learn in a holistic way and through reflection on experience. The learning that occurs is global and personal and is not always easy to measure. Often the learner will be encouraged to establish personal goals for the experience and these can be used as criteria, or at least a starting point, to examine what learning has occurred. In a sense the reflection process itself is designed to "bring forth" what learning is taking place, but the reflection process is also part of the learning. For this reason it is important not to make students feel that they are being evaluated or graded during the reflection process, even though this process provides for the teacher some good feedback on what the student is actually learning. For evaluation purposes, and for grading, it is probably best to have the student produce some written products, some diaries or journals, some projects associated with their work, or a final paper in which the student steps back from and describes the learning that has occurred. What the teacher is looking for in the student's work is insight about the experience and growth in self-awareness.

Betsy Warner has Greg Adams engaged in a variety of activities in his overseas service experience in Brazil that provide her with information about how he is doing: what he is observing, how he is responding, and what efforts he is actually making to solve problems and act on his concerns. At the end of the experience, Greg has a number of media—journals, informal notes, papers, and further research—to document what he has learned.

Dolores Martinez and her mother are interested primarily in help with the candy business, but if Dolores decides that she wants credit for this experience that could be used toward an associate degree, she will need to pull together some materials to document her evidence of learning. In this case she will have a wealth of materials to draw on from the business: samples of the new balance sheets, payroll records, a business plan, and so forth. She may be required to provide for Hiroshi Ikeda, at the end of six months, a brief paper that describes what she has learned about managing a small business and to document this with appendixes of materials that illustrate what plans and procedures have been established at the candy store.

Ralph Graham keeps a journal with regular entries, which he uses to reflect on his experience of ministry in a parish setting. In addition, from time to time, Sue Best may ask him to produce additional brief papers as well as a final paper in which he is asked to stand back from the experience and elaborate what he has learned about being a pastor and what he has learned about himself in that role. Sometimes she asks students to write a brief critique of her role in facilitating the reflection process.

From this brief review of the examples in the chapters on the teaching strategies, it can be seen that the types of learning that occur differ from strategy to strategy and that the methods of evaluation should also vary. It makes little sense to speak of grading and evaluation techniques apart from a specific learning paradigm. One key to success in using teaching strategies is to establish creative forms of evaluation that provide useful information both for the student and the teacher. With information about student learning in hand, we can return to the composite perspective once again to ask: How good is the fit between the composite perspective and the selection of the teaching strategy? In what ways should the implementation of the strategy be modified to take into account the evaluation information and the composite perspective? Thus the cybernetic cycle is complete: The use of the strategy can be improved or a new strategy can be chosen.

THE IMPACT OF TEACHING ON LEARNING

The techniques for assessing student learning presented above grow out of the paradigms of learning that serve as a basis for the five teaching strategies. Although it is important for us as individual teachers to become more skillful in our teaching and to be able to gain more direct feedback about what learning is occurring as a result of our teaching, the institutions where we teach are increasingly concerned about providing evidence that teaching has a *cumulative* effect on student learning. To put the matter bluntly, postsecondary institutions today are being asked to demonstrate that the students who study on their campuses are "getting an education." To "get an education" may mean something quite different at the Art Institute of the South and at Mid-West University; but all institutions today, from the small proprietary school to the large public research university, are being asked to describe their anticipated educational outcomes for students and to demonstrate that they are making efforts to assess student learning in light of those stated outcomes.

This concern about assessing student learning is part of a larger movement called "the quest for quality," which reaches beyond colleges and universities to many other institutions that provide products and services to the public.[7] More recently the measurement of quality in higher education was transformed from a natural concern within institutions to an obligation, when the federal government required national and regional accreditation associations to examine what institutions of higher education are doing to measure student outcomes.[8] With the passage of Public Law 101-542, The Student Right-to-Know and Campus Security Act of 1990, colleges and universities are now required to track the progress of students toward meeting degree requirements within "normal time" and to report "graduation rates." Peter Ewell notes three themes in this quest for a "new accountability" in institutions of higher education:

- increased emphasis on explicit linkages between higher education and achieving wider societal goals of renewed economic development and global competitiveness,
- altering the focus of accountability for higher education from equitable access and efficient operation toward "return on investment,"

- an emerging emphasis on "consumer protection" in higher education through publicly available information on student outcomes and comparative student performance.[9]

Although the merits of the "quality movement" are being debated— it is surely not all good or all bad—there is an emerging awareness that assessment of student learning is no longer a luxury but a necessity on every campus.

This poses an interesting set of measurement problems for postsecondary institutions and their faculties. On the one hand, individual faculty members will be expected to focus their efforts more on describable student learning and will need to develop more sophisticated methods of assessing that learning in their classes. On the other hand, the departments, programs, and colleges within which teachers teach, and the institution as a whole, will need to devise methods of assessing the cumulative effects of teaching on students. Thus student learning outcomes may be thought of as existing at certain levels or in tiers:

- classroom or structured out-of-class learning outcomes that result from students being registered in particular courses,
- general learning outcomes, such as growth in certain skills in written and spoken communication, mathematics, foreign language, and core knowledge growing out of enrollment in general education programs,
- discipline-based learning in specific domains of knowledge and/or development of professional competencies resulting from enrollment in specific programs and concentrations,
- general student development outcomes such as cognitive development, growth in ego and social-emotional development, maturity in moral judgement, historical awareness, problem-solving ability, and critical thinking, which result from the cumulative experience of going to college.

Assessing these outcomes is no easy task and will require efforts to measure learning that cut across conventional institutional structures and employ innovative methods of gathering and synthesizing data about student learning. Because this kind of assessment focuses on growth and institutional impact—what Alexander Astin refers to as "talent development"—it will be necessary to do much more than most institutions currently do to obtain entry-level, base-line measures of students in order to assess *progress* and demonstrate the "value added" through the educational experience.[10]

Fortunately, there is a long tradition of studying the impact of college on students, and we are not without some sense of how to proceed in these matters.[11] Furthermore, the results of this research are encouraging. The recent literature on college impact has been brought together and analyzed in the work of Ernest Pascarella and Patrick Terenzini in *How College Affects Students*.[12] Their conclusions are that students do indeed change from freshman to senior years, and on a very broad range of variables and in an integrated way. Among other changes, students grow in verbal and quantitative skills; in knowledge of subject matter; in their interests in art, culture, and ideas; and in self-understanding and self-definition. They become more open, tolerant, and nonstereotypical in their thinking about others who are different from themselves. They also begin to shift away from the instrumental value of education (as preparation for an occupation) toward a greater appreciation of the intrinsic rewards of education. Although the gains of these areas are not dramatic, they are significant and consistent. Even more impressive than the small gains in each area are the pronounced breadth of interconnected gains in general areas. Perhaps there is hope!

One clear implication growing out of this increased interest in assessing student learning is that teaching is coming to be seen more and more as a collective enterprise for which we as teachers are being held collectively responsible. The days are gone when we can go to class, teach our subject, and hope that some of our students will "get it." It is no longer possible to avoid probing questions about the amount and quality of student learning. For these reasons, it is important that we conceive of our teaching in terms of student learning, and that we organize what we do by employing teaching strategies based on paradigms of learning.

If the impact of teaching on student learning is viewed increasingly as a collective enterprise, then the improvement of teaching is likely to be seen more and more as a collective need of whole faculties and a matter of institutional policy. Although there are now thriving faculty development programs at many institutions, and although there is a growing body of literature on faculty development and several vigorous national professional organizations,[13] current faculty development efforts at most institutions are largely directed toward *individual* faculty members, usually on a voluntary basis. A variety of faculty development services are offered to individuals, with the hope that those most in need will participate and be "helped" in some way, so that collectively the instructional mission of the institution will be strengthened. Although most institutions will want to continue the essentially voluntary nature of faculty development activities because it is unlikely faculty will ever be coerced into improving anything, institutions will increasingly seek to allocate scarce resources in ways that increase the numbers who participate in significant discussions about enhancing student learning. Faculty development will come to be seen less as a general service to individuals who wish to avail themselves of it, and more as a necessity for everyone, a high institutional priority for improving student learning. Faculty development, therefore, is surely not just a remedial activity for the few, but a central activity for all, the vehicle for what the Japanese call *kaizen*—continuous improvement.[14] With apologies to John Donne, no teacher is an island, and any colleague's poor teaching diminishes mine. Like it or not, we are all in this together and "better teaching," carefully crafted to produce "more learning," is everyone's business.

CONCLUSIONS

It is hoped that the perspectives and teaching strategies provided in this book will be of use to teachers who are seeking new conceptual frameworks for talking and thinking about teaching and learning. The perspectives provide some lenses for looking at the subject, the setting, and the students. The learning paradigms provide a professional language—sets of concepts and categories—for deepening the dialogue about learning. The teaching strategies serve to enlarge the repertory of what we can attempt and what we will surely be able to do more successfully through practice. By developing a composite perspective on our instructional situation, we can match the appropriate teaching strategies to the desired outcomes of instruction and to the possibilities and limitations of our particular situation. By using broader and more sophisticated evaluation methods, we can gain useful feedback about our teaching that we can use to adjust our selection and implementation of teaching strategies. As teaching becomes more focused on learning, perhaps the cumulative impact of our teaching will be greater, and the students we teach, individually and collectively, will develop their talents in more demonstrable ways.

NOTES

1. Daniel Bell, *The Reforming of General Education* (New York: Doubleday, Anchor, 1968), p. xiii. Although retold here with different words, the essence of the story has been retained.

2. Thomas Kuhn, *The Structure of Scientific Revolutions*, 2nd ed., (Chicago: University of Chicago Press, 1970). For source material paraphrased here, see especially pp. 45 and 35. The quotations are from pp. 50-51 and p. 148, respectively.

3. Joseph Schwab, "The Practical: A Language for Curriculum," *School Review*, November 1969, reprinted in Martin Lawn and Len Barton, *Rethinking Curriculum Studies* (New York: John Wiley, 1981), p. 311 in reprinted version.

4. The study is found in Omer Milton, *Will That Be on the Final?* (Springfield, IL: Charles E. Thomas, 1982).

5. The study is cited by Omer Milton, H.R. Pollio, and J.A. Eison in *Making Sense of College Grades: Why the Grading System Does Not Work and What Can be Done about It* (San Francisco: Jossey-Bass, 1986).

6. Some of the useful recent discussions of student evaluation, testing, and grading are found in Bette Erickson and Diane Strommer, *Teaching College Freshmen* (San Francisco: Jossey-Bass, 1991), Chapter 9, "Evaluating Student Learning"; Stephen Brookfield, *The Skillful Teacher* (San Francisco: Jossey-Bass, 1991), Chapter 10, "Giving Helpful Evaluations"; and T. Dary Erwin, *Assessing Student Learning and Development* (San Francisco: Jossey-Bass, 1991), Chapter 4, "Selecting Assessment Methods."

7. Daniel Seymour, *On Q: Causing Quality in Higher Education* (Phoenix, AZ: American Council on Education and Oryx Press, 1993).

8. U.S. Department of Education, "Secretary's Procedures and Criteria for Recognition of Accrediting Agencies," *Federal Register*, 1988, 53 (127), 25088-25099. Cited in T. Dary Erwin, *Assessing Student Learning and Development: A Guide to the Principles, Goals, and Methods of Determining College Outcomes* (San Francisco: Jossey-Bass, 1991).

9. Quoted from Peter Ewell and Dennis Jones, *Assessing and Reporting Student Progress: A Response to the New Accountability* (Denver: SHEEO, 1991).

10. Alexander Astin, *Achieving Educational Excellence* (San Francisco: Jossey-Bass, 1988) and *Assessment for Excellence* (Phoenix, AZ: American Council on Education and Oryx Press, 1991).

11. The original study that set in motion the research in this field was Phillip Jacob, *Changing Values in College* (New York: Harper & Bros., 1957). Two earlier summaries of the research on the impact of college are Kenneth Feldman and Theodore Newcomb, *The Impact of College on Students* (San Francisco: Jossey-Bass, 1969) and Howard Bowen, *Investment in Learning: The Individual and Social Value of American Higher Education* (San Francisco: Jossey-Bass, 1977).

12. Ernest Pascarella and Patrick Terenzini, *How College Affects Students: Findings and Insights from Twenty Years of Research* (San Francisco: Jossey-Bass, 1991), Chapter 13, "How College Makes a Difference," pp. 556-635.

13. The original classic on faculty development is the now somewhat dated two-volume work by W.H. Berquist and S.R. Phillips, *A Handbook for Faculty Development* (Washington, DC: Council for the Advancement of Small Colleges, vol. I, 1975; vol. II, 1979). More recent useful works are Jack Schuster and Daniel Wheeler and Associates, *Enhancing Faculty Careers: Strategies for Development and Renewal* (San Francisco: Jossey-Bass, 1990); Emily Wadsworth, ed., *A Handbook for New Practitioners* POD Network, (Stillwater, Oklahoma: New Forum Press, 1990); Edwin L. Simpson, *Faculty Renewal in Higher Education* (Malabor, Florida: Robert Krieger Publishing, 1990). For a comprehensive bibliography containing articles and books on faculty development see Jack Schuster and Daniel Wheeler and Associates, *Enhancing Faculty Careers*, "A Guide to the Literature on Faculty Development," pp. 298-328. The professional organizations include: Professional and Organizational Network in Higher Education (POD), Teaching and Learning Center; 121 Brenton Hall; University of Nebraska—Lincoln; Lincoln, NE 68588-0623, and The International Society for Exploring Teaching Alternatives (ISETA); 137 Engineering Sciences Building; West Virginia University; Morgantown, WV 26506.

14. Seymour, *On Q*, p. 78.

Index

by Linda Webster

Accountability, 15, 365-66
Active listening, 258-59
Ad hominem arguments, 221
Adler, Alfred, 323
Affective outcomes, 28
Age theory, of development, 64-65
Amado, Jorge, 133
Analogical thinking, 222-26
Analogies, 223-24
Androgogy, 87-88
Anomie, 17-18
Apathy, in groups, 261-62
Appeal to authority, 221
Appeal to pity or pride, 221
Appeal to tradition, 221
Aptitude, 72, 75, 77-78
Arguments, 188, 221-22
Aristotle, 177, 220
Arizona State University, 126
Art, 134, 141-42, 152-54, 166. *See also*
    Interior design
Art institute
    assessment of learning at, 359, 362-
        63
    goals at, 27
    groups and teams in, 248-49, 280-83
    interior design course at, 4, 248-49,
        280-83, 362-63
    lecturing and explaining in, 134,
        141-42, 152-54, 166
    objectives at, 30
    organizing principle in, 37
Assertions, 187-88

Assessment of learning, 123-25, 186-
    87, 355-64, 366-67
Association of American Colleges, 85
Astin, Alexander, 52-53, 366
Attention mechanisms, 140-44
Auditory memory, 161
Authority, teacher as, 49
Ayer, A.J., 219

Back, Richard, 299
Bacon, Francis, 177
Barbe, Walter, 81
Bartlett, F.L., 136
Begging the question, 221
Behavioral objectives, 113-16
Behaviorism
    compared with cognitive psychol-
        ogy, 136-37
    rewards and punishments, 106-13
    shaping complex behavior, 101-6
    and Skinner, 100-1
Beliefs, 188
Bell, Daniel, 342-43
Belth, Marc, 219-20, 222-23, 225-26
Benne, Kenneth, 256
Berelson, Bernard, 245
Beyer, Barry, 187
Bion, W.R., 252
Birnbaum, Robert, 51-52
Black box, 136-37, 138
Bloom, Benjamin, 123-24
Bottom-up processing, 146, 151
Brain hemispheres, 78, 87

Brain research, 310-17
Brainstorming, 264-64
Breadth, of subject, 28
Breuer, Josef, 323
Briggs, Kathleen, 80
Briggs-Myers, Isabel, 80
Bronte, Charlotte, 97
Brophy, Jere, 10
Business courses, 175-76, 181-82, 212-17, 303-4, 318-20, 332-35, 361, 364
Buzz group, 265

CAEL. *See* Council for the Advancement of Experiential Learning (CAEL)
CAI. *See* Computer-assisted instruction (CAI)
Card stacking, 221
Carnap, Rudolph, 219
Carnegie Council, 52
CD-ROM disc, 121-22
Centrality and balance, of subject, 28
Chaffee, Ellen, 53-54
Change process, 245-46
Cherry, C., 140
Chickering, Arthur, 64-65, 66-67
Chunking, 160
CIRP. *See* Cooperative Institutional Research Program (CIRP)
Clark, Burton, 51, 54
Classrooms. *See* Setting
Climate
   of classroom, 46
   of institutions, 54
Cluster colleges, 36, 44n13
Coaching. *See* Training and coaching
Cocktail party phenomenon, 140
Cognitive development, 68-72
Cognitive outcomes, 28
Cognitive psychology
   attention mechanisms, 140-44
   development of, 135-37
   information processing model, 137-39, 144-59
   memory, 139, 159-68
   and thinking about thinking, 176-77
College. *See also* Higher education
   assessment of learning in, 358, 360, 361

criterion-referenced evaluation in, 125
experience and reflection in, 301-3, 317-18, 327-32
goals in, 26
inquiry and discovery in, 176, 182, 226-33
instructional design in, 127-28
lecturing and explaining in, 135, 143-44, 156-59, 167-68
literature course at, 2-3
organizing principle in, 37
training and coaching at, 98-99, 103-5, 112, 125, 127-28
Colleges within a college, 36
Colloquium, 265
Communication, in groups, 253-61
Communications engineering, 137
Community college
   assessment of learning in, 358-59, 362, 364
   assessment of student learning in, 360-61
   CAI in, 122-23
   criterion-referenced evaluation in, 126
   experience and reflection in, 303-4, 318-20, 332-35
   goals in, 26-27
   groups and teams in, 247-48, 270-75
   inquiry and discovery in, 175, 181, 196-201
   instructional design in, 128
   organizing principle in, 37
   training and coaching at, 99-100, 105-6, 112-13, 122-23, 126, 128
   wellness course at, 3, 247-48, 270-75, 362
Competency-based curriculum, 35, 44n12
Competitive groups, 265-66
Complex behavior, shaping of, 101-6
Computer-assisted instruction (CAI), 119-23
Computer science, 137, 144-45, 161-62
Conflict, in groups, 259-61
Connotative language, 220-21
Cooperative Education, 306
Cooperative groups, 265-66

Cooperative Institutional Research Program (CIRP), 61
Council for the Advancement of Experiential Learning (CAEL), 300
Counseling, 322-27
Creative thinking, 179-80
Criterion-referenced evaluation, 123-25, 123-26
Critical thinking, 179
Cultural diversity, 16-17, 41
Cultural pluralism, 41
Culture
    of classroom, 46
    of institutions, 53-54
    student cultures, 61
Curriculum. *See* Subject

Deal, Terence, 53
Deception, 222
Decision making, 8-9, 207-12
Deductive reasoning, 188-92
Demographics, 28-29, 135, 142-43, 154-56, 166-67, 359-60
Denotative language, 220-21
Depth, of subject, 28
Descartes, René, 177
Development
    age theory of, 64-65
    cognitive development, 68-72
    ego development, 65-66
    social and emotional development, 62-68
    stage theories of, 62-68
Dewey, John, 37, 44n13, 69, 177, 306
Dialogical thinking, 180
Dickens, Charles, 25
Diction, 221-22
Directed thinking, 178
Disabled students, 14, 81-83
Disciplines, academic, 32-33, 54-55, 178
Discovery. *See* Inquiry and discovery
Dramatization, 266-67
Durkheim, Emile, 17

Egan, Gerard, 324-26
Ego development, 65-66
Ego ideal, teacher as, 50
Eisner, Elliot, 7
Eliot, Charles, 43n4

Ellis, Albert, 323-24
Emotional development, 62-68
Encoding, 163
Encounter groups, 283-85
Entrapment, 209
Environment. *See* Setting
Episodic memory, 161
Erikson, Erik, 63-64
Esalen Institute, 251
Ethnicity of students, 14, 83-84, 86-87
Euphemism, 221
Evaluation. *See* Assessment of learning
Ewell, Peter, 365-66
Exaggeration, 221
Existential therapy, 323
Experience and reflection
    and assessment of learning, 363-64
    examples of, 301-6, 317-22, 363-64
    as holistic learning, 310-22
    learning through experience, 299-306
    reflection-in-action, 306-9
    reflection process, 322-39
    summary of, 354
    types of experience-based learning, 300-1
Expert system, 121
Expert, teacher as, 49
Explaining. *See* Lecturing and explaining
Extinction, 108, 109

Facial expressions, 259
Facilitator, teacher as, 49-50
False dichotomy, 221
Feedback for teachers, 9-10
Field experience, 304-6, 320-22, 335-39, 364
Flexibility, of subject, 28
Forgetting, 165
Formative evaluation, 356-57
Frames, in information processing, 149-50
Frequency, 211
Freud, Sigmund, 252, 288, 310, 312, 322-23, 340n6

Gage, N.L., 7
Gambler's Fallacy, 211

Games, 267
Gaps, in subject, 28
Gardner, Howard, 74-75
Garfield, James A., 5
Gender of students, 14, 15, 67, 85-86
General education, 31, 43n4
Gestalt Psychology, 136, 146-47
Gestalt therapy, 323
Get-acquainted activities, 263
Glasser, William, 323
Globalization, 16-17
Goals
    examples of, 26-27
    and subject, 26-27
    of teams, 277
Goffman, Erving, 256
Good, Thomas, 10
Gould, R., 66
Grading. *See also* Assessment of learning
    and inquiry strategy, 186-87
    norm- versus criterion-referenced
        evaluation, 123-25
Great books, 33-34
Group presentations, 265
Groups and teams
    apathy in, 261-62
    and assessment of learning, 362-63
    benefits of, 245-46
    brainstorming, 264-64
    characteristics of, 243, 253-62
    characteristics of teams, 276-79
    in classroom settings, 262-67
    cohesiveness of, 254-55, 287
    communication in, 253-61
    conflict in, 259-61
    cooperative and competitive
        groups, 265-66
    definition of, 242-43
    drawbacks to using, 246-47
    examples of, 247-49, 270-75, 362-63
    games, 267
    get-acquainted activities, 263
    group presentations, 265
    group therapy process, 285-289
    individuals in, 257-58
    leadership in, 267-70, 279
    listening in, 258-59
    living and learning in groups, 242-44

nonverbal communication in, 259
norms in, 257
origins of formal use and study of,
    249-52
participants and observers, 265
for personal growth, 276, 283-92
process functions of, 254, 256-57,
    268-69, 270
productivity of, 255
role play and dramatization, 266-67
roles of group members, 256-58
size of, 243-44
spiral model of idea development
    in, 253
stages of, 253
stages of encounter groups, 284-85
structure of, 255-56, 268-69, 277
summary of, 353
task functions of, 254, 255, 256,
    268, 270
teacher's role in use of, 267-75
teams used for projects, 276-83
types of, 244
use of, 244-51
working as partners or triads, 263-
    64
Group therapy, 252, 285-289
Groupthink, 246-47
Guilt/virtue by assocation, 221

Halpern, Diane, 201-2, 205
Hardy, Thomas, 46
Hart, Leslie, 312-15, 316
Havinghurst, Robert, 66-67
Hawthorne Effect, 250
Hayakawa, S.I., 218
Hemingway, Ernest, 342
Heuristics, 183-84
Hidden curriculum, 28
Higher education. *See also* College;
    Community college; University
    classification of institutions, 52
    differences in institutions, 51-56
Humanistic psychology, 251
Humanities, 176, 182, 226-33, 349-50,
    361. *See also* Literature
Human Relations Movement, 250-51
Hypotheses, 192, 193-94

Iconoic memory, 161

"If, then" statements, 191
Imagery, as memory technique, 163-64
Inductive reasoning, 191-95
Information presentations, 133-35
Information processing model, 137-39, 144-59
Inquiry and discovery
    and assessment of learning, 360-61
    classroom settings for teaching thinking, 184-87
    decision making, 207-12
    encouraging students to think, 173-76
    examples of, 175-76, 181-82, 196-201, 212-17, 226-33, 360-61
    guidelines for, 185-86
    problem solving, 201-7
    summary of, 352-53
    teaching thinking, 182-84
    thinking about thinking, 176-82
    thinking and language, 217-33
    thinking and reasoning, 174, 177, 187-201
    types of thinking, 178-81
Instruction. *See* Teaching
Instructional design, 126-28
Intelligence
    compared with thinking, 183
    definition of, 72-74
    everyday intelligence, 73
    interaction with aptitude and motivation, 77-78
    multiple intelligences, 74-75
Interior design, 4, 27, 30, 37, 248-49, 280-83, 362-63
Irrelevant reasons, 221-22

James, William, 136
Janis, Irving, 247
Joyce, James, 60
Jung, Carl, 80, 251

Keller, Fred, 126
Kennedy, Allen, 53
Kinesics, 259
King, Patricia, 69-72
Kitchener, Karen, 69-72
Knapp, Mark, 47, 48-49
Knowledge
    compared with thinking, 178

in information processing, 148-52
    role in society, 16
Knowles, Hulda, 242, 243
Knowles, Malcolm, 87-88, 242, 243
Kolb, David, 78-79, 306-7, 340n3
Kuhn, Thomas, 12-13, 343-44
Kurfiss, Joanne, 183-84

Labeling, 221
LaFasto, Frank, 276
Language
    learning of, 315-16
    and thinking, 217-33
Larson, Carl, 276
Leaderless Group Discussion (LGD), 269
Leadership, 267-70, 279, 288-89
Leading questions, 221
Learned helplessness, 77
Learners. *See* Students
Learning
    assessment of, 123-25, 186-87, 355-64
    teaching's impact on, 365-68
Learning hierarchy, 118-19
Learning paradigms, 342-45
"Learning Style Inventory, " 78-79
Learning styles, 78-83
Least restrictive environment, 82
Lecturing and explaining
    and assessment of learning, 359-60
    attention mechanisms, 140-44
    cognitive psychology, 135-37
    examples of, 134-35, 141-44, 152-59, 359-60
    information processing model, 137-39, 144-59
    memory, 139, 159-68
    presenting information, 133-35
    summary of, 351-52
Lee, Calvin, 52-53
Left-brain functions, 78, 87
Levinson, Daniel, 66
Lewin, Kurt, 246, 250-51, 306
LGD. *See* Leaderless Group Discussion (LGD)
Lipman, Matthew, 177
Listening in groups, 258-59
Literature, 2-3, 26, 29, 37, 349-50, 361
Locus of control, 77

Loevinger, Jane, 65-66
Logical positivism, 219-20
Long-term memory, 139, 159, 160-66
Lorayne, H., 163-64
Lucas, J., 163-64

Maclean, Paul D., 310-11
Mager, Robert F., 114
Mainstreaming, 82
Management courses, 175-76, 181-82, 212-17, 303-4, 318-20, 332-35, 361, 364
Mann, Richard, 49-50
Maslow, Abraham, 251
Mastery learning, 123-26
Mathematics, 99-100, 105-6, 112-13, 115, 122-23, 126, 128, 358-59
May, Rollo, 323
Mayo, Elton, 250
Meaning making, in information processing, 147-48
Means-ends analysis, 204-5
Memory, 139, 159-68
Memory techniques, 163-66
Mental sets, 207
Metacognition, 184
Metaphors, 224-26
Method of loci, 164
Miller, G.A., 160
Minority students, 14, 83-84, 86-87
Misinterpretation, 221
Mission, of institutions, 53
Models, 222-23
Montessori, Maria, 81
Moos, Rudolph, 46-47
Moreno, J.L., 252, 267
Morrison, Toni, 173
Motivation
    and reinforcement, 110-11
    of students, 72, 75-78, 110-11
Music appreciation, 98-99, 103-5, 112, 115, 125, 127-28, 358
Myers-Briggs Type Indicator, 80-81

NAEP. *See* National Assessment of Educational Progress (NAEP)
National Assessment of Educational Progress (NAEP), 173
National Training Laboratory for Group Development (NTL), 251

Negative reinforcement, 107, 109
Neugarten, Bernice, 67
Newell, A., 137, 202
Nickerson, Raymond, 174, 183, 192, 195, 218
Nondirected thinking, 178
Nonverbal communication, 259
Norm-referenced evaluation, 123
Norms in groups, 257
NTL. *See* National Training Laboratory for Group Development (NTL)
Null curriculum, 28

Objectives
    behavioral objectives, 113-16
    examples of, 28-30
    for subject, 27-30
Oceanography, 175, 181, 196-201, 360-61
Older students, 14, 66-68
Operant conditioning, 101-13, 136
Organizing principle, 31-37

Pandemonium system, 145, 151
Panel, 265
Paradigm, 12-13, 343-44
Participants and observers, 265
Partners, working as, 263-64
Pascarella, Ernest, 367
Pedagogy, 87-89. *See also* Teaching
Perls, Fritz, 323
Perry, William, 69
Personal growth group, 276, 283-92
Personalized System of Instruction (PSI), 126-27
Phenix, Philip, 32
Philosophy, 177, 188-95, 219-20
Philosophy of education, 39
Physical science, 135, 143-44, 156-59, 167-68, 360. *See also* Oceanography
Piaget, Jean, 62, 174, 306
Plath, Sylvia, 1
Pollyanna Principle, 209
Popularity, 221
Positive reinforcement, 107-9
Postman, Neil, 185, 186-87
Pressey, Sidney L., 120
Probabilistic thinking, 209-11

Problem solving, 201-7
Projects, 276-83
Propaganda, 221
Proxemics, 259
PSI. *See* Personalized System of Instruction (PSI)
Psychomotor memory, 161
Psychomotor outcomes, 28
Psychotherapy, 322-27
Punishment, 110

Quoting out of context, 221

Rand Corporation, 137
Rational emotive therapy, 323-24
Reality therapy, 323
Reasoning, 174, 177, 187-201. *See also* Inquiry and discovery
Reflection. *See* Experience and reflection
"Reflective Judgment Model, " 69
Reflective judgment, stages of, 69-72
Rehearsal, 163
Reich, Wilhelm, 251
Reinforcement, 106-13
Rewards, 106-13
Riesman, David, 52
Right-brain functions, 78, 87
Ringlemann Effect, 246
Risky shift phenomenon, 247
Rogers, Carl, 251, 284, 323
Role play, 266-67
Rote learning, 163
Round table, 265

Sagan, Carl, 78, 311
Sapir-Whorf Hypothesis, 217-18
Sarason, Seymour, 46
Scanner, electronic, 144-45
Schemas, in information processing, 149-51
Schön, Donald, 307-9
Schwab, Joseph, 344-45
Science. *See* Oceanography; Physical science
Scope, of subject, 28
Scripts, in information processing, 149-50
Selfridge, O., 145
Self-talk, 217

Semantic association, 164-65
Semantic memory, 161
Seminary
    assessment of learning at, 363, 364
    experience and reflection in, 304-6, 320-22, 335-39
    goals at, 27
    groups and teams in, 249, 289-92
    objectives at, 30
    organizing principle in, 37
    social change course at, 4-5, 249, 289-92
Sensory modalities, 81-83
Sequence, of subject, 28
Setting
    classroom settings, 47-51
    examples of, 2-5
    and goodness of fit with teachers, 56-57
    importance of, 46-47
    institutional settings, 51-56
    questions on, 11, 347-48
    spatial arrangements, 48-49
Shaping of complex behavior, 101-6
Shaw, J.C., 137
Sheehy, Gail, 66
Sheets, Paul, 256
Short-term memory, 139, 159-60
Simon, H.A., 137, 202
Skill development, 97-100
Skinner, B.F., 7, 100-1, 107, 120, 126, 176
Skinner box, 100, 101
Smith, Frank, 315-16
Social change, 36
Social change course, 4-5, 27, 30, 37, 249, 289-92, 363
Social class of students, 83-84, 86-87
Social development, 62-68
Social loafing, 246
Social problems curriculum, 36, 44n13
Socializing agent, teacher as, 49
Sociology, 2, 26, 28-29, 36-37, 135, 142-43, 154-56, 166-67, 301-3, 317-18, 327-32, 359-60, 363-64
Spatial arrangements, 48-49
Special education, 82
Split-half method, 205-6
Spontaneity theater, 252

Status and Education of Women project, 85-86
Steiner, Gary, 245
Stereotype, 221
Sternberg, Robert, 73, 74
Student Right-to-Know and Campus Security Act, 365
Students
    aptitude of, 72, 75, 77-78
    cognitive development of, 68-72
    as consumers, 14-15
    cultures of, 61
    disabled students, 14, 81-83
    diversity in student body, 60
    as individuals, 61-62
    as influence on curriculum, 37-38
    intelligence of, 72-75
    learning styles of, 78-83
    minority students, 14, 83-84, 86-87
    motivation of, 72, 75-78, 110-11
    older students, 14, 66-68
    pedagogies and teaching strategies for, 87-89
    personal development of, 34-35
    questions on, 11, 348
    sensory modalities of, 81-83
    social and emotional development of, 62-68
    social class of, 83-84, 86-87
    "traditional" students, 60
    women students, 14, 15, 67, 85-86
Subject
    breadth of, 28
    centrality and balance of, 28
    definitions of, 25-26
    depth of, 28
    examples of, 2-5
    flexibility of, 28
    gaps in, 28
    goals established for, 26-27
    and hidden curriculum, 28
    influences on curriculum, 37-41
    objectives clarified for, 27-30
    and organizing principle, 31-37
    questions on, 11, 42, 347
    scope of, 28
    sequence of, 28
    societal influences on, 38
    student influences on, 37-38
Swassing, Raymond, 81

Swimming, 98, 103, 111-12, 114, 117-18, 125, 127, 358
Syllogisms, 188-90, 192
Symposium, 265
Systems analysis, 137
Systems approach to learning, 126

Task analysis, 116-19
Tavistock Institute, 252
Teaching
    as art, 6-7
    author's assumptions about, ix-xi
    composite perspective on, 347-50
    decision making in, 8-9
    definition of, 5-6
    diversity in, 1-5
    driving and controlling factors in, 350
    examples of, 2-5, 349-50
    experience and reflection, 299-339, 354, 363-64
    and feedback, 9-10
    and goodness of fit with setting, 56-57
    groups and teams, 242-93, 353, 362-63
    impact of, on learning, 365-68
    inquiry and discovery, 173-234, 352-53, 360-61
    instructional model for employing teaching strategies, 345-47
    lecturing and explaining, 133-68, 351-52, 359-60
    need for improvement of, 14-18
    perspective of experienced teachers, 10-11
    as profession, 7-8
    roles of teacher, 49-50
    as science, 7
    and societal trends, 16-18
    strategies of, 12-14, 87-89, 342-68
    training and coaching strategy, 97-128, 350-351, 357-59
Teaching machines, 120
Teams. *See* Groups and teams
Technical Rationality, 307-9
Terenzini, Patrick, 367
T-group, 251, 283
Therapy. *See* Psychotherapy

Thinking skills. *See* Inquiry and discovery
Thoreau, Henry David, 242
Thorndike, E.L., 100-1, 176
Tierney, William, 53-54
Top-down processing, 146, 147-49, 151
Tower of Hanoi Problem, 204-5
Training and coaching
  and assessment of learning, 357-59
  behavioral objectives, 113-16
  behaviorism, 100-13
  computer-assisted instruction, 119-23
  criterion-referenced evaluation and mastery learning, 123-26
  examples of, 98-100, 103-6, 111-13, 125-26, 358-59
  instructional design, 126-28
  rewards and punishments, 106-13
  shaping of complex behavior, 101-6
  skill development, 97-100
  summary of, 350-51
  task analysis, 116-19
Transformation group, 276, 283-92
Travers, W.W., 44n12
Triads, working as, 263-64

University. *See also* Higher education
  assessment of learning in, 358, 359-60, 361
  criterion-referenced evaluation in, 125
  goals in, 26
  inquiry and discovery in, 175-76, 181-82, 212-17
  instructional design in, 127
  lecturing and explaining in, 135, 142-43, 154-56, 166-67
  organizing principle in, 36-37
  sociology course at, 2
  training and coaching at, 98, 103, 111-13, 125, 127
University of California, Santa Cruz, 44n13
University of Chicago, 177, 251
University of Cincinnati, 306
University of Wisconsin, Green Bay, 44n13

Videodisc, 121-22
Vienna Circle, 219
Visual communication, 134, 141-42, 152-54, 166, 359

Watson, John B., 100, 176
Weingartner, Charles, 185, 186-87
Wellness course, 3, 26-27, 29, 37, 247-48, 270-75, 362
Western Electric, 250
Wishful thinking, 209
Wlodkowski, Raymond, 75-76
Women students, 14, 15, 67, 85-86
Wright, Frank Lloyd, 47
Wundt, Wilhelm, 136

Yalom, Irvin D., 286

ISBN 0-89774-813-1

90000